All in One®

Recommended by **Teachers** Trusted by **Toppers**

HOME SCIENCE

Class 11

EVERYTHING YOU NEED TO SCORE

- Simplified NCERT Theory
- NCERT & Other Important Questions
- CBQs; MCQs, A-R, Case Based
- Sample Question Papers

CBSE Exams 2026

Author
Saumya Aggarwal

arihant
SUCCESS AND NOTHING LESS

arihant
SUCCESS AND NOTHING LESS

ARIHANT PRAKASHAN
(School Division Series)

卐 *ADMINISTRATIVE & PRODUCTION OFFICES*

Regd. Office

'Ramchhaya' 4577/15, Agarwal Road, Darya Ganj, New Delhi -110002
Tele: 011- 47630600, 43518550; Fax: 011- 23280316

卐 *Head Office*

Kalindi, TP Nagar, Meerut (UP) - 250002, Tel: 0121-7156203, 7156204

卐 *SALES & SUPPORT OFFICES*

Agra, Ahmedabad, Bengaluru, Bareilly, Chennai, Delhi, Guwahati, Hyderabad, Jaipur, Jhansi, Kolkata, Lucknow, Nagpur & Pune.

PO No : TXT-XX-XXXXXXX-X-XX

Published By Arihant Publications (India) Ltd.

For further information about the books published by Arihant, log on to www.arihantbooks.com or e-mail at info@arihantbooks.com

Follow us on

卐 *PRICE* ₹350.00

PRODUCTION TEAM

Publishing Managers	*Cover Designer*	*Inner Designer*
Mahendra Singh Rawat & Keshav Mohan	Salman Shaikh	Ankit Tyagi
Project Head	*Page Layouting*	*Proof Reader*
Monika Bhasin	Chintoo Kumar	Anurag Vashist

Index *cum* Study Planner

One Book- Endless Features

to Help you Succeed

In this Chapter

At the start of each chapter, all the chapter topics have been listed , so that students may know what they are going to study.

Understanding the Self

inside the CHAPTER

- What is Self?
- What is Identity?
- Introduction
- Biological and Physical Changes Affecting Identity
- Socio-Cultural Contexts
- Emotional Changes
- Cognitive Changes

Check Point 01

1. What term is used to signify the self worth that an individual places on themselves?
2. What describes a sense of who we are?
3. Self overestimation is the characteristics of which self?
4. Identity development and crisis arise during which phase of adolescence?

Check Points

To assess your step by step learning of chapter check point questions are incorporated in between the theory.

A. What Makes Me 'I'
(Who am I?)

Right from birth to adolescence, a child's understanding of the self develops from no understanding or awareness of self to a concrete understanding and awareness of self by the completion of adolescence. During this time, a child is influenced by physical, socio-cultural, emotional and cognitive factors. He/She also faces conflicts in identity during adolescence.

We all have many things in common with our parents, siblings, other relatives and friends while each one of us is also a unique person, different from all others. This sense of being unique gives us our sense of self — the sense of 'I' which is different from 'you', 'them' and 'others'.

What is Self?

The sense of self refers to the sense of who we are and what makes us different from everyone else. During adolescence we start thinking more than ever about 'Who am I?' and 'What makes 'me' different from others?' At this stage, we try to define our 'self', more than any other stage.

Dimensions of Self

Some of the aspects that we use to define ourselves are discussed below

- **Physical** We use our physical aspects to differentiate ourselves from others. For example, 'I am tall'.
- **Mental Abilities** Sometimes we differentiate ourselves according to the mental abilities, emotions or feelings we possess. For example, 'I can count easily' or 'I cry very often about small things'.
- **Potential/Capabilities** We may also describe ourselves in terms of things we can do. For example, 'I can drive a car'.

Though there are several dimensions of self, we can broadly classify these dimensions into the **personal** and the **social**. The personal self includes all those aspects which relate only to you. On the other hand, the social self includes those aspects in which you are involved with others, be it family, friends or society as a whole. Social self relates to aspects like sharing, cooperation, unity, etc.

So, the term **self** refers to the totality of a person's experiences, ideas, thoughts and feelings with regard to herself/himself. It is the characteristic way in which we define ourselves. **The idea that we hold of ourselves is the notion of the 'self'.**

Complete Theory in Each Chapter

Each chapter has Complete, Easy to Understand and Simplified theory covering latest syllabus and rationalised NCERT Textbook. Theory is developed in such a way that it perfectly rectifies the complexity of NCERT Text making it suitable for all types of students.

One Book- Endless Features

to Help you Succeed

NCERT Folder

To make students completely understand NCERT books, solutions of all the NCERT exercises have been given in each chapter in NCERT Folder. Accuracy, Detailing and Simplicity of Solution are the major features of this section.

NCERT FOLDER

A. What Makes Me 'I'

1. Explain what you understand by the term 'self'. Discuss its various dimensions giving examples.

Ans. Some of the aspects or dimensions that we use to define ourselves are discussed below

- **Physical** We use our physical aspects to differentiate ourselves from others. For example, 'I am tall'.
- **Mental Abilities** Sometimes we differentiate ourselves according to the mental abilities, emotions or feelings we possess. For example, 'I can count easily' or 'I cry very often about small things'.
- **Potential/Capabilities** We may also describe ourselves in terms of things we can do. For example, 'I can drive a car'.

So the term self refers to the totality of a person's experiences, ideas, thoughts and feelings with regard to herself/himself. It is the characteristic way in which we define ourselves. The idea that we hold of ourselves is the notion of the 'self'.

2. Why is it important to understand the self?

Ans. It is important to understand the self because when we have a better understanding of ourselves, we are able to experience ourselves as unique and separate individuals. People who understand themselves have a positive outlook in life and they are open to any sort of changes as well as build on their areas of strength. They are capable of managing their emotions, behaviours, thoughts among others and identify areas where improvement is necessary.

Chapter Practice

To make students completely prepared for examination, this Exercise contains Exam Pattern Questions. This exercise covers all types of questions, like, MCQs, Case Based Questions, Assertion-Reason, VAS, SA & LA Type Questions. All the questions are fully explained helping students to understand, how to write the answers to get full marks in the exam.

CHAPTER PRACTICE

Objective Type Questions

Multiple Choice Questions (MCQs)

1. These attributes of a person that make the person different from others.
(a) Social identify (b) Personal identity
(c) Self esteem (d) Self concept

Ans. (b) Personal identity

2. Which of the following is the description of oneself?
(a) Self concept (b) Self esteem
(c) Social self (d) Physical self

Ans. (a) Self concept

3. "In this stage of life, children's self evaluations become more complex". Which stage is being referred to in the statement?
(a) Infancy
(b) Early Childhood
(c) Middle Childhood
(d) Adolescence

Ans. (c) Middle Childhood

4. Which among the following is seen as a critical time for identity development?
(a) Childhood (b) Adolescence
(c) Schooling (d) None of these

Ans. (b) Adolescence

5. During this period, physical and biological changes occur which leads to puberty.
(a) Pubescence (b) Infancy
(c) Middle Childhood (d) Early Childhood

Ans. (a) Pubescence

6. "Boys who do not have adequate growth of facial hair, as compared to other boys, often feel peculiar about it." What kind of changes are being referred in this statement?
(a) Cognitive changes
(b) Physical changes
(c) Emotional changes
(d) Biological changes

Ans. (c) Emotional changes

CHAPTER ASSESSMENT

Objective Type Questions

1. Adolescence is a critical time for .... part of development?
(a) Personal (b) Identity
(c) Social (d) Political

2. .... is the time in the life of an adolescent when sexual maturity takes place.
(a) Adolescence (b) Puberty
(c) Pubescence (d) None of these

3. .... development means the growth of a child's ability to think and reason.
(a) Emotional (b) Physical
(c) Mental (d) Cognitive

Very Short Answer Type Questions

1. Explain the role of parenting in adolescence.
2. What are the two types of identity? Explain.
3. Why adolescent faces an identity crisis? List three factors.

Short Answer Type Questions

1. What are the differences between male and female physical and biological change.
2. What are the impacts of relationships on adolescents?
3. Explain any three dimensions of self with example.

Long Answer Type Questions

1. What are the different stages of 'self' during middle childhood?
2. What are the characteristics of an adolescent's sense of self?
3. "Culture is responsible for shaping the adolescent identity". Explain the statement with examples.

Chapter Assessment

At the end of the chapter, these unsolved questions are for practice and assessment of students. By practising these questions students can assess their preparation level for the Chapter.

Latest Course *Structure*

Paper: One | Time: 3 Hrs | Max. Marks : 70

No.	Units	Marks	No. of Periods
I	Introduction to Home Science	02	04
II	Understanding oneself : Adolescence	20	35
III	Understanding Family, Community and Society	15	35
IV	Childhood	15	24
V	Adulthood	18	28
	Total	**70**	**126**
	Practical	**30**	**28**
	Grand Total	**100**	**154**

UNIT I Introduction to Home Science

UNIT II Understanding Oneself : Adolescence

Ch. Understanding the Self

A. 'Who am I'?

B. Development and Characteristics of the Self (Development characteristics and needs of adolescents)

C. Influences on Identity

Ch. Food, Nutrition, Health and Fitness

Ch. Management of Resources

Ch. Fabric Around Us

Ch. Media and Communication Technology

UNIT III Understating Family, Community and Society

Ch. Concerns and needs in diverse contexts:

A. Nutrition, Health and Hygiene

B. Resources Availability and Management

UNIT IV Childhood

Ch. Survival, Growth and Development

Ch. Nutrition, Health and Well-being

Ch. Our Apparel

UNIT V Adulthood

Ch. Health and Wellness

Ch. Financial Management and Planning

Ch. Care and Maintenance of Fabrics

Unit I: Introduction To Home Science

- What is Home Science
- Areas of Home Science
- Home Science is important for both boys and girls
- Career options of Home Science

Unit II: Understanding Oneself: Adolescence

Chapter : Understanding the Self

- What is Self?
  - Personal dimension
  - Social dimension
  - Self- concept
  - Self esteem
- What is Identity?
  - Personal identity
  - Social identity
- Self during Infancy: characteristics
- Self during early childhood: characteristics
- Self during middle childhood: characteristics
- Self during adolescence: characteristics

- Identity development
- Identity crisis
- Real vs Ideal self

- Influences on identity
  - Developing a sense of self and identity
  - Influences on formation of identity
    - Biological and physical changes
    - Socio-cultural context
    - Emotional changes
    - Cognitive changes

Chapter : Food, Nutrition, Health and Fitness

- Introduction
- Definition of
  - Food
  - Nutrition
  - Nutrients
- Balanced diet
  - Definition
  - RDA
- Health and Fitness
- Using Basic food Groups for planning Balanced Diets
  - Food guide pyramid
- Vegetarian food Guide
- Dietary patterns in Adolescence
  - Irregular meals and skipping meals
  - Snacking
  - Fast foods
  - Dieting
- Modifying diet related behaviour
  - Diet journal
  - Exercise
  - Substance use and abuse
  - Healthy eating habits
  - Snacks
  - Drinking water
- Factors influencing eating behaviour
- Eating disorders at adolescence
- Key terms and their meaning

Chapter : Management of Resources

- Introduction
- Classification of resources
  - Human/non-human resources
  - Individual/ shared resources
  - Natural/community resources
- Human and non-human resources
  - Human resources
    - Knowledge
    - Motivation/ interest
    - Skills/ strength/ aptitude
    - Time
    - Energy
  - Non-human resources
    - Money
    - Material resources
- Individual and shared resources
  - Individual resources
  - Shared resources
- Natural and community resources
  - Natural resources
  - Community resources
- Characteristics of resources
  - Utility
  - Accessibility
  - Interchangeability
  - Manageable
- Managing Resources
  - Management process
  - Planning
  - Steps in planning
  - Organising
  - Implementing
  - Controlling
  - Evaluation

Chapter : Fabric Around Us

- Definition of yarns, fibres, textile products, finishing
- Introduction to fibre properties
- Classification of textile fibres
  - Filament/staple fibres
  - Natural/Manufactured (manmade) fibres
- Types of Natural Fibres
  - Cellulosic fibres
  - Protein fibres
  - Mineral fibres
  - Natural rubber
- Types of Manufactured Fibres
  - Regenerated cellulosic fibres
  - Modified cellulosic fibres
  - Protein fibres
  - Non-cellulosic fibres
  - Mineral fibres
- Some Important fibres and their properties
  - Cotton
  - Linen
  - Wool

- Silk
- Rayon
- Nylon
- Polyester
- Acrylic
- Elastomeric fibres
- Yarns
- Yarn processing
  - Cleaning
  - Making into a sliver
  - Attenuating, drawing out and twisting
- Yarn terminology
  - Yarn number
  - Yarn twist
  - Yarn and thread
- Fabric production
  - Weaving
  - Knitting
  - Braiding
  - Nets
  - Laces
- Textile Finishing
  - Finishing with colour
  - Printing

Chapter : Media Communication Technology

- Communication and Communication Technology
  - What is Communication
  - Classification of communication
  - How does communication takes place
- What is media
  - Media classification and functions
- What is communication technology
  - Classification of communication technologies
  - Modern communication technologies

Unit III : Understanding Family, Community and Society

Chapter : Concerns and Needs in Diverse Contexts

A. Nutrition, Health and Hygiene

- Health and its Dimensions
  - Social health
  - Mental health
  - Physical health
- Health care Indicators of Health
- Nutrition and Health
- Importance of nutrients
- Factors affecting nutritional well being
  - Food and nutrient security
  - Care for the vulnerable
  - Good health for all
  - Safe environment
- Nutritional Problems and their consequences
  - Malnutrition
  - Under nutrition
  - Over nutrition
- Hygiene and Sanitation
  - Personal Hygiene
  - Environmental Hygiene
  - Food Hygiene
  - Water safety-Qualities of potable water, methods of water purification(Boiling, chlorine, storage and electric filter ,RO)

B. Resources Availability and Management

- Time Management
  - Definition of time plan
  - How good is your time management (Activity)?
  - Steps in making time plan
  - Tips for effective time management
  - Tools in time management---Peak load period, Work curve, Rest /break periods, Work simplification
- Space Management
  - Space and the home
  - Principles of space planning

Unit IV: Childhood

Chapter : Survival Growth and Development

- The meaning of survival
- Growth and development
- Areas of development
  - Physical development
  - Motor development
  - Cognitive development
  - Sensory development
  - Language development
  - Social development
  - Emotional development
- Good Nutrition
- Stages in development
  - Neonate
    - Reflexes
    - Sensory capabilities
- Development across stages from infancy to adolescence
  - Physical and motor development
  - Language development
  - Socio –emotional development
  - Cognitive development
    - Mental processes involved in thinking
    - Stages of cognitive development

- Sensory motor stage
- Pre-operational stage
- Concrete operational stage
- Formal operational stage

Chapter : Nutrition, Health and Well-being

- Introduction
- Nutrition, Health and Well-being during infancy (birth – 12 months)
  - Dietary requirements of infants
  - Breast feeding
    - Benefits of breast feeding
  - Feeding the low birth weight infants
  - Complementary foods
  - Guidelines for complementary feeding
  - Immunisation
  - Common health and nutrition problems in infants and young children
- Nutrition, Health and well-being of preschool children (1-6 years)
  - Nutritional needs of preschool children
  - Guidelines for healthy eating for pre-schoolers
  - Planning balanced meals for preschool children
  - Some examples of low-cost snacks
  - Feeding children with specific needs
  - Immunisation
- Nutrition, Health and well-being of school-age children (7-12 years)
  - Nutritional requirements of school children
  - Planning diets for school-age children
  - Factors that influence diet intake of preschool- and school-age children
  - Healthy habits
  - Health and nutrition issues of school age children

Chapter: Our Apparel

- Clothing functions and the selection of clothes
  - Modesty
  - Protection
  - Status and prestige
  - Adornment
- Factors affecting selection of clothing in India
  - Age
  - Climate and season
  - Occasion
  - Fashion
  - Income
- Understanding children's basic clothing needs
  - Comfort
  - Safety
  - Self help
  - Appearance
  - Allowance for growth
  - Easy care
  - Fabrics
- Clothing requirements at different childhood stages
  - Infancy (birth to six months)
  - Creeping age (6 months to one year)
  - Toddlerhood (1-2 years)
  - Preschool age (2-6 years)
  - Elementary school years (5-11 years)
  - Adolescents (11-19 years)
  - Clothes for children with special needs

Unit V: Adulthood

Chapter : Health and Wellness

- Importance of health and fitness
- Healthy & Unhealthy diet
- BMI
- Do's and Don'ts for health promoting diets
- Fitness
- Importance of exercise and physical activities in adulthood
- Wellness
- Qualities of a person who is rated high on wellness
- Dimensions of wellness
  - Social aspect
  - Physical aspect
  - Intellectual aspect
  - Occupational aspect
  - Emotional aspect
  - Spiritual aspect
  - Environmental aspect
  - Financial aspect
- Stress and coping with stress
- Simple techniques to cope with stress
  - Relaxation
  - Talking with friends/family
  - Reading
  - Spirituality
  - Music
  - Hobby
  - Yoga

Chapter : Financial Management and Planning

- Financial management
- Financial planning
- Management
- Money and its importance

- Family Income
  - Money income
  - Real income: Direct and Indirect income
  - Psychic income
- Income management
- Budget
- Steps in making budget
- Advantages of planning family budgets
- Control in money management
  - Checking to see how well the plan is progressing
    - Mental and mechanical check
    - Records and accounts
  - Adjusting wherever necessary
  - Evaluation
- Savings
- Investment
- Principles underlying sound investments
  - Safety to the principle amount
  - Reasonable rate of interest
  - Liquidity
  - Recognition of effect of world conditions
  - Easy accessibility and convenience
  - Investing in needed commodities
  - Tax efficiency
  - After investment service
  - Time period
  - Capacity
- Savings and investment avenues
  - Post office
  - Banks
  - Unit Trust of India
  - NSC
  - Mutual funds
  - Provident funds
  - Chit fund
  - Life insurance and medical insurance
  - Pension scheme
  - Gold, house, land
  - Others (new schemes)
- Credit
- Need of credit
- 4C's of credit: character, capacity, capital means, collateral

Chapter : Care and Maintenance of Fabrics

- Mending
- Laundering
  - Stain removal
    - Vegetable stains
    - Animal stains
    - Oil stains
    - Mineral stains
    - Dye bleeding
  - Techniques of stain removal
    - Scraping
    - Dipping
    - Sponging
    - Drop method
  - Reagent for stain removal
  - Common stains and method of removing
- Removal of dirt: the cleaning process
  - Soaps and detergents
  - Methods of washing: friction, kneading & squeezing, suction, washing by machine
- Finishing
  - Blues and optical brighteners
  - Starches and stiffening agents
- Ironing
- Dry cleaning
- Storage of textile products
- Factors affecting fabric care
  - Yarn structure
  - Fabric construction
  - Colour and finishes
- Care label

Note :

- *Wherever required latest data/figures to be used.*
- *Latest RDA's to be used.*

Practicals

Practicals should be conducted alongside the concepts taught in theory classes

LIST OF EXPERIMENTS

PRACTICALS FOR CLASS XI

1. Understanding oneself with reference to:
   (a) Physical development in terms of age, height, weight, hip and chest circumference.
   (b) Sexual maturity (Age at menarche, Development of breasts : girls). Growth of beard, change in voice:boys)
2. Observe developmental norms: (Physical, Motor, Language and social - emotional) birth to three years.
3. List and discuss 4-5 areas of agreement and disagreement with
   (a) Mother
   (b) Father
   (c) Siblings/ Friends
   (d) Teacher
4. (a) Record own diet for a day
   (b) Evaluate qualitatively for adequacy
5. Preparation of different healthy snacks for an adolescent suitable in her/his context.
6. (a) Record one day's activities relating to time use and work
   (b) Prepare a time plan for yourself
7. Plan a budget for a given situation/purpose.
8. (a) Record the fabrics and apparel used in a day
   (b) Categorise them according to functionality
9. Relationship of fibre properties to their usage:
   (a) Thermal property and flammability
   (b) Moisture absorbency and comfort
10. (a) Analyse label of any one garment with respect to: Clarity, fiber content, size and care instructions.
   (b) Prepare one care label of any garment.
   (c) Analyze two different fabric samples for color fastness.

Scheme for Practical Examination **_30 Marks_**

1. Observe developmental norms: (Physical, Motor, Language and social emotional) birth to three years. *5 marks*

   Or

   List and discuss 4-5 areas of agreement and disagreement with
   (a) Mother
   (b) Father
   (c) Siblings/ Friends
   (d) Teacher
2. Preparation of healthy snacks for an adolescent. *7 marks*
3. Plan a budget for a given situation/ purpose. *3 marks*
4. Prepare a time plan for yourself. 3 marks
5. Relationship of fibre properties to their usage: *5 marks*
   (a) Thermal property and flammability
   (b) Moisture absorbency and comfort

   Or

   Prepare one care label of any garment.
6. File *5 marks*
7. Viva *2 marks*

01 CHAPTER

Human Ecology and Family Science

Home Science is an interdisciplinary subject which focuses in to enhance the quality of life.

YOUR STUDY GOALS

1.1 Introduction
1.2 Concept of Home Science
1.3 Career Options in Home Science

YOUR PRACTICE GOAL

- Objective Type Questions (12 Qs ; MCQs, A-R, Statements, Matching, Case Based)
- Subjective Questions (9 VSAs, 5 SAs, 4 LAs)

1.1 Introduction

- The term **Human Ecology**[1] **and Family Sciences** (HEFS) combines two important concepts.
  - First, it refers to a **branch of biology** (Human Ecology) that studies the relationships between living organisms and their environment.
  - Second, it denotes the complex interactions between an organism and its surroundings.
- The term **living organism** refers to human beings. Therefore, the term 'Human' comes before **Ecology** indicating that ecology studies how humans interact with their environment.
- The subject also studies the changing relationships that children, **adolescents**[2] and adults have with different physical, economic, social and psychological aspects of their surroundings.

Family Sciences

- The **family**[3] is central to most individuals' lives. It is within the family that children are nurtured and develop into independent adults. HEFS aims to guide students in understanding individuals within the context of their families, which are critical social units of society.

---

1 **Ecology** The study of interactions between living organisms and their environment.
2 **Adolescents** The transitional phase between childhood and adulthood marked by physical and emotional changes.
3 **Family** A social unit where individuals are nurtured and relationships are developed.

- This subject focuses on the interaction between human beings, the families and the society with the environment. This interaction creates a strong relationship that includes physical, psychological, social cultural and economic aspects.

Modernisation of the Subject

- Home Science has traditionally been taught in higher secondary schools and universities. However, as subjects have developed, their names and content have been updated. For example, **Life Sciences** is now often used instead of **Biological Science**.
- Similarly, the content of Home Science at the school level needed to be updated and given a new name to move away from its traditional focus on the home and tasks typically done by girls and women. The University Grants Commission (UGC) started this update at the university level many years ago.

History of Home Science in India

- In the early 20th century, many institutions across India started offering courses in foods and nutrition, clothing and textiles and extension education.
- In 1932, these courses were grouped under the name **Home Science** when **Lady Irwin College** was established in Delhi. This college aimed to **promote women's education** at a time when few girls attended school and higher education for women was rare.
- The college was named after **Lady Dorothy Irwin**, the wife of the British Viceroy, Lord Irwin, who also supported the initiative.
- Lady Irwin College was founded with the support of several prominent women, including **Sarojini Naidu, Rajkumari Amrit Kaur and Kamaladevi Chattopadhyay.** These women were leaders in the movement for India's independence.
- The college's mission was to address social and educational inequalities that prevented women from reaching their full potential.
- Home Science was never meant to be just about the 'home'. It was rather meant to be an interdisciplinary field aimed at helping students improve their own quality of life[4] and that of others.
- However, over time, people, including non-home science professionals, started associating it mainly with cooking, laundry and childcare. While higher education updated the curriculum and professional standards years ago, at the high school level, the subject continued to be linked with gender roles (gender-typing)[5] and seen as focused on 'cooking and laundry'.

1.2 Concept of Home Science

The term **Home Science** literally means **science related to the home.** The home includes the house and all the family members living in it. Science refers to systematic study. Therefore, Home Science is the systematic study of matters related to the family and home.

Home Science is the discipline that structures and responds to the needs of the home and its family members. Its goal is to enhance the happiness and prosperity of family life.

It is a multidisciplinary[6] field that includes topics such as health, nutrition, child care, textile and garment design and the effective use of resources, along with other subjects related to home management.

4 Quality of Life The overall well-being and satisfaction of individuals, influenced by physical, emotional and social factors.
5 Gender-typing Assigning roles and expectations based on traditional gender norms and stereotypes.
6 Multidisciplinary An approach combining various modern fields of study to address complex issues.

Areas of Home Science

- **Human Development** It includes the **overall development of children**. It explores their physical, mental, social and emotional growth. It also addresses family roles, values and responsibilities that nurture a supportive environment. Understanding these aspects leads to healthy relationships and effective parenting.
- **Resource Management** This area focuses on efficiently using **family resources,** like money, time and energy. We learn to make informed decisions for the household and about consumer education. Topics include selecting quality products, recognising adulteration and identifying unethical trading practices. The Consumers Protection Act helps protect consumer rights.
- **Food and Nutrition** It covers **nutrition and dietary health**. We learn about essential nutrients, their functions and health issues from deficiencies. Meal planning, cooking methods and dietary needs for different ages. This knowledge helps us make informed food choices and promotes family health.
- **Textile Science** It examines textiles and clothing. It includes types of fibers, garment design, maintenance and storage techniques. We also learn proper washing and cleaning methods. Understanding **fabric properties** is essential for hygiene and extending the life of clothing.
- **Communication and Extension** Under this, we learn about **improving backward rural areas** and the various **employment opportunities** available. This includes small and household industries, using new technology in farming and modern communication methods. It also emphasises women's empowerment and social welfare initiatives. This enables us to contribute positively to our communities.

Quick Test 1

1. What does the term 'branch of biology' primarily study?
2. Which term refers to assigning roles based on traditional gender norms?
3. Name the area of Home Science deals with family roles and effective parenting?
4. Mention the name of the college, who introduced Home Science courses in India in 1932?

Importance of Home Science for both Boys and Girls

- **Interdisciplinary Field** Home Science improves the quality of personal and family life by teaching valuable skills that are useful in everyday situations. It is not just about traditional roles, but it prepares both boys and girls to handle various responsibilities at home. This helps them manage daily tasks effectively and confidently.
- **Equal Opportunities** It ensures that both boys and girls have the same access to learning and resources. This approach helps create a level playing field, allowing all individuals to pursue their interests and succeed in various professions.
- **Shared Responsibilities** With the changing societal norms, home management is a shared responsibility among all family members. Knowledge of Home Science is crucial for everyone involved in household tasks. It enables them to collaborate effectively and maintain a well-managed, comfortable living environment for the entire family.
- **Personal and Financial Growth** Home Science education empowers youth to become successful householders, responsible citizens and entrepreneurs. This leads to personal satisfaction and improved family finances.

1.3 Career Options in Home Science

- Home Science provides students with important skills and knowledge they can use in their careers.
- It covers areas like nutrition, health, textiles and financial management, preparing students for various **job opportunities**. This practical education encourages critical thinking and problem-solving, making graduates ready for a range of careers.

Few options are listed area wise

Field Options	Self Employment Opportunity
Human Development	▪ Child counsellor ▪ Work in ICDS/NGO ▪ Open day care center ▪ Work with NGO in the child care projects
Foods and Nutrition	▪ Chef ▪ Dietician ▪ Nutritional consultant ▪ Cooking classes
Resource Management and Design application	▪ Consumer activist ▪ Interior decorator ▪ Funiture designer
Fabric Apparel and Science	▪ Fashion designer ▪ Fabric technologist ▪ Opening up tie and dye/block printing unit
Community Development and Extension	▪ Social entrepreneur ▪ Work in government projects

Quick Test 2

1. In modern society, who shares home management responsibilities?
2. Name the field that involves careers like social entrepreneur and working in government projects?
3. This area in Home Science offers careers such as consumer activist and interior decorator. Identify the area.

Mind Map

1 History of Home Science in India

- In the early 20th century, India started offering courses related to food, nutrition and clothing.

Lady Irwin college established in 1932

- Aims to promote women's education.
- Address social and educational inequalities.
- Help to improve quality of life.

2 Concept of Home Science

- Systematic study of matters related to the family and home.
- Enhance the happiness and prosperity of family life.
- Multi disciplinary field
  - Health
  - Nutrition
  - Child care
  - Textile and Garment
  - Effective use of resources

3 Area of Home Science

Human Development

Overall Development of Children

- Explores physical, mental, emotional and social growth.
- Addresses family roles, values and responsibilities.

Resource Management

Effective use of Family Resources

- It includes money, time and energy.

Communication and Extension

Improve Backward Rural Areas

- Various employment opportunities.
- Use new technology in farming.
- New communication methods.

Food for Nutrition

Nutrition and Dietary Health

- Meal planning
- Cooking method
- Dietary needs for different ages.

Textile Science

Examines Textile and Clothing

- Types of fibres
- Garment design
- Maintenance
- Storage techniques

4 Importance of Home Science

Inter-disciplinary Field

- Improves the quality of personal and family life.
- Manage daily tasks.

Equal Opportunities

- Both boys and girls have the same access to learning and resources.

Shared Responsibilities

- Collaborate effectively.
- Maintain comfortable environment.

Personal and Financial Growth

- Empower youth to become successful and responsible citizens.
- Improves family finances.

5 Career Options

- Child counsellor
- Work in NGO
- Nutritional consultant
- Interior decorator
- Fashion designer
- Social entrepreneur

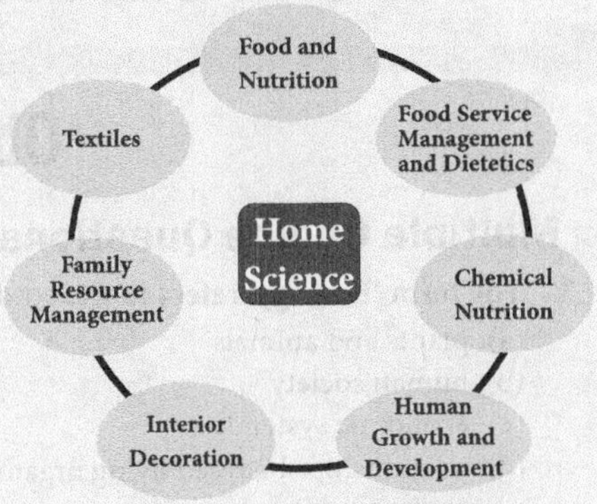

Career in Home Science

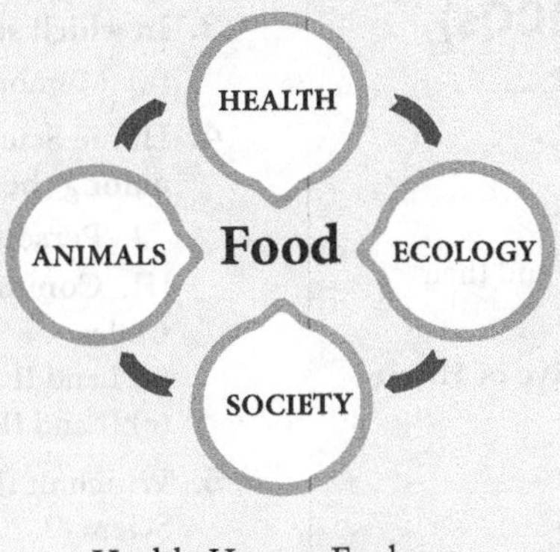

Health-Human Ecology

NCERT Folder

Exercise

1. Do you know about the subject Home Science? Yes or No? List five terms/concepts that you associate with home science.

(i) .... (ii) ....
(iii) .... (iv) ....
(v) ....

Ans Yes, I know about the subject Home Science.

Five terms/concepts that are associated with Home Science are as follows

(i) Nutrition (ii) Resource management
(iii) Child development (iv) Textile science
(v) Home management

2 At the end of the year after you have studied this book 'Human Ecology and Family Sciences' list five areas of study that you would associate with the subject.

(i) .... (ii) ....
(iii) .... (iv) ....
(v) ....

Ans (i) Human development (ii) Food and nutrition
(iii) Family dynamics (iv) Consumer education
(v) Community development

Review Exercise

1. Explain the terms 'Human Ecology' and 'Family Sciences'.

Ans. Human Ecology studies the interactions between humans and their environment. It focuses on how these interactions impact well-being.

Family Sciences examines the roles, relationships and dynamics within families. It highlights the importance of family as a fundamental social unit.

2. Do you agree that adolescence is a 'turning point' in one's life?

Ans. Yes, adolescence is a critical period characterised by significant physical, emotional and social changes. It shapes identity, influences future relationships and impacts educational and career choices, making it a turning point.

3. Name the eminent women who conceived of starting the first Home Science college in India.

(i) .... (ii) ....(iii) .... (iv) ....

Ans. (i) Sarojini Naidu
(ii) Rajkumari Amrit Kaur
(iii) Kamaladevi Chattopadhyay
(iv) Lady Dorothy Irwin

Exam Pattern Questions

Objective Type Questions

Multiple Choice Questions (MCQs)

1. The term 'Ecology' refers to the study of ....

(a) plants and animals
(b) human society
(c) economic systems
(d) relationships between living organisms and their environment

2. Which among the following is an objective of Home Science?

(a) Improve family life
(b) Promote industrial growth
(c) Advance scientific research
(d) Develop economic policies

3. In which state Lady Irwin College is situated.

(a) Mumbai (b) Delhi (c) Bihar (d) Punjab

4. Home Science education can contribute to which among the following?

I. Personal development II. Family well-being
III. Community development **Competency Based Que**

Codes

(a) I and II (b) Only II
(c) II and III (d) All of these

5. Which of the following is not a career option in Home Science?

(a) Fashion designer (b) Engineer
(c) Dietician (d) Child counselor

6. Find the incorrect statement from the following **Competency Based Que**

(a) Several courses were grouped together under the name 'Home Sciences' in 1936.
(b) Lady Irwin college was established at Delhi.
(c) The lady Irwin College aimed to address social and educational inequalities against women.
(d) Home Science is an interdisciplinary field.

7. Select the correct pair. **Competency Based Que**

(a) Consumer activist- Food and nutrition
(b) Nutritional consultant - Human development
(c) Fabric technologist - Resource management
(d) Social entrepreneur - Community development

8. The term 'Home Science' literally means science related to the home. Identify two possible implications of imparting Home Science education. **Competency Based Que**

I. Traditional gender roles will get strengthened
II. It will lead to individual empowerment
III. It will possibly result in huge economic growth
IV. It will possibly raise the quality of life

Choose the correct option from the following.

(a) I and II (b) II and IV
(c) II and III (d) III and IV

9. Match the elements in List I with those in List II. **Competency Based Que**

List I	List II
A. Human development	1. Focuses on budgeting and efficient use of resources.
B. Resource management	2. Involves improving rural areas and women empowerment
C. Communication and extension	3. Studies childrens' physical and emotional growth
D. Textile science	4. Covers fabrics, garment care and design

Codes

	A	B	C	D		A	B	C	D
(a)	1	2	3	4	(b)	3	1	2	4
(c)	4	3	2	1	(d)	2	1	4	3

Assertion-Reason Questions

Direction (Q. Nos. 10-11) In the questions given below, there are two statements marked as Assertion (A) and Reason (R). Read the statements and choose the correct option.

Codes

(a) Both A and R are true and R is the correct explanation of A.
(b) Both A and R are true, but R is not the correct explanation of A.
(c) A is true, but R is false.
(d) A is false, but R is true.

10. Assertion (A) All the members of the family make good efforts for the fulfillment of their needs.

Reasons (R) There is a beautiful inclusion of Art and Science in Home Science.

11. Assertion (A) By studying many areas of Home Science, we can better manage our available resources.

Reasons (R) This subject suggest us the right way to solve any problem.

Case Based Questions

Modernisation of the Subject

12. Home Science has traditionally been taught in higher secondary schools and universities. However, as subjects have developed, their names and content have been updated. For example, Life Science is now often used instead of Biological Science. similarly, the content of Home Science at the school level needed to be updated and given a new name to move away from its traditional focus on the home and tasks typically done by girls and women. The University Grants Commission (UGC) started this update at the university level many years ago.

(i) Why was Home Science updated at the school level?

(a) To focus only on cooking and childcare.
(b) To enhance its relevance beyond traditional gender roles.
(c) To reduce the number of courses offered.
(d) To make it mandatory for all students.

(ii) What is one of the goals of modernising Home Science?

(a) To promote only women's education.
(b) To prepare students for diverse professional opportunities.
(c) To eliminate practical skills from the curriculum.
(d) To restrict enrollment to female students only.

(iii) Choose the correct pair with respect to the subject that has undergone a name change to update its content and move away from traditional gender roles?

(a) Physics - Life Science
(b) Biological Science - Life Science
(c) Home Economics - Home Science
(d) Home Science - Family Studies

(iv) **Assertion** (A) The University Grants Commission (UGC) has played a key role in updating Home Science education.

Reason (R) The UGC aims to maintain outdated educational practices.

Codes

(a) Both A and R are true, and R is the correct explanation of A.
(b) Both A and R are true, but R is not the correct explanation of A.
(c) A is true, but R is false.
(d) A is false, but R is true.

Answers

1. (d) relationships between living organisms and their environment
2. (a) Improve family life 3. (b) Delhi
4. (d) All of these
5. (b) Engineer
6. (a) Several courses were grouped together under the name 'Home Sciences' in 1936.
7. (d) Social entrepreneur - Community development
8. (b) II and IV
9. (b) 3 1 2 4
10. (b) Both A and R are correct but R is not the correct, explanation of A.
11. (b) Both A and R are correct, but R is not the correct explanation of A.
12. (i) (b) To enhance its relevance beyond traditional gender roles.
    (ii) (b) To prepare students for diverse professional opportunities
    (iii) (b) Biological Science - Life Science
    (iv) (c) A is true, but R is false

Subjective Questions

Very Short Answer Type Questions

1. What is human ecology?

Ans. Human ecology is the study of how humans interact with their environment.

2. Which part of science provides a wholesome knowledge?

Ans. Home Science is the part of science that provides a wholesome knowledge.

3. What is the goal of Home Science?

Ans. The goal of Home Science is to enhance the happiness and prosperity of family life.

4. The greatest misconception about Home Science is that it is meant only for which category?

Ans. The greatest misconception about Home Science is that it is meant only for girls.

5. What was the main aim of Lady Irwin College?

Ans. The main aim of Lady Irwin College is to promote women's education and address social inequalities.

6. Give two advantages of Home Science.

Ans. Two advantages of Home Science are

(i) Home Science empowers its students to enhance their own quality of life.

(ii) In Home Science one can learn several skills that can enable them to set up home based enterprises like boutique, creche, etc.

7. What career can one pursue in foods and nutrition?

Ans. Dietician is one career option that can be pursued in foods and nutrition.

8. 'Education in Home Science can help individuals to conduct nutrition awareness programme in their community'. Give two ways in which education in home science can assist in this task. **Competency Based Que**

Ans. Two ways in which Home Science education can help in conducting nutrition awareness programme are as follows

(i) Individuals can use their knowledge in nutrition to design educational workshops that teach families about healthy meal planning and essential nutrients.

(ii) Individuals can collaborate with local schools and health centers to reach a wider audience, ensuring their programme addresses community-specific dietary needs.

9. Meera is passionate about women's empowerment and wants to develop training programmes for rural women. How can her background in Home Science facilitate her initiatives? **Competency Based Que**

Ans. Meera can use her Home Science background to create training programmes focused on health, nutrition and income-generating skills.

By empowering women with practical knowledge, she can help them achieve economic independence and improve their family's quality of life.

Short Answer Type Questions

1. What is the role of Home Science in managing day to day family affairs?

Ans. During the last few decades human relations have been changing drastically. Our life becomes more mechanised and stressful. Various family problems like domestic violence, abuse, crime, etc. are increasing due to the change in family values and ethics.

Home Science tries to educate and acquire the ability to manage these crises at right times with proper steps.

2. Name the five different areas of specialisation in Home Science.

Ans. The five major areas of specialisation in Home Science are

(i) Human development

(ii) Family and community resource management

(iii) Food and nutrition (iv) Textile science

(v) Extension education

3. Sanjay is a college student considering a career in Home Science but is uncertain about its relevance. How can Home Science benefit him? **Competency Based Que**

Ans. Home science can benefit Sanjay by offering him important life skills, such as managing money and understanding nutrition. This field combines different subjects, preparing him for various careers, from dietitian to community worker.

Home Science is relevant today because it helps people balance work and home life, especially as more women work outside the home.

It also teaches how to use modern services and technology effectively. Additionally, it equips him to handle family issues, like stress and conflict.

4. Aman is exploring career options after completing his degree in home science. Suggest any four career options for him. **Competency Based Que**

Ans. Career paths for Aman can include

(i) **Child Counselor** Aman can use his knowledge of human development and family dynamics to provide counselling services to children and families.

(ii) **Dietician** His understanding of nutrition and food science can lead him to a career as a dietician, offering nutritional advice and creating meal plans.

(iii) **Fashion Designer** Aman's knowledge of textiles and garment design can be applied to a career in fashion design, creating clothing and accessories.

(iv) **Community Development** His skills in resource management and extension education can be utilised in community development roles, working on projects to improve the lives of people in rural areas.

5. Kaustubh is conducting an orientation programme for students related to the subject Home Science.

(a) How can he explain the meaning of 'Home Science' to students?

(b) How can he insist the importance of this subject for family life?

(c) How can he justify the multi-disciplinary nature of the subject?

Ans. (a) He can explain to student that the term 'Home Science' literally means 'science related to the home. The home includes the house and all the family members living in it and Science refers to systematic study. Therefore, Home Science is the systematic study of matters related to the family and home.

(b) He can insist that Home Science is the discipline that structures and responds to the needs of the home and its family members. Its goal is to enhance the happiness and prosperity of family life and hence knowledge of this subject will enhance their quality of life.

(c) He can tell students that Home Science is a multi-disciplinary field that includes topics such as health, nutrition, child care, textile and garment design and the effective use of resources, along with other subjects related to home management.

Long Answer Type Questions

1. 'There are several mis-conceptions regarding the subject of Home Science that it is related only with cooking, laundry and childcare'. Justify this statement. **Competency Based Que**

Ans. Home Science has evolved into a very vast and detailed area of study. But people have many mis-conceptions about the subject. These are

(i) There is a common mis-conception that Home Science is limited to cooking, laundry and needlework. The fact is that cooking, laundry and needlework are only a small part of what is taught in Home Science.

(ii) Another mis-conception is that Home Science is meant only for girls. Many people think that since Home Science teaches only about the home, it should be studied by girls only.

Due to the gradual change in the structure of our society, men have to learn to share the responsibilities.

2. Analyse the socio-cultural implications of the establishment of home science as a formal discipline in India, particularly in relation to women's education and empowerment during the early 20th century. Competency Based Que

Ans. The establishment of Home Science in India, especially with the founding of Lady Irwin College in 1932, was a major step forward for women's education. It addressed the social barriers that limited women's access to higher education. By offering courses in foods and nutrition, clothing and textiles, and extension education, the college aimed to equip women with important skills for participating in society.

Although it was initially seen as focused on domestic tasks, Home Science helped challenge traditional gender roles. The involvement of leaders like Sarojini Naidu highlighted its importance for promoting women's rights and their participation in society.

3. What knowledge is imparted in different areas of Home Science? Discuss in detail.

Ans. Home Science can be defined as education for better living. It is a dynamic and ever growing field of education. It covers mainly five major areas. These areas are

(i) **Human Development** Human development deals with the development of a child from childhood to old age. Physical, motor, emotional, linguistic, cognitive and social developments of human beings are included in this.

(ii) **Family and Community Resource Management** Under family and community resource management time, money, energy and space management are the main topics for study. Consumer education, housing and equipment, interior decoration are also included.

(iii) **Food and Nutrition** Home Science covers food service, nutrition both clinical and community nutrition, institutional food services. Detailed information related to food is included in it. Nutrition provides the knowledge of various nutrients, their compositions, functions, sources, requirements and deficiency status.

(iv) **Textile Science** It includes all details about textile fibres and fabrics, fabric construction processes, viz, spinning, weaving, printing, dyeing, etc. Basic principles of apparel designing and construction are also taught in home science.

(v) **Communication and Extension** This includes media for communication programme planning and evaluation, preparation of audio-visual aid, social work, teaching about women empowerment, how to make rural women financially independent, small scale industries, new techniques of agriculture, etc.

Home Science is essential to sustain and improve one's quality of life, irrespective of the gender difference of the individual.

4. Your sister wants to know more about career options in Home Science. She also thinks that Home Science is a career option for only girls. Competency Based Que

(a) Tell her how Home Science is important for both boys and girls.

(b) What is the significance of Home Science?

Ans. (a) Home Science is important for both boys and girls in following ways

- It offers vocational and professional avenues for both boys and girls.
- Both genders have to apply knowledge in day to day life to improve the standard of living.
- Both need to manage available resources in an efficient manner.
- It also helps in increasing the rate of success in a highly competitive world.
- It helps in levelling the field and treating both girls and boys with equal share of opportunities.

(b) The significance of Home Science can be explained as follows

- **Use of Scientific Knowledge** Home Science elaborates the use of scientific knowledge in the areas of health, nutrition, textile, psychology, housing, managerial skills. This knowledge is required by homemaker in their daily life for managing and maintaining the household.
- **Economic Necessities** Today more and more women are working outside the home. At the same time, men are managing and handling the house. So, managing and balancing both household and professional life is essential for them.

SELF ASSESSMENT TEST

Objective Type Questions

1. Home Science is a ..... field of study.
   (a) multi-disciplinary
   (b) scientific
   (c) technological
   (d) None of these
2. In which year Lady Irwin College was established?
   (a) 1952
   (b) 1960
   (c) 1944
   (d) 1932
3. Which of the following is not a core area of Home Science?
   (a) Human development
   (b) Resource management
   (c) Food nutrition
   (d) Economics
4. Home Science also offers more scope for .... opportunities.
   (a) self-employment
   (b) employment
   (c) education
   (d) professional

Very Short Answer Type Questions

5. What is the primary focus of human ecology?
6. What is the central focus of family sciences within HEFS?
8. Name the various areas that Home Science deals with.
7. When was Home Science formally recognised in India?

Short Answer Type Questions

9. What does human development include in Home Science?
10. Why is Home Science important for all genders?
11. 'Resource management is important in Home Science'. Examine.
12. What are the opportunities that a student can get after studying resource management and design application?

Long Answer Type Questions

13. Explain what is Home Science and how many areas of specification does it have? **Competency Based Que**
14. Analyse the two ideas that are wrongly associated with the subject of Home Science? **Competency Based Que**
15. Explain the role Home Science play in promoting healthier lifestyles? **Competency Based Que**

02

CHAPTER

Understanding the self is the overall idea we have about, who we are and our judgements about ourselves. It influenced by both biological and environmental factors but social interaction is the key for the development.

YOUR STUDY GOALS

2.1 What Makes me 'I'
2.2 Development and Characteristics of the Self
2.3 Influences on Identity : Developing a Sense of Self

YOUR PRACTICE GOAL

- Objective Type Questions (23 Qs ; MCQs, A-R, Statements, Matching , Case Based)
- Subjective Questions (20 VSAs, 7 SAs, 10 LAs)

Understanding the Self

2.1 What Makes Me 'I'

- We share similarities with our parents, siblings and friends, but each of us is unique. This uniqueness shapes our sense of self-**the feeling of 'I'** that distinguishes us from others.
- Our sense of self develops over time. The way we think about and describe ourselves can change as we grow.

Meaning of Self

- The sense of self is our awareness of who we are and what makes us unique. During adolescence, we try to define our sense of self more than ever before. We start to think more about questions like Who am I and what makes me different from others?
  - We describe ourselves through our physical features, emotions, beliefs, potential and capabilities. This reflects various aspects of our physical, emotional and mental selves.
  - We also define ourselves by our roles and relationships, such as being a family member or student, highlighting our social self within the community.
- These descriptions reveal that the self has **multiple dimensions.** They are broadly divided into personal and social dimensions
  - **Personal Self** It has those aspects which relate only to an individual.

- **Social Self** It involves our relationships and interactions with others. It emphasises the importance of sharing and co-operation in our relationships.

The term self refers to the totality of a person's experiences, ideas, thoughts and feelings with regard to himself/herself. It reflects how we define ourselves and our understanding of who we are.

Self Concept and Self Esteem

Self-concept It describes who we are. It answers the question Who am I? Self-concept includes our qualities, feelings, thoughts and abilities.

Self-esteem It is an important aspect of self-concept. Self-esteem refers to how we judge ourselves based on our own standards, which are influenced by society. It reflects our evaluation of self-worth.

Meaning of Identity

- Identity is our sense of who we are and it stays with us throughout our lives.
- As time goes by, we experience physical changes, meet new people and develop relationships. This leads to shifts in our beliefs, values and preferences. This indicates that we are not exactly the same person we were in the past.
- Despite these changes, we retain a strong sense of continuity and sameness and a feeling that we have been the same person throughout our life. Identity has two main parts
  (i) **Personal Identity** This includes the characteristics that make us different from others.
  (ii) **Social Identity** It connects a person to a group-whether professional, social or cultural. For example, identifying as Indian links us to people in the country, while identifying as Gujarati or Mizo highlights shared characteristics with people in that state.
  These group affiliations, such as being a Gujarati, Hindu, Muslim or a professional like a teacher or lawyer, are different dimensions of our social identity.
  The self is thus multi-dimensional in nature. It changes as we grow from a child to an adolescent.

2.2 Development and Characteristics of the Self

Our self and identity is not something that we are born with. It grows over time through our experiences, choices and relationships. As we grow, we shape our identity based on what we learn and how we connect with the world. We develop ourselves as we go through different stages of life. Different stages of life are discussed below

Self during Infancy (0-2 Years)

- At birth, infants are not aware of their unique existence. They do not realise they are separate from the world around them. They lack self-awareness, self-understanding and self-recognition. This means that they do not have a mental picture of themselves. For instance, the infant looks at their hand but doesn't understand it belongs to them.
- The sense of self develops slowly during **infancy**[1]. By around 18 months, they develop the ability of **self-recognition** i.e. they begin to recognise themselves in a mirror or a photo.
- In the later half of their second year, infants start using the words 'I,' 'me' and 'mine.' They say things like 'my toy' or 'my mother' to show **ownership**. They also describe what they are doing, like 'me eating.'

1 **Infancy** It is the earliest stage of human development, spanning from birth to approximately two year of age.

Self during Early Childhood (2-6 Years)

By age 3, children can talk well, so we can understand their self-awareness by talking to them. Researchers have identified five main ways young children see themselves

- **Physical Descriptions** Children use physical descriptions of their self or material possessions to differentiate themselves from others. They may use descriptive words like 'tall', or 'big' or refer to the clothes they wear or the toys they have. Their **self-descriptions** are in absolute terms. This means that they don't compare themselves to others. For example, they say, 'I am tall' instead of 'I am taller than Kiran.'
- **Abilities** They describe themselves in terms of **things they can do**. For example, they might say, 'I can ride a bike' or 'I can count.' Their self understanding contains active descriptions of themselves.
- **Simple/Concrete Terms** They describe themselves in clear and straightforward ways. They define themselves in terms of things they can do or what is visible to them. For instance, they might say, 'I have a toy' or 'I have a television.'
- **Overestimation** Children often over-estimate themselves. They often think they can do more than they actually can. For example, they might say, 'I am never scared' or 'I know all the poems,' even if they don't remember them all.
- **Inability to Recognise** Young children don't always understand that they can have both **good and bad qualities** (attributes). They may not realise they can be nice one moment and mean the next moment.

Self during Middle Childhood (6-12 Years)

During middle childhood, children's understanding of themselves becomes more complex. Five key changes are

- **Internal Characteristics** Children start to describe themselves using their internal characteristics, like their preferences and personality. For example, they might say, 'I am good at making friends' or 'I work hard to finish my homework.' They are less likely to name physical characteristics.
- **Social Identity** The child's descriptions include social descriptions and identity. They may define themselves in **terms of groups** they belong to. For instance, they might say, 'I am in the music choir at school.'
- **Social Comparisons** They describe themselves in **comparative** rather than absolute terms, i.e. they begin to compare themselves to others. For example, instead of saying, 'I am fast,' they might say, 'I can run faster than Kiran.'
- **Real vs. Ideal Self** They start to understand the difference between their real Self[2] and ideal self[3], i.e., who they are and who they want to be. They can recognise their real abilities compared to those they aspire to have.
- **Realistic Self-descriptions** Their self-descriptions become more accurate. This is because they can see things from other people's perspectives.

Self during Adolescence (Above 12 Years)

- During adolescence, understanding of the self becomes more complex. This stage is crucial for identity development. Psychologist **Erik H. Erikson** noted that at each life stage, we must complete certain tasks to progress. For example, during late infancy and early childhood (between 2-4 years old), an important task is learning to control bowel and bladder functions.
- Without this ability, it would be hard for the child to take part in most social and community activities. While in adolescence, the main task is to **develop a clear sense of identity**.

2 Real Self It refers to an individuals authentic, genuine and actual self image.
3 Ideal Self It refers to an individual conceptualisation of their perfect or desired self image.

- There is an enhanced focus on the development of the self during adolescence. The stage of adolescence is critical for several reasons
  (i) **Self-exploration** Adolescence is a time when a person is more focused on getting to **know themselves** than at any other point in their life. They are very concerned about understanding who they are.
  (ii) **Formation of Identity** By the end of adolescence, individual's start to form a lasting **sense of self** and can confidently say, "This is who I am".
  (iii) **Influences on Identity** During this time, rapid **biological changes** and **new social expectations** or demands also shape a person's identity.

Adolescence and Identity Development

Adolescents are expected to behave more like adults and take on responsibilities related to family, work or marriage.

- **Cultural Differences** Different cultures handle the change in various ways. For example, Western cultures emphasise independence and separating from parents. On the other hand, non-Western cultures, like Indian culture, focus on staying connected with family.
- **Role Confusion**[4] In all cultures, adolescence is often marked by challenges and disagreements. They might not like to be treated 'like a child' but still seek comfort like a child at times. Parents might tell the adolescent to 'act like an adult,' but their actions might show that they don't fully see them as grown-up yet.
  - Expectations from family and society can differ for boys and girls depending on family expectations in their culture.
  - The **mixed/conflicting expectations** from family and society, along with an adolescent's changing needs and emotions, can make it hard to develop a clear sense of self during this time. This can lead to role confusion or identity confusion. Since everyone is different, people respond to these situations in their own ways.
  - This makes it hard for adolescents to focus on tasks. They have trouble starting or finishing work and generally find it hard to stick to schedules.
- **Identity crisis** Feelings of identity crisis happen when adolescents **feel a gap** between what is expected of them now and how they used to behave earlier. The difficulties that the adolescent experiences in the process of developing an identity are a normal part of development.
  For some adolescents, especially those working in family businesses, the transition to adulthood may not seem very big. For example, a child helping on a farm may not notice much change in their responsibilities from age 12 to 16, except that they might take on more tasks.

Characteristics of an Adolescent's Sense of Self

The following characteristics of an adolescent's sense of self are

- **Abstract**[5] **Descriptions** Adolescents focus less on physical characteristics like 'tall' or 'big'. Instead, they focus more on **inner-qualities**, describing themselves as 'quiet', 'sensitive' or 'brave.'
- **Contradictions** They often have conflicting self-descriptions, such as 'I am calm but get easily disturbed' or 'I am both quiet and talkative.'
- **Fluctuating Sense of Self** As adolescents experience different situations and respond to different experiences, their understanding about their own-self fluctuates over situations and over time.

4 **Role confusion** It refers to uncertainity or conflity about one's social role, responsibilities or expectations.
5 **Abstract** It refers to the intangible concepts or ideas.

- **Ideal Vs. Real Self** An adolescent's self includes both an 'ideal self' and a 'real self.' Everyone has an idea of how they would like to be, which is called the 'ideal self.' For example, a girl might want to be tall, but in reality, she is quite short. The 'ideal self' becomes more important during this time.
- **Increased Self-consciousness** Adolescent are more self-conscious and focused on themselves than children. They often feel like they are always **'on stage,'** thinking that everyone is noticing them. This is why many adolescents are very concerned about how they look.

Quick Test 1

1. What is social self?
2. Which term is used for our sense of who we are and that stays throughout our lives?
3. The ability of self-recognition develops at which age?
4. Which psychologist noted that at each life stage, we must complete certain task to progress?

2.3 Influences on Identity : Developing a Sense of Self

- The self is shaped by what we learn about ourselves from our experiences and from what others say about us. Every person lives within a network of relationships-these include those within the family, school, workplace and community. Our sense of self develops through interactions with the people around us and our own actions. Thus, **multiple people shape the development of our-self.**
- Construction of the self is a **continuous and dynamic process**. The word construction implies that the self is not something we are born with but what we create and develop as we grow.

  The sense of self develops from the early years in the following ways
  - **Personal Identification** From the earliest days, parents address children by a specific name in various situations, helping them associate the name with themselves. They also point to the child in mirrors and photographs, using pronouns like 'you' and 'your.'

    As the child learns to speak, they start using pronouns like 'me' and 'mine,' understanding that 'you' and 'your' refer to others. Parents also play games that involve pointing to and naming body parts. This helps the child gradually see themselves as distinct and separate from others.
  - **Effect of Actions on Surroundings** As infants grow, they realise that their actions affect the world around them. For example, when they touch a toy, it moves. This helps them understand that they are separate from other people and things.
  - **Relationship between Cause and Effect** As the child grows older and learns to talk, parents encourage him/her to provide statements and reasons. For example, they ask questions like, Why did you do this? or How do you feel? These questions help the child to understand their experiences and the reasons behind their actions. This helps in the process of defining themselves.
  - **Re-construction of Selfhood and the Sense of Identity** Throughout the day, the child meets and interacts with various people. These experiences help the child understand their abilities. They provide feedback about the child's behaviour. For instance, when a father tells his 6-years-old child, "That was a good thing to do. You are a good boy," it reinforces the child's self-beliefs.

Thus, the child builds and changes **(constructs and re-constructs)** their sense of self through conversations and interactions with caregivers and others.

- **Developing a Sense of Self and Identity** Each person has a unique identity for a few reasons

(i) **Unique Genes** Except for identical twins, everyone has a different mix of genes.

(ii) **Different Experiences** We all have different life experiences that shape us.

(iii) **Individual Responses** Even if we go through similar experiences, we react to them in different ways.

The factors that influence how we develop our identity can be grouped into four main categories

Biological and Physical Changes

- Adolescence is characterised by **physical and biological changes** in the body that occur in a specific sequence. These changes lead to sexual maturity, known as **puberty**[6].
- For girls, sexual maturity is marked by **menarche**[7] or the first menstruation. Boys do not have a specific event like this, but the production of sperm can indicate puberty.
- Puberty happens at different average ages in different cultures. A common sign of puberty for both boys and girls is a maximum increase in height. This occurs just before menarche for girls and before other adult characteristics for boys.
- The period of physical and biological changes leading to puberty is called **pubescence.** This typically ranges from ages 11 to 13 for girls and 13 to 15 for boys.

Typical changes during puberty for girls and boys

Girls	Boys
Initial enlargement of breasts	Beginning growth of testes
Straight, pigmented pubic hair	Straight, pigmented and kinky pubic hair
Kinky pubic hair	Early voice changes
Menarche	First ejaculation of semen
Growth of axillary hair	Development of beard
Initial enlargement of breasts	Marked voice changes

Physical changes during puberty are universal. However, their psychological and social effects differ by culture and individual experiences.

Socio-Cultural Contexts

- Physical changes in the body and changing social expectations are the two main factors that influence identity formation during adolescence. However, the impact of these changes on identity varies based on cultural, social and family contexts.
- Different societies react differently to the physical changes of adolescence. In traditional Indian society, girls often face restrictions at puberty, while boys typically have more freedom. Some types of entertainment or jobs are not considered suitable for girls. The elements of the self and the identity of a girl from a traditional community would be very different from that of a girl living in urban areas.

Comparison of Cultures

- **India Vs. West** In Western cultures, like the US and UK, adolescents are encouraged to be independent and often move out of their family homes. In contrast, many Indian adolescents remain dependent on their parents. Their family maintains control over their lives.
- In traditional Indian society, adolescents often define themselves by their family roles, **using 'we'** instead of 'I.' Self-reflection is less common and neither encouraged nor tolerated. Many Indians define themselves primarily in one or the other roles that they play-son/daughter, mother/father, sister/brother. For example, while talking about her views on marriage, an adolescent girl would say, 'In our family marriages are arranged by parents, rather than saying, 'I would prefer my parents to arrange my marriage'. This contrasts with Western cultures, where **individual expression** is more valued.

---

6 **Puberty** It is the physical, emotional and psychological transition form childhood to adolescence, typically occurring between the age 10-19.

7 **Menarche** It refer to a girls first menstrual period, marking the beginning of her re-productive life.

Traditional Vs. Modern Communities

The development of self in adolescents varies significantly between different cultural settings. In India, experiences can differ greatly among communities.

- In India, many adolescents, especially in rural and tribal areas, start contributing to the family income and take on adult roles. However, they do not separate from their families. Instead, their efforts to earn money are often focused on helping their family members.
- In traditional communities with limited job opportunities and little technological advancement, adolescents are trained in family occupations, such as weaving. They are also expected to take on adult responsibilities like working, marrying and having children. In these communities, adolescents often draw their identity from their families and typically do not face much conflict with elders. This leads to fewer confusions about their sense of self.
- In contrast, communities with more job options and technological advancements, adolescents may need extended training for their chosen careers. This can extend their dependence on parents. It leads to increase in the period of adolescence and delay in transition to adulthood.
  Apart from this, the increase in choices and exposure to alternate lifestyles may bring the adolescent in conflict with parents and other authority figures in society. The impact of these cultural influences will vary from family to family and person to person.

Family Shapes Adolescent Identity

- During adolescence, identity formation is strengthened when family relationships encourage adolescents to have their own opinions and provide a secure environment. This gives them a safe base to explore the broader social world.
- Research shows that firm and affectionate parenting supports healthy identity development. **Affectionate parenting** means parents are warm, loving and supportive of their child's efforts and achievements. They often praise the child, show enthusiasm for their activities and respond sensitively to their feelings and viewpoints.
- At the same time, such parents are firm in setting rules and discipline. This parenting style leads to independence and self-reliance in children.
- A family atmosphere that balances **individuality**[8] and **connectedness**[9] is crucial for adolescent identity development. Individuality allows for personal opinions, while connectedness involves being sensitive and open to others' views.

Influence of Peers/Friends on Adolescent Identity

- During adolescence, individuals develop a strong need for support and acceptance from their peers. Sometimes, the values of parents and friends may conflict, leading the adolescent to lean more towards their friends. This can cause tension in the parent-child relationship.
- **Peer pressure** can have both positive and negative effects. The negative impact is seen when adolescents engage in harmful behaviours like smoking, using drugs or alcohol or bullying. However, both peers and parents often play complementary roles in fulfilling different needs of adolescents.

Emotional Changes

- Adolescents go through significant emotional changes as they grow. This is mainly due to **biological and physical developments.**
- They often focus on their appearance or physical body, believing others notice every detail of their behaviour and body. For example, a teenager with acne feels very conscious and thinks that everyone is watching.

8 Individuality It refer to the unique characteristics, traits and qualities that distinguish one person from another.
9 Connectedness It refer to the state of being linked, joined or united with others.

- Adolescents react differently to bodily changes. For example, a boy might feel self-conscious if his facial hair grows more slowly than others, while another boy may not be bothered by it. Feeling proud or comfortable with physical development boosts self-esteem. However, dis-satisfaction can hinder focus on other areas like studies, leading to lower performance and self-esteem.
- A negative self-image can cause insecurity and negative feelings about one's body. For instance, a physically disabled adolescent might not feel less capable than others, while a well-built boy might still feel inadequate because he believes his body isn't 'good enough.'
- Adolescents often experience **mood swings**[10], sometimes wanting to be with family and friends and other times preferring to be alone. They may also have sudden bursts of anger as they try to understand many changes they are going through.

Cognitive Changes

The development of thinking or cognition, undergoes significant changes from infancy to adolescence

- **Early Childhood** Children start without a clear sense of self and gradually begin to describe themselves in simple, absolute terms.
- **Middle Childhood** Self-descriptions become more comparative. This allows the child to see himself/herself in comparison to others.
- **Around Age 11** Children develop more realistic self-views, distinguishing between who they are (real self) and who they want to be (ideal self).
- **Adolescence** Teenagers gain the ability to think abstractly. This allows them to consider ideas and situations beyond what they currently see and experience. They can imagine different possibilities and their outcomes without needing to try everything out. This ability helps them connect their present with their imagined future. For example, a teenager can think about potential careers that match their interests and plan their studies accordingly.

  Adolescence is an important stage for developing identity. It involves many changes and opportunities. Healthy adolescents can manage these changes effectively and reach their full potential. Proper food and nutrition are essential for good health during this period.

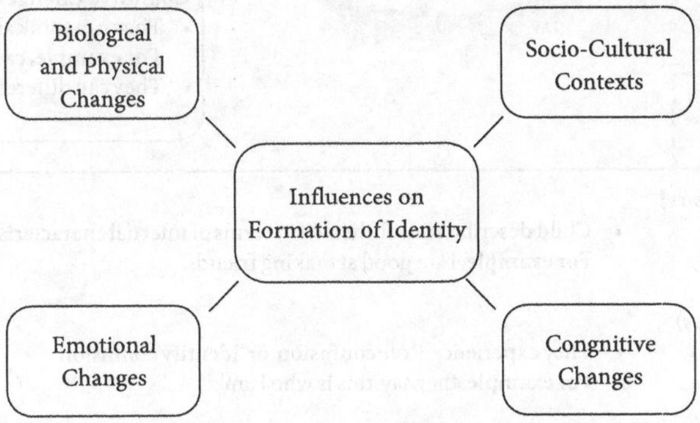

▲ *Formation of Identity*

Quick Test 2

1. List two ways in which the sense of self develops from early years.
2. Mention one factor that influences formation of identity.
3. What is the meaning of pubescence?
4. What is the negative impact of peer pressure?

10 **Mood swings** It refer to sudden, intense changes in emotional state.

Mind Map

UNDERSTANDING THE SELF

1 Meaning of Self

Our awareness of who we are and what make us unique.

Personal Self
- It has those aspects which are only related to an individual.
- **For example,** individual belief, interest and attitudes.

Social self
- It involves relationship and interaction with others.
- **For example,** interact with family members, friends and co-workers.

Identity

Self -Concept
- It is self description.
- **For example,** tall and beautiful.

Self-Esteem
- It is our thinking and standards of ourselves.
- **For example,** Like and value yourself and recognise your strengths.

2 Development and Characteristics of the Self

Development of Self During Infancy (0-2 Years)
- Multidimensional in nature.
- Self starts developing in infancy.
- By 18 months, infants start self recognition like my, mine and me.

Development of Self During Early Childhood (2-6 Years)
- Children use physical description of their self.
  For example, tall and big.
- Their self understanding contains active description of themselves.
  For example, I can ride bicycle.

Development of Self During Middle Childhood (6-12 Years)
- Child self evaluation becomes complex.
- Children began to make social comparisons.
  For example, I can run faster than Isha.
- Child describe himself/herself in terms of internal characteristics.
  For example, I am good at making friends.

Development of Self During Adolescence (Above 12 Years)
- Self understanding becomes more complex.
- They create a sense of selfhood and identify.
- Adolescent enhanced their focus on development of self.
- They experience 'Role confusion' or 'Identify confusion'.
  For example, they say 'this is who I am'.

3 Develop a Sense of Self

Personal Identification
- Parents address their child by specific names.
- It helps them to associate the name with themselves.

Effects of Actions or Surroundings
- Infants grow and realise that their actions affect the world around them.

Relationship Between Cause and Effect
- As the children grows parents encourage them to talk, express themselves and give reasons.

Reconstruction of Selfhood and the Sense of Identify
- Child meets and interact with people and get the feedback to reconstruct the selfhood.

4 Influences on Identity Formation in Adolescent

Biological and Physical Changes
- These changes lead to sexual maturity, known on puberty.
  - First menstruation considered puberty in girls.
  - Production of sperm considered puberty in boys.
- The period of these changes leading to puberty is called pubescences.
  - Age range for girls 11 to 13 years.
  - Age range for boys 13 to 15 years.

Socio - Cultural Contexts
- Physical changes in the body and social expectations influences the Identity formation.
  For examples restriction on girls, freedom of boys.
- Peer pressure can be both positive and negative.
- Increase in exposure may bring them in conflict.

Emotional Changes
- A sense of pride develops positive self-image.
- A sense of insecurity develops negative self-image.

Cognitive Changes
- They can think abstractly.
  For example, career planning
- They can differentiate between 'Ideal' and 'Real' self.

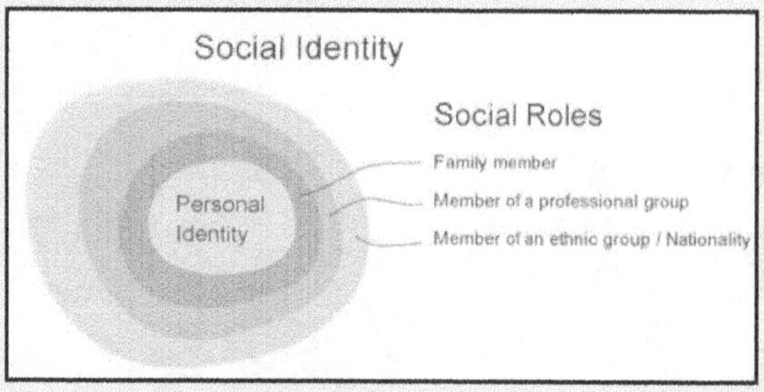

Identity

Three Components of Self-Concept

NCERT Folder

Intext Questions

1. Complete the following sentences starting with – I am.

(i) I am ....

(ii) I am ....

(iii) I am ....

(iv) I am ....

(v) I am ....

(vi) I am ....

(vii) I am ....

(viii) I am ....

(ix) I am ....

(x) I am ....

Ans. (i) I am tall. (ii) I am happy.

(iii) I am fat. (iv) I am intelligent.

(v) I am beautiful. (vi) I am caring.

(vii) I am thin. (viii) I am fair.

(ix) I am creative.

(x) I am sporty.

2. Are you the same person that you were-five-years ago? Reflect on this for some time, and write your views and the reasons for these views in the space below.

Ans. No, I'm not the same person I was five-years-ago. I have undergone several significant changes during the last five years

(i) **Physical Changes** My body has undergone tremendous transformations. I've grown taller, my voice has changed and my facial features have become more defined. These physical changes have significantly impacted my self-perception and confidence.

(ii) **Emotional Maturity** Five years ago, I was more impulsive and emotional. Now, I've learned to manage my emotions better, think critically and respond more thoughtfully to challenging situations.

(iii) **Interests and Passions** My interests have shifted dramatically. I used to be obsessed with video games, but now I'm more into reading, writing and exploring different hobbies.

(iv) **Relationships** My relationships with family and friends have evolved. I've made new friends and some old friendships have faded. My communication style and conflict resolution skills have improved.

(v) **Personal Values and Beliefs** As I've learned more about the world, I've developed my own set of values and beliefs. I've become more open-minded, empathetic and aware of social issues.

These changes make me realise that I'm constantly evolving. While my core values and personality remain same, my perspectives, interests and relationships have transformed significantly.

Exercises

A. What Makes Me 'I'

1. Explain what you understand by the term 'self'. Discuss its various dimensions giving examples.

Ans. The term self refers to the totality of a person's experiences, ideas, thoughts and feelings with regard to herself/himself. It is the characteristic way in which we define ourselves. The idea that we hold of ourselves is the notion of the 'self'.

Some of the aspects or dimensions that we use to define ourselves are discussed below

- **Physical** We use our physical aspects to differentiate ourselves from others. For example, 'I am tall'.
- **Mental Abilities** Sometimes we differentiate ourselves according to the mental abilities, emotions or feelings we possess. For example, 'I can count easily' or 'I cry very often about small things'.
- **Potential/Capabilities** We may also describe ourselves in terms of things we can do. For example, 'I can drive a car'.

2. Why is it important to understand the self?

Ans. It is important to understand the self because when we have a better understanding of ourselves, we are able to experience ourselves as unique and separate individuals. People who understand themselves have a positive outlook in life and they are open to any sort of changes as well as build on their areas of strength. They are capable of managing their emotions, behaviours, thoughts among others and identify areas where improvement is necessary.

B. Development and Characteristics of the Self

1. Describe, giving examples, the characteristics of the self during

(i) infancy **(ii) early childhood**

(iii) middle childhood **(iv) adolescence**

Ans. (i) The characteristics of the self during infancy are as follows

- The infant has no self-awareness, self-understanding or self-recognition. For example, the child may see his/her own hand but has no concept the hand belongs to him/her.
- Similarly, the child does not realise that he/she is separate from what or who he/she sees around it. The sense of self gradually emerges during infancy.
- Recognition of his/her own image in a mirror or his/her own photo happens around the age of 18 months. By the end of the second year infants begin to use the personal pronouns 'I', 'me', 'my' and 'mine' to
- Indicate possession of persons or objects ('my toy', 'my mother').
- Describe themselves ('I am tall').
- Actions they are doing ('I am eating').
- Their experiences ('I see a house').

(ii) The characteristics of early childhood are as follows

- They use physical descriptions of their self or material possessions to differentiate themselves from others. Their self-descriptions are in absolute terms, as they do not see themselves in comparison with others ('I am tall').
- They describe themselves in terms of things they can do ('I can count'). Thus, their self-understanding contains active descriptions of themselves.
- Their self descriptions are in concrete terms, as they define themselves in terms of things they can do or what is visible to them ('I have a toy car').
- They often over-estimate themselves. Thus, a child may say, 'I know all the poems', but may not remember them completely.
- They are unable to recognise that they can possess different attributes at different points in time. For instance, the child may not understand that certain actions or activities are 'good' at a certain time and 'bad' at another time.

(iii) The characteristics of middle childhood are as follows

- The child shifts towards describing itself in terms of its internal characteristics. The child is more likely to name its psychological characteristics (such as preferences or personality traits) in its self-definition and less likely to name physical characteristics.
- They may define themselves in terms of groups they belong to.
- Children begin to differentiate themselves from others in comparative rather than absolute terms. Thus, they begin to think about what they can do in comparison with others.
- They can differentiate between their actual competencies and those they want to have or those which they think are most important.
- The self-descriptions become more realistic as compared to those of the pre-school child. This may be because of the ability to see things and situations from the point of view of others.

(iv) The characteristics of adolesence are as follows

- They are likely to lay less emphasis on describing themselves in physical terms. Instead, they emphasise the abstract or inner aspects of their personality. Thus, they may describe themselves as quiet, sensitive, cool headed, brave, emotional or truthful.
- They may describe themselves as 'I am calm but get, easily disturbed' or 'I am quiet and also talkative.'
- As they experience diverse situations and respond to different experiences, their understanding about their own self-fluctuates over situations and over time.
- Each individual has an idea of what and how one would ideally like to be, towards which one would like to develop (the 'ideal self'). For instance, a girl may want to be tall but is actually quite short.
- They are self-conscious and pre-occupied with themselves.

2. "Adolescence is a time when all adolescents experience identity crisis". Do you agree with this statement? Give reasons for your answer.

Ans. This statement is true because adolescence is accompanied with dilemmas and disagreements. For instance, an adolescent may rebel against being treated 'like a child', but at the same time may itself seek comfort as a child would.

Even the parents may reinforce this contradiction as they may often tell the adolescent to 'behave like a grown-up' but other actions by them may indicate to the adolescent that they do not think of him/her as a grown-up.

This may be somewhat different for girls and boys depending on the expectations of the family and the culture one belongs to.

Thus, the adolescent experiences conflicting feelings and also receives conflicting messages and social expectations from the people around it. This causes all adolescents to experience an identity crisis.

C. Influences on Identity
How do We Develop a Sense of Self?

1. Discuss the concepts of puberty and pubescence. Explain the major physical and biological changes in girls and boys during puberty.

Ans. Puberty occurs at different average ages in different cultures. A criterion of puberty that has been found useful for both boys and girls is that of maximum yearly increase in height. The age of most rapid growth comes just before menarche for girls and before appearance of certain adult characteristics in boys.

This period, during which physical and biological changes occur, leading to puberty, is called pubescence. For most girls this period ranges from 11 years to 13 years. For boys it is 13 years to 15 years.

The major physical and biological changes in girls and boys during pubescence are given in the table below in chronological order from first to last.

Girls	Boys
Initial enlargement of breasts	Beginning growth of testes
Straight, pigmented pubic hair	Straight, pigmented and kinky pubic hair
Kinky pubic hair	Early voice changes
Age of maximum growth	First ejaculation of semen
Menarche	Kinky pubic hair
Growth of axillary hair	Age of maximum growth
	Growth of axillary hair
	Marked voice changes
	Development of the beard

2. What is the role of family in shaping the personality of the adolescent?

Ans. The family plays an important role in shaping the personality of the adolescent

(i) Identity formation is enhanced by family relationships where adolescents are encouraged to have their own point of view and where there is a secure relationship between family members which provides the adolescent with a secure base from which one explores their widening social environment.

(ii) Firm and affectionate parenting which is characterised by parents that are warm, loving and supportive of the child's effort and accomplishment leads fostering healthy development of identity. Such parents often praise the adolescent, show enthusiasm in his/her activities, respond sensitively to his/her feelings, personality and his/her points of view.

(iii) The ways in which conflict and disagreement are negotiated within the family are important blueprints for dealing with issues in other arenas.

(iv) When parents are firm in the discipline of an adolescent, such a parenting style fosters independence and self-reliance in adolescents.

It has been observed that a family atmosphere that promotes both individuality and connectedness is important for the identity development of the adolescent. Sometimes parental and peer values can be in conflict with each other and the adolescent may tend to lean more towards friends. This can cause dis-harmony in parent-child relationships.

3. To what extent does culture shape the adolescent identity? Explain with examples.

Ans. Culture shapes the adolescent identity significantly

- If we compare Western culture with Indian culture, we can understand, why this happens. In conservative Indian households the onset of puberty places many restrictions on the girls compared to boys.
- Certain avenues of entertainment or work are not seen as appropriate for adolescent girls. The elements of the self and the identity of a girl from an orthodox community would be very different from that of a girl living in an un-orthodox community.
- In Western culture, adolescents are expected to be fairly independent. Often they are expected to move away from the family to set up their own home.
- This is not so in Indian culture, in which most adolescents continue to be fairly dependent on parents as they are expected to be and the family continues to exercise control over them.

4. List the major emotional and cognitive changes during adolescence.

Ans. The major emotional changes during adolescence are

- Pre-occupation with their physical body
- Feeling conscious about themselves
- Mood swings

The major cognitive changes during adolescence are

- Developing advanced reasoning skills and ability to think hypothetically using a logical thought process.
- Developing abstract thinking.
- Considering many points of view, thus being able to compare or debate ideas or opinions.

Exam Pattern Questions

Objective Type Questions

Multiple Choice Questions (MCQs)

1. .... refers to the totality of a person's experiences, ideas, thoughts and feelings with regard to oneself.

(a) Identity (b) Self
(c) Adolescence (d) Childhood

2. .... refers to our judgement of ourselves according to the standards we have set for ourselves which are largely influenced by society.

(a) Self-esteem (b) Self-concept
(c) Identity crisis (d) Congnative identity

3. These attributes of a person that make the person different from others.

(a) Social identity (b) Personal identity
(c) Self-esteem (d) Self-concept

4. Which of the following is Not related to personal identity?

(a) The unique attributes that distinguish you from others
(b) Characteristics linking you to a cultural group
(c) Attributes making you different from others
(d) Personal traits that make you distinct from others

5. A child tells his mother that he is taller than Aman. At what stage does a child starts comparisons?

(a) Infancy (b) Early childhood
(c) Middle childhood (d) Adolescence

6. Which of the following are true regarding children's self-descriptions in early childhood?

I. Their self-descriptions often focus on tangible attributes and activities.
II. They tend to describe themselves in relative terms, comparing with others.
III. They often have a more realistic view of their abilities compared to older children.

Competency Based Que

Codes
(a) Only I and II (b) Only I
(c) Only II and III (d) None of these

7. "In this stage of life, children's self-evaluations become more complex". Which stage is being referred to in the statement? **Competency Based Que**

(a) Infancy (b) Early childhood
(c) Middle childhood (d) Adolescence

8. Which among the following is seen as a critical time for identity development?

(a) Childhood (b) Adolescence
(c) Schooling (d) None of these

9. Which of the following characterise self during middle childhood? **Competency Based Que**

I. Absolute self-descriptions
II. Identity development
III. Social descriptions
IV. Social comparisions

Codes
(a) I and II (b) II and III
(c) III and IV (d) I and IV

10. During this period, physical and biological changes occur which leads to puberty.

(a) Pubescence (b) Infancy
(c) Middle childhood (d) Early childhood

11. Which of the following changes are similar in both the boys and girls during puberty **Competency Based Que**

(i) Menarche
(ii) Early voice changes
(iii) Enlargement of breasts
(iv) Straight, pigmented and kinky pubic hair

Choose the correct option from the following

(a) (i) and (ii) only (b) (ii) only
(c) (iv) only (d) (ii) and (iv) only

12. Catherine, who lives in America, goes to her friend's place at midnight while Tanya, who lives in India is not allowed to stay out after 8 pm. Why is it so? **Competency Based Que**

(a) Difference in culture
(b) Catherine is intelligent
(c) Tanya is not old enough
(d) Tanya likes to stay at home

13. An adolescent fighting at home that he wants a bike because all his friends have one. This is the influence of **Competency Based Que**

I. Society **II. Family**
III. Peer groups **IV. Teachers**

Codes
(a) Only 1 and II (b) Only III
(c) Only I and IV (d) None of these

14. **"Boys who do not have adequate growth of facial hair, as compared to other boys, often feel peculiar about it." What kind of changes are being referred in this statement?** **Competency Based Que**

(a) Cognitive changes
(b) Physical changes
(c) Emotional changes
(d) Biological changes

15. **Choose the correct pair of stages of development with the cognitive changes that occurs during these stages.** **Competency Based Que**

(a) Early childhood: can distinguish the real and ideal self.
(b) Adolescence : does not have a clear sense of self.
(c) Around 11 years : ability to think abstractly.
(d) Middle childhood: self description are more comparative.

16. **Match the following.**

List-I	List-II
A. Cognitive development	1. Ability to think and reason
B. Emotional development	2. Changes in the body
C. Socio culture development	3. Mood swings
D. Biological development	4. Different sections of society responding differently

Codes

	A	B	C	D		A	B	C	D
(a)	1	2	3	4	(b)	1	4	2	3
(c)	2	1	4	3	(d)	1	3	4	2

Assertion-Reason Questions

Direction (Q. Nos. 17-20) In the questions given below, there are two statements marked as Assertion (A) and Reason (R). Read the statements and choose the correct option.

Codes

(a) Both A and R are true and R is the correct explanation of A.
(b) Both A and R are true, but R is not the correct explanation of A.
(c) A is true, but R is false.
(d) A is false, but R is true.

17. **Assertion** (A) The evaluation of our self-worth is known as self-concept.

Reason (R) Self-concept includes our qualities, feelings, thoughts and abilities.

18. **Assertion** (A) Each person has a unique sense of development of a sense of self and identity.

Reason (R) Every person has unique genes, different experiences and individual responses to situations.

19. **Assertion** (A) Adolescent can be a period of isolation and frustration.

Reason (R) There are increased conflicts between children and their family.

20. **Assertion** (A) Adolescents are very conscious of their apperance.

Reason (R) They find it hard to make good friends.

Case Based Questions

21. **Read the passage given below and answer the following questions.**

Jatin is a 16 years old adolescent boy who suffers from anxiety, stress, depression and exhibit anti social behaviour. The conflicting expectations of family and society along with peer pressure has made him lack the positive outlook. He is much concerned about his appearance and looks making his ideal self more important.

(i) Jatin may experience anxiety and stress mainly because which of the following?

(a) Family expectations (b) Societal expectations
(c) Peer pressure (d) All of these

(ii) Which of the following is not a likely consequence of conflicting family and societal expectations for Jatin?

(a) Increased self-esteem (b) Anxiety and stress
(c) Role confusion (d) Identity issues

(iii) Assertion (A) Jatin's problems with anxiety and depression and depression are unrelated to the developmental changes typical of adolescence.

Reason (R) Adolescents commonly experience mood swings and identity issues as part of normal development. **Competency Based Que**

Codes

(a) Both A and R are true and R is the correct explanation of A.
(b) Both A and R are true, but R is not the correct explanation of A.
(c) A is true, but R is false.
(d) A is false, but R is true.

(iv) Assertion (A) The lack of a positive outlook in Jatin's life is likely linked to his self-image concerns.

Reason (R) Adolescents with poor self-image often struggle with maintaining a positve outlook due to their dis-satisfaction with their appearence and self-worth. **Competency Based Que**

Codes

(a) Both A and R are true and R is the correct explanation of A.
(b) Both A and R are true, but R is not the correct explanation of A.
(c) A is true, but R is false.
(d) A is false, but R is true.

22. **Read the passage given below and answer the following questions.**

Kashmira is a 14 years old girl who loves to dress up and takes a lot of care about her external appearances. Due to some health issues, she had to take a lot of medicines. Some of the medicines didn't suit her due to which she had to suffer through acne all over her face. None she doesn't wish to go to school and cover her face whenever she goes out in case of emergency. She feels that everyone else is beautiful and nobody wants to be her friend. She is facing an identity crisis.

(i) What is an incorrect approach to supporting a friend dealing with an identity crisis due to appearance issues?

(a) Offering empathy and understanding while discussing their feelings.
(b) Encouraging them to isolate themselves to avoid social embarrassment.
(c) Providing practical advice on managing their condition and improving their appearance.
(d) Suggesting professional counseling or therapy if necessary.

(ii) At this stage, Kashmira's identity is mostly influenced by which of the following? **Competency Based Que**

I. Biological change **II. Physical change**
III. Chemical change **IV. Geographical change**

Codes

(a) I and II (b) II and III
(c) III and IV (d) I and IV

(iii) **Assertion** (A) Kashmira's reluctance to go to school and her need to cover her face are signs of low self-esteem and an identity crisis.

Reason (R) Adolescents who experience changes in their physical appearance due to health issues may struggle with their self-image and social interactions.

Competency Based Que

Codes

(a) Both A and R are true, and R is the correct explanation of A.
(b) Both A and R are true, but R is not the correct explanation of A.
(c) A is true, but R is false.
(d) A is false, but R is true.

(iv) **Assertion** (A) An adolescent often faces identity crisis.

Reason (R) This is the time when the person is pre occupied with trying to know oneself.

Competency Based Que

Codes

(a) Both A and R are true and R is the correct explanation of A.
(b) Both A and R are true, but R is not the correct explanation of A.
(c) A is true, but R is false.
(d) A is false, but R is true.

23. **Read the given passage and answer the following questions.**

The time when sexual maturity is reached is called Puberty. Menarche (first menstruation) is usually considered the point of sexual maturity in girls. There is no corresponding definite event marking puberty for boys, although a criterion is sometimes used in the production of spermatozoa.

Puberty occurs at a different average age in different cultures. A criterion of puberty that has been found useful for boys and girls is that of maximum yearly increase in height. The age of most rapid growth comes just before menarche for girls and before certain adult characteristics in boys. This period during which physical and biological changes occur, leading to puberty is called pubescence. For most girls this period ranges from 11 years to 13 years and for boys it is 13 years to 15 years.

(i) The peaking of sexual maturity is called …………

(a) menarche (b) pubescence
(c) puberty (d) ovulation

(ii) Which of the following is not a criterion used to mark puberty in boys?

(a) Production of spermatozoa
(b) Menarche
(c) Peak height velocity
(d) Development of adult secondary sexual characteristics

(iii) **Assertion** (A) There is no common marker between boys and girls to ascertain the start of puberty.

Reason (R) The period during which physical and biological changes occur rapidly, leading to puberty is called pubescence. **Competency Based Que**

Codes

(a) Both A and R are true and R is the correct explanation of A.
(b) Both A and R are true, but R is not the correct explanation of A.
(c) A is true, but R is false.
(d) A is false, but R is true.

(iv) **Assertion** (A) Menarche is considered the point of sexual maturity in girls.

Reason (R) Menarche marks the onset of menstruation, which indicates the beginning of reproductive capability.

Codes **Competency Based Que**

(a) Both A and R are true and R is the correct explanation of A.
(b) Both A and R are true, but R is not the correct explanation of A.
(c) A is true, but R is false.
(d) A is false, but R is true.

Answers

1. (b) Self
2. (a) Self-esteem
3. (b) Personal identity
4. (b) Characteristics linking you to a cultural group
5. (b) Early childhood
6. (b) Only I
7. (c) Middle childhood
8. (b) Adolescence
9. (c) III and IV
10. (a) Pubescence
11. (d) (ii) and (iv) only
12. (a) Difference in culture
13. (b) Only III
14. (c) Emotional changes
15. (d) Middle childhood: self description are more comparative
16. (d) 1 3 4 2
17. (d) A is false but R is true.
18. (a) Both A and R are true and R is the correct explanation of A.
19. (a) Both A and R are true and R is the correct explanation of A.
20. (c) A is true, but R is false
21. (i) (d) All of these
    (ii) (a) Increased self-esteem
    (iii) (c) A is false, but the R is true.
    (iv) (a) Both A and R are true and R is the correct explanation of A.
22. (i) (b) Encouraging them to isolate themselves to avoid social embarrassment.
    (ii) (a) I and II
    (iii) (a) Both A and R are correct and R is the correct explanation of A.
    (iv) (a) Both A and R are true and R is the correct explanation of A.
23. (i) (c) puberty
    (ii) (b) Menarche
    (iii) (d) A is false, but R is true.
    (iv) (a) Both A and R are true and R is the correct explanation of A.

Subjective Questions

Very Short Answer Type Questions

1. How can the concept of the self be defined? In what ways does it distinguish an individual from others in terms of personal identity and uniqueness?

Ans. The self is a sense of who we are and what makes us unique from others. It is sour personal identity that differentiates us from 'you', 'them' and 'others'. The self consists of experiences, thoughts and feelings about who we are as individuals.

2. How is self-esteem defined? In what ways is it connected to the self-concept?

Ans. Self-esteem is the judgement we make about overselves based on the standards we set influenced by society. It is a critical aspect of self-concept reflecting our self-evaluation and sense of worth.

3. What two concepts are related to the self?

Ans. The two concepts related to the self are the concepts of one's identity and one's personality.

4. What are the social aspects of identity?

Ans. The social aspects of identity are those aspects of the person that link the person to a group that is professional social or cultural. For example : when you think of yourself as an Indian you linked yourself with the group of people living in a country. And when you describe yourself as Gujarati, means you are sharing some characters with the people living in the state.

5. What are the two main identity under which all the identity of the self can be grouped?

Ans. The two main identity under which all the identity of the self can be grouped are personal and social identity.

6. You observe a 20 months old infant in front of a mirror with a red dot on her cheek. She touches the mirror instead of her own face. What does this behaviour indicate about her self-awareness? **Competency Based Que**

Ans. The infant has not yet developed self-awareness. Infants typically begin to recognise themselves in a mirror and understand that they are separate individuals around 18-24 months. The behaviour of touching the reflection indicates the child still lacks self-recognition.

7. What are the things for which infants begin to use personal pronouns like 'I', 'me' 'my' and 'mine' by the time they are two-years-old?

Ans. By the time infants are two-years-old, they start using personal pronouns for the following things

- Indicating possession of persons or objects ('my toy', 'my mother').

- Describing themselves.
- Actions they are doing ('I am eating').
- Their experiences.

8. Why and how do children in the stage of early childhood (2 - 6 years) describe themselves?

Ans. Children in the stage of early childhood (2 - 6 years) describe themselves so as to differentiate themselves from others.

However, their self-descriptions are in absolute terms, as they do not see themselves in comparison with others. In addition, they describe themselves in terms of things they can do, what they possess or what is visible to them.

9. When a child reaches the middle childhood (6 - 12 years) stage in life, it describes itself through his 'internal characteristics'. What does this mean?

Ans. When a child reaches the middle childhood, he shifts towards describing himself in terms of his preferences, personality traits and other characteristics which are not directly visible, but avoids describing himself by its external appearance or physical characteristics. These preferences, personality traits and other characteristics which are not directly visible are termed as 'internal characteristics'.

10. What is the range of age during which changes due to puberty are usually observed in boys and in girls?

Ans. Pubescence for girls usually occurs from 11 years to 13 years of age. Pubescence for boys usually occurs from 13 years to 15 years of age.

Hence, the age during which changes due to puberty are usually observed in boys and girls ranges from 11 to 15 years.

11. Vishal, aged 10, says, "I wish I could draw like Ramesh, but I'm good at finishing my homework." What developmental milestone does this illustrate?

Ans. Vishal's ability to differentiate between his actual competencies (finishing homework) and his ideal self (drawing like Ramesh) indicates that he is developing the capacity to compare his real self with his ideal self. This is a key characteristic of middle childhood.

12. How can self-esteem impact an adolescent's academic performance?

Ans. Self-esteem can affect academic performance by influencing motivation and confidence. High self-esteem can lead to better performance, while low self-esteem may result in decreased effort and lower academic achievement.

13. What role do cognitive changes play in the development of identity during adolescence?

Ans. Cognitive changes allow adolescence to think abstractly and imagine future possibilities. This helps them to link their present actions with future goals and refine their sense of identity.

14. List four aspects of self by which adolescents may describe themselves.

Ans. Following are the four aspects of self by which adolescents may describe themselves

(i) Physical self-for example, 'I am tall'
(ii) Mental self-for example, 'I get irritated very easily'
(iii) Social self-for example, 'I am friends with a lot of people'
(iv) Cognitive self- for example, 'I am capable of becoming a doctor'.

15. Name the factors which influence the formation of identity of adolescents.

Ans. The factors which influence the formation of Identity of adolescents are

- Biological and physical changes
- Socio-cultural contexts
- Emotional changes
- Cognitive changes

16. In what two ways is identity of adolescents influenced by their physical changes?

Ans. Identity of adolescents is influenced by their physical changes' by making them feel

- awkward and shy
- highly conscious about themselves

17. A 15-years-old says, "I'm sensitive and emotional, but I can also be strong when needed." How does this description 'align with the understanding of self during adolescence? **Competency Based Que**

Ans. This description aligns with the adolescent's ability to understand and express abstract characteristics of their personality. Adolescents move away from physical descriptions and focus more on internal traits like sensitivity and emotional strength.

18. Why might an adolescent's sense of self vary between traditional and modern cultural settings?

Ans. Traditional settings may emphasis familial roles and less personal reflection. On the other hand, modern settings may offer more individual freedom and diverse experiences, leading to varied self-perceptions.

19. What is meant by individuality and connectedness. How do these values in family contributes to the development of adolescent?

Ans. Individuality means having greater opportunity and ability to have one's own point of view and Connectedness suggests greater sensitivity to and respect for others' views and openness to others' views.

It has been seen that a family atmosphere that promotes both individuality and connectedness is important for the development of identity of adolescent.

20. 'Adolescents are pre-occupied with their physical body'. Justify the statement with example. **Competency Based Que**

Ans. Adolescents go through significant emotional changes as they grow due to biological and physical developments. They often focus on their appearance or physical body and believes that others notice every detail of their behavior or body. For example- a teenager with acne feels very conscious and thinks that everyone is watching.

Short Answer Type Questions

1. How does the sense of self develop during early childhood?

Ans. The sense of self develops in early childhood through interactions with caregivers and experiences in the environment. Initially, parents and caregivers address the child by name and associate it with the child's reflection in mirrors and photographs. This helps the child recognise themselves as a separate individual. Parents also use pronouns like 'you' and 'me,' and play games that involve identifying body parts, which further helps the child differentiate themselves from others. As the child grows, they begin to understand that their actions affect the environment.

For example, moving a toy by touching it helps them realize they can interact with the world. By around 18 months, the child identifies themselves in the mirror and understands that they are distinct from others.

2. A 6-years-old child helps clean up after dinner and receives positive feedback from their parents. How does this feedback influence their self-concept and identity development? **Competency Based Que**

Ans. Positive feedback from parents reinforces a child's self-concept by validating their behaviour and abilities. When the 6-years-old is praised for helping, they internalise the idea that they are capable and good. This affirmation strengthens their sense of self-worth and encourages further positive actions. Such interactions are crucial for shaping identity, as the child's beliefs about themselves evolve based on the approval and feedback they receive. This contributes to a more confident and socially aware sense of self.

3. Adolescence is seen as a critical time for identity development. **Competency Based Que**

(i) What are the two social traits which develop during adolescence?

(ii) List two social aspects about one-self that are under focus during adolescence.

Ans. (i) Two social traits which develop during adolescence are

(a) **Searching for Identity** Adolescents try to work out who they are and where they fit in the world. This search can be influenced by gender, peer group, cultural background, media, school and family expectations.

(b) **Wanting more Independence** This influences the decisions the adolescent takes and the relationships it has with family and friends.

(ii) Two social aspects of ourselves which we look at during adolescence are

(a) In terms of the roles we perform.

(b) The relationships we are involved with, like son/ daughter, brother/sister.

4. (i) It is important to stress that the difficulties that the adolescent experiences in the process of developing an identity are a normal part of development. justify this statement.

(ii) The stage of adolescence is critical for identity development. Provide three reasons to support this statement.

Ans. (i) The challenges adolescents face in developing their identity are a normal part of growing up. It is common for them to experience conficlting emotions as they deal with changes in expectations and behaviour.

The sense of identity crisis or role confusion arises when adolescents feel a gap between what they are expected to do now versus in the past.

However, for some, particularly those in family occupations, this transition may be smoother, with fewer emotional struggles as their roles evolve gradually.

(ii) The stage of adolescence is critical for identity development due to three key reasons.

(a) Adolescents become more focused on self-discovery, dedicating significant time to understanding who they are. This pre-occupation with knowing one-self is stronger than in earlier life stages.

(b) By the end of adolescence, individuals typically establish a relatively stable sense of self. This allows them to confidently assert, 'This is who I am' reflecting a clearer understanding of themselves.

(c) During this period, rapid biological changes and evolving social expectations heavily influence the formation of their identity. These significant changes influence an adolescent's identity by introducting new roles, responsibilities and expectations, which they must integrate into their self-concept.

5. In conservative Indian households, how are girls treated during adolescence? Why do adolescents develop a fluctuating-sense of self about themselves? **Competency Based Que**

Ans. In conservative Indian households, during adolescence many restrictions are applied on a girl child and certain areas of entertainment or work are not allowed to them. Their freedom of movement is also restricted.

Adolescents develop a fluctuating-sense of self about themselves because they experience diverse situations and respond to different experiences differently.

The confict between the expectations from one's family and society and one's own changing needs may give rise to a fluctuating sense of self.

6. A teenager feels self-conscious about their appearance due to body changes during adolescence. How can these physical changes impact their emotional well-being and sense of self? **Competency Based Que**

Ans. Physical changes during adolescence, such as growth spurts and hormonal shifts, can significantly affect a teenager's emotional well-being and self-perception. For example, a teen who feels self-conscious about their appearance, like acne or lack of facial hair, may experience a decline in self-esteem.

This negative self-image can lead to insecurity, affecting their social-interactions and academic performance.

On the other hand, accepting and feeling comfortable with their body positively rainforces their sense of self, boosting confidence and emotional stability.

7. If an adolescent is confused about his/her role or identity, what kinds of problems can he/she face? What may be two reasons due to which an adolescent gives more importance to his/her peers than his/her family? **Competency Based Que**

Ans. If an adolescent is confused about his/her role or identity, the kinds of problems can he/she face are

- Inability to concentrate on the work at hand.
- Difficulty in starting or finishing work on time.
- General difficulty in coping with schedules.

Two reasons due to which an adolescent gives more importance to his/her peers than his/her family are

(i) **Peer Pressure** During the day, an adolescent spends more time with peers than with family members. Thus, the peers influence directly affects the perspectives and values of the adolescent.

(ii) **Pressure to Conform** The adolescent faces the pressure to conform to social norms set by the peer group, irrespective of the family's social outlook.

Long Answer Type Questions

1. Explain any five dimensions of the self by giving one example of each. **Competency Based Que**

Ans. Five dimensions of the self are as follows

(i) **Physical** In this aspect of self, you describe your bodily self. An example of this is, 'I am 160 cm tall' or 'My body is peer-shaped with a slim waist.'

(ii) **Emotional** In this dimension, you refer to your feelings and emotions. An example of this is, 'I am feeling very sad due to my aunt passing away, as I was her favourite nephew.'

(iii) **Mental** In this aspect of self, you describe yourself in terms of your mental abilities. An example of this is, 'I am very quick at mental calculations.'

(iv) **Social** In this dimension of self, you describe yourself in relation to others, in terms of the roles you perform and the relationships you are involved in. An example of this is, 'I am a student of St. Gregorios Public School, Dwarka'.

(v) **Beliefs or Religion** In this aspect of self, you describe yourself by the religion you follow or your beliefs. An example of this is, 'I am a Methodist Christian.'

2. Describe how a child develops its self and identity from infancy to middle childhood.

Ans. Right from infancy, parents address their child by a particular name or names in a variety of situations. Thus, the child begins to associate the name with himself/herself. Along with himself/herself, parents also point to the child in the mirror and in photographs with that name. They use the pronouns 'you' and 'your' and when the child is able to speak, the use of the pronouns 'me' and 'mine' appears. The child understands that 'you' and 'your' refer to another person.

As the child grows during infancy, he/she begins to realise that his/her actions have an effect on the environment. Then, as the child grows older and can talk, the parents encourage the child to make self-statements and ask him/her to give reasons.

These questions help the child understand what he/she is experiencing or the reasons for certain actions; in this way they help the child in defining the self. During the course of the day, the child has several encounters with people and objects around him/her which help him/her to develop an idea about his/her abilities. People also give the child a feedback about his/her behaviour and abilities.

All this feeds into the child's beliefs about himself/herself. So, he/she constructs and re-constructs selfhood and a sense of identity through the verbal-social interactions he/she has with caregivers and others.

3. Explain five characteristics of early childhood which children use to describe themselves, giving an example of each. **Competency Based Que**

Ans. Refer to the text under the heading 'Self During Early Childhood'.

4. Rohan is a 10 years old kid who became the monitor of his class. He came home and told his mother, "I am better than other kids that's why teacher made me the monitor". **Competency Based Que**

(i) What are the characteristics of age?

(ii) Which stage of self is Rohan at?

(iii) Distinguish between early childhood and middle childhood.

Ans. (i) Some of the characteristics of middle childhood are

(a) **Distinguish Real Self from Ideal Self** They can differentiate between their actual competencies and those that they want to have or those which they think are most important.

(b) **Realistic Self-descriptions** The self-descriptions become more realistic as compared to those of the pre school child. This may be because of the ability to see things and situations from the point of view of others.

(ii) Rohan is at middle childhood stage. At this stage of life, children's self-evaluations become more complex.

This stage ranges from 6 to 12 years.

(iii) There are many differences between early childhood and middle childhood. Some of them are

(a) During early childhood children use physical descriptions of their material possessions to differentiate themselves from other whereas in middle childhood child shift towards describing himself in terms of his/her internal characteristics.

(b) In early childhood they describes themselves in term of things they can do where as in middle childhood they define them selver in term of of groups they belong to.

5. Tom a 13-years-old, is struggling with his identity and feels conflicted about his social roles.

(i) What are some signs Tom might show if he is experiencing identity confusion?

(ii) How can Tom's self-concept be affected by conflicting expectations from his family?

(iii) What strategies might help Tom cope with identity confusion? **Competency Based Que**

Ans. (i) Tom may show signs of identity confusion, including trouble focusing, frequent mood changes and an unclear sense of direction in life. He might find it difficult to set clear 'goals' or understand what he truly wants. This inner struggle could extend to social situations, where he may feel unsure of his role and place among others.

(ii) Tom's self-concept can be affected by conflicting expectations from his family. He may feel stuck between fulfilling family expectations and seeking his own independence, leading to stress and confusion.

The pressure to conform to traditional family roles while also trying to develop his own identity can be over-whelming. As he struggles to balance these conflicting demands, he might find it challenging to determine what his family expects of him versus what he truly desires for himself. This internal conflict creates emotional tension, leaving Tom uncertain about how to move forward.

(iii) To cope with identity confusion, Tom can engage in open discussions with trusted adults or mentors, allowing him to express his feelings and gain valuable guidance. Setting achievable personal goals can help provide clarity arid direction. Participating in activities that-align with his passions and interests will further reinforce his sense of identity.

Additionally, developing self-awareness through introspection and seeking support from friends or counselors can offer emotional relief and practical advice as he goes through this challenging phase as he goes through this challenging phase.

6. What five characteristics does the adolescent's sense of self have? Explain with examples.

Ans. Five characteristics of the adolescent's sense of self are

(i) **Abstract Self-descriptions** They are likely to lay less emphasis on describing themselves in physical terms. Instead, they emphasise the abstract or inner-aspects of their personality.

Thus, they may describe themselves as quiet, sensitive, cool headed, brave, emotional or truthful.

(ii) **Carry Several Contradictions** They may describe themselves as 'I am calm but get easily disturbed' or 'I am quiet and also talkative.'

(iii) **Fluctuating Sense of Self** As they experience diverse situations and respond to different experiences, their understanding about their own self fluctuates over situations and over time. For instance, in one situation they may feel afraid, but at another time in a different situation they may feel brave.

(iv) **Ideal Self Becomes Prominent** Each individual has an idea of what and how one would ideally like to be, towards which we would like to develop (the 'ideal self'). For instance, a girl may want to be tall but is actually quite short.

(v) **Become Self-conscious** They are self-conscious and pre-occupied with themselves. This gives them a feeling of always being noticed, which causes them to become over-concerned about their physical appearance.

7. Riya, a 14-years-old girl, lives in a traditional Indian family where she is expected to help with household chores. However, she also wants to pursue a career in science and sometimes feels that her aspirations are not taken seriously by her family.

(i) How might Riya's cultural context contribute to her experience of role confusion?

(ii) What steps can Riya take to balance her household responsibilities and her career aspirations?

(iii) How could family support help Riya overcome her identity confusion? **Competency Based Que**

Ans. (i) In Riya's case her cultural background emphasises family interdependence, often leading to gendered expectations. These expectation scan conflict with her personal aspirations, contributing to her role confusion. Balancing household duties with career goals becomes challenging when traditional family roles limit her independence.

(ii) Riya can start by managing her time effectively, making space for both her household duties and academic ambitions. She can also initiate conversations with her family, explaining her passion for science and how it can positively affect her and the family's future.

(iii) Family support plays a crucial role in helping Riya resolve her identity confusion. If her family encourages her education and aspirations, it will give her the confidence to pursue her goals while maintaining a sense of belonging within the family.

8. How do interactions of the adolescent with his/her family members, its peer group and other members of society affect their identity?

Ans. The relationships that adolescents have with their peers, family and other members of society play a vital role in their identity development.

As adolescents try to form their unique identities, they draw away from their parents, although parents still play a significant role in their identity formation.

Adolescence can be a period of increased conflict between parents and their children.

On the other hand, peer groups offer their members the opportunity to develop social skills; however, they can also be the source of negative influences, such as peer pressure. Other members of society create the pressure on adolescents to conform to expected norms of behaviour. Thus, their identity develops due to interactions with all these groups.

9. How do emotional changes during adolescence affect the identity of the adolescent? Explain with examples.

Ans. Adolescents experience many emotional changes during the process of growing up. Many of these changes are the result of biological and physical changes.

There are individual differences in the way adolescents react to bodily changes. For instance, boys who do not have adequate growth of facial hair as compared to other boys, often feel peculiar about it.

A proper physical growth gives adolescents a sense of pride and confidence. Further, if they are dis-satisfied with their appearance beyond a point, they are not able to concentrate on work and studies, a negative self-image can cause a person to feel insecure and also generate a negative feeling about the body.

Adolescents also experience mood swings. Sometimes their mood changes from feeling confident and happy to feeling irritated and depressed in a short span of time. These mood swings may occur due to shifting levels of hormones during puberty.

10. What cognitive changes affect the identity of an adolescent? Explain.

Ans. Cognitive development means the growth of a child's ability to think and reason. The growth happens differently in late childhood and in adolescence. By the time the child enters adolescence, he/she can differentiate between the 'real' and the 'ideal' self. During adolescence, he/she can think beyond what is present and what he/she sees and experiences.

The implication for identity formation is that adolescents can imaginatively link up their present with a future they imagine for themselves. They can think of the possible careers that they can take up as an adult which suit them.

In addition, in this stage of life, the individual's thoughts start taking more of an abstract form. This allows adolescents to think and reason with a wider perspective. Their, cognitive improvement is relatively sudden. Due to this, creative thinking as well as examination of their own thoughts and feelings are developed.

SELF ASSESSMENT TEST

Objective Type Questions

1. Adolescence is a critical time for .... part of development.
   (a) personal
   (b) identity
   (c) social
   (d) political
2. Which of the following is the time in the life of an adolescent when sexual maturity takes place.
   (a) Adolescence
   (b) Puberty
   (c) Pubescence
   (d) None of these
3. .... development means the growth of a child's ability to think and reason.
   (a) Emotional
   (b) Physical
   (c) Mental
   (d) Cognitive
4. **Assertion** (A) Defining of oneself in terms of roles and relationship is part of social self.
   Reason (R) The social self only involves individual mental abilities, excluding emotional and physical aspects.
   Codes
   (a) Both A and R are true and R is the correct explanation of A.
   (b) Both A and R are true, but R is not the correct explanation of A.
   (c) A is true, but R is false.
   (d) A is false, but R is true.

Very Short Answer Type Questions

5. What is the primary way the sense of self-develops in individuals?
6. Explain the role of parenting in adolescence.
7. Describe briefly the common emotional change experienced during adolescence?

Short Answer Type Questions

9. Examine the differences between male and female physical and biological change? **Competency Based Que**
8. 'The self is multi-dimensional in nature'. Explain? **Competency Based Que**
10. What is the difference in identity development between traditional Indian cultures and Western cultures during adolescence? Elaborate with suitable examples. **Competency Based Que**

Long Answer Type Questions

11. Explain the different stages of 'self' during middle childhood? **Competency Based Que**
12. "Culture is responsible for shaping the adolescent identity". Explain the statement with examples. **Competency Based Que**
13. "Cognitive development means the growth of a child's ability to think and reason". Describe the cognitive changes that take place in adolescents. Examine the given statement with examples. **Competency Based Que**

03 CHAPTER

Adolescence brings many changes including a significant increase in the growth rate of our body caused by the hormonal activity.
This growth affects every organ of our body and hence we need more nutrients. The nutrient needs increase during childhood, reach its highest point in adolescence and stabilise or even lower in adulthood.

YOUR STUDY GOALS

3.1 Introduction
3.2 Balanced Diet
3.3 Health and Fitness
3.4 Using Basic Food Groups for Planning Balanced Diets
3.5 Vegetarian Food Guides
3.6 Dietary Patterns in Adolescence
3.7 Modifying Diet Related Behaviour
3.8 Factors Influencing Eating Behaviour
3.9 Eating Disorders at Adolescence

YOUR PRACTICE GOAL

- Objective Type Questions (23 Qs ; MCQs, A-R, Statements, Matching, Case Based)
- Subjective Questions (15 VSAs, 8 SAs, 6 LAs)

Food, Nutrition, Health and Fitness

3.1 Introduction

We consume various foods like dal, chapatti, bread, rice, vegetables and milk. All these different kinds of food provide us with nutrients to keep us healthy and active. Understanding what to eat is key to staying healthy.

The science of food, nutrients and their effect on health is called **nutrition**. Nutrition and health are closely connected. Health largely depends on proper nutrition and nutrition depends on the food we eat. Therefore, food is the key factor for health and fitness.

Food, Nutrition and Nutrients

- **Food** Food is anything solid or liquid that, when swallowed and digested, provides nutrients and keeps the body healthy. It is the basic necessity of life. Food provides energy, helps in growth, repairs tissues, protects from diseases and regulates body functions.
- **Nutrition** Nutrition is the study of food including the nutrients and other substances it contains and how these work in our body. This includes ingestion[1], digestion, **absorption, metabolism** and excretion. These are the physiological state[2] and dimensions of nutrition. However, it also has social, psychological and economic dimensions.

1 Ingestion The process of taking food into the body.
2 Physiological State State when nutrient needs increase because of normal physiological events such as pregnancy and lactation.

- **Nutrients** Nutrients are components in food that the body needs in specific amounts. These include carbohydrates, proteins, fats, minerals, vitamins, water and fibre. We need a variety of nutrients to stay healthy. Most foods contain more than one nutrient, such as milk, which has proteins and fats. Nutrients are classified as **macro-nutrients** and **micro-nutrients** based on the amount needed by the body each day.

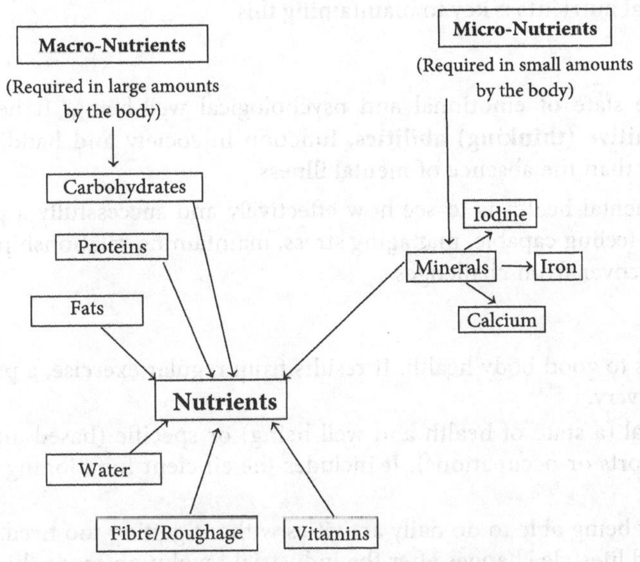

▲ *Basic Nutrients in Our Food*

3.2 Balanced Diet

- A balanced diet includes a variety of foods in the right amounts and proportions. It is essential in order to meet daily needs for nutrients like proteins, carbohydrates, fats, vitamins, minerals, water and fiber.
- It helps **maintain good health and provides a reserve of nutrients** for times of shortage. This reserve covers days when we fast or have short-term nutrient deficiencies.
- If a balanced diet meets the Recommended Dietary Allowances[3] (RDAs), the safety margin is already included, as RDAs are set with extra allowances in mind.

Recommended Dietary Allowances (RDA) = Requirements + Safety Margin

A balanced diet focuses on

- Includes a variety of foods.
- Provides nutrients in the right amounts.
- Supports and maintains good health.
- Helps keep a healthy body weight for height.
- Ensures to meet the RDA for all nutrients.
- Ensures a safety margin for nutrients.

3 Recommended Dietary Allowances These are the allowances of nutrients which cover the needs of practically all healthy individuals. These are not requirements for any individual but guidelines which tell us the amount of nutrients to be consumed daily.

3.3 Health and Fitness

According to the **World Health Organisation (WHO),** health is a state of complete physical, emotional and social well-being, not just the absence of disease. This definition has remained the same since 1948. We all aim to achieve positive health, which is a balance of physical, social and mental well-being. Eating the right amounts of essential nutrients is key to maintaining this.

Mental Health

- Mental health is the state of emotional and psychological well-being. It helps a person use their **emotional and cognitive (thinking) abilities,** function in society and handle everyday life. Mental health involves more than the absence of mental illness.
- One way to assess mental health is to see how effectively and successfully a person functions. Good mental health means feeling capable, managing stress, maintaining relationships and having the ability to bounce back or recover from challenges.

Physical Fitness

- Physical fitness refers to good body health. It results from regular exercise, a proper diet and enough rest for physical recovery.
- Fitness can be general (a state of health and well-being) or specific (based on the ability to perform specific aspects of sports or occupations). It includes the efficient functioning of the heart, lungs and muscles.
- Earlier, fitness meant being able to do daily activities without getting too tired. However, automation, more leisure time and lifestyle changes after the industrial revolution made this definition insufficient. Now, fitness is about the body's ability to work efficiently in both work and leisure. It also means being healthy, resisting diseases and handling emergencies.

Fitness is divided into five categories: aerobic fitness, muscular strength, muscular endurance, flexibility and body composition.

Importance of Being Physically Fit

Being physically fit is important because it can improve your health in many ways including

- Being fit helps people handle mental and emotional challenges.
- A fit person feels strong and energetic.
- Fitness allows one to meet everyday physical demands while having extra energy for sudden challenges like running to catch a bus.

Thus, health is complete mental, physical and social well-being, while fitness is the ability to perform physical tasks. A well-nourished and fit person learns better and has more energy, stamina[4] and self-esteem. Eating healthy and exercising regularly helps maintain fitness. Teenagers aged 12 to 18 with poor eating habits and undernutrition may develop eating disorders.

Quick Test 1

1 What is the science of food and nutrients called?
2 Name any one macro-nutrient.
3 What aspect of health involves emotional and psychological well-being?
4 What are the five categories of fitness?

4 Stamina The ability to do something that involves a lot of physical or mental effort for a long time.

3.4 Using Basic Food Groups for Planning Balanced Diets

One simple way to plan a balanced diet is by dividing foods into groups. It is important to make sure that each group is included in the meals. Each food group contains different foods with common characteristics. These characteristics may relate to the food's source, its function in the body or the nutrients it contains.

Five Food Groups Classification in India

- Foods can be grouped based on the main nutrients they provide. This classification can differ between countries due to various factors. In India, **a five food group classification** is used to help plan meals. This classification considers factors like food availability, cost, meal patterns and common deficiency diseases.
- Not all foods in each group have the same nutrient content. Therefore, it's important to include a variety of foods from each group in the diet. This nutrient-based classification ensures that all nutrients are available to the body and offers more variety.

  The five basic food groups recommended by the **Indian Council of Medical Research** (ICMR) are
  - Cereals, grains and products
  - Pulses and legumes
  - Milk and meat products
  - Fruits and vegetables
  - Fats and sugars

	Food Group	Main Nutrients Supplied
I.	**Cereals, Grains and Products** Rice, Wheat, Ragi, Bajra, Maize, Jowar, Barley, Rice flakes, Wheat flour.	Energy, Protein, Invisible fat, Vitamin-B1, Vitamin-B2, Folic acid, Iron, Fibre.
II.	**Pulses and Legumes** Bengal gram, Black gram, Green gram, Red gram, Lentil (whole as well as dals) Cowpea, Peas, Rajmah, Soyabeans, Beans.	Energy, Protein, Invisible fat, Vitamin-B1, Vitamin-B2, Folic acid, Calcium, Iron, Fibre.
III.	**Milk, Meat and Products** Milk and products Curd, Skimmed milk, Cheese.	Protein, Fat, Vitamin-B12, Calcium.
	Meat and products Chicken, Liver, Fish, Egg, Meat.	Protein, Fat, Vitamin-B2.
IV.	**Fruits and Vegetables** **Fruits** Mango, Guava, Tomato ripe, Papaya, Orange, Sweet lime, Watermelon.	Carotenoids, Vitamin-C, Fibre.
	Vegetables (Green Leafy) Amaranth, Spinach, Drumstick leaves, Coriander leaves, Mustard leaves, Fenugreek leaves	Invisible fats, Carotenoids, Vitamin-B2, Folic acid, Calcium, Iron, Fibre.
	Other Vegetables Carrots, Brinjal, Ladies finger, Capsicum, Beans, Onion, Drumstick, Cauliflower.	Carotenoids, Folic acid, Calcium, Fibre
V.	**Fats and Sugars** **Fats** Butter, Ghee, Hydrogenated oils, Cooking oils like Groundnut, Mustard, Coconut.	Energy, Fat, Essential Fatty Acids.
	Sugars Sugar, Jaggery	Energy

Note

One gram of carbohydrate and protein provides 4 calories each. On the other hand, fat offers 9 calories. This shows that fat gives more energy than carbs and protein.

Guidelines for Using the Basic Food Groups

The five food group system helps us plan and check balanced diets. It's an easy daily guide for learning about nutrition. Some simple guidelines are

Guidelines for Using the Basic Food Groups

- **Include All Food Groups** Add at least one serving from each food group in every meal.
- **Limit Cereals** Cereals should not make up more than 75% of your total calories.
- **Add Fresh Foods** Include uncooked vegetables and fruits in your meals.
- **Make Smart Choices** Choose different foods within each group as not all foods in a group have the same nutrients.
- **Combine for Protein** If the meal is vegetarian, mix foods like cereals and pulses. Consider adding small amounts of milk or yogurt.
- **Drink Milk** Include at least one serving of milk for calcium and nutrients. Milk has almost all nutrients except iron, Vitamin C and fiber.

- When planning balanced diets, choose food from each group in the right amounts. Eat enough cereals and pulses. Include plenty of fruits and vegetables. Consume animal foods in moderation. Use oils and sugars sparingly.

Food Guide Pyramid

- The food guide pyramid visually shows how to balance our daily diet. It depicts variety, moderation and proportions. Each section represents the number of servings we should eat.
  - **Grains at the Base** The broad base at the bottom means grains should be eaten in large amounts. They form the **foundation of a healthy diet.**
  - **Fruits and Vegetables** Fruits and vegetables are next in line. They are important but should be eaten in smaller amounts compared to grains.
  - **Meats and Dairy** Meats and dairy appear near the top. A few servings of each can provide important nutrients like protein, vitamins and minerals, without adding too much fat and cholesterol.
  - **Limit Fats and Sweets** Fats, oils and sweets are at the top of the pyramid, showing they should be used sparingly/in less quantity.

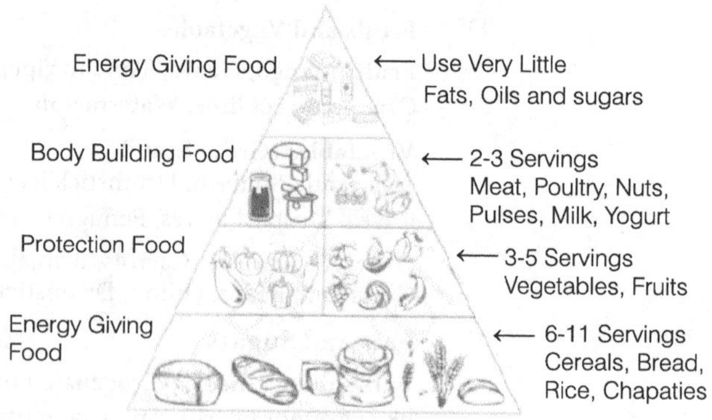

▲ Food Guide Pyramid

- Alcoholic beverages are not included in the pyramid, but if consumed, they should be limited. Spices, coffee, tea and diet soft drinks provide few nutrients but can enhance flavour and enjoyment in meals when used wisely.
- The daily food guide and pyramid focus on grains, vegetables and fruits. These are all plant-based foods. **About 75% of daily servings should come from these three groups**. This approach helps people get complex carbohydrates, fiber, vitamins and minerals while keeping fat low. It also simplifies meal planning for vegetarians.

3.5 Vegetarian Food Guides

- Vegetarian diets mainly focus on **plant foods**. These include grains, vegetables, legumes, fruits, seeds and nuts. Some vegetarians also eat eggs and dairy products.
- People who avoid meat and dairy can still use the daily food guide to create a balanced diet.
- The food groups are similar and the number of servings remains the same.
- Vegetarians can choose alternatives to meat, such as legumes, seeds, nuts, tofu and eggs. Legumes and at least one cup of dark leafy greens provide iron, which is often found in meats.
- If vegetarians do not drink cow's milk, they can use soy milk. This product, made from soybeans, offers similar nutrients when fortified with calcium, vitamin D and vitamin B12.

The food guide pyramid emphasises foods from the five food groups in the three lower sections. Each group provides some nutrients, but not all. No food group can replace another. All groups are important for good health.

The pyramid serves as a daily outline for what to eat. It is a general guide, not a strict rule. It encourages eating a variety of foods to get the nutrients and consuming the right amount of calories to maintain a healthy weight.

3.6 Dietary Patterns in Adolescence

- Healthy eating is very important for teenagers' health and well-being. Nutritional needs increase during adolescence due to rapid growth and changes in the body that occur during puberty. Good nutrition is important for emotional and physical health. It helps prevent future chronic illnesses like obesity, heart disease, cancer and diabetes.
- Studies show that adolescents often get less vitamin A, thiamine, iron and calcium than they need. They also consume more fat, sugar, protein and sodium as compared to required amount.
- It's essential to recognise common eating habits in adolescents. Understanding these patterns helps evaluate their diets and ensure they meet health requirements.
- Although the practice of eating in between meals is often criticised, research indicates that teens can get a significant amount of nutrition from foods consumed outside of the traditional meals. More significant than the time or location of meals is the selection of foods. Fresh fruits and vegetables, along with whole-grain goods, should be prioritised in order to supplement the high-protein and high-energy items they typically select.
- Some common eating habits **(idiosyncrasies)** include skipping meals, eating fast food regularly, avoiding fruits and vegetables, snacking frequently and dieting. By addressing each of these issues individually, it can be ensured that we meet our minimum nutritional requirements.

Irregular Meals and Skipping Meals

- Teenagers miss more meals and eat away from home as they grow up. This shows their need for independence. The evening meal is usually the most consistent.
- In some families with limited resources, teens may not get enough meals, leading to nutrient deficiencies. Breakfast is often skipped by teenagers and young adults under 25. Girls are more likely to miss breakfast, lunch and evening meal than boys because they want to be thin and often on diet. Many believe that skipping meals will help control their weight.
- However, this can backfire. This is because by mid-morning or lunch time they may be so hungry that they overcompensate for the **saved kilocalories**. This means that they eat more than they would have otherwise. Skipping breakfast can slow down metabolism, which may lead to weight gain and poor performance.

Snacking

- Snacking is likely a **survival strategy** for teens. It doesn't have to be a bad habit. Snacking can help keep energy levels up, especially for active and growing adolescents.
- Many teens don't eat three regular meals each day because of the skipping meal factor. In this case, snacking can help them get important nutrients. However, relying only on snacks is not healthy.

Fast Foods

- Teens, especially in cities, often eat fast food because it's convenient and social. They may think it's trendy.
- However, fast food is usually high in fat and has **empty calories.** It's important to make smart food choices, even at fast food restaurants.

Nutritional Limitations of Fast Foods

The following factors are major nutritional limitations of fast food meals

- **Calcium, Riboflavin, Vitamin A** These important nutrients are low unless milk or a milkshake is ordered.
- **Folic Acid, Fiber** Fast food has very few sources of these key nutrients.
- **Fat** Many meal combinations have a high percentage of energy from fat.
- **Sodium** Fast food meals are often high in sodium, which is not good for health.
- **Energy** Common meal combinations have more energy as compared to other nutrients.

Fast foods can provide some nutrients, but they do not fully meet the nutritional needs of teenagers. Both teens and health professionals should understand that fast foods can be acceptable when eaten wisely and as part of a balanced diet.

However, if fast food becomes the main part of the diet, it can lead to problems. **Nutrient imbalances** might not show up right away but can affect health later on. There is growing evidence that what teenagers eat now can impact their health in the future.

Dieting

- **Obesity Risks** Obesity is a serious issue among teenagers. Without action, 80% of overweight teens will stay overweight as adults. This will increase their risk for diabetes, high blood pressure, high cholesterol and sleep apnea(sleep disorder).
- **Unhealthy Dieting** Dieting without expert guidance can lead to serious problems, including eating disorders in teens. Signs of unhealthy dieting include skipping meals, binge eating, fasting and using laxatives[5] or diet pills. These behaviours can cause cycles of weight loss and regain. This increases the chance of developing eating disorders and obesity. It can also lower self-esteem and cause psychological issues. These problems may lead to heart risks and even death.
- **Promoting Healthy Eating** To tackle dieting issues, replace the term diet with healthy eating. Incorporating healthy habits and regular exercise into daily life can reduce the need for dieting.
- **Media Influence** Adolescents influenced from media about thinness. Girls are bombarded with messages from the media about what is considered a beautiful bodys and ways to achieve a lower body weight. This may result in unhealthy and unnecessary attempts to loose weight.

5 Laxative A substance that promotes bowel movements and relieves constipation.

3.7 Modifying Diet-Related Behaviour

Adolescence is a time when young people start to question authority and establish their identity. Eating habits can be a way for teenagers to express their individuality. Many rejects healthy home-cooked meals and choose to eat out, often with friends.

It is easier for us to change lifestyle and diet patterns if we are convinced that we want to do so.

Some ways through which healthier eating habits can be practised are

- **Limit TV Time** Television watching should be limited to one or two hours a day. This includes video games and computer use. Watching TV doesn't burn many calories and often leads to irregular or erratic eating habits, as people tend to snack while watching. This can cause both **overeating and undereating**.
- **Healthy Eating Habits** Aim to eat three balanced meals each day, plus two nutritious snacks and should not skip meals.
- **Snacking** Limit snacks to two per day. Choose low-calorie options like raw fruits and vegetables. Try to avoid high-calorie snacks like chips and fried foods. However, it is fine to enjoy our favourite snacks occasionally.
- **Drink Water** Aim to drink four to six glasses of water each day, especially before meals. Water has no calories and helps **create a feeling of fullness.** Limit soft drinks and fruit juices, as they are high in calories (150-170 calories per serving)
- **Diet Journal** Keep a weekly record of food and drink intake, TV and game time and exercise. Weigh yourself each week to track progress.
- **Exercise** This is essential for a healthy life. Participating in extracurricular activities such as sports helps to keep activity levels high. Here are some tips to stay active
    - Walk or ride a bicycle for short distances.
    - Use stairs instead of elevators.
    - Exercise for 20-30 minutes, 3-4 times a week. Activities like walking, jogging, swimming, playing sports or doing yoga are all good options.
- **Substance Use and Abuse** Substance abuse, such as tobacco, alcohol and drugs, is a major public health issue among adolescents. These substances can harm nutrition and health. Nutrition intervention, support and counselling would play a major role in the physical and psychosocial rehabilitation process.

Nutritional Challenges for Adolescents in Rural Areas

- **Active Roles** Rural boys and girls often help with farming and caring for animals. Girls also look after younger siblings and assist with cooking and cleaning, while boys help with agricultural tasks. Then there are the tasks of collecting fodder for the cattle, firewood and water. In tribal areas many people are dependent on forest products like berries, flowers, leaves and roots. They spend time gathering and processing these products.
- **High Energy Needs** Because they are very active, rural adolescents have higher energy and protein needs to support their growth during this stage.
- **Risk of Malnutrition** Many adolescents in poorer rural communities are at high risk of malnutrition. Girls, in particular, often experience anemia and need iron-rich foods to stay healthy.
- **Wealthier Families** Adolescents from richer rural families may face similar issues as those in urban areas. They tend to be less active (sedentary) and often consume more high-fat and high-carbohydrate foods.

Adolescence and Anemia

- Anemia affects around two billion people worldwide, mostly due to **lack of iron**. It mainly impacts women and girls. According to the National Family Health Survey-3 (2005-06), 56% of adolescent girls are anemic, compared to 30% of boys. The rates of anemia are rising compared to previous surveys from 1991-92.
- In developing countries like India, anemia is more common due to poverty, poor diets, certain illnesses, frequent pregnancies and lactation[6] and limited access to healthcare.
- Adolescence is a good time to address anemia. Girls need to improve their iron levels before pregnancy. Both boys and girls can learn about anemia through schools and media. This information can promote iron-rich foods and supplements when needed.

3.8 Factors Influencing Eating Behaviour

By the time teenagers reach adolescence, many factors influence their eating habits. These habits are formed in complex ways. As teens gain more independence and join social activities, their food choices are affected. They start buying food for themselves and start preparing their own meals. They often eat rapidly and away from home.

- **Parental Role** Parents should offer a variety of healthy foods while children are growing up. Teens need some freedom to use the kitchen, which is important for both boys and girls.
- **Peer Influence** Friends can support healthy eating but can also create stress. Peer influence and support can be helpful for overweight teenagers. However, the same peers can also target such adolescents for teasing.
- **Vulnerability to Advertising** Teenagers are influenced by food commercials. Many ads promote sugary and fatty foods. Thus, teens need to be careful about their choices.
- **Easy Food Access** The ease of obtaining food that is ready to eat also influences the eating habits of teenagers. Through home delivery/vending machines, at movies, melas and sporting events, at fast food outlets and convenience groceries, food is available at numerous times throughout the day. As a result, teens may eat more frequently and choose less healthy foods. It's important to keep an eye on this trend.

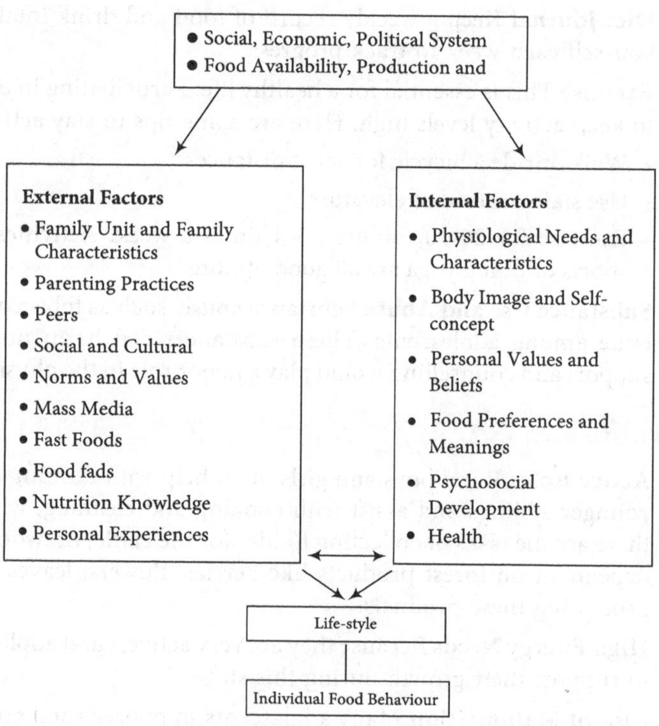

▲ *Factors Affecting Foob Behaviour of Adolescents*

6 **Lactation** The period when the mother nurses her infant.

3.9 Eating Disorders at Adolescence

Adolescence comes with rapid physical growth and changes in body image. This makes eating disorders a major concern. These changes can worsen self-esteem issues. Some common eating disorders are

Anorexia Nervosa

- It is often seen in adolescents who struggle with body image. This disorder interrupts the development of a healthy body image.
- Take Sonam as an example. Sonam wants the perfect body and has ignored her parents' and teachers' advice. She has stopped eating and is obsessed with being very thin.
- Despite having a normal weight, she feels the pressure to look like actresses and models. She struggles with low self-esteem, feels depressed and has withdrawn from her family and friends. She doesn't realise she is undernourished and insists she is fat. This is a clear case of **anorexia nervosa,** which can lead to severe health risks, even death.

In girls, anorexia can delay menstruation, stunt growth and lead to weak bones (osteoporosis).

Bulimia

- It is another eating disorder. It often starts in late adolescence or early adulthood after unsuccessful weight loss attempts. People with bulimia eat large amounts of food in a short time (binge eating) and then try to get rid of the food by vomiting or taking laxatives.
- While it's more common in females, about 5 to 10 percent of cases occur in males as well. Both anorexia and bulimia can cause serious health issues, such as convulsions, kidney failure, irregular heartbeats and dental problems.
- One way to protect against these disorders is to appreciate one's uniqueness. Valuing oneself can be life-saving. Important dietary steps include eating balanced meals, increasing fiber intake and using supplements to address nutrient deficiencies.

Conclusion

- The physical, social and emotional changes during adolescence can greatly affect a teen's nutrition and eating habits. While young people may not think about nutrition for long-term health, learning good dietary principles can help them lead healthier lives now and in the future. Health is crucial for young people, influencing their access to other important resources.

Quick Test 2

1. How many food groups are recommended by ICMR?
2. What percentage of daily servings should come from plant-based foods?
3. Write the names of key nutrients do cereals provide?
4. Which mineral is often deficient in adolescent girls?
5. Mention the factors, which influence eating behavior.

Mind Map

FOOD, NUTRITION, HEALTH AND FITNESS

1 Food, Nutrition and Nutrients

Food
- Basic necessity of life.
- Provides energy and helps in growth.

Nutrition
- It includes ingestion> digestion> absorption> utilisation by the body.

Nutrients
- Components in food which body needs in specific amounts.
- **For example,** Carbohydrates, proteins, fats, vitamins and water.

Two Types of Nutrients

Marco-Nutrients
- Require in large amount.
- **For example,** Protein.

Micro-Nutrients
- Require in small amount.
- **For example,** Iodine.

2 Balanced Diet
- Variety of foods.
- Provide nutrients in right amounts.
- Meets the RDA for all nutrients.
- Maintain good health.

3 Health and Fitness

Mental Health
- Good mental health means
  - Feeling capable
  - Managing stress
  - Ability to bounce back

Physical Fitness
- Regular exercise, proper diet, enough rest is important for good health.
- Categories of physical fitness
  - Aerobic fitness
  - Muscular strength
  - Muscular endurance
  - Flexibility
  - Body composition

4 Using Basic Food Groups for Planning and Balanced Diets

Food Guide Pyramid
- Energy giving food (Fat, oil, sugar) - Use very little
- Body building food (meat, nuts, pulses, milk, yogurt) - Eat in small amount
- Protection food (vegetables and fruits) - eat in small amount
- Energy giving food (cereals, bread, rice, rotis) - Eat in large amount

Guidelines for Using the Basic Food Groups.
- Include all food groups
  - Limit cereals
  - Add fresh foods
  - Choose different foods within each group
  - Drink milk

Five Food Groups

(i) Cereals', grains and products
(ii) Pulses and legumes
(iii) Milk, meat and products
(vi) Fruits and vegetables
(v) Fats and sugars

5 Vegetarian Food Guide
- Vegetarian diets mainly bows on plants foods.
- They can choose alternatives to meat such as legumes, seeds, fruits, nuts.
- They can use soya milk.

6 Dietary Patterns in Adolescence
- Irregular meals and skipping meals.
- Snacking is generally a survival technique for teens.
- Unhealthy diet pattern increases the risk of obesity, which is serious health issue.

7 Modifying Diet-Related Behaviours
- Limit television viewing and avoid overeating and undereating.
- Eat three balanced meals each day and two nutrients snacks.
- Drink four to six glasses of water each day.
- Avoid tobacco, alcohol and drugs.

8 Nutritional Challenges for Adolescents in Rural Areas
- Adolescent in rural areas often help in farming which needs higher energy and protein based foods.
- Poorer rural communities specially girls are at high risk of malnutrition (need iron rich foods to stay healthy).

9 Factors Influencing Eating Behaviour

External Factors
- Family unit
- Nutrition knowledge
- Parenting practices
- Personal experiences
- Social and cultural influence
- Norms and values
- Peers acceptances
- Influence of mass media
- Fast foods
- Food fads

Internal Factors
- Physiological needs
- Body image and self concept
- Personal values and beliefs
- Individual food behaviour
- Health

10 Eating Disorders at Adolescence

Anorexia Nervosa
- Often see in adolescent who struggle with body image.

Bulimia
- Start in late adolescence.
- People wait Bulimia eat large amount of food in short time, and try to rid of the food by vomiting.

NCERT Folder

Intext Questions

1. Differentiate between the terms RDA and requirement.

Ans. Recommended Dietary Allowance (RDA) is the level of intake of essential nutrients that, on the basis of scientific knowledge, is judged to be adequate to meet the known daily nutrient needs of practically all healthy persons.

The RDAs include a safety margin or reserve of nutrients to withstand short durations of deprivation when they are not supplied by the diet.

However, the term 'requirement' means the actual daily nutrient needs of each nutrient. It does not include the safety margin kept in the RDA for short-term deprivation of any nutrient.

2. Explain how the use of food groups simplifies planning of balanced meals.

Ans. The use of food groups simplifies planning of balanced meals as follows

- A food group consists of a number of food items having some nutrients which are common to all foods in the group.
- A balanced meal includes items from all food groups. Each food group has a vast variety of items in it.
- Selecting any one or two such items for a particular meal from each food group will provide a balanced meal.
- Such items will depend on availability, cost, seasonality and other factors.

Thus, knowing the food group to which each item belongs simplifies planning of balanced meals.

3. List ten foods which belong to the protective food group, stating reasons for your choice.

Ans. The protective food group consists of those nutrients which help to protect our body from injury, harm or disease. This group is the fruits and vegetables group, which contain vitamins and minerals.

Ten foods which belong to the protective food group are

Fresh fruits watermelon, sweet lime, orange, papaya, etc. They contain vitamin C.

Green leafy vegetables spinach, coriander leaves, etc. They contain carotenoids, vitamin B2, folic acid, calcium and iron.

Other vegetables carrot, brinjal, capsicum, onion, etc. They contain carotenoids, folic acid and calcium.

4. Discuss the factors that influence eating behaviour at adolescence.

Ans. The factors that influence eating behaviour at adolescence can be classified into two categories, external and internal factors

(i) **External factors** include, the family unit and family characteristics, parenting practices, influence of the peers, social and cultural norms, availability of fast foods, prevalent food fads, the knowledge that the adolescent has about nutrition and the personal experiences of the adolescent.

(ii) The **internal factors** include, the adolescent's physiological needs and characteristics, body image and self-concept, personal values and beliefs, food preferences and meanings, psychosocial development and health status.

5. Explain the two eating disorders that may arise at adolescence. What would be the best way to prevent their occurrence?

Ans. The two eating disorders that may arise at adolescence are

(i) **Anorexia Nervosa** It is a disorder tied to body image distortion. Some adolescents, particularly girls, feel that their appearance matters a lot and that people judge them by their looks, rather than their inner self. They are obsessed with their weight and feel that they are fatter than acceptable and hence they force themselves to lose weight unnecessarily by restricting their food intake.

It leads to health complications like osteoporosis, reduced height, delayed onset of menstruation, damaged kidneys and heart disorders.

(ii) **Bulimia** Adolescents with this problem will eat a large amount of food in a short time, i.e. binge on eating. Then they will do something to get rid of the food like vomiting, exercising too much or using medicines like laxatives.

If not treated, this 'binge and purge' cycle can lead to serious, long-term health problems because acid in the mouth from vomiting can cause tooth decay, gum disease and loss of tooth enamel. Any type of purging can lead to osteoporosis, kidney damage, heart problems, renal failures or even death.

The best way to prevent their occurrence would be to

- educate adolescents to appreciate their own uniqueness of body.

- They should adopt healthy attitudes and behaviours about body shape and weight.
- They should not judge others and themselves based on body weight or shape.
- They should critically view the media and its messages about self-esteem and body image.
- They can value themselves based on their goals, accomplishments, talents and character.

Activity

1. List ten foods that you commonly eat. Identify the food group to which each food belongs. Then list the macro-nutrients and micro-nutrients present in the foods listed. Identify the foods which are the richest sources of energy.

Ans. Ten food items that I normally eat are

S. No.	Food Item	Food Group	Macro-nutrients	Micro-nutrients	Remarks
1	Wheat chapatti	Cereals, grains and products	Carbohydrates, proteins, invisible fat and fibre	Vitamins B1 and B2, folic acid and iron	Foods which are the richest sources of energy are wheat chapatti, rice, groundnut oil and sugar.
2	Rice				
3	Bengal gram	Pulses and legumes	Carbohydrates, proteins, invisible fat and fibre	Vitamins B1 and B2, folic acid, calcium and iron	
4	Rajmah				
5	Milk	Milk, meat and products	Protein and fat	Vitamin B12 and calcium	
6	Ripe tomato	Fruits and vegetables	Fibre	Vitamin C	
7	Spinach		Invisible fat and fibre	Carotenoids, vitamin B2, folic acid, calcium and iron	
8	Capsicum		Fibre	Carotenoids, folic acid, calcium and iron	
9	Groundnut oil	Fats and sugars	Fat	Nil	
10	Sugar		Carbohydrate	Nil	

2. List 10 signs of good health. Evaluate yourself using the following format.

Ans.

Signs of good health	Rating of yourself		
S. No.	**Satisfactory**	**Normal**	**Below Normal**
1. Feeling energetic	✓		
2. Healthy skin		✓	
3. Rarely getting sick		✓	
4. Regular and deep sleep	✓		
5. Healthy weight			✓
6. Able to handle normal levels of stress			
7. Maintaining healthy relationships		✓	
8. Ability to think clearly and concentrate	✓		
9. Strong and healthy hair and nails		✓	
10. Good oral health			✓

3. Record your diet for a day. Evaluate each meal in terms of inclusion of the five food groups. Do you think the diet is balanced? Use the following format to write your response.

Ans. A typical example of an adolescent's diet during a day is given below

Meal/Menu	Inclusion of Five Food Groups	Comment on whether Meal is Balanced/Not Balanced
Breakfast Bread, Butter, Milk and Egg	Groups I, III and V are included	Not balanced
Mid-morning Snack Fruit	Only Group IV is included	Not balanced
Lunch Rice, Dal, Curd, Vegetables and Salad	All five groups are included	Balanced
Evening tea Hot vegetable snack and Tea	Groups I, III, IV and V are included	Not balanced
Dinner Wheat chapatti, Vegetables and Salad	Groups I, IV and V are included	Not balanced

4. Interview members of your family such as your grandmother, mother or aunt to collect information about

(a) Food taboos giving reasons why taboos are followed.

(b) Food practices during fasting and festivity from the region of India to which you belong.

(c) Preparations during fasting.

Ans. Tabulate the information as follows.

Region	Occasion (nature of fast)	Preparation	Nutrients present
West Bengal	Navratri (9 days fast)	Sabudana khichdi, fruits	Carbohydrates, Vitamins, Potassium, Fibre
Delhi	Karwachauth (1 day fast)	Sargi (sweet dish) in morning and poori, Curry, Halwa at night	Carbohydrates, Proteins, and Sugar
Uttar Pradesh	Ekadashi (1 day fast)	Sabudana vada, Falahari missal, Fruit juices and Coconut-water	Carbohydrates, Protein, Fibre and Electrolytes
Bihar	Chhath fast (3 day fast)	Thekua (wheat flour cookies), Kharra (sweet rice dish), Fruits salads, Sharbat	Carbohydrates, Fibre, Vitamins and Minerals

5. Give two inferences on the basis of the information tabulated.

Ans. Based on the information tabulated, here are two inferences

(i) Regional fasts in India emphasise traditional and nutrient-rich foods, ensuring that individuals maintain their health and well-being while observing fasting rituals.

(ii) Most fasts include foods high in carbohydrates (e.g., rice, wheat flour, tapioca), fiber (e.g., fruits, vegetables, legumes) and protein (e.g., nuts, lentils), indicating a focus on sustaining energy and overall nutritional balance during periods of fasting.

These inferences highlight the significance of traditional Indian fasting practices in promoting health and well-being.

Exam Pattern Questions

Objective Type Questions

Multiple Choice Questions (MCQs)

1. Anything solid or liquid which, when swallowed, digested and assimilated in the body, provides it with essential substances called nutrients. What is it?

(a) Nutrition (b) Carbohydrates
(c) Food (d) Minerals

2. Find the incorrect statement from the following

(a) Carbohydrates, proteins and fats are macro-nutrients.
(b) Micro-nutrients are required in small amounts by the body.
(c) Nutrients like iodine, iron and calcium are required in very large amounts by the body.
(d) Fibre or roughage is also a kind of nutrient.

3. Health is the state of complete physical, emotional and social well-being and not merely the absence of diseases or infirmity. This definition of health is given by

(a) UNICEF (b) WHO (c) UNESCO (d) FAO

4. Full form of ICMR is

(a) Indian Cure Most Mediated Research
(b) Indian Council of Medical Research
(c) Indian Council of Meteor Research
(d) Indian Cure for Most Readymade Products

5. A five-food group classification by ICMR is used in India to help plan meals. Identify the food categories under this classification.

(i) Deep fried snacks and canned vegetables
(ii) Milk, meat and products
(iii) Fruits and vegetables
(iv) Packaged food items

Choose the correct option from the following

(a) (i) and (ii) (b) (ii) and (iv)
(c) (ii) and (iii) (d) (iii) and (iv)

6. About half of our diet should include which of the following?

(a) Fruits and milk (b) Grains and vegetables
(c) Fats and sugar (d) Milk and cheese

7. Rajesh is a vegetarian which is why he doesn't like meat but he also says that he is a vegan. What does this imply?

(a) Rajesh eats only green vegetables. **Competency Based Que**
(b) Rajesh sometimes doesn't like to eat even vegetables.
(c) Rajesh doesn't eat or drink cow/buffalo milk products.
(d) None of the above

8. The soy milk used by vegan is fortified with which of the following?

I. Calcium II. Vitamin D
III. Fats IV. Vitamin K

Codes

(a) I and II (b) II and III
(c) III and IV (d) I and IV

9. Which of the following combination is both high and undesirable in fast foods?

I. Fibre II. Fat
III. Sodium IV. Calcium

Codes

(a) I and II (b) II and III
(c) III and IV (d) I and IV

10. Which of the following is not a reason for higher malnutrition rates in rural adolescents?

(a) High activity levels leading to increased energy needs
(b) Sedentary lifestyle with low physical activity
(c) Higher protein requirements due to growth
(d) Limited access to iron rich foods leading to anemia

11. Which of the following is an external factor that influence the eating behaviour?

(a) Psychological development
(b) Body image
(c) Parenting practice
(d) Food preferences

12. Reena lives in a village near Jabalpur and she is ill since few days. On getting tested, she has a deficiency of red cells in her blood. What is the name of this body condition? **Competency Based Que**

(a) Diabetes
(b) Anemia
(c) Thyroid
(d) High blood pressure

13. Which of the following pair is not correctly matched?

(a) Physical fitness – Regular exercise
(b) Specific fitness – Task oriented
(c) Mental fitness – Ability to handle difficult situations with calmness
(d) Limiting television – Helps in concentration

14. Match the following.

List-I	List-II
A. Macro-nutrient	1. Iodine
B. Micro-nutrient	2. Carbohydrates
C. Soya milk	3. Sodium
D. Fast food	4. Vitamin B12

Codes

	A	B	C	D		A	B	C	D
(a)	1	2	3	4	(b)	2	1	3	4
(c)	2	1	4	3	(d)	1	3	2	4

Picture Based Questions

15. Look at the picture and pick the correct name.

(a) Food pyramid
(b) Food clubing
(c) Food triangle
(d) Food dieting chart

16. Look at the picture below and identify the problem that this adolescent is going through. Pick the correct option.

(a) Anaemia
(b) Anorexia nervosa
(c) Obesity
(d) None of these

Assertion-Reason Questions

Direction (Q. Nos.17-21) In the questions given below, there are two statements marked as Assertion (A) and Reason (R). Read the statements and choose the correct option.

Codes

(a) Both A and R are true and R is the correct explanation of A.
(b) Both A and R are true, but R is not the correct explanation of A.
(c) A is true, but R is false.
(d) A is false, but R is true.

17. Assertion (A) A balanced diet provides a reserve of nutrients for times of shortage on days when we fast or have short-term nutrient deficiencies.

Reason (R) Recommended dietary allowance has been formulated keeping in mind our requirements and safety margin.

18. Assertion (A) The food guide pyramid is a graphic representation of the daily food guide.

Reason (R) The size of each section represents the number of daily servings recommended.

19. Assertion (A) Irregular meals and skipping meals is a common eating habit in adolescents.

Reason (R) Adolescent girls want to be thin and often diet and belives that this would help control their weight.

20. Assertion (A) Rejection of healthy home food and eating outside, in order to conform to peer pressure, is common during adolescence.

Reason (R) It is necessary to eat food only at home to stay healthy.

21. Assertion (A) There are high chances of malnourishment in children of rural areas among the poor communities.

Reason (R) Children in rural areas perform multiple tasks which require high protein levels but are not able to afford proper diet.

Case Based Questions

22. Read the passage given below and answer the following questions.

Anemia afflicts an estimated two billion people worldwide, mostly due to iron deficiency. It primarily affects women and girls. The latest National Family Health Survey–3 (NFHS-3) conducted in 2005-06 has revealed 56% of adolescent girls and 30% of adolescent boys are anemic.

(i) Anemia occurs due to the deficiency of ....

(a) Vitamin k
(b) Vitamin B_2
(c) Iron
(d) Calcium

(ii) Which of the following groups is the most likely to have anemia?

(a) Men
(b) Women
(b) Children
(d) Older adults

(iii) Which of the following is a cause of anemia?

I. Poverty
II. Inadequate diet
III. Illiteracy
IV. Fast food

Codes

(a) I and II
(b) II and II
(b) II and IV
(d) I and IV

(iv) **Assertion** (A) Anemia primarily affects women and girls. Nearly 56% of adolescent girls are found to be anemic.

Reason (R) Women experience blood loss due to menstruation and if iron is not supplemented adequately in diet, this can make them anemic.

(a) Both A and R are true and R is the correct explanation of A
(b) Both A and R are true, but R is not the correct explanation of A
(c) A is true, but R is false
(d) A is false, but R is true

23. Read the passage given below and answer the following questions.

Vegetarian diets rely mainly on plant foods: grain, vegetables, legumes, fruits, seeds, and nuts. Some vegetarian diets include eggs, milk products. Or both. People who do not eat meats or milk products can still use the daily food guide to create an adequate diet. The food groups are similar and the number of servings remains the same. Vegetarians can select alternatives to meat such as legumes, seeds, nuts, tofu and for those who eat them, eggs. Legumes, and at least one cup of dark leafy greens, help to supply the iron that meats usually provide. Vegetarians who do not drink cow's milk can use soy milk' a product made from soyabeans that provides similar nutrients if it has been fortified with Calcium, Vitamin D, and Vitamin B12 (i.e., these nutrients are added).

(i) **Which among the following are the primary food sources in a vegetarian diet?**

I. Meat, fish and poultry
II. Grain, vegetables, legumes, fruits, seeds and nuts
III. Dairy products and eggs
IV. Processed foods

Codes
(a) II and III only
(b) I , III and IV only
(c) II and IV only
(d) II only

(ii) **Which of the following is a suitable alternative to meat for vegetarians?**

(a) Dairy products only
(b) Legumes, seeds, nuts and tofu
(c) Fish and poultry
(d) Processed food only

(iii) **Given below are two statements labelled as Assertion (A) and Reason (R).**

Assertion (A) Vegetarians who do not drink cow's milk can use soy milk as an alternative.

Reason (R) Soy milk provides similar nutrients to cow's milk when fortified with calcium, vitamin D and vitamin B12.

(a) Both A and R are true and R is the correct explanation of A.
(b) Both A and R are true but R is not the correct explanation of A.
(c) A is true but R is false.
(d) A is false but R is true.

(iv) **What is essential for vegetarians to include in their diet to supply iron?**

(a) Red meat and poultry
(b) Legumes and dark leafy greens
(c) Fish and seafood
(d) Eggs and dairy products

Answers

1. (c) Food
2. (c) Nutrients like iodine, iron and calcium are required in very large amounts by the body.
3. (b) WHO
4. (b) Indian Council of Medical Research
5. (c) (ii) and (iii)
6. (b) Grains and vegetables
7. (c) Rajesh doesn't eat or drink cow/buffalo milk products.
8. (a) I and II
9. (b) II and III
10. (b) Sedentary lifestyle with low physical activity
11. (c) Parenting practice
12. (b) Anaemia
13. (d) Limiting television-Helps in concentration
14. (c) 2, 1, 4, 3
15. (a) Food pyramid
16. (c) Obesity
17. (b) Both A and R are true, but R is not the correct explanation of A.
18. (a) Both A and R are true and R is the correct explanation of A.
19. (a) Both A and R are true and R is the correct explanation of A.
20. (c) A is true, but R is false.
21. (a) Both A and R are true and R is the correct explanation of A.
22. (i)-(c), (ii)-(b), (iii)-(a), (iv)-(a).
23. (i)-(d), (ii)-(b), (iii)-(a), (iv)-(d).

Subjective Questions

Very Short Answer Type Questions

1. What are the functions of food?

Ans. The functions of food are to supply energy, enable growth and repair of tissues and organs, protect the body from disease and regulate body functions.

2. What are nutrients and how can they be classified?

Ans. Nutrients are the constituents in food that must be supplied to the body in suitable amounts.

They can be classified as macro-nutrients (required in large amount every day) and micro-nutrients (required in small amount every day) on the basis of the required quantity to be consumed by us everyday.

3. What is included in a balanced diet? What is its main function?

Ans. A balanced diet includes a variety of foods in adequate amount and correct proportions to meet the day's requirements of all essential nutrients.

Its main function is to promote and preserve good health while also providing a safety margin or reserve of nutrients to withstand short duration of deprivation.

4. What are the two major classes of micro-nutrients required by our body?

Ans. The two major classes of micro-nutrients required by our body are vitamins and minerals.

5. Explain what do you understand by mental health.

Ans. Mental health is a state of emotional and psychological well-being in which a person is able to use cognitive and emotional capabilities, function in society and meet the ordinary demands of everyday life.

However, the absence of a recognised mental disorder is not necessarily an indicator of mental well-being.

6. What are the two aspects of physical fitness?

Ans. The two aspects of physical fitness are

(i) General fitness, which is a state of health and well-being.

(ii) Specific fitness, which is task-oriented, based on the ability to perform specific aspects of sports or occupations.

7. What can be the common features of differents foods present in same food groups?

Ans. A food group consists of different food which have common characteristics. The common features may be the source of food, the physiological function performed and the nutrients present.

8. Sameer, a 17-years-old from Bangalore, is concerned about his calcium intake as he dislikes dairy products. What alternative sources of calcium should Sameer consider for his diet? **Competency Based Que**

Ans. Sameer can enhance his calcium intake by consuming non-dairy sources like green leafy vegetables (e.g., spinach and fenugreek), fortified plant-based milks and nuts (such as almonds). Including sesame seeds and tofu in his diet will also help meet his calcium needs effectively.

9. What nutrients are adolescents likely to take less or more than their required quantities in their normal diets? What should they do instead?

Ans. Adolescents take less vitamin A, thiamine, iron and calcium than recommended in their normal diets. They consume more fat, sugar, protein and sodium than required. They should instead consume more fresh vegetables and fruits as well as whole-grain products.

10. 'It has been shown that teenagers obtain substantial nourishment from food eaten outside of the traditional meals.' How choice of food is important in this context for adolescent?

Ans. The choice of food that adolescent makes is of greater importance than the time or place of eating. Emphasis should be placed on fresh vegetables and fruits as well as whole grain products to complement the food high in energy value and protein that they commonly choose.

11. What are the alternative food items for vegans, i.e. vegetarians who do not consume cow/buffalo milk or its products?

Ans. The alternative food items for vegans are as follows

(i) They can select alternatives to meat such as legumes, seeds, nuts and tofu (a soyabean product).

(ii) They can select alternatives to milk and its products by using soya 'milk'. It is a product made from soyabeans that provides similar nutrients and has been fortified with calcium, vitamin D and vitamin B12.

12. Imagine Rahul, a college student who frequently eats fast food due to his busy schedule. What are four major nutritional limitations of relying heavily on fast food that he should be aware of? **Competency Based Que**

Ans. Four major nutritional limitations of fast foods

(i) Calcium, riboflavin and vitamin A are low unless milk or a milkshake is added.

(ii) Folic acid and fibre are lacking in most fast foods.

(iii) Fat and sodium are high in most fast food meal combinations.
(iv) Common fast food meal combinations contain excess energy in comparison to other nutrients.

13. How does unhealthy dieting negatively affect health of adolescents?

Ans. Unhealthy dieting or dieting without expert guidance can lead to serious problems including eating disorders and obesity in teenagers.

Unhealthy dieting can cause cycles of weight loss and regain. Some of the signs of unhealthy dieting are as follows

- Skipping meals
- Binge eating
- Fasting
- Using laxatives or diet pills

14. Consider Priya, a high school student who has been struggling with substance abuse issues. Which substances are most commonly abused by adolescents like Priya? What steps should be taken to rehabilitate her and support her recovery effectively? **Competency Based Que**

Ans. Substances most widely abused by adolescents like Priya are tobacco, alcohol and marijuana/ other addictive drugs.

To rehabilitate the affected person, nutritional intervention, support and counselling are required.

15. Meera frequently watches food commercials that promote sugary snacks. How might these advertisements affect her dietary choices? **Competency Based Que**

Ans. Exposure to food commercials that promote sugary snacks can influence Meera's dietary choices by increasing her desire for these products.

Advertising often emphasises taste and convenience, which can overshadow nutritional value. This might lead Meera to consume more sugary snacks, which are high in empty calories and low in essential nutrients.

Short Answer Type Questions

1. What do you understand by the term RDA? Mention six properties of a balanced diet.

Ans. The term 'RDA' means the Recommended Dietary Allowance (RDA) for a person, which comprises the daily nutritional requirements of a person plus a margin of safety.

Six properties of a balanced diet are

(i) It includes a variety of food items.
(ii) It meets the RDA for all nutrients.
(iii) It includes nutrients in correct proportions.
(iv) It provides a safety margin for nutrients.
(v) It promotes and preserves good health.
(vi) It maintains acceptable body weight for the relevant height.

2. What are macro-nutrients? List the macro-nutrients required by the body everyday along with any two items of common consumption containing each of these macro-nutrients.

Ans. Macro-nutrients are those nutrients which are required in large amount by the body everyday. The nutrients that are needed in large amount are

(i) Carbohydrates, found in rice and wheat.
(ii) Proteins, available in abundance in pulses and eggs.
(iii) Fats, in milk and eggs.
(iv) Water, almost all food items contain this in different proportions.
(v) Fibre, usually found in all cereals and fruits.

3. How is health defined by WHO? What is the difference between health and fitness?

Ans. As defined by WHO, "Health is the state of complete physical, emotional and social well-being and not merely the absence of diseases or infirmity".

The difference between health and fitness is that health is a state of complete mental, physical and social well-being, whereas fitness is the ability to meet the demands of a physical task.

4. Aarav, a teenager, is frequently skipping breakfast and prefers fast food. **Competency Based Que**

(i) How might this affect his nutritional intake?
(ii) What adjustments can he make?

Ans. (i) Aarav's habit of skipping breakfast can lead to irregular metabolism and overeating later in the day. This can potentially contribute to weight gain and poor nutritional status.

Fast food, though convenient, is often high in fats, sugars and sodium which can exacerbate nutrient deficiencies and increase the risk of chronic diseases.

(ii) To improve his nutrition, Aarav should aim to have a balanced breakfast daily, including. whole grains, fruits and proteins.

Reducing fast food intake and opting for healthier snacks like fruits and nuts will also help. Consistent, nutritious meals will support better growth and overall health.

5. On what condition are fast foods nutritionally acceptable? List six internal factors influencing eating behaviour in adolescents.

Ans. Fast foods are nutritionally acceptable on the condition that they are consumed judiciously and as a part of a well-balanced diet, but should not be the mainstay of the diet.

Six internal factor influencing eating behaviour in adolescents are

(i) Physiological needs and characteristics
(ii) Body image and self-concept
(iii) Personal values and beliefs
(iv) Food preferences and meanings
(v) Psychosocial development
(vi) Health status

6. Aisha is influenced by advertisements that showcase glamorous images of thin bodies. How might this impact her eating behaviour and self-esteem? **Competency Based Que**

Ans. Aisha's exposure to advertisements that emphasise thinness can negatively impact her eating behaviour and self-esteem. She might feel pressured to conform to unrealistic body ideals, which can lead to unhealthy dieting practices, disordered eating and decreased self-esteem.

It is important for Aisha to receive support in developing a positive body image and understanding that health is not solely defined by appearance. Promoting self-acceptance and educating her about healthy eating habit can help her focus on overall well-being rather than appearance alone.

7. Aarav spends more than four hours daily watching television and playing video games. How might this affect his eating habits and health? **Competency Based Que**

Ans. Aarav's extended television and video game time can lead to erratic eating patterns, such as mindless snacking or overeating.

The sedentary nature of these activities also contributes to reduced physical activity, potentially leading to weight gain and poor overall health.

Limiting screen time to 1-2 hours daily and incorporating more physical activities can help Aarav establish helathier eating habits and improve his well-being. Encouraging breaks for physical exercise and promoting mindful eating can also mitigate the negative effects of extended screen time.

8. What are the two categories of factors influencing eating behaviour of adolescents? Explain any two factors of the category which is not dependent of the individual.

Ans. The two categories of factors influencing eating behaviour are external factors and internal factors.

Two factors which are external to the individual are

(i) **Peer Influence** Peers can strongly affect eating behaviour by promoting certain food trends or social pressures. They can offer support and encouragement for healthy choices but may also create stress or encourage unhealthy eating habits through teasing or group norms.

(ii) **Parenting** While the family provides the initial foundation for eating habits, parental guidance and the availability of nourishing food choices play a crucial role. Parents can help offering a range of healthy foods and giving teenagers the freedom to use the kitchen, which influences their food choices and independence.

Long Answer Type Questions

1. What are the five basic food groups formed by ICMR and what are their functions? Also list one consideration for using each of these food groups in planning a meal for a family.

Ans. The five basic food groups, their functions and considerations for their use in planning a meal for a family are given below

Basic Food Group	Function	Consideration
Cereals, millets and tubers	Providing energy	Choose whole grain cereals instead of refined cereals
Pulse and legumes	For body building	Give these to vegetarians along with nuts
Milk and milk products, eggs, meat and fish	For body building	Include one serving of milk or milk products in any form
Vegetables and fruits	For giving protection	Include green leafy vegetables in any form
Oils and fats, nuts, sugar and jaggery	Providing energy	Limit the use of ghee, butter, oil and sugar

2. Why is healthy eating very important for an adolescent? Explain six guidelines for planning meals to ensure healthy eating based on the five basic food groups.

Ans. Healthy eating is very important for an adolescent. This is because, during adolescence, a growth spurt occurs due to the activity of hormones that affect every organ of the body.

Six guidelines for planning meals to ensure healthy eating based on the five basic food groups are as follows

(i) Include at least one or a minimum number of servings from each food group in each meal.

(ii) Make choices within each group, as foods within each group are similar but not identical in nutritive value.

(iii) If the meal is vegetarian, use suitable combinations to improve the overall protein quality of the diet.
For instance, we can serve cereal-pulses combination or include small quantity of milk or curd in the meal.
(iv) Include uncooked vegetables and fruits in the meals.
(v) Include at least one serving of milk to ensure a supply of calcium and other nutrients as milk contains all nutrients except iron, vitamin C and fibre.
(vi) Ensure that cereals should not supply more than 75 per cent of total calories.

3. Riya is given the task of planning a diet for her teenage sibling Aman. List and explain five issues that she should keep in mind while planning the diet of an adolescent child. **Competency Based Que**

Ans. Five issues that Riya should keep in mind while planning the diet of an adolescent child are as follows

(i) To include variety, colour, taste appeal and adequate nutrition to the adolescent, we will provide food stuffs like missi roti, rice pulao, pav bhaji, etc at different meals.
(ii) To provide adequate amount of fibre in the menu by including fruits and salads along with the meals.
(iii) Ensure that neither too heavy nor too light meals are given at any time. Breakfast will be the heaviest meal of the day, while dinner will be the lightest.
(iv) The total supply of nutrients will be divided into three equal parts, with one part being given in breakfast, another during lunch and the third during evening tea time and dinner.
(v) Spicy and deep fried foods will be avoided.

4. How does eating behaviour manifest itself in adolescents? What healthy dietary practices should they adopt to maintain good health?

Ans. During adolescence, eating behavior is often influenced by a desire for independence and peer pressure. Teenagers may reject home-cooked meals, preferring fast food or snacks that are high in calories but low in nutrients. They may also eat erratically, skipping meals or overeating, especially while watching TV or using screens.

To maintain good health, adolescents should adopt healthy dietary practices. This includes eating three balanced meals each day and limiting snacks to two healthy options like fruits or vegetables. Drinking plenty of water (four to six glasses daily) helps maintain hydration and reduces unnecessary calorie intake from sugary drinks. Limiting TV time to one or two hours daily can also help avoid unhealthy eating habits. Regular exercise, such as walking, cycling, or playing sports, is essential for overall health. Keeping a food journal can help track eating habits and make it easier to adopt healthier choices.

5. Diya is actively involved in farming and household duties in a rural setting.
(i) Why does she need more nutritional intake compared to adolescents living in urban environments?
(ii) What steps can she take to meet her specific nutritional needs effectively? **Competency Based Que**

Ans. (i) Diya requires more nutrition than urban adolescents due to the high level of physical activity involved in her rural lifestyle, including farming, cattle-rearing and household chores. This increased physical exertion leads to higher caloric and protein needs.
Rural areas often have limited access to a diverse range of food, which can contribute to nutritional deficiencies.
(ii) To meet her increased nutritional needs, Diya should include a variety of locally available nutrient-dense foods in her diet, such as legumes, pulses and animal products, to provide adequate protein and energy.
Consuming iron-rich foods like dark leafy greens and fortified cereals can help prevent anemia, which is prevalent in rural areas.

6. Preeti is an adolescent girl, who eats a large amount of food in a short time and then she vomits or use laxatives to get rid of that food intake. She does this in order to reduce weight.
(i) Which eating disorder is she suffering from?
(ii) State some factors influencing eating behaviour.
(iii) Which other eating disorder does adolescents suffer from? **Competency Based Que**

Ans. (i) She is suffering from Bulimia. Bulimia is a type of eating disorder. Adolescents with this problem will eat a large amount of food in a short time.
(ii) Eating behaviour is influenced by both external and internal factors.
External Factors Family, parenting practices, peers social and cultural norms, mass media, etc.
Internal Factors Physiological needs, body image and self concept, personal values and beliefs, etc.
(iii) The other eating disorder adolescents may suffer is anorexia nervosa.

SELF ASSESSMENT TEST

Objective Type Questions

1. Which of the following are the functions of food?
(a) Protect the body from disease
(b) Regulate body functions
(c) Supply energy
(d) All of these

2. The balanced diet meets the RDA for a person as RDA = Requirements + Margin of safety
The full form of RDA is ....
(a) Right Dietary Allowances
(b) Recommended Dietary Allowances
(c) Required Diet for Adolescents
(d) Reasonable Dietary Allowance

3. What is a potenhal negative effect of skipping breakfast?
(a) Increased metabolism
(b) Better weight management
(c) Overcompensation in later meals
(d) Enhanced cognitive performance

Very Short Answer Type Questions

4. What is Nutrition?

5. Define mental health.

6. Which category of the fruit and vegetable group supplied the maximum amount of iron?

Short Answer Type Questions

7. Discuss the role of peer influences in adolescent dietary choices and how it can be managed. **Competency Based Que**

8. List out the four major nutritional limitations of fast foods and explain. **Competency Based Que**

Long Answer Type Questions

9. Explain the major eating peculiarities of adolescents.

10. "Positive health is a perfect blend of physical, social and mental health". Elaborate. **Competency Based Que**

11. Explain the food guide pyramid with figure.

12. Compare and contrast the dietary challenges faced by adolescents in rural and urban areas.

04

CHAPTER

We need to manage our resources in an effective manner to complete and achieve our goals.

Management of Resources

▼ **YOUR STUDY GOALS**

▼ **YOUR PRACTICE GOAL**

- Objective Type Questions (18 Qs ; MCQs, A-R, Statements, Matching, Case Based)
- Subjective Questions (10 VSAs, 7 SAs, 5 LAs)

4.1 Introduction

In our daily lives, we engage in various activities like travelling to school, studying, cooking and washing clothes. To complete these tasks, we need resources such as knowledge, money, energy, materials, time, property and skills. Things which we use to complete tasks and achieve our goals are called **resources**.

Anything we use while carrying out any activity becomes a resource. On the other hand, anything which is not used by us is not a resource. For example, a bicycle which has not been used for long and is just lying at your place may not be a resource for you. However, it may be a resource to someone else.

Classification of Resources

Resources can be classified in different ways such as

- Human/Non-human resources
- Individual/Shared resources
- Natural/Community resources

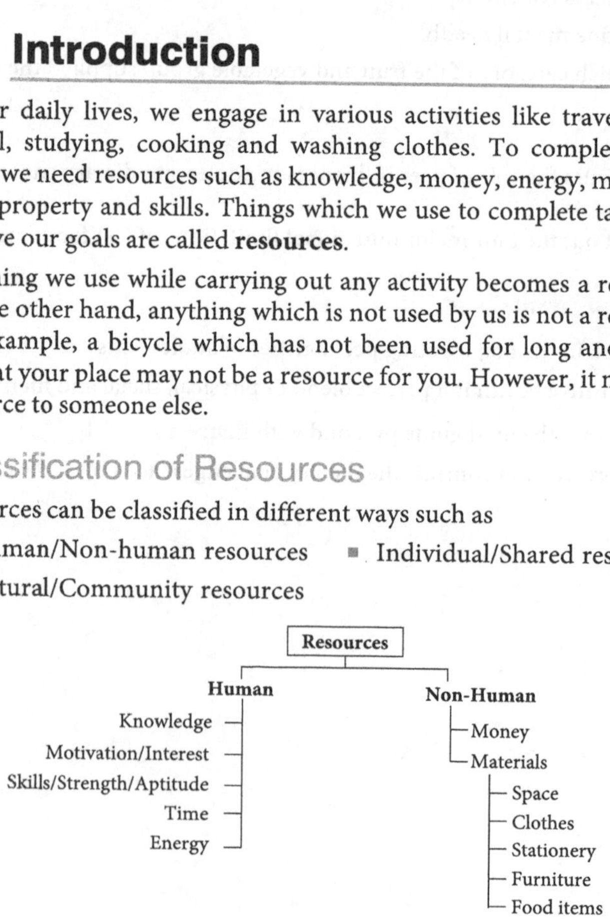

▲ *Classification of Resources*

Human Resources and Non-Human Resources

Human Resources

Human resources are essential for completing any activity. These resources can be developed **through training and self-development**. For example, you can gain knowledge about a specific field or task and develop skills that will help you build **aptitude**[1].

This can be of different types

- **Knowledge** It is a resource that we use throughout our lives and is essential for successfully completing any activity. For example, a cook needs to know how to use a stove before cooking and a teacher needs to have a strong understanding of their subject to teach effectively. If a teacher does not have good knowledge of his/her subject, then he/she cannot become an effective teacher. It's important to keep learning and acquiring knowledge throughout life.
- **Motivation/Interest** The saying **"Where there is a will, there's a way"** means that to accomplish any task, one must be motivated and interested in doing it. For example, if a student is not interested in learning, they might make excuses and not complete the task, even if other resources are available. Our motivation drives us to pursue hobbies like dance, painting, reading and art.
- **Skills/Strength/Aptitude** Not everyone is skilled in all activities. Each person has strengths in certain areas, allowing them to perform better. For example, pickles made by different people will taste different depending on their skill. However, we can learn and develop new skills through practice and training.
- **Time** Time is a resource that is arailable to everyone equally. There are 24 hours in a day and each person uses their time in their own way. Once time is lost, it can't be regained. Therefore, it the most **valuable resource**. Managing time well to reach your goals is very important. We need to plan carefully and use the time we have to complete our tasks.

  Time can be divided into three parts i.e. **work time, non-work time** and **rest or leisure time**. It is important to balance these three parts to achieve your goals. Balancing them helps us stay physically fit, emotionally strong and mentally alert. One should know when they are most productive and use that time wisely to achieve your goals.
- **Energy** It is important for growth and **physical outputs**[2]. Energy levels vary from person to person based on factors like physical fitness, mental state, personality, age and lifestyle. To use energy effectively, it is important to plan and think through the activities to complete the tasks efficiently.

Non-Human Resources

- **Money** Everyone needs money, but it is not distributed equally. Some people have more money than others. Since money is limited, it should be spent wisely to fulfill our needs.
- **Material Resources** Material resources means any material which we used to complete our task. For example furniture, space, clothes, stationery and food items.

Individual and Shared Resources

- **Individual Resources** These are resources that are available to an individual for his/her personal use. They can be either **human or non-human resources**. Examples include your own skills, knowledge, time, your school bag and your clothes.
- **Shared Resources** These are resources that are accessible to many members of a community or society. Shared resources can be **natural or community based**.

---

1 **Aptitude** It is a person's natural or aquired curicity to learn and understand or perform task.

2 **Physical outputs** It refers to the quantity of goods or services, produced in a given time period.

Natural and Community Resources

- **Natural Resources** These are the resources that come from nature, such as water, mountains and air. These resources are available to everyone. It is our responsibility to use them wisely to protect the environment.
- **Community Resources** These are the resources that an individuals can use as a member of a community or society. They are usually provided by the government and can be either human or non-human. Examples include services from government hospitals, doctors, roads, parks and post offices. Every individual should use these resources responsibly and also help them to maintain.

Quick Test 1

1. What are the three main classifications of resources?
2. Identify the three parts into which time can be divided.
3. List any one characteristic of shared resources.
4. Name a natural resource that is essential for life.

4.2 Characteristics of Resources

Resources can be categorised in different ways, but they also share some common features. Characteristics of the resources are as follows

- **Utility** Utility means importance of the usefulness of any resource, which help us in achieving our goals. Whether a resource is useful or not depends on the goal and the situation. For example, cow dung is often seen as waste, but it can be used as fuel or to make manure.
- **Accessibility** Some resources are available easily than others. The availability of resources also changes over time. This means that the accessibility of resources varies from person to person and from time to time. For example, every family has money as a resource. While some families have enough money to meet their needs, others may have limited funds.
- **Interchangeability** Almost all resources have substitutes[3]. This means if one resource is not available, it can be replaced by another. For example, if your school bus does not arrive on time, you could go to school in a car, tractor, bullock cart or scooter. So, the same task can be done using different resources.
- **Manageable** Resources can be managed. Since resources are limited, they should be managed carefully and effectively to get the best use out of them. Resources should be used in a way that gives us the most benefit with the least amount of use. For example, we should avoid using two or three buckets of water to wash clothes if we can do it with just one bucket.

4.3 Managing Resources

- It is important to remember that no resource is unlimited. All resources have limits, so we need to use them wisely to achieve our goals more quickly and efficiently. Resources should not be wasted or misused. To reach our goals, effective **resource management** is essential.
- Managing resources means making the most of what we have. For example, everyone has 24 hours in a day. Some people plan their day and use every hour to work towards their goals, while others waste time and do not get much work done.

3 Substitutes It means that if a person or thing is not available, than it can be replaced by another.

The Management Process

The management process involves five aspects, planning, organising, implementing, controlling and evaluation.

Planning

- Planning is the first step in any management process. It helps us to create the path to reach our goals. In simple terms, planning means **creating a plan** to achieve specific goals and using the available resources. Planning involves choosing the right actions to take. To plan effectively, you should ask yourself these four basic questions and the answers of these questions will help you to create a plan
  - What is your present situation? This means looking at where you are now and understanding what you currently have and what you want in the future.
  - Where do you want to reach? This involves setting clear goals or targets that you want to achieve, considering both your current situation and future needs.
  - What is the gap? This is the difference between where you are now and where you want to be. You need to cover this gap to reach your goal.
  - How can you reach your desired goals? Answering this question will help you figure out how to cores the gap. This involves making a plan to achieve your goals.

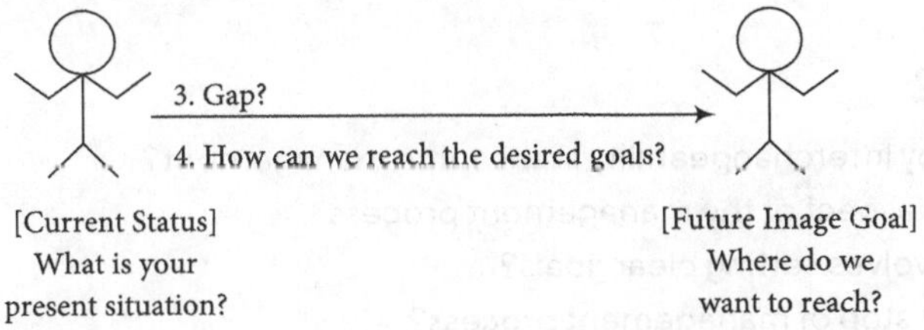

Steps in Planning

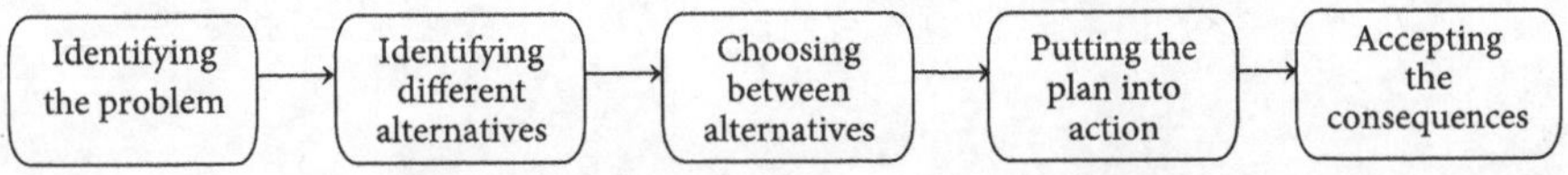

For example, if you have only one month left before your annual exams and you have not finished your revision (current situation) and your goal is to score good marks. In this situation, you need to study five subjects in that time (the gap). You would think about how to achieve this goal (create a plan), which might include deciding how many hours to study each subject, prioritising subjects and cutting back on other activities.

Organising

- Organising means **collecting and arranging** the right resources to carry out plans effectively and efficiently. For example, if your goal is to study and achieve good marks, it is important to organise all the resources you need to support your efforts. This includes gathering your books and notes, setting up a comfortable study space with good lighting and ensuring you have the necessary stationery.

Implementing

- This stage involves putting the prepared plan into **action**. In the example of studying for your exams, implementing means actually starting to study by using the resources which you have organised, such as books, notes and stationery. This is where you follow your plan and begin working towards your goal of achieving good marks.

Controlling

- Controlling means **checking** to ensure that your activities are producing the results you want. It involves monitoring your progress to see if the plan you put into action is working as intended.
  This step is important because it **provides feedback** and helps you **identify any mistakes.**
  For example, while following your study plan, if you find that you can't finish your assigned chapter because you are watching television, this feedback indicates that you need to reduce distractions. To improve your results, you would decide not to watch TV, play games or chat with friends during study hours, as these activities can interfere with your planned study time.

Evaluation

- In the final stage, you look at the **results** after putting your plan into action. You compare what you achieved with what you wanted to achieve. This helps you see what worked well and what did not, so you can improve next time.
  For example, when you get your marked answer sheets back after an exam, you evaluate them based on how well you prepared and the scores you aimed for. If your scores in some subjects are lower than you expected, you try to figure out why. At the same time, you look for what you did well that helped you get good marks in other subjects. You can then use those strengths to address your weaknesses and aim for better results in your next exam.

Quick Test 2

1. What is meant by interchangeability in resource management?
2. Identify one key aspect of the management process.
3. Which phase involves setting clear goals?
4. Which is the last step of management process?

Mind Map

MANAGEMENT OF RESOURCES

1 Classification of Resources

Human Resources

Knowledge
- We use this knowledge throughout our lives and it is essential for success.

Motivation / Interest
- This help us to move forward in life.

Skill/Strength/Aptitude
- It differentiate one person from another.
- People learn skill according to their interest.

Time
- Time is equally given to us.
- It depends on us how we use our time.

Energy
- It depends on person's physical fitness, age, lifestyle and mental state.

Non-Human Resources

Money
- Everyone needs money to fulfill their goals and desires.
- This resources is not equally available to everyone.
- We should spent it wisely.

Material Resources
- It means the material which we use to complete our work.
- **For examples** For study we need - pen, notebook, books etc.

Natural Resources
- Available in our surrounding For example, plants, water and air.
- Equally present for all human beinges.
- We should use them wisely to protect our environment.

Community Resources
- An individual can use these resources as a member of community or society.
- Provided by the government and can be either human or non-human.
- **For examples**, Government hospitals, doctors, roads, park, post office, etc.

Individual Resources
- Available for personal use by an individual.
- They can be human or non-human resources.
- **For examples** our own skill, knowledge, time, clothes etc.

Shared Resources
- Accessible to many members of society.
- They can be natural or community based.
- **For examples** Library, water etc.

2 Characteristics of Resources

Utility
- It means the usefulness of resources in achieving goal.
- Resource is useful or not depends on the goal or situation.
- **For example** Cow dung can be use as manure.

Accessibility
- Accessability of resources varies from person to person and from time to time.
- **For example** Money is not easily available to all the persons.

Interchange ability
- Almost all resources have substitutes.
- **For example** If your school bus does not arrive on time then you can go to school by car, scooter or tractor.

Manageable
- Resources are limited.
- They should be managed carefully and effectively
- **For example** We can switch off the lights when not in use.

3 Managing Resources

Planing
- First step in management process.
- Resources are limited and to complete our work we need to manage our resources.
- Management Process involves five steps.
- It means creating a plan to achieve the goal by using the available resources.
- Steps.

  Identify the problem → Identify different alternatives → Choosing between alternatives → Putting the plan into action → Accepting the consequences.
- **For example** If you have only one month left for exam then you need to divide time for each subject on priority basis.

Organising
- Collecting and arranging the right resources to carry out plans.
- **For example** If you want to achieve good marks then you need to organise the resources such as books, notes and stationary.

Implementation
- Carrying out the prepared plan into action.
- Follow your plan and start working.
- **For example** Now start study by using the resources you have organised.

Controlling
- It helps to monitor the outcome of activities.
- It ensures that if only problem arises then how we need to overcome from that problem.
- **For example** While studying if you can't complete your task then you need to reduce your T.V. time, game time or chat time.

Evaluation
- This is the final stage, which tell us the result.
- This gives the feedback that what you achieved and what you want to achieve.
- This help to improve next time.
- **For example** After getting your answer sheet you will evaluate about how well you prepared and where you need the improvement.

NCERT Folder

Intext Questions

1. Think of your own self and make a list of the human resources you have. Use the following guidelines to reflect on this. (Pg-51)

(i) Knowledge – which areas are you knowledgeable about

(ii) Motivation/interest- what activities do you enjoy doing most

(iii) Skills/strengths/aptitude – what are you particularly good at doing

(iv) Time- which periods of the day are you most active

(v) Energy- Do you largely feel energetic or tasteless/tired?

Ans. **(i) Knowledge**

- **Basic knowledge** Mathematics, Science, Hindi, English, and Social Science
- Culture
- Basic computer skills (MS Office, Internet)
- Art and architecture
- Basic life skills (cooking, first aid)

(ii) Motivation/Interest

- Playing cricket and football
- Reading Hindi literature and comics
- Listening to bollywood music
- Learning new languages (Spanish)
- Participating in school debates

(iii) Skills/Strengths/Aptitude

- Problem-solving and aptitude skills
- Communication and public speaking
- Teamwork and leadership
- Time management
- Drawing and painting

(iv) Time

- **Most active periods** Morning (7-10 am) and evening (4-6 pm)
- **Available time for learning** Weekends and daily 1 hour in the evening
- **Dedicated time for self-care** Daily 30-minutes exercise

(v) Energy

- Generally, feel energetic throughout the day
- Experience a dip in energy levels post-lunch (1-2 pm)
- Recharge with short breaks, sports and spending time with friends

2. List the resources you would need in order to secure good makes and study well. Compare your list with others. (Pg-53)

Ans. The following is a list of resources I would need to secure good marks as an Indian Class Xth student

(i) Human Resources

- Teachers' guidance and support
- Parents' encouragement and motivation
- Peer group study sessions
- My own time management and discipline

(ii) Non-Human Resources

- Textbooks and study materials
- Stationery (notes, pens, pencils)
- Internet and computer/laptop
- Mobile phone with educational apps
- Library access
- Online resources (NCERT website, study guides)
- Comfortable study space at home

Comparison of my list with my others reflect several similarities and dissimilarities

(iii) Similarities

- All of us need teachers' guidance and support
- We all rely on textbooks and study materials
- Internet and computer/laptop are essential for research and online learning
- Mobile phones with educational apps are common

(iv) Differences

- Some friends have private tutors for extra support
- A few have access to online courses and webinars
- Some use digital tools like flashcards and mind maps
- Others prioritise library access and study groups.

3. Your wish to arrange a farewell party for Class XII students. Identify your resources and state the aspects you will keep in mind at each stage of the management process in organising the party. (Pg-55)

Ans.

Farewell Party For Class XII Students

S.No.	Resources Available	Planning	Organising	Implementation	Controlling	Evaluation
(i)	Human- Non human	Venue? Menu?	Division of responsibility	(i) Decorating the venue (ii) Keeping the food ready	Checking if the decoration is being done as per the plan?	Assess if the venue is looking good or not?
(ii)	Teachers (guidance and supervision)	Decide venue (school auditorium or private hall)	Book the venue and catering service	Supervise the decoration and food of the venue.	Monitor the decoration process and catering services	Check all the arrangements
(iii)	Catering staff (Food preparation)	Decide the date, time and menu	Arrange for food	Prepare food and beverages	Check food quality and quantity	Assess food quality and student satisfaction
(iv)	Decorators (Venue decoration)	Create budget and allocate funds	Arrange for decorations	Set up sound system, music and other activities	Ensure sound system and music are working	Evaluate the decoration was it good or not
(v)	Furniture and seating	Form an organising committee to plan seats	How many seats are required	Arrange seating and furniture	Check all seats	Evaluate if any one left and not get the seat
(vi)	Camera and photography equipments	Assign tasks responsibilities and placing of camera	Co-ordinate with photographer	arrange camera placing	Address any last-minute issues	Review the quality of the photographs
(vii)	Farewell day	Plan entertainment and activities	Prepare a schedule and time	Welcome Class XII students and teachers	Ensuring the correct order of performances	Note the success and shortcoming of the event for future references

Exercises

1. Define a resource.

Ans. A resource is anything which we use while carrying out any activity to accomplish our goals like time, energy, knowledge, interest, etc.

2. Classify resources in three different ways giving the definition of each resource and two examples of each.

Ans. Resources can be classified in the following three ways

(i) **Human and Non-human Resources**

(a) **Human** These are resources present in humans which are central to any activity and can be developed through training and self-development.
Two examples of human resources are knowledge and skills.

(b) **Non-human** These are resources not present in humans but which are required to carry out our activities.
Two examples of non-human resources are money and material resources.

(ii) **Individual and Shared Resources**

(a) **Individual** These are resources which are available to any person for personal use.
Two examples of individual resources are your knowledge and your clothes.

(b) **Shared** These are resources which are available to many members of the community or society.
Two examples of shared resources are community parks and the air in the atmosphere.

(iii) **Natural and Community Resources**

(a) **Natural** These are resources which are available in nature available for use by all of us. Two examples of natural resources are rivers and mountains.

(b) **Community** These are resources which are available to any person as a member of the community or society. Two examples of community resources are consultancy provided by government hospitals and roads.

3. Why should resources be managed?

Ans. Resources should be managed because they are limited and finite, so we need to utilise the available resources more effectively to achieve our goals faster and more efficiently.

4. Explain the steps in the management process, using one example to clarify each step.

Ans. The steps in the management process are

(i) **Planning** It is the first step in any management process. It helps us to visualise the path to reach our goals. In it, we produce a scheme for action to achieve specified goals by using the available resources. It involves selecting the course of action.

For example, a clothing brand wants to increase its sale by 50% until next year. For this, the company will have to prepare a proper plan. It will have to select a course of action considering all the risks and profits.

(ii) **Organising** It means collecting and arranging the appropriate resources to implement the plans effectively and efficiently.

For example, now the company will have to select one best alternative from all the available alternatives. The company may have alternatives like reducing price, increasing advertisement and promotion, after sale services, unique styles, etc.

Supposedly, the brand selects increasing advertisement as the best option. Now, it will implement this.

(iii) **Implementing** Here we carry out the prepared plan. For example, the brand will now create TV advertisement, hire models, actors, for promotion, give lucrative services, etc. It will implement all the things that were earlier planned.

(iv) **Controlling** It means monitoring the outcome of activities to make sure that the plans are being implemented correctly.

It provides feedback and helps to check errors. The feedback helps us to revise our plan of action, if necessary, to achieve the goal.

For example, a proper feedback mechanism will be developed by the brand throughout its branches so that actual customer response, revenue collection, employee response, etc. could be known.

(v) **Evaluating** In this stage, the outcome that we have arrived at after putting the plan into action is evaluated. The end result of the action taken is compared with the result desired.
For example, It will now check the profits earned. Here, it will get to know whether the actual sale is equal to the planned sale or not.

Exam Pattern Questions

Objective Type Questions

Multiple Choice Questions (MCQs)

1. **We need this to carry out our day to day activities. What is being referred to in the statement?**
(a) Planning (b) Management
(c) Resources (d) None of these

2. **Resources are limited and people have .... needs.**
(a) limited (b) exhausting
(c) infinite (d) None of these

3. **'Motivation' is which type of resource?**
(a) Non-human resource (b) Human resource
(c) Shared resource (d) Natural resource

4. **'This resource is available to everyone equally. It is the most valuable resource because once lost it cannot be regained'. Which resource is being referred in the statement?** **Competency Based Que**
(a) Energy (b) Time
(c) Skills (d) Motivation

5. **Identify the dimensions of time.** **Competency Based Que**
I. Work time II. Exercise time
III. Rest and leisure time IV. Movie time
Codes
(a) I and II (b) II and III
(c) I and III (d) III and IV

6. **'This resource gives a sense of security to the family and help them achieve what they want. It is not equally distributed'. Name the resource with respect to the statement.** **Competency Based Que**
(a) Money (b) Material Resource
(c) Strength (d) Aptitude

7. **Which among the following is not included in individual resources?**
(a) Skills (b) Knowledge
(c) Clothes (d) Parks

8. **Cow dung is considered waste. However it can be used to prepare humus (manure). Which characteristic of resources does this symbolise?** **Competency Based Que**
(a) Accessibilty (b) Interchangeability
(c) Manageable (d) Utility

9. **To attain a better standard of living, what must one do?**
(a) Effectively plan (b) Closely evaluate
(c) Manage resources well (d) Balance time

10. **Planning is the first step in any management process which helps us to visualize the path to reach our goals. Identify the basic steps in planning among the following** **Competency Based Que**
I. Identifying different alternatives
II. Collecting and arranging appropriate resources
III. Identify the problem
IV. Action to carry out the plan
Codes
(a) I and II (b) II and IV
(c) II and III (d) II, III and IV

11. **When we actually performing the planned activity for a goal we call it?**
(a) Implementation (b) Controlling
(c) Organising (d) Evaluation

12. **Match the following.** **Competency Based Que**

Characteristics of Resources	Meaning
A. Utility	1. Substitutes of all resources
B. Accessibility	2. Resources managed for effective utilisation
C. Interchangeability	3. Usefulness of resources to achieve the goal
D. Manageable	4. Resources available easily to everyone

Codes

	A	B	C	D		A	B	C	D
(a)	1	2	3	4	(b)	3	4	1	2
(c)	2	1	4	3	(d)	4	3	2	1

Assertion-Reason Questions

Direction (Q. Nos. 13-15) In the questions given below, there are two statements marked as Assertion (A) and Reason (R). Read the statements and choose the correct option.

Codes
(a) Both A and R are true and R is the correct explanation of A.
(b) Both A and R are true, but R is not the correct explanation of A.
(c) A is true, but R is false.
(d) A is false, but R is true.

13. **Assertion** (A) A bicycle which has not been used for long and is just lying at someone's place is also a resource for them.

Reason (R) Anything which is not used by us is not a resource.

14. **Assertion** (A) Human resources can be developed through training and self-development.

Reason (R) Knowledge and time are examples of human resources.

15. **Assertion** (A) For sustaining individual growth and physical output, energy is essential.

Reason (R) To conserve energy and to use it most effectively, one must carefully plan through the activity.

Case Based Questions

16. Read the passage given below and answer the following questions.

There is only one month left for your examination and you have not completed your revision. Your aim is to score good marks and to achieve this you need to study different subjects in specified time periods.

You would think of a way of achieving this goal which includes number of hours, subjects, curtailing other activities so on.

On the basis of above information provided answer the following questions.

(i) **Which among the following is included in planning?**

I. Collecting resources
II. Implementing
III. Identifying the problem
IV. Choosing alterative

Codes

(a) I and II (b) II and III (c) III and IV (d) I and IV

(ii) **What do we need to cover to reach our goal?**

(a) Present situation (b) Gap
(c) Future situation (d) Syllabus

(iii) **It is first step in any management process. Which step is being referred to in the statement?**

(a) Organising (b) Evaluating
(c) Planning (d) Controlling

(iv) **Assertion** (A) Planning is the most important step of the management proces.

Reason (R) It helps us to visualise the path of actions to reach our goals.

Codes

(a) Both A and R are true and R is the correct explanation of A.
(b) Both A and R are true, but R is not the correct explanation of A.
(c) A is true, but R is false.
(d) A is false, but R is true.

17. Read the passage given below and answer the following questions.

A cook must have knowledge of how to operate cooking gas before she/he starts preparing food. A teacher who does not have knowledge of his/her subject, cannot teach the students properly. On the other hand, student will not try to learn a subject if he is not interested in it. He may continue to give excuses for not studying that subject. He may waste his time doing other unproductive stuff. Time being the most valuable resource, must not be wasted.

(i) **Which of the following resources are mentioned in the above passage?**

(a) Interest (b) Knowledge
(c) Time (d) All of these

(ii) **Knowledge is a form of .... resource.**

(a) human (b) community
(c) natural (d) shared

(iii) **What does the student need to study the subject?**

(a) Knowledge (b) Interest
(c) Skill (d) Aptitude

(iv) **Assertion** (A) 'Where there is a will there is a way'.

Reason (R) To accomplish any task, the person must be interested in doing it.

Codes

(a) Both A and R are true and R is the correct explanation of A.
(b) Both A and R are true, but R is not the correct explanation of A.
(c) A is true, but R is false.
(d) A is false, but R is true.

18. Read the passage given below and answer the following questions.

Planning is the first step in any management process. It helps us to visualise the path to reach our goals. In other words, to plan is to produce a scheme for action to achieve specific goals by using the available resources. Planning involves selecting the course of action. To plan effectively to achieve a goal, you must ask the following four basic questions. The answers to these questions will help you to develop a plan.

- What is our present situation? This involves assessing the present situation, analysing what one has at present and what one would like to have in future.
- Where do we want to reach? This involves setting specific goals or targets which we desire to achieve keeping in mind the present and future needs.

- Gap. This is the difference between our present situation and the desired situation. We need to cover this gap in order to achieve our goal.
- How can we reach our desired goals? Answering this question will help you to decide how to cover this gap. This involves making a plan to achieve goals.

On the basis of the information provided above, answer the following questions.

(i) We use planning to reach

(a) a place (b) a goal
(c) a distinction (d) a point in the future

(ii) The difference between our present situation and the desired situation is

(a) a goal (b) a resource
(c) a gap (d) None of these

(iii) Which of the following is not a characteristic of effective planning ?

(a) Using available resouces
(b) Selecting a random cause of action
(c) Developing a scheme for action
(d) Setting targets

(iv) Assertion (A) It is important to get feedback.
Reason (R) Feedback helps you to revise your plan of action so you can achieve your goals. **Competency Based Que**

Codes

(a) Both A and R are true and R is the correct explanation of A
(b) Both A and R are true, but R is not the correct explanation of A
(c) A is true, but R is false
(d) A is false, but R is true

Answers

1. (c) Resources
2. (c) infinite
3. (b) Human resource
4. (b) Time
5. (c) I and III
6. (a) Money
7. (d) Parts
8. (d) Utility
9. (c) Manage resource well
10. (d) II, III and IV
11. (a) Implementation
12. (b) 3 4 1 2
13. (d) A is false but R is true.
14. (b) Both A and R are true, but R is not the correct explanation of A.
15. (b) Both A and R are true, but R is not the correct explanation of A.
16. (i) (c) III and IV (ii) (b) Gap
(iii) (c) Planning
(iv) (a) Both A and R are true and R is the correct explanation of A
17. (i) (d) All of these
(ii) (a) human
(iii) (b) Interest
(iv) (a) Both A and R are true and R is the correct explanation of A
18. (i) (b) a goal (ii) (c) a gap
(iii) (b) Selecting a random cause of action
(iv) (a) Both A and R are true and R is the correct explanation of A

Subjective Questions

Very Short Answer Type Questions

1. What do you mean by human resources?

Ans. Human resources are central for currying out any activity. Resources can be developed by any person by their abilities and training. For example gaining knowledge of any field.

2. Priya wants to prepare for her exams but struggles to concentrate. She has all the study materials. Which resource is she lacking and how can she address this issue? **Competency Based Que**

Ans. Priya is lacking motivation or interest. She can address this by setting small goals, taking breaks and rewarding herself after completing each task.

3. At what time during the day should a student plan study time?

Ans. A student should plan study time for the time period when the student is able to work best i.e., at the peak time. Some students work best in early morning hours whereas others work most efficiently during late night.

4. How do persons who do not plan their activities misuse their time resource?

Ans. Persons who do not plan their activities will not understand how much time during the day they should allocate to each activity.
Consequently, they spend too much time on one activity, thus leaving less time to perform other activities properly and effectively. Thus, they misuse their time resource.

5. Define non-human resources?

Ans. Non-human resource are the resources, which everyone needs to fulfill their goals and desire to complete their work. For example-money, material.

6. Which non-human resources can be bought with money?

Ans. The non-human resources which can be bought with money are material resources i.e., items like space, furniture, clothes, stationery, food items, etc.

7. Which resources are available to many members of the community or society?

Ans. Shared resources are available to many members of the community.

8. Rohan wants to start a new business, but he's unsure about the necessary resources. What resources does Rohan need to consider to start his business successfully? **Competency Based Que**

Ans. Rohan needs to consider human resources such as knowledge, skills, motivation, time and energy and non-human resources such as money, material resources, space and community resources to start his business successfully.

9. Vikas wants to organise a school event but struggles to allocate tasks effectively. Which management process is he failing at? **Competency Based Que**

Ans. Vikas is struggling with the process of organising.

10. What is the last stage of the management process?

Ans. Evaluating is the last stage of the management process.

Short Answer Type Questions

1. A student has only one month left for their annual examination and needs to study five subjects. What strategies can the student employ to manage their time and energy effectively, ensuring good grades? **Competency Based Que**

Ans. The student can create a study schedule, prioritizing subjects, setting realistic goals, and allocating time for revision and practice. They should also maintain a healthy lifestyle, exercise regularly, and take breaks to conserve energy.

2. Shashi wants to learn a new language. Discuss the human and non-human resources she will utilise to achieve this goal. **Competency Based Que**

Ans. To learn a new language, Shashi will need various human and non-human resources.

(i) **Human Resources**

(a) **Motivation** A strong desire to communicate with speakers of the language.

(b) **Knowledge** Understanding effective language learning strategies.

(c) **Support** Seeking guidance from teachers or language exchange partners.

(ii) **Non-human Resources**

(a) **Money** Money to arrange for various materials.

(b) **Materials** Textbooks, apps and online courses for structured learning.

3. Aman wants to start a new hobby, painting.

(i) What human resources does Rohan need to develop to excel in painting, and how can he acquire them?

(ii) What non-human resources does Rohan require to start painting and why are they essential?

(iii) How can Rohan ensure his painting hobby aligns with his overall goals and priorities? **Competency Based Que**

Ans. (i) Rohan needs to develop his knowledge, skills and motivation. He can acquire these by taking painting classes, practicing regularly, reading art books and joining a painting community.

(ii) Rohan requires material resources such as paints, brushes, canvas, easel and a dedicated space. These resources are essential for creating artwork, experimenting with techniques and expressing creativity.

(iii) Rohan can reflect on his values, interests, and long-term objectives to ensure painting aligns with them. He should consider how painting enhances his life, provides relaxation and fosters personal growth.

4. "Utility means the importance or usefulness of a resource in helping one achieve a goal."

(a) Explain the concept of utility in resource management, providing examples.

(b) How does understanding utility help in effective resource management? **Competency Based Que**

Ans. (a) Utility refers to the importance or usefulness of a resource in achieving a goal. For instance, knowledge of marketing has high utility for a business owner aiming to increase sales.

Similarly, a painter's skill in colour mixing has high utility in creating artwork.

(b) Understanding utility enables individuals to prioritise resources, allocate them efficiently and make informed decisions. By recognising the utility of each resource, individuals can optimise their use, minimise waste, and maximise output.

5. What is the interchangeability characteristic of a resource? Explain it by using the example of your school bus.

Ans. The interchangeability characteristic of a resource means that the same function can be performed by a number of different resources.

For example if you are normally travelling to school in your school bus, it is a resource for you. However, in case you are late and miss the bus, one of your parents may leave you to your school in their own car or motorcycle.

Thus, the school bus has been interchanged with your family's personal transport vehicle.

6. What are the implications of the statement, 'all resources are finite? **Competency Based Que**

Ans. The implications of this statement is that we need to utilise resources effectively to achieve our goals faster and efficiently. Because resources are limited and should not be misused or wasted.

Thus, effective management of resources is important. This is possible only by getting the most out of the resources available to us.

7. Imagine you have organised a party for your loved ones.

(i) After the party is over, how can you check if your planning and execution were effective?

(ii) What key things should you look at to find ways to improve for future parties or events? **Competency Based Que**

Ans. (i) To see how well you did, compare what actually happened during the party with what you wanted to achieve. This means looking at both the good and not so good parts of your planning and execution. Think about how your preparations matched the results.

If some parts did not meet your expectations, make a note of them. However, also remember the things that went well.

(ii) By focusing on your strengths and working on any weaknesses, you can improve your planning for future events and make them even better.

Long Answer Type Questions

1. Describe the five types of human resources and give an example of each of these resources.

Ans. Five types of human resources are

(i) **Knowledge** It is used throughout one's life and is a pre-requisite for carrying out any activity successfully.

An example is my excellent knowledge of all the topics taught in Class XI Home Science.

(ii) **Motivation/Interest** To accomplish any task, the worker must be motivated and interested in doing it. An example is my deep interest in studying Home Science because I want to make a career in it later on in life.

(iii) **Skills/ Strength/ Aptitude** All individuals may not be skilled in performing all activities. Each one of us has an aptitude in certain areas. We can therefore carry out activities in these areas better as compared to others. But we can acquire skills we do not have through learning and training. An example is my poor skill in cooking, which I can improve by proper training in a cooking training programme.

(iv) **Time** This resource is available to everyone equally. It is the most valuable resource because time once lost cannot be regained. We need to continuously plan and be able to utilise the available time to finish the desired tasks.

An example is the time available to me for revision of the syllabus of anyone subject in preparation for the final exam.

(v) **Energy** For sustaining individual growth and physical output, energy is essential. Energy levels vary from person to person according to their physical fitness, mental condition, personality, age, family background and their standard of living. To conserve energy and to use it most effectively, one must carefully think and plan through the activities so that one can complete a task efficiently.

An example is the energy I maintain to revise my subjects thoroughly for the final exam. I do this by conserving energy which was earlier used in playing outdoor games, by reducing my playing time to half of what it used to be earlier.

2. Four well-known resources are time, money, energy and space. How will you categorise each of these resources into whether it is human/ non-human, individual/ shared or natural/community. **Competency Based Que**

Ans. The four resources can be categorised are as follows

(i) **Time** It is a human resource because every person has it. However, it is also an individual resource because every person reserves a different time for each activity.

(ii) **Money** It is a non-human resource because it is not equally distributed among different people. Thus, it is also an individual resource.

(iii) **Energy** Energy levels vary from person to person, so it is an individual resource. Everyone has some energy, so it is also a human resource.

(iv) **Space** It is a non-human resource because it is not equally distributed among different people. However, it can be shared or individual, depending on the status of persons having that space. Certain spaces belong to the community. In such a case, space is also a community resource.

3. Consider Rani, a small business owner in Jaipur. What are four key characteristics on resources that she should keep in mind while managing her boutique?

Competency Based Que

Ans. Key characteristics of resources that Rani should keep in her mind while managing her boutque are as follows

(i) **Utility** Resources must be useful for achieving goals. Rani should assess how each resource, such as fabric and marketing funds, can effectively contribute to her business objectives.

(ii) **Accessibility** The availability of resources can very widely. Rani needs to recognise that some resources are more accessible than others, depending on her location and timing. For example, her budget might be tighter at the end of the month , affecting her purchasing choices.

(iii) **Interchangeability** Many resources have substitutes. Rani should be aware that if a particular material is unavailable, she can often find alternatives that fulfill the same function. This will ensure that her boutique remains stocked.

(iv) **Manageability** Resources require effective management for optimal use. Rani must strategise how to maximise her resources, ensuring she gets the best results with minimal input. For instance, using efficient methods to reduce waste and costs in her operations.

4. Riya has carefully made a schedule distributing equal time to studies as well as extra curricular activities.

(i) Why it is important to manage resources?

(ii) Which aspects does the management process involves?

(iii) What are the steps involved in planning?

Competency Based Que

Ans. (i) It is important to manage resources because all resources are finite, we need to utilise resources efficiently. This is possbile only by getting the most out of the resources available to us.

(ii) The management process mainly involves five aspects i.e. planning, organising, implementing, controlling and evaluation.

(iii) **Steps in Planning** The basic steps in making the plan are

(a) Identifying the problem.

(b) Identifying different alternatives for achieving the target.

(c) Choosing between the alternatives which will make the target achievable.

(d) Acting to carry out the plan i.e. putting the plan into action.

(e) Accepting the consequences or results.

5. A local community plans to establish a community garden, requiring coordination among residents, local authorities and resource allocation.

(i) Describe the human and non-human resources necessary for the community garden's success, explaining their roles.

(ii) Explain how effective resource management can ensure the community garden's long-term sustainability, providing examples.

Competency Based Que

Ans. (i) The human and non-human resources necessary for the success of the community garden are as follows

- Human resources include knowledge (gardening expertise), skills (landscaping, maintenance), motivation (community engagement), time (volunteering) and energy (physical labor) of residents, volunteers and local authorities.
- Non-human resources include money (funding, grants), material resources (seeds, tools, water), space (land allocation) and community resources (local government support). These resources will facilitate garden design, planting, maintenance and sustainability.

(ii) Effective resource management involves coordinating volunteer efforts, allocating tasks, ensuring resource availability, monitoring progress, and evaluating outcomes. This enables the community to maintain the garden efficiently, address challenges and ensure continued community engagement and support.

For instance, implementing a rotation system for watering and weeding in the garden ensures consistent maintenance. Regular meetings and feedback sessions help identify areas for improvement.

Additionally, resource management enables adaptation to changing weather conditions, pest management and crop rotation, ensuring the garden remains productive and sustainable.

SELF ASSESSMENT TEST

Objective Type Questions

1. To accomplish any task, the worker must be ....
   (a) charged (b) motivated
   (c) on time (d) ready
2. Which among the following includes durable and perishable goods?
   (a) Material resources (b) Money resources
   (c) Non-human resources (d) Human resources
3. Which among the following process includes demarcating and dividing the activities into small units?
   (a) Implementation (b) Planning
   (c) Organisation (d) Controlling

Very Short Answer Type Questions

4. How are human resources developed?
5. 'We are open to acquiring knowledge throughout our lives.' Explain briefly. **Competency Based Que**
6. Why is time the most valuable resource?
7. Differentiate between Natural and Community resources.

Short Answer Type Questions

8. What activities may be included in non-rest time. At what time during the day should it be planned?
9. On what basis are energy levels of a person different from those of another person? Explain. **Competency Based Que**
10. During the planning stage of managing resources, how can we reach our desired goals?

Long Answer Type Questions

11. Describe what is the aptitude for a task or a subject? How can it be developed?
12. 'Human resources are known as central for completing any task'. Examine this statement.
13. 'There is always a substitute for each and every resources'. Explain this statement.
14. List the resource management procedures. Which one of them is carried out at the end? Explain how it is carried out.

05 CHAPTER

Fabric Around Us

Fabrics are important for us as it would enable us to make wise selection of clothes.

YOUR STUDY GOALS

5.1 Introduction
5.2 Fibre Properties
5.3 Classification of Textile Fibre
5.4 Yarns
5.5 Fabric Productions
5.6 Textile Finishing
5.7 Some Important Fibres

YOUR PRACTICE GOAL

- Objective Type Questions (23 Qs ; MCQs, A-R, Statements, Matching, Case Based)
- Subjective Questions (15 VSAs, 10 SAs, 6 LAs)

5.1 Introduction

- Fabrics are all around us and are important in our lives. They give comfort and warmth, bring colour and decorative style and add texture.
- Things such as bedsheets, pillow covers, soft towels, school dresses and even school course, school bags are all made from different types of fabric. In our homes, we find fabrics in curtains, kitchen dusters, floor mops and rugs.
- Fabrics come in various types, weights and thicknesses. They are selected according to their intended use. Fabrics are composed of **yarns**, which are thin, thread-like structures.
- When we pull apart a piece of fabric, we can observe the yarns twisted together. By untwisting a yarn we can see tiny, fine hair-like structures called **fibres**. These fibres serve as the fundamental building blocks of fabrics.
- Fibres, yarns and fabrics are collectively known as textile[1] products. After fabric production, it can be further processed to improve its appearance through cleaning, whitening, or colouring or to improve its shine and texture. This process is called **finishing**.
- Various fabrics have different methods of use and care. The performance of a fabric depends on the type of fibre, yarn, fabric construction and finishing techniques used.

1 Textiles It is a general term for all types of fabrics and materials made from yarns and fibres.

5.2 Fibre Properties

A fibre is useful, when it is available in large quantities and be affordable. The properties of fibres affect the final fabric.

- The most essential property is its **spinnability**. This refers to how easily a fibre can be turned into yarn and then into fabric. This depends on its length, strength, flexibility and surface structure.
- Consumers look for certain qualities in fibres. These includes colour, luster/shine, weight, moisture retention, dye absorption and elasticity.
- Care and maintenance of the fabric are also important. Factors like **abrasion resistance**[2], reactions to chemicals and detergents, heat resistance and resistance to biological organisms are important factors for consumers.

▲ *Fabric to fibre*

5.3 Classification of Textile Fibre

Textile fibres can be classified as follow

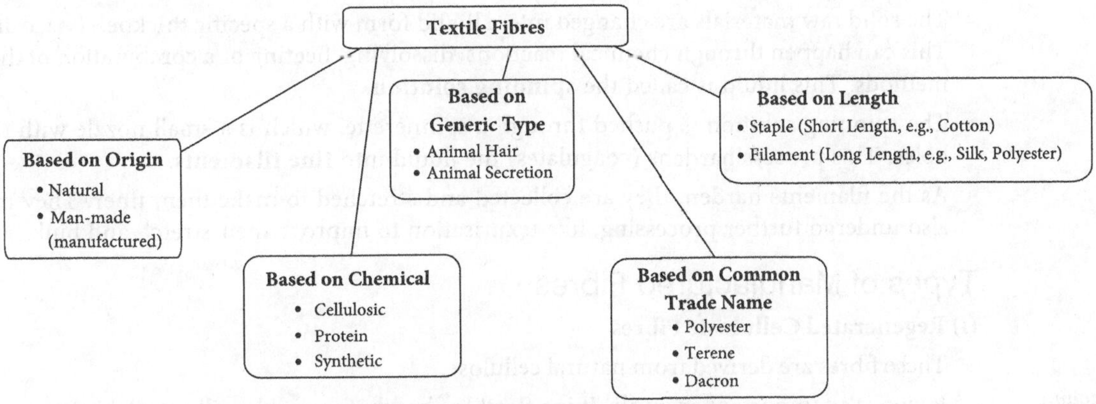

▲ *Chart of the classification of textile fibre*

Natural Fibres

Natural fibres are those found in nature. They can be divided into four main types

(i) **Cellulosic**[3] **Fibres** They are derived from plant cellulose.

(a) **Seed Hair** Examples include cotton and kapok.

(b) **Bast Fibres** Examples include flax (linen), hemp and jute.

(c) **Leaf Fibres** Examples include pineapple and agave (sisal).

(d) **Nut Husk Fibres** Example include coir, which comes from coconuts.

(ii) **Protein Fibres** They are derived from living organisms.

(a) **Animal Hair** Includes wool and special hair from goats and camels. It also includes fur.

(b) **Animal Secretion** The main example is silk.

2 Abrasion resistance It refers to how well a fabric can resist damage from rubbing or scratching.
3 Cellulosic It means to fibres made from plant materials that contain cellulose, like cotton and linen.

(iii) **Mineral Fibre** They are derived from **natural minerals** containing mineral salts. An example is asbestos.

(iv) **Natural Rubber** Natural rubber is made from natural rubber, tree barks and vines juice or latex. It is also known as **'Indian rubber'**.

Manufactured Fibres

- Manufactured fibres, or man-made fibres, are created by humans. The first manufactured fibre was Rayon[4] which was made in 1895. Most others were developed in the 20th century.
- The idea of creating fibres likely came from wanting to make something like silk. Silkworms eat mulberry leaves and digest them. They then release a liquid through two openings (spinnerettes). This liquid hardens and becomes the silk filaments[5] that form cocoons. This led people to think that if a cellulose material was processed, it could produce a silk-like fibre. Therefore it was referred as **artificial silk or art silk**.
- The earliest manufactured fibres were created by converting non-fibrous materials into fibrous forms, mainly from **cellulosic substances** like cotton waste or wood pulp. The second group of fibres was made entirely from chemicals. Regardless of the raw material used, the basic steps to convert it into fibres are the same.

Steps for Conversion into Fibrous Form

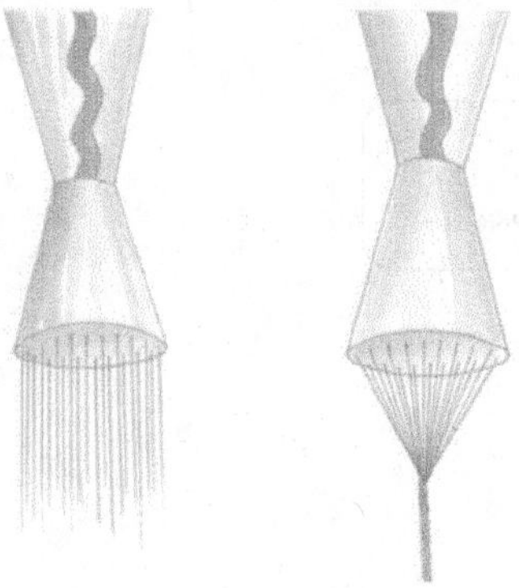

▲ *Spinnerette Machine*

- The solid raw materials are changed into a liquid form with a specific thickness(viscosity). This can happen through chemical reactions, dissolving, heating or a combination of these methods. This liquid is called the **spinning solution**.
- The spinning solution is pushed through a spinnerette, which is a small nozzle with tiny holes. This process hardens (coagulates) the liquid into **fine filaments**.
- As the filaments harden, they are collected and stretched to make them finer. They may also undergo further processing, like texurisation to improve their stretch and bulk.

Types of Manufactured Fibres

(i) **Regenerated Cellulosic Fibres**

These fibres are derived from natural cellulose.

Rayon is an important example. It is a flexible fibre that resembles silk, available in different forms

(a) **Viscose Rayon** The most common type, known for its softness.

(b) **Cuprammonium Rayon** Known for its strength and smooth texture.

(c) **High Wet Modulus Rayon** It improved strength when wet, which makes it suitable for various applications.

(ii) **Modified Cellulosic Fibres**

These are chemically altered forms of cellulose.

(a) **Acetate** A semi-synthetic fibre that is soft and has a luxurious feel.

(b) **Secondary Acetate** A less common variant with different properties.

(c) **Triacetate** Known for its resilience and resistance to wrinkles.

(iii) **Protein fibres**

Azlon A regenerated protein fibre made from natural sources like soy or milk proteins, offering a sustainable alternative to traditional fibres.

4 Rayon It means a man- made fibre made from cellulose, designed to look like silk.
5 Filament It is a long, continuous strand of fibre, typically used in making synthetic fabrics.

(iv) **Non-Cellulosic (Synthetic) Fibres**

These fibres are entirely synthetic.

(a) **Nylon** A strong, elastic fibre commonly used in clothing and industrial applications.

(b) **Polyester** It includes

Terelene Known for its durability and quick-drying properties.

Terrene Another variant with similar characteristics.

(c) **Acrylic** It used as a wool substitute. It includes

Orlon Known for its warmth and softness.

Cashmilon A softer acrylic variant that mimics cashmere.

(d) **Modacrylic** A modified acrylic fibre that is flame-resistant.

(e) **Spandex** Known for its exceptional elasticity, commonly used in active wears and fitted garments.

(f) **Rubber** Used primarily in elastic products due to its stretch ability.

5. **Mineral Fibres**

(a) **Glass Fibres** It is known for the strength and lightweight properties and referred as fibreglass.

(b) **Metallic Fibres** Lurex is used to add sparkle to fabrics.

Check Point 1

1. What are the basic building blocks of textiles?
2. Name the process that improves a fabric's appearance and texture.
3. Which was the first manufactured fibre, made in 1895.
4. What is a spinnerette?

5.4 Yarns

- Fibres alone cannot be used for most consumer products, except for items like surgical cotton, pillow stuffing, quilts, mattresses and cushions. To convert fibres into the fabrics we see, they must be made into a continuous strand.
- Some fabrics, like **felts or non-wovens,** are made directly from fibres. However, most fibres are processed into an intermediate stage called **yarn**.
- Yarn is a continuous strand of textile fibres or filaments. It is suitable for **knitting**[6], weaving or **intertwining** to form textile fabrics.

Yarn Processing

- Yarn processing from natural staple fibres is called **spinning**. Spinning is the last stage in processing. In the past, young unmarried girls often spun the finest yarn because of their nimble fingers (means who can move their fingers quickly). The term **'spinster'** for unmarried women comes from this context.
- The process of converting fibres into yarn involves several stages
  - **Cleaning** Natural fibres like cotton and wool often have impurities (like seeds or twigs). These are removed and the cleaned fibres are sorted and rolled into loose sheets called **laps**.
  - **Making into a Sliver** The laps are straightened using carding and combing, similar to brushing hair. Carding untangles the fibres, while combing removes smaller impurities and short fibres. The lap then goes through a funnel-shaped device which leads to formation of sliver. It is a rope-like mass of loose fibres, about 2-4 cm in diameter.

6 **Knitting** It is a technique for creating fabric by interlocking loops of yarn with needles.

- **Attenuating, Drawing Out and Twisting** The continuous strand of fibres then needs to be sized. This is called **attenuation**. Multiple slivers are combined for uniformity and drawn out to make them longer and finer. If a blended yarn (like cotton and wool) is needed, slivers from different fibres are mixed.

  The final sliver remains the same size as the original. The sliver is then taken to the roving machine, where it is further stretched until it reaches 1/4 or 1/8 of its original diameter. A slight twist is added to keep the fibres together.
- **Spinning** In this stage, the strand is shaped into yarn. It is stretched to the desired fineness and twisted, then wound onto cones.

▲ *Cotton Spinning*

- All manufactured fibres start as filaments. Yarn can consist of a single filament or a multifilament yarn, which is made by twisting multiple filaments together. Filaments can also be cut into shorter staple-length fibres. These shorter fibres are spun just like natural fibres and are called spun yarns. Staple-length fibres are needed for blended/mixed fabrics, such as **terecot** (terene and cotton), **terewool** '(terene and wool), or **polycot** (rayon and cotton).

Yarn Terminology

Some term are common in yarn production. These are as follows

- **Yarn Number** There are numbers like 20, 30 or 40 on thread reels. A higher number means the thread is finer. This number shows the relationship between the weight of the fibre and the length of yarn made from it.
- Yarn Twist When fibres are made into yarn, a twist is added to keep them together. This is measured as **t.p.i. (twist per inch)**. Loosely twisted yarns are softer and shinier, while tightly twisted yarns can have ridges, like in denim jeans.
- **Yarn and Thread** Yarn and thread are similar but used differently. 'Yarn' is the term used when making fabric, while thread refers to the product used to stitch pieces of fabric together.

5.5 Fabric Production

- There are many types of fabric available in the market. They differ based on the basic fibre used, such as cotton or wool and the type of yarn .
- Most fabrics are made from yarns, but some are produced directly from fibres. The two main types of these fabrics are **felts** and **non-wovens** (or bonded fibre fabrics).
  - Felts and non-wovens are made by laying fibres in a **matt** after carding and combing. The fibres stick together to form a matt that can be made in various thicknesses and shapes.
- Most fabrics require yarns for their creation. The primary methods for making fabrics are weaving and knitting.
- While weaving and knitting are the most common techniques, other methods like braiding and knotting are used less frequently.

Weaving

- Weaving is the oldest textile art, originally used for making mats and baskets. A woven fabric is made from two sets of yarns that cross each other at right angles, forming a strong structure. This process happens on machines called **looms.**
- One set of yarns is placed on the loom and determines the fabric's length and width. These are called **warp yarns**. The loom keeps these yarns at a fixed tension (tight) and evenly spaced. The second set of yarns is called **filling yarns,** which are woven in and out to create the fabric.
- The simplest way to weave is to have the filling yarn go over and under. Each warp yarn in one row, then reverse the process in the next row. By changing warp yarns the filling yarn goes over or under, and by this different patterns can be made. Special attachments like dobby or jacquard can help to create detailed designs. These designs become clearer when different coloured yarns are used for warp and filling.
- Some designs use an extra yarn that runs parallel to the warp or **filling yarns.** This yarn can be looped during weaving, which can either be left uncut (like in towels) or cut later (like in velvets and corduroy).
- The direction of the yarns in woven fabric is called the **grain.** Warp yarns run along the **length of the fabric (the selvedge**). While, filling yarns run across the **width (the weft)**. When we buy fabric, it has two cut sides and two bound sides. The bound sides are the selvedges, and the fabric is strongest along these edges.

Knitting

Knitting involves the interlooping of at least one set of yarns. This can be done by hand using two needles for **flat fabrics** or four needles for **circular fabrics**. Machines can also be used for knitting. The process creates a series of loops along the knitting needle or machine bed, with each row interlooping with the previous row.

Types of Knitting

The two basic types of knitting are

- **Filling or Weft Knitting** It is a method where the yarn moves across the width of the material. This allows the creation of articles that can be shaped during construction.
- **Warp Knitting** It is a technique used in industrial knitting machines that is similar to weaving looms. It involves a set of yarns (like warp yarns) interlooping with adjacent yarns. This method produces continuous lengths of material, which can be cut and stitched, in contrast to weft knitted fabric.

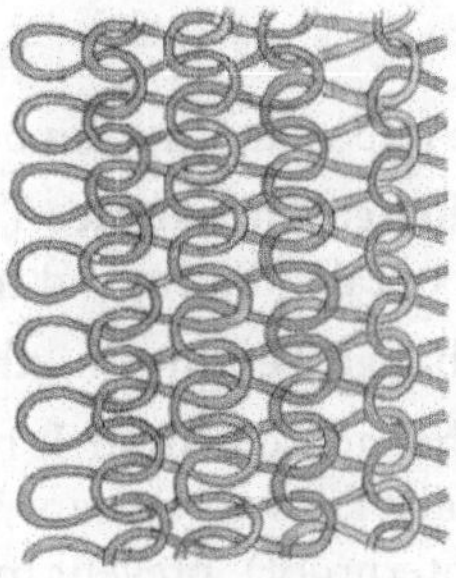
Weft Knitting

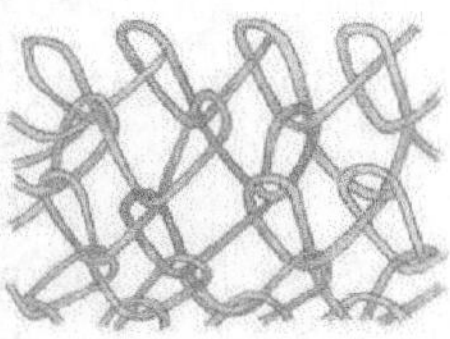
Warp Knitting

Characteristics of Knitted

The Characteristics of knitted fabrics are

- Knitted fabrics can be produced quickly and have greater elasticity (stretch) due to their looped structure. This makes them **suitable for fitted items** like vests, underwear and socks.
- They are **breathable(porous)** and allow air circulation, which enhances comfort. Knitted fabrics also provide freedom of movement, making them ideal for sportswear.

Braiding

Braided fabrics have a **diagonal pattern** on the surface. They are made by weaving three or more yarns together. These yarns start from one point and lie parallel before they intertwine. We can see braids in items like shoelaces, ropes, wire insulation and decorative trimmings.

Nets

Nets are **open fabrics** with large geometric holes between the yarns. They are made by tying the yarns together (inter-knotting), either by hand or with machines.

Laces

Lace is an **openwork fabric** made of a network of yarns that create complex designs. It is made through different techniques, including twisting, looping and knotting.

Quick Test 2

1. Who historically spun fine yarn due to nimble fingers?
2. This is the oldest textile art, originally used for making mats and baskets. Identify the process being referred to here.
3. Knitted fabrics are ideal for sportswear. List down one reason.
4. What fabric has large geometric holes between the yarns?

5.6 Textile Finishing

- When fabric comes straight from the loom, it often looks different from what we see in stores. Most fabrics available for sale have been treated with one or more Textile finishing[7] processes. Except for white fabrics.
- A finish is any treatment applied to the fabric that can change its appearance, texture or behaviour for specific uses. Finishes that are considered absolutely necessary are called **routine.**
- Finishes can be either durable or renewable. **Durable finishes** like dyeing do not get removed on washing or drycleaning. **Renewable finishes,** like starching or blueing, need to be reapplied repeatedly because they get removed on washing.

Functions of Finishes

Some important finishes based on their functions are as follows

- **Change Appearance** Techniques like cleaning (scouring and bleaching) , straightening and smoothing (like calendering and tentering) alter how the fabric looks.
- **Change Textures** Methods like starching, sizing and special calendering affect the feel of the fabric.
- **Change Behaviour** It refers to fabric finishes that enhance performance. This includes treatments that make fabrics resistant to wrinkles (wash and wear, permanent press), repel water (water repellent or waterproof), prevent moth damage, resist fire and reduce shrinkage (sanforisation).

Special Finishes

Finishing with Colour

Colour is often the most important factor when choosing fabric, whether for clothing or home use. Substances that add colour to fabric in a way that doesn't easily wash out are called **dyes**. The dyeing method depends on the chemical nature of both the fibre and the dye, as well as the desired effect.

Colour can be applied in different stages

- **At the fibre Stage** This is for creating yarns of different colours or designed felts.
- **At the Yarn Stage** This is used for woven patterns like checks and stripes.
- **At the Fabric Stage** This is the most common method for solid colours, as well as for designs like batik, tie-dye and printing.

7 Textile finishing The processes applied to fabrics after they are made to improve their appearance of performance, such as cleaning, dyeing or making them softer.

Printing

- This is a more specialised form of dyeing. According to the design, it involves applying colour only in specific areas of the fabric. Printing uses special tools to transfer colour only to specified parts. This allows for multiple colours on the same fabric.
- Printing can be done using hand tools like blocks, stencils or screens. It can also be done on an industrial level with methods like roller printing or automatic screen printing.

5.7 Some Important Fibres

Fibres both man-made and natural are very useful in our life. Some of the fibres are discussed below

Cotton

- Cotton is the most commonly used fibre for clothing and home textiles. India was the first country to grow and use cotton and it remains one of the largest cotton-producing regions.
- Cotton fibres come from the seed pods of the cotton plant. Each seed has many tiny hairs attached to it. When the seeds ripen, the pod bursts open.
- The seeds are separated from the fibres through a process called **ginning**. The fibres are then packed into large bundles called bales for **spinning**.

Properties of Cotton

- Cotton is a natural fibre made of cellulose and is classified as a **staple fibre**. It is relatively short, with lengths ranging from 1 cm to 5 cm. This makes the yarn or fabric appear dull and feel slightly rough. Cotton is also heavier than most other fibres.
- It absorbs moisture well and dries quickly, making it comfortable to wear in summer.
- Cotton is available in a wide variety of fabrics with different weights, textures, structures and finishes. Some common cotton fabrics include muslin, cambric, poplin, long cloth (latha), casement, denim, sheeting material and furnishing material.

Linen

Linen is a **bast fibre** made from the stems of the **flax plant**. Bast refers to the soft part found inside the bark.

- To get the fibres, the stems of the flax plant are soaked in water for a long time. This is done to break down the soft parts in a process called **retting**.
- After retting, the hard and woody parts are removed. The linen fibres are then collected and prepared for spinning.

Properties of Linen

- Linen is a cellulosic fibre, so it shares many properties with cotton. The fibres are longer and finer than cotton, which makes the yarn stronger and shinier (lustrous) Like cotton, linen absorbs moisture well, making it comfortable to wear. However, it absorbs dye easily, so the colors are not very bright.

> The flax plant is grown in only a few places around the world and takes longer to process. Thus, linen is used less than cotton.
>
> Jute and hemp are also bast fibres like linen, but they are coarser and less flexible. Thus, they are mainly used for making ropes, bags and similar products.

Wool

- Wool comes from the hair of sheep. It can also be collected from other animals like goats, rabbits and camels. These fibres are known as speciality hair fibres. Different sheep breeds produce different types of wool. Some breeds are raised specifically for their high-quality fibres.

- Removing the hair from the animal is called **shearing**. This is usually done once or twice a year, depending on the climate. During shearing, care is taken to keep the hair in one piece, known as **fleece**. This makes it easier to sort the fibres because hair from different parts of the body varies in length and thickness.
- After sorting, the fibres are cleaned to remove dirt, grease and sweat/perspiration. This cleaning process is called **scouring**. Next, process is called **carbonisation**. In this process it removes any plant material like leaves and twigs. After these steps, the fibres are sent for spinning.

Properties of Wool

- Wool is a natural protein fibre. The fibres can range from 4 cm to 40 cm in length. They can be coarse or fine, depending on the sheep breed and where the hair is taken from. Wool has a natural crimp or waviness that gives it elasticity and stretch.
- Wool is not as strong as some other fibres. However, it has good resilience and can return to its shape (elasticity).
- The surface of wool has scales that repel water. It can absorb a lot of water but doesn't feel wet on the outside. This quality makes wool comfortable in humid and cold weather.

Wool is often blended with cotton, rayon and polyester to improve its care and maintenance.

Silk

- Silk is a natural filament fibre made by silkworms. Silk produced under controlled conditions, like mulberry silk, is smooth with longer fibres. This results in a finer and shinier fabric. On the other hand, **wild silk** is coarser, stronger and has shorter fibres. This leads to a thicker fabric, like **tussar silk**.
- To produce high-quality silk, the cultivation of silk worms is carefully managed. This process is called **sericulture**. Since silk is a filament fibre, it doesn't need to be spun like other fibres. Instead, it is carefully reeled from the cocoon. Yarns are made by twisting several filaments together. If the filaments break or if the insects break the cocoon, the broken pieces are spun like cotton. This is known as spun silk.
- It is believed that silk was discovered when a cocoon accidentally fell into a Chinese princess's tea. She found that she could pull out a long, continuous fibre. The Chinese kept the process of making silk a secret for over 2,000 years, until around 500 A.D.

Properties of Silk

- Silk is a natural protein fibre and its natural colour ranges from off-white to cream. Wild silk is brownish. Silk filaments are long, fine, smooth and have a high lustre or sheen(shine). They contain a natural gum that gives silk a crisp texture.
- Silk is one of the stronger fibres used in fabrics. It has good elasticity and can stretch moderately.

Rayon

Rayon is a manufactured cellulosic fibre. It is called cellulosic because it is made from wood pulp. It is manufactured because the wood pulp is treated with chemicals and then turned into fibres.

Properties of Rayon

- Since rayon is a manufactured fibre, its size and shape can be controlled. It has a uniform diameter and looks clear and shiny.
- Rayon shares many properties with cotton because it is a cellulosic fibre. However, it is weaker and less durable.
- One main advantage of rayon and other manufactured cellulosic fibres is that they can be made from waste materials and look similar to silk.

Nylon1

- Nylon was the **first true synthetic fibre**. This means it is completely made from chemicals. It was first used for toothbrush bristles.

- In 1940, nylon fabrics were introduced, starting with socks and stockings, which became very popular. After that, it was used for many types of fabrics and helped inspire the creation of other synthetic fibres.

Properties of Nylon

- Nylon filaments are usually smooth and shiny, with a uniform thickness/diameter.
- Nylon is very strong and resists wear and tear(resists abrasion). This makes it suitable for items like brushes and carpets.
- Nylon is **highly elastic**. Very fine and clear fibres are used for 'one-size' garments like stockings.
- Nylon is a popular fabric for clothing, including socks, undergarments, swimsuits, gloves, nets and sarees. It is a leading fibre for making hosiery and lingerie. For outerwear, it can be blended with other fibres.

Polyester

Polyester is a manufactured synthetic fibre. It is also known as **Terylene or Terene**.

Properties of Polyester

- Polyester fibres have a uniform thickness, a smooth surface and a rod-like shape. They can be made in different strengths, lengths and diameters based on what is needed. The fibres are partially transparent and shiny.
- Polyester does not absorb water easily, so it has a low moisture regain. Because of this, it can be uncomfortable to wear in hot, dry weather.
- One of the best features of polyester is that it resists wrinkles. It is commonly blended with rayon, cotton, wool and sometimes spun silk.

Acrylic

Acrylic[8] is another synthetic fibre. It looks so much like wool that even an expert may have trouble in identifying the difference between the two. It is often called **Cashmilon** and is cheaper than wool.

Properties of Acrylic

- The length, thickness and fineness of acrylic fibres can be controlled by the manufacturer.
- The fibres can be made with different levels of crimp and shine.
- Acrylic is not very strong; its strength is similar to cotton.
- The fibres can elongate or stretch a lot and have good elastic recovery.
  Acrylic is used as a substitute for wool and is commonly found in children's clothing, blankets and knitted items.

Elastomeric fibres

- There are some lesser-known fibres that are **elastic and rubber-like**. They can be produced in various forms.
- The natural version includes rubber, while the synthetic version is spandex or Lycra. These fibres are often blended with other fibres that have low elasticity. Thus Understanding fabrics is important for adolescents because it helps them to choose clothes wisely.

Quick Test 3

1. What type of finish requires re-application after washing?
2. From which plant does linen fibre originate?
3. Which fibre is often used as a substitute for wool in clothing?
4. Which type of fibre is spandex or Lycra?

8 Acrylic It means a synthetic fibre often used as a substitute for wool, known for its warmth and softness.

Mind Map

FABRICS AROUND US

1 Fibre Properties

Fibres, Yarns and Fabrics are Collectively Known as Textile Products.

Properties of Fibre

- It should be spinable. (easy to convert into yarn and later into fabric).
- It should be economical.
- Includes, colour, luster/shine, weight, etc.

2 Classification of Textile Fibres

Natural Fibres

Cellulosic Fibres

- Derived from plant cellulose.
- **For examples**

(i) Seed hair- cotton, kapok

(ii)Best fibres- linen, hemp, jute

(iii)Leaf fibres- Pineapple, sisal

(iv)Nut husk fibres- coir (coconuts)

Protein Fibres

- Derived from living organism.
- Also called animals fibres
- **For examples**

(i) Animal hair- wool, special hair (goat, camel) fur

(ii)Animal secretion-silk

Mineral Fibre

- Derived from natural mineral.
- **For example** - Asbestos

Natural Rubber

- Made from natural rubber tree barks and latex.

Manufactured Fibres (man-made)

- Made of physical and chemical compositions.
- First manufactured fibre was Rayon.

Process of Manufacturing Fibres

- Solid raw material converted into a liquid form called the spinning solution.
- Spinning solution passed through a spinneret which turn it into fine filaments.
- Filaments become and stretched for further fineness.

3 Yarns

Yarn Processing

Cleaning

- Impurities are removed.
- Clean fibres are ruled into loose sheets called laps.

Making into a Silver

- Laps are straightened by combing.
- Then it converted into rope like mass of loose fibre.

Attenuating, Drawing out and Twisting

- Multiple silver are combined and make them long fibre.
- Twisting the fibre to keep it together.

Spinning

- Strand is shaped into yarn.
- It stretched for desired fineness.

Yarn Terminology

Yarn Number

- Numbers like 20, 30 ,40 on thread reels.
- Higher number means thread is finer.

Yarn Twist

- Twist is added to keep them together.

Yarn and Thread

- Yarn- used to make fabric.
- Thread- used when to stitch pieces of fabric together.

4 Fabric Production

Weaving

- A woven fabric consists of two sets of yarns which are interlaced at right angles to form a compact construction.

Nets

- Open mesh fabrics.
- Made by inter-knotting of yarns.

Knitting

- It is the interlooping of atleast one set of yarns.
- Done by hand using a set of two needles for that fabrics or set of four needles for circular fabrics.

Lace

- It is a an open work fabric.
- Combination of procedures include yarn twisting, interlooping and knotting.

Braiding

- Made by plaiting three or more yarns.
- They appear in items such as shoelaces, ropes etc.

5 Textile Finishing

Types of Textile Finishes

Basic Finishes

- These are necessary.
- Durable and renewable.

Special/Functional Finishes

- These finishers change the behaviour of the fabrics.
- It includes wash and wear, permanent press, water repellent, moth proof, fine proof and anti-shrink.

Dyeing and Printing of Fabrics

- Substances which add colour to the fabric and not easily wash out are known as dyes.
- Printing can be done by, black printing , screen printing, machine printing, stencil printing

6 Important Fibres

Cotton

- Natural cellulosic, staple fibre
- Shortest fibre
- Good conductor of heat
- Comfortable for summer
- Lack flexibility

Linen

- Natural cellulosic fibre
- It is longer and finer than cotton
- Not so bright

Wool

- Natural and protein fibre
- Obtained from sheep hair
- Flexible
- Woolen garments shrink

Silk

- Natural animal fibre
- Queen of textiles
- Stronger than all natural fibres

Rayon

- Man made/manufactured fibre
- Mixed with all types of fibres
- Shape can be controlled

Nylon

- Man made fibre
- Highly elastic fibre
- Used in apparel, socks, gloves etc

Polyester

- Manufactured synthetic fibre
- Partially transparent
- Wrinkle resistance

Acrylic

- Man made fibre
- Similar to wool
- Not very strong
- Use as substitute for wool

Elastomeric Fibres

- These are elastic and rubber like fibre
- Famous for their good elasticity and elongation qualities

NCERT Folder

1. Name five articles of everyday use that are made from different types of fabrics?

Ans. The five articles which are made from different types of fabrics and are used everyday are as follows

(i) Bedsheets (ii) Shoes
(iii) Blankets (iv) Hand bag
(v) Socks

2. How are textile fibres classified? Briefly discuss their characteristics.

Ans. Textile fibres are classified by their chemical origin. These fall into two groups-natural fibres and manufactured fibres.

(i) **Fibres from Natural Sources** The fibres obtained from nature, i.e., plants or animals, are known as natural fibres. e.g., cotton, wool, linen, silk, etc.
Fibres obtained from plant source are called cellulosic fibre e.g., cotton and linen. The fibres that come from animal sources are known as protein fibres, e.g., wool and silk.

(ii) **Man-made Fibres** The fibres which are made in laboratories using chemicals are known as man-made fibres. These are of following two types.

(a) **Regenerated Fibres** These fibres are made from extremely small cotton fibres or any other fibre source such as wood pulp, milk protein, etc.

(b) **Synthetic Fibres** These are made using various petrochemical products. Nylon, acrylic and polyester are all synthetic fibres.
The fibres we have listed above are short or long. The short length fibres are called staple fibres and are measured in inches or centimeters, e.g., cotton, wool and linen.
The long fibres are known as, filaments and are measured in yards/meters, e.g., silk and all man-made fibres.

3. What is a yarn? Explain different methods of yarn processing?

Ans. Yarn is a long unbroken length of interlaced fibres suitable for use in the production of fabric, embroidery, crochet, weaving, etc. It is made up of numerous strands of material wrapped together.
Different methods of yarn processing are

(i) **Cleaning** It means cleaning the impurities from natural fibres like leafy matter, twigs or suint in wool. These fibres are then sorted out and converted into rolled sheets of loose fibres called laps.

(ii) **Carding/Combing** Fibres in the laps are unrolled and then straightened to disentangle the fibres which is known as carding/combing.

(iii) **Conversion to Sliver** The fibres are then rolled into a rope of 2-4 cms in diameter. This is done by passing the fibres through a funnel shaped device. The rope is called sliver.

(iv) **Attenuating** Several slivers are combined to make the fibres longer. Though their thickness remains the same. Attenuating is done in the roll machine where slivers are drawn to make them longer and finer i.e. $\frac{1}{4}$ or $\frac{1}{8}$ or its original diameter.

(v) **Twisting** The fine slivers are then twisted to keep the fibres together. After the desired amount of twist, the yarns are wounded on cones.

4. List the processes in fabric production.

Ans. Fabric production can be done by various methods like by natural methods and by machines.
The list of processes in fabric production is as follow

- **Made directly from fibres** Fabrics are formed by laying the fibres in the form of a Matt and then the adhesion (fixing) is carried out between them. e.g., belts and non-woven or bonded fibre fabrics.
- **Weaving** A woven fabric consists of two sets of yarns that are interlaced at right angles to each other, to form a compact construction. It is done on machines called looms. One set of yarns is fitted on the loom, which determines the length and width of the fabric to be woven. These are called warp yarns. The loom helps to maintain these yarns at a fixed tension and even space. The second yarn, which is the filling yarn, is then interlaced to form the fabric.
- **Knitting** Knitting is the interloping of at least one set of yarns. It may be done by hand using a set of two needles for flat fabrics or a set of four needles for circular fabrics or on machines. The process consists of making a series of loops along the knitting needle or machine bed. Each successive row is formed by interlooping with the first row of loops.
- **Braiding** Braided fabrics have a diagonal surface effect and are made by plaiting three or more yarns that originate from a single location and lie parallel before interlacing occurs. Braids appear in items such as shoelaces, ropes, insulation for wires and trimmings.

5. Mention any three properties of each of the following fibres.

(i) Cotton (ii) Linen (iii) Wool
(iv) Silk (v) Rayon (vi) Nylon
(vii) Acrylic

Ans. The properties are as following

(i) **Cotton**
- It allows heat and air to pass through and absorbs sweat easily.
- Cotton is light in weight.
- Cotton is available in fabrics of varying types of weights, fineness and structures.

(ii) **Linen**
- Linen absorbs moisture easily and therefore it is comfortable to wear it in summers.
- The fibre is longer and finer than cotton.
- It requires longer processing time.

(iii) **Wool**
- Wool is the only fibre which has sulphur.
- Wool has low strength but has good resilience and elastic recovery.
- Wool has surface scales which are water repellant in nature.

(iv) **Silk**
- Silk looks luxurious because of its softness, strength and lustrous quality.
- It is a bad conductor of heat.
- It is made up of a natural protein fibre.

(v) **Rayon**
- It is a good conductor of heat.
- Rayon has greater elasticity than cotton.
- Rayon is resistant to most insects except silver fish.

(vi) **Nylon**
- Nylon has good elastic recovery.
- It is easy to wash and does not wrinkle easily.
- It is not affected by moth and mildew.

(vii) **Acrylic**
- It has high elasticity.
- It is similar to cotton in strength.
- It is available in varied length, diameter and fineness.

Exam Pattern Questions

Objective Type Questions

Multiple Choice Questions (MCQs)

1. These are hair like strands which are fit to be made into a fabric. What is the statement referring to?

(a) Clothes (b) Wool (c) Fibres (d) Linen

2. Which among the following is a textile product?

(a) Fibre (b) Yarns (c) Fabrics (d) All of these

3. A textile manufacturer wants to convert raw materials into fibres to produce synthetic yarn. What process would they use to achieve this? Competency Based Que

(a) Spinning the raw materials directly into fibres
(b) Dissolving the raw materials into a liquid spinning solution and then pushing it through a spinnerette
(c) Heating the raw materials to create fibres directly
(d) Weaving the raw materials into fibres

4. Which among the following are non-synthetic fibres? Competency Based Que

I. Nylon II. Azlon
III. Viscose IV. Spandex

Codes

(a) I and II (b) II and III (c) III and IV (d) I and IV

5. It is the conversion of fibres into yarn.

(a) Manufacturing (b) Regenerating
(c) Yarn production (d) Yarn processing

6. Which of the following statements is incorrect regarding yarn processing from natural staple fibres? Competency Based Que

(a) The process of converting fibres into yarn involves cleaning, making into a sliver, attenuating, drawing out, twisting and spinning.
(b) Carding and combing are used to tangle the fibres.
(c) The sliver is a rope-like mass of loose fibres, about 2-4 cm in diameter.
(d) The final stage of yarn processing is spinning.

7. Yarns made up from staple fibres are known as ....

(a) spun yarn (b) filament yarn
(c) spiral yarn (d) cord yarn

8. Interlooping of at least one set of yarn is called.

(a) Braiding (b) Knitting
(c) Nets (d) Lace

9. **Which process is used for removing paleness or the pre-existing colour of the fibre and making it pure white?**

(a) Tentering (b) Sizing
(c) Singeing (d) Bleaching

10. **Meera bought a fabric and she wants to get a kurti stiched out of that fabric. She gives her size to the tailor and also wants to change the appearance of the fabric by bleaching.**

What is this end process of changing the form of the fabric called? **Competency Based Que**

(a) Bleaching (b) Weaving
(c) Finishing (d) Printing

11. **These type of fibres are measured in inches as they are short in length. Which type of fibres are being referred to in the statement?**

(a) Filament (b) Staple
(c) Natural (d) Manufactured

12. **The bast fibre is ....**

(a) Cellulosic (b) Protein
(c) Mineral (d) None of these

13. **Which of the following is also known as man-made fibre?**

(a) Vegetable fibres (b) Animal fibres
(c) Protein fibres (d) Manufactured fibres

14. **Match the following.** **Competency Based Que**

	Fibres		Examples
A.	Mineral fibre	1.	Spandex
B.	Metal fibre	2.	Silk
C.	Animal fibre	3.	Asbestos
D.	Synthetic fibre	4.	Stainless steel

Codes

	A	B	C	D		A	B	C	D
(a)	3	4	2	1	(b)	1	3	4	2
(c)	2	1	3	4	(d)	4	2	1	3

Picture Based Question

15. **Identify the machine given in the picture below.**

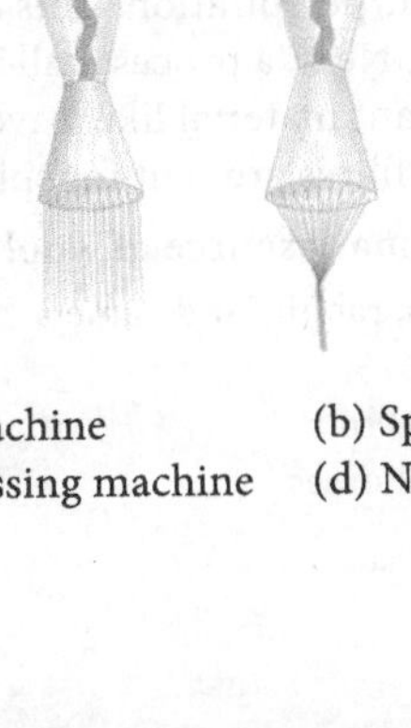

(a) Knitting machine (b) Spinnerette machine
(c) Yarn processing machine (d) None of these

Assertion-Reason Questions

Direction (Q. Nos.16-20) In the questions given below, there are two statements marked as Assertion (A) and Reason (R). Read the statements and choose the correct option.

Codes

(a) Both A and R are true and R is the correct explanation of A.
(b) Both A and R are true, but R is not the correct explanation of A.
(c) A is true, but R is false.
(d) A is false, but R is true.

16. **Assertion** (A) Fibres can be directly used to make most consumer textile products.
Reason (R) Fibres can be easily converted into usable forms without intermediate processing.

17. **Assertion** (A) Weaving and knitting are the primary methods of fabric production.
Reason (R) These methods utilise yarns to create fabric through interlacing or intertwining.

18. **Assertion** (A) Durable finishes like starching are removed after washing.
Reason (R) Starching is a type of renewable finish.

19. **Assertion** (A) Rayon is quite suitable for summer wear.
Reason (R) It is a good conductor of heat.

20. **Assertion** (A) fibres with high abrasion resistance require less maintenance.
Reason (R) Abrasion resistance enhances durability and reduces wear.

Case Based Questions

21. **Read the passage carefully and answer the given questions**

Manufactured fibres, or man-made fibres, are created by humans. The first manufactured fibre was Rayon which was made in 1895. Most others were developed in the 20th century. For a long time, Rayon was called 'artificial silk' or 'art silk.'

The idea of creating fibres likely came from wanting to make something like silk. Silkworms eat mulberry leaves and digest them. They then release a liquid through two openings (spinnerettes). This liquid hardens into silk filaments that form cocoons. This led people to think that if a cellulose material was processed, it could produce a silk-like fibre.

The earliest manufactured fibres were created by converting non-fibrous materials into fibrous forms, mainly from cellulosic substances like cotton waste or wood pulp. The second group of fibres was made entirely from chemicals. Regardless of the raw material used, the basic steps to convert it into fibres are the same.

(i) What inspired the development of manufactured fibres?
(a) Desire to replace cotton
(b) Need for stronger fibres
(c) Attempt to replicate silk
(d) Demand for cheaper textiles

(ii) What were the primary materials used to create the earliest manufactured fibres?
(a) Chemicals only
(b) Cellulosic substances like cotton waste or wood pulp
(c) Natural fibres like cotton and wool
(d) Synthetic polymers

(iii) Assertion (A) Rayon was initially called 'artificial silk' or 'art silk.'
Reason (R) Rayon's texture and appearance resemble silk.
Codes **Competency Based Que**
(a) Both A and R are true and R is the correct explanation of A.
(b) Both A and R are true, but R is not the correct explanation of A.
(c) A is true, but R is false.
(d) A is false, but R is true.

(iv) Assertion (A) Manufactured fibres were first developed in the 19th century.
Reason (R) Rayon, the first manufactured fibre, was invented in 1895. **Competency Based Que**
Codes
(a) Both A and R are true and R is the correct explanation of A.
(b) Both A and R are true, but R is not the correct explanation of A.
(c) A is true, but R is false.
(d) A is false, but R is true.

22. Read the passage given below and answer the following questions.

A woven fabric consists of two sets of yarns which are interlaced at right angles to each other, to form a compact construction. It is done on machines called looms. One set of yarns is fitted on the loom, which determines the length and width of the fabric to be woven. These are called warp yarns. The loom helps to maintain these yarns at a fixed tension and even space. The second yarn, which is the filling yarn, is then interlaced to form the fabric. The simplest interlacing is when the filling yarn moves over and under one warp yarn alternately in one row and reverses the process in the second row. By passing the filling yarn over and under different number of warp yarns, in a specified sequence, different designs can be created. Attachments like the dobby or jacquard to the loom can help to create figurative designs as well. These designs become clearer when different coloured yarns are used for warp and filling.

(i) .... determines the length and width of the fabric to be woven.
(a) Loom (b) Dobby
(c) Warp yarn (d) Filling yarn

(ii) Assertion (A) Attachments like the dobby or jacquard to the loom can help to create figurative designs as well.
Reason (R) These designs become clearer when different coloured yarns are used for warp and filling.
Codes **Competency Based Que**
(a) Both A and R are true and R is the correct explanation of A
(b) Both A and R are true, but R is not the correct explnation of A
(c) A is true, but R is false
(d) A is false, but R is true

(iii) Acrylic is similar to which among the following?
(a) Lycra (b) Polymer
(c) Linen (d) Cotton

(iv) Production of good quality silk is called
(a) fleecing (b) weaving
(c) ginning (d) sericulture

23. Read the passage carefully and answer the questions that follow

Wool comes from the hair of sheep. It can also be collected from other animals like goats, rabbits and camels. These fibres are known as speciality hair fibres. Different sheep breeds produce different types of wool. Some breeds are raised specifically for their high-quality fibres.

Removing the hair from the animal is called shearing. This is usually done once or twice a year, depending on the climate. During shearing, care is taken to keep the hair in one piece, known as fleece. This makes it easier to sort the fibres because hair from different parts of the body varies in length and thickness.

After sorting, the fibres are cleaned to remove dirt, grease and sweat/perspiration. This cleaning process is called scouring. Next, a process called carbonisation removes any plant material like leaves and twigs. After these steps, the fibres are sent for spinning.

(i) What is the primary source of wool?
(a) Sheep, goats, rabbits and camels
(b) Sheep only
(c) Goats and rabbits
(d) Camels and horses

(ii) **Which of the following pairs is correct?**
(a) Spinning – keeping sheep hair in fleece
(b) Scouring – Removing plant material
(c) Carbonisation – Cleaning wool fibres
(d) Shearing – Removing hair from animals

(iii) **Assertion** (A) Wool fibres are sorted after shearing.
Reason (R) Hair from different parts of the body varies in length and thickness. **Competency Based Que**
Codes
(a) Both A and R are true and R is the correct explanation of A.
(b) Both A and R are true, but R is not the correct explanation of A.
(c) A is true, but R is false.
(d) A is false, but R is true.

(iv) **Assertion** (A) Carbonisation is done to remove dirt and grease from wool fibres.
Reason (R) Carbonisation removes plant material like leaves and twigs. **Competency Based Que**
Codes
(a) Both A and R are true and R is the correct explanation of A.
(b) Both A and R are true, but R is not the correct explanation of A.
(c) A is true, but R is false.
(d) A is false, but R is true.

Answers

1. (c) Fibres
2. (d) All of these
3. (b) Dissolving the raw materials into a liquid spinning solution and then pushing it through a spinnerette
4. (d) I and IV
5. (d) Yarn processing
6. (b) Carding and combing are used to tangle the fibres.
7. (a) spun yarn
8. (b) Knitting
9. (d) Bleaching
10. (c) Finishing
11. (b) Staple
12. (a) Cellulosic
13. (d) Manufactured fibres
14. (a) 3421
15. (b) Spinnerette machine
16. (d) A is false, but R is true.
17. (a) Both A and R are true and R is the correct explanation of A.
18. (d) A is false, but R is true.
19. (a) Both A and R are true and R is the correct explanation of A.
20. (a) Both A and R are true and R is the correct explanation of A.
21. (i) (c) Attempt to replicate silk
(ii) (b) Cellulosic substances like cotton waste or wood pulp
(iii) (a) Both A and R are true and R is the correct explanation of A.
(iv) (d) A is false, but R is true.
22. (i) (c) Warp yarn
(ii) (b) Both A and R are true, but R is not the correct explanation of A
(iii) (d) Cotton
(iv) (d) sericulture
23. (i) (a) Sheep, goats, rabbits and camels
(ii) (d) Shearing – Removing hair from animals
(iii) (a) Both A and R are true and R is the correct explanation of A.
(iv) (d) A is false, but R is true.

Subjective Questions

Very Short Answer Type Questions

1. What are fibres?

Ans. Fibres are hair like strands which are fit to be made into a fabric.

2. What is meant by Man-made fibres?

Ans. Man-made fibres are produced by using chemical compounds and through chemical reaction.

3. Mineral fibres are obtained from natural minerals. Give any one example of mineral fibre.

Ans. Asbestos and glass fibres are examples of mineral fibres.

4. What do you understand by the term 'artificial silk'?

Ans. The term 'artificial silk' refers to man-made artificial fibre called 'rayon'. Main raw material used in the manufacture of rayon is cellulose which is obtained from cotton linters and wood pulp, etc.

5. What is carding in the yarn processing stage?

Ans. It is a process that disentangles and straightens

6. What does T.P.I stand for in yarn terminology.

Ans. T.P.I stand for twist per inch

7. What is a loom?

Ans. Loom is the device or machine used to weave.

These looms are what hold the longitudinal warp threads in place as the weaver weaves the 'filling' or weft threads through them.

The weaver can choose different colours to create specific patterns.

8. Neha wants to create a uniques design for a cushion cover using a weaving technique. What weaving technique could she use for a textured effect?

Ans. Neha could use a jacquard loom to create unique and intricate designs and textures.

9. A textile factory wants to produce fabric for upholstery using industrial knitting machines. What technique would be suitable?

Ans. Warp knitting would be suitable to produce fabric for upholstery using industrial knitting machines.

10. Rani is planning to make a summer dress. She wants a fabric that is breathable and comfortable. What type of fabric should she choose.

Ans. She should choose cotton or a light knitted fabric for comfort ability and breathability.

11. Why is textile finishing important?

Ans. Textile finishing is important because they improve the appearance of fabric. It also improves the touch or feel of the fabric and makes the fabric suitable for a specific use.

12. Rahul wants to create a striped pattern on his cotton shirt. At what stage should the colour be applied?

Ans. For woven patterns like checks and stripes the colour should be applied at the yarn stage.

13. Cotton fibre is obtained from which part of the plant?

Ans. Cotton is obtained from pods of cotton plant.

14. What is 'sericulture'?

Ans. Sericulture is the raising of silk worms for the purpose of manufacturing silk.

15. Ria wants to buy activewear pants that stretch comfortably. Which type of fibre should she look for?

Ans. For activewear pants that have stretching capability, elastomeric fibres such as spandex or Lycra are best suited.

Short Answer Type Questions

1. Rahul is exploring various types of fabrics for his clothing business. **Competency Based Que**

(a) What factors should Rahul consider when selecting fabrics for his business?

(b) How do the properties of fibres affect the final fabric?

(c) What is the significance of abrasion resistance in fabric selection?

Ans. (a) Rahul should consider several factors, including the type of fibre, yarn, fabric construction and finishing techniques.

(b) Fibre properties significantly impact the final fabric. Essential properties include spinnability, colour, luster, weight, moisture retention, dye absorption and elasticity.

- Spinnability determines how easily fibres can be converted into yarn.
- Colour and luster influence the fabric's appearance.
- Weight affects its warmth and texture.
- Moisture retention and dye absorption impact the fabric's comfort and colourfastness.
- Elasticity determines the fabric's flexibility and recovery.

(c) Abrasion resistance is crucial in fabric selection as it indicates a fabric's ability to withstand damage from rubbing or scratching. Fabrics with high abrasion resistance are suitable for heavy-use applications, such as upholstery or workwear. In contrast, low-abrasion resistance fabrics are better suited for delicate or infrequently used items.

2. Textile fibres can be classified based on origin. **Competency Based Que**

(i) Explain the difference between natural and man-made fibres.

(ii) Examples of natural fibres and their sources.

Ans. (i) Natural fibres are derived from natural sources, such as plants (cotton, flax) or animals (wool, silk). These fibres often offer breathability, softness, and warmth.

On the other hand, Man-made fibres, like polyester and nylon, are created through chemical processes. They typically provide durability, wrinkle resistance and easy care.

(ii) Examples of natural fibres include cotton (seed hair), flax (bast fibre), silk (animal secretion), wool (animal hair) and coir (nut husk fibre).

These fibres are obtained from various sources, such as plants (cotton, flax), animals (wool, silk) or minerals (asbestos).

3. How is silk produced?

Ans. Silk is produced by silkworms, which are the larvae of the silk moth. The process begins when the female moth lays eggs. These eggs hatch into tiny caterpillars, called silkworms. The silkworms feed on mulberry leaves and grow larger. After about 4-6 weeks, they are ready to spin silk.

To make silk, the silkworm secretes a liquid from its glands that hardens into a long, continuous thread when it touches air. The silkworm wraps itself in this thread to create a protective cocoon. Each cocoon can contain up to 1,000 meters of silk thread.

After the cocoon is formed, it is carefully boiled in hot water to soften the sericin (a protein that holds the threads together). The silk threads are then unwound, cleaned, and spun into yarn. This yarn can be woven into fabrics like silk clothing, bed sheets, and other luxurious textiles.

4. What are the main techniques of fabric construction?

Ans. Main techniques of fabric construction involves

(i) **Weaving** It is the process of interlacing yarns in different ways.

(ii) **Knitting** It is a technique of producing a three-dimensional fabric from a yarn.

(iii) **Braiding** It is a type of fabric made by plaiting three a more yarns in such a way that they cross one another in a diagonal formation.

5. A consumer wants to purchase sustainable textiles. **Competency Based Que**

(i) What eco-friendly textile options are available?

(ii) How do textile finishing processes impact sustainability?

Ans. (i) Eco-friendly options include natural fibres like organic cotton, hemp, and jute. Recycled synthetic fibres, Tencel and plant-based rayon are also sustainable choices.

(ii) Textile finishing processes can impact sustainability through chemical treatments, water consumption, and waste generation. Consumers should look for eco-friendly finishes, organic certifications and sustainable production methods.

6. Describe in brief the stages through which finishing with colour is possible.

Ans. The method of dyeing depends on the chemical natures of the fibre and the dye and the type of effect desired. Colour application can be done at the following stages

- **At fibre stage** for yarns of different colours or designed felts.
- **At the yarn stage** for woven checks, stripes or other woven patterns.
- **At fabric stage** the most common method for solid colour dye, as also for designed dyeing like batik, tie and dye and printing.

7. Neelam wants to incorporate linen into her summer clothing line. What benefits of linen should she highlight? **Competency Based Que**

Ans. Neelam should highlight several benefits of linen for summer clothing line. As a best fibre derived from the flax plant, linen is breathable and ideal for hot weather. It has moisture-absorbing properties, ensuring comfort by keeping the skin dry. Linen's fibres are longer and finer than cotton, resulting in stronger, more lustrous fabric. This offers an elegant look.

Overall, linen is comfortable, eco-friendly and a stylish choice for summer wear.

8. List some basic features of silk.

Ans. Some basic features of silk are

(i) Silk is one of the stronger fibres used in making fabrics. It has good elastic recovery and moderate elongation.

(ii) Silk is a natural protein fibre and the natural colour of silk is off white to cream. Wild silk is brownish in colour.

(iii) Silk filaments are very long, fine, smooth and have a relatively high lustre or sheen. It contains a natural gum which gives silk a crisp texture.

9. How will you identify a rayon fibre?

Ans. A rayon fibre can be recognised with its shine and it has lengthwise parallel. It is shiny like silk but sometimes it can be dull also.

Rayon is a good conductor of heat hence it can be worn in summers also. Length of rayon fibres can be controlled as desired. Long filaments and staple fibres both can be obtained. Rayon is normally white and shiny.

10. Rani is an aspiring textile designer working on a project about different fabrics. She has a fabric sample that she suspects might be nylon. To ensure her project is accurate she needs to identify whether her sample is indeed nylon. How can Rani identify if her fabric sample is made of nylon. **Competency Based Que**

Ans. Rani can identify if her fabric sample is made of nylon by examining its texture and properties. Nylon filaments are typically smooth and shiny with a uniform diameter. Additionaly, if the fabric has a high level of elasticity and resembles fine, transparent fibres , it is likely nylon.

Long Answer Type Questions

1. What is the difference between natural fibre and synthetic fibre?

Ans. Difference between natural fibre and synthetic fibre are

Natural Fibre	Synthetic Fibre
All natural fibres come from nature only.	Synthetic fibres are completely man-made.
Length of these fibre is nature given.	Length of the fibre is controlled by man.
Fibres are found in staple or filament form.	It is found in filament form in but sometimes it could be converted into cut length.
Natural fabric is comfortable to wear.	Synthetic textile product is not as comfortable as natural product.
There could be dust and impurities in natural fibre.	No dust or impurities contain in synthetic fibre.

2. You went to an industry where yarn processing is taking place. It means conversion of fibres into yarns. In the very first step, they are removing the impurities from natural fibres.

(i) What is this step known as? Disucss.

(ii) What is yarn processing?

(iii) Which others steps are involved in yarn processing? **Competency Based Que**

Ans. (i) The first step involved in yarn processing is cleaning. It means cleaning the impurities from natural fibres like leafy matter, twigs or suint in wool. These fibres are then sorted out and converted into rolled sheets of loose fibres called laps.

(ii) Yarn processing is the conversion of fibre into yarn. It is also called spinning as it involves twisting the fibres around a spindle. Unmarried girls in Europe were commonly involved in spinning the finest yarn because of their nimble fingers. It led to the coining of the term 'spinster'.

(iii) Yarn processing involves the following steps

Making into a Sliver The laps are unrolled and straightened by the process of carding and combing.

- The process is similar to combing and brushing hair.
- This process also helps in removing the impurities and short fibre. At the end, it passes through a funnel shaped device which helps to convert it into a sliver. Sliver is a rope like mass of loose fibres.

Attenuating When the fibres have been converted into a continuous strand, it needs to be made to the size required. This is called attenuation.

3. Preeti, a fashion designer, wants to create a new clothing line that combines comfort, durability and style.

(i) Describe the characteristics of knitted fabrics that make them suitable for Rahul's clothing line, and explain the difference between weft knitting and warp knitting.

(ii) Choose three natural fibres and discuss their properties, suitability and potential applications in Rahul's clothing line. **Competency Based Que**

Ans. (i) Knitted fabrics are ideal for Rahul's clothing line due to their elasticity, breathability and comfort. Weft knitting involves inter looping yarns across the width of the material, allowing for shaping during construction.

Warp knitting, used in industrial machines, involves inter looping yarns similar to weaving looms, producing continuous lengths of material.

(ii) Rahul can consider the following natural fibres for his clothing line

- **Cotton** Cotton is a breathable, moisture-absorbing fibre suitable for casual wear. Its natural comfort and durability make it ideal for everyday clothing, such as t-shirts, jeans and undergarments.
- **Linen** Linen is a strong, lustrous fibre that absorbs moisture well, making it perfect for summer clothing. Its breathability and cooling properties make it suitable for garments like shirts, dresses and pants.

- **Silk** Silk is a smooth, lustrous, and elastic fibre suitable for high-end or formal wear. Silk's natural temperature regulation properties also provide comfort in various environments.

4. A textile manufacturer wants to enhance the appearance, texture, and performance of its fabrics for various applications.

(i) Explain the concept of textile finishing and discuss the differences between durable and renewable finishes, providing examples of each.

(ii) Describe the various methods of changing fabric texture through finishing processes, highlighting their effects on fabric behavior.

Competency Based Que

Ans. (i) Textile finishing involves various treatments that alter fabric appearance, texture or behavior to meet specific requirements. Finishes can be categorised into durable and renewable. Durable finishes, such as dyeing, printing and water repellency treatments, remain effective through multiple washings and dry cleanings. Renewable finishes, including starching, blueing and sizing lose their effectiveness after washing and require reapplication.

(ii) Various finishing processes alter fabric texture, impacting its behavior and suitability for different applications. Methods include

- **Starching** adds temporary stiffness and smoothness
- **Sizing** strengthens fabric for easier handling and sewing
- **Calendering** smoothes and straightens fabric using heat and pressure
- **Tentering** stretches and dries fabric to prevent shrinkage

5. Describe the suitability of woollen fibre.

Ans. Wool is an important natural fibre. The suitability of wool is explained in the following way

(i) Wool is a bad conductor of heat i.e., woollen clothes trap the body heat, so these are to be worn in cold winter.

(ii) Wool is a soft fibre and is used to make sweaters, caps, gloves, suits, pants, coats, dresses, socks, lining of shoes and jackets. It is also used for making carpets, rugs and blankets, etc.

(iii) Woollen clothes are not wrinkeled easily and hence do not require frequent ironing.

(iv) The stretchability and elasticity of woollen clothes are helpful in both maintaining the shape and durability of the garment.

(v) Wool is used in other ways, for example, terrywool is made by blending wool with terylene, cotswool is made by blending wool with cotton.

6. Aditi is redesigning her living room and is considering polyester for curtains. Can you provide insights on the key characteristics of polyester fabric, including its duralility, maintenance, appearance?

Competency Based Que

Ans. Polyester is an artificial fibre made by chemical process. The other names of polyester are terylene, decron.

The main characteristics of polyester are

(i) Polyester is available from transparent to off white and its luster may be from very dull to shiny bright.

(ii) It is quite strong and can last for a long time.

(iii) It has good resistance to friction.

(iv) It does not have affinity to dyes. Hence, it can not be dyed easily.

(v) It is a bad conductor of heat.

SELF ASSESSMENT TEST

Objective Type Questions

1. Which term is used to describe the process that improves a fabric's appearance and qualities?
   (a) Weaving (b) Spinning
   (c) Finishing (d) Dyeing
2. Fibres are typically interwoven to form which of the following?
   (a) Yarns (b) Threads
   (c) Textiles (d) Nets

Very Short Answer Type Questions

3. Name the different fibres choosen for making yarns.
4. Define knitting.
5. How did the word spinster originate?
6. What do you understand by the term 'finishing'?

Short Answer Type Questions

7. Classify textile fibres based on their origin.
8. What are the different methods of constructing a fabric?
9. How is calendering different from sanforising?
10. Differentiate between nets and laces.

Long Answer Type Questions

11. Explain basic mechanism of weaving.
12. Explain the various yarn terminologies and the differences between yarn and thread.
13. Suggest the difference between knitting, felting and weaving.
14. "Dyeing and printing have great importance in fabric construction". Discuss how? **Competency Based Que**

06

CHAPTER

Media and communication are essential parts of our daily lives, helping us share information, ideas and emotions.

Media and Communication Technology

▼ **YOUR STUDY GOALS**

▼ **YOUR PRACTICE GOAL**

- Objective Type Questions (19 Qs ; MCQs, A-R, Matching, Case Based)
- Subjective Questions (11 VSAs, 8 SAs, 7 LAs)

6.1 Introduction

Media[1] and communication is an important field of study that has an impact on adolescent lives. Media and communication, gradually becomes an integral part of our lives and it adds quality to our lives.

Meaning of Communication

- The word communication comes from the Latin word **communis**, which means **common**. Thus, it involves sharing ideas in a way that both the sender/communicator and receiver understand.
- Communication is the process of thinking, observing, understanding, analysing and sharing feelings or ideas with others through different methods in various situations. It includes seeing, listening, exchanging thoughts, knowledge and emotions either with oneself or others.
- Effective communication creates a **shared understanding** of the message among the people involved in the communication. It is a continuous process that happens in all areas of life, like at home, school or in the community.

1 **Media** It refers to the ways, means or channels of transmitting message from the sender to the receiver.

Classification of Communication

The classification of communication can be understood by the chart given below

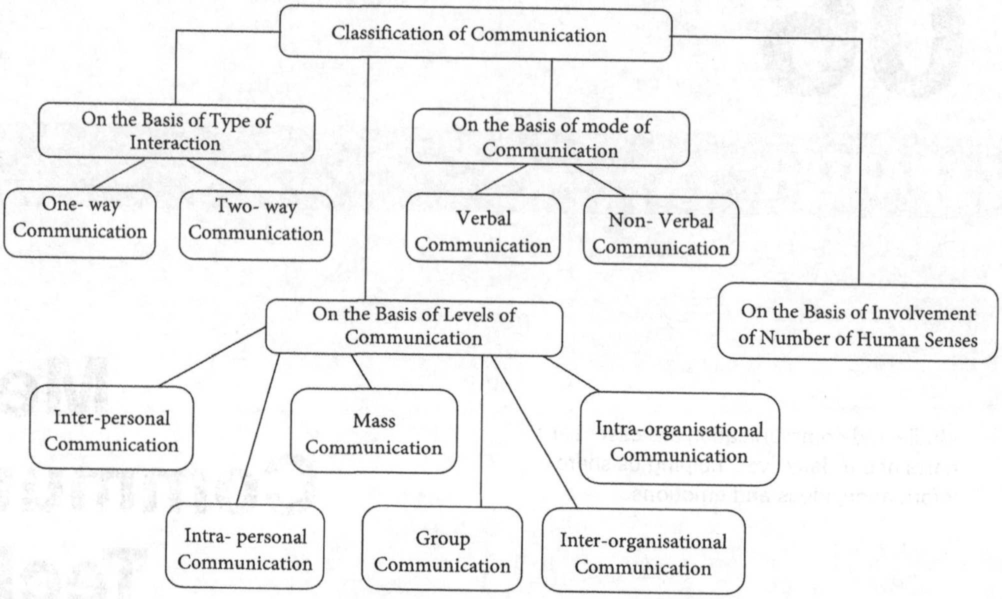

▲ *Classification of Communication*

I. On the Basis of the Type of Interaction

There are two types of interactions

(i) One-way Communication

- In one way communication receiver receives the information, but the receiver either never able to respond or cannot respond immediately. Thus, information remains one way.
  - For examples speeches, lectures, listening to music on the radio, watching TV programmes or using the internet to search for information.

(ii) Two-way Communication

- Communication happens between two or more people where there is an exchange of ideas and information, etc. It can be **either verbally or silently**. For examples, talking on the phone, discussing plans with family, or chatting online.
- The cry of the body is a message that he/she is hunger. This is an example of two-way communication, as the mother responds by feeding the baby.

II. On the Basis of Levels of Communication

There various level of communication are

(i) Intra-personal Communication

- This refers to communicating with oneself. It is a mental process of observing, analysing and drawing conclusions.
- It helps individuals reflect on their present, past and future behaviour. It is an **ongoing process**. For example; mentally rehearsing before an interview or exam.

(ii) Inter-personal Communication

- This is the exchange of thoughts and ideas between two or more people in a **face-to-face situation**.
- It can happen in both formal and informal settings. This communication method includes body movements, facial expressions, gestures, posture, written text, and spoken words. For example; talking to a friend about study problems or participating in a panel discussion.
- Inter-personal communication is effective because of the following reasons
  - There is **direct contact** between communicator and communicate. This makes it easier to persuade, motivate and convince the communicate (receiver) of the idea or thought.
  - **Instant feedback** is possible in this form of communication.

(iii) Group Communication

- This form of communication is **direct and personal,** such as inter-personal communication. However, it involves communication between more than two people.
- It encourages participation, decision-making and self-expression. Group communication increases the individual's impact in a gathering, thus enhancing one's status in the group.
- It also helps with socialising, motivation and relaxation.
- Audio-visual aids can improve group communication.

(iv) Mass Communication

- Spreading thoughts, ideas and innovations to large sections of society has become easier due to the advancements in technology.
- Mass communication can be defined as the process of **multiplying messages** with the help of any mechanical device and spreading them to the masses. For examples, include radio, TV, satellite communication, newspapers and magazines.
- The audience in mass communication is large, **heterogeneous**[2] and anonymous. They are spread across wide areas and are not directly connected to the communicator in time and space. Because of this, getting correct, complete and immediate feedback is not possible. Instead, feedback is slow, cumulative, expensive and delayed.

(v) Intra-organisational Communication

- Organisational communication takes place in structured environments or settings.
- Like people, organisations also form and maintain relationships. They communicate at different levels within their departments or sections. Every organisation has different levels or hierarchy of ranks working together for achieving common goals.
- The information flow in such organisations is expected to be **two-way** at the same level and **one-way** across different levels.

(vi) Inter-organisational Communication

- This refers to the communication system developed by one organisation to communicate with other organisations. This is done with the aim of working in **co-operation** and **co-ordination** with each other.
- For example, for assistance in developmental activities of the country, both technical and financial support is provided by international agencies. On the other hand, administrative support is given by the Central Government and State Governments.

It is important to note that in both intra-organisational and inter-organisational setups, communication does not take place among the departments or organisations. Rather, it is human beings working in these organisations who communicate with each other. Therefore, understanding of the **human factor** is very important.

2 **Heterogeneous** It means censisting of different kinds of people or things.

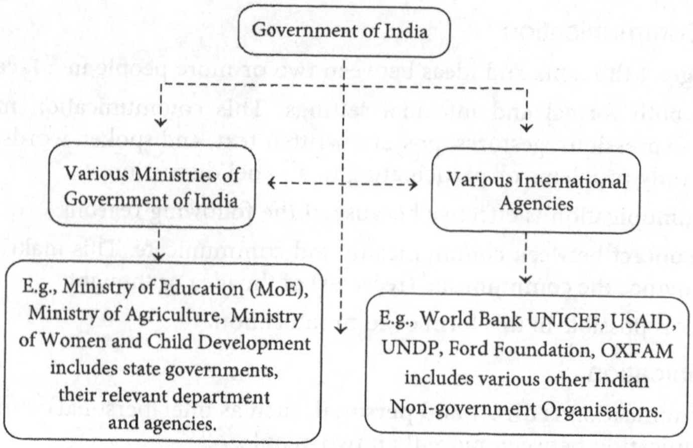

▲ *Communication System among various organisations*

III. On the Basis of Modes of Communication

There are two modes of communication i.e, verbal and Non-verbal

(i) Verbal Communication

- It includes auditory means or verbal modes like **speaking** and **singing**.
- Factors like the **tone of voice** are of significance in verbal communication.
- Research shows that on an average, an individual spends about **70 per cent** of her/his active time in communicating verbally, i.e., listening, speaking and reading aloud.

(ii) Non-verbal Communication

- Non-verbal communication includes **gestures**, facial expressions, posture, eye contact, touch, para-language, writing, clothing, hairstyles, architecture, symbols and sign language. For example; smoke signals used by some tribal groups.

IV. On the Basis of Involvement of Number of Human Senses

- Various studies have shown that involving more senses in the learning process makes learning clearer, easier to understand and more lasting.
- Thus, involvement of more number of senses makes the learning more clearly understandable and permanent. For example watching a live or televised folk or classical dance helps us learn about our traditional heritage more easily and interestingly than reading about it in a book.

Our Senses and Communication

People retain 10% of what they	Read	Visual
People remember about 20-25% of what they	Hear	Audio
People keep in mind about 30-35% of what they	See	Visual
People remember 50% and more of what they have	Seen, Heard	Audio-Visual
People remember 90% and more of what they have	Seen, Heard and Done	Audio-Visual
Involvement of more number of senses makes the learning more clearly understandable and permanent		

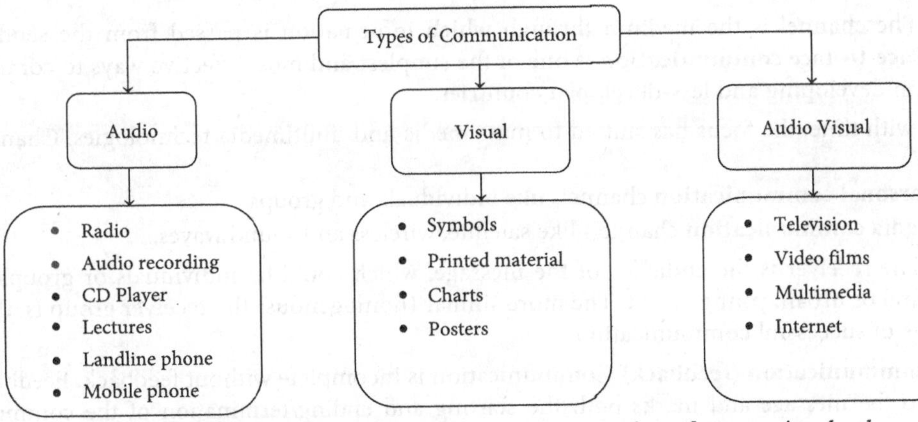

▲ *Classification of Communication based on number of senses involved*

Process of Communication

Communication is the process of **sending information** from a sender to a receiver with the use of a medium.

- It allows the exchange of information through different methods, ensuring both sender and receiver understand it correctly, clearly and completely.
- In the process of communication **feedback** from the audience is also important for future planning, just like market surveys before launching a product.
- Communication events **occur in sequence**. One way to explain it as: who says, what, to whom, when, in what manner under what circumstances and with what effect.
- The communication process follows a specific order to complete the cycle. The basic elements of any communication process in general are arranged in a definite order to complete the cycle.
- The basic elements must be managed for effective communication. These are explained in **the SMCRE model** of communication.

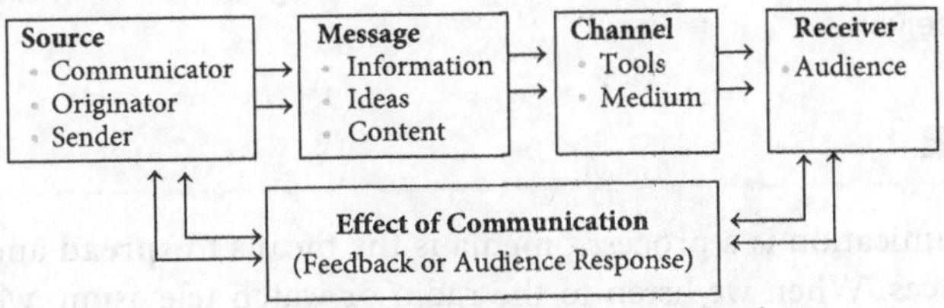

▲ *The SMCRE Model of Communication*

The elements of the SMCRE model of communication are described below

- **Source** The source is the person who starts the communication process. She/he plays a key role in making the communication effective. The source sends a message to a specific group of audience in a way that ensures correct interpretation of the message and gets the expected response.

  The source could be a teacher, parents, friend, classmate, extension worker, leader, administrator, writer, farmer or a tribal person with indigenous knowledge.
- **Message** The message is the information or content which the communicator wants from the audience to understand or act on. It could be any technical, scientific or general information related to any field of knowledge or daily life.

  A good message should be simple, clear, specific and authentic. It should also be timely, appropriate and suitable for the selected channel and the audience.

- **Channel** The channel is the medium through which information is passed from the sender to the receiver. **Face-to-face communication** is one of the simplest and most effective ways to communicate, especially in developing and less-developed countries.

  However, with time, the focus has shifted to mass media and multimedia technologies. Channels can be

  - **Inter-personal communication** channels like individuals and groups.
  - **Mass media communication** channels like satellite, wireless and sound waves.
- **Receiver** The receiver is the audience of the message, which could be individuals or groups, men or women, rural or urban, young or old. The more similar (homogenous) the receiver group is, the higher the chances of successful communication.
- **Effect of communication (feedback)** Communication is incomplete without feedback. Feedback is the response to the message and marks both the starting and ending/termination of the communication process. The process ends or terminates when the expected response is received, thus, it completes the cycle.

  If the response of the intended audience does not give the desired results, rethinking and recasting of message is important and the entire communication process is repeated.

  Some examples of feedback are

  (i) Teacher asking students questions after a lesson to see if they understood it.

  (ii) Letters to editors from readers in newspapers and magazines.

  (iii) Television Ratings Points (TRPs) showing viewer feedback for a programme.

Quick Test 1

1. What is communicating with onself known as?
2. Give two examples of mass media communication.
3. The SMCRE model of communication stands for?
4. What is the content or information a communicator wishes to receive, accept or act upon?
5. Mention the medium of communication through which the information flows from the sender to the receiver.

6.2 Media

- While communication is a process , media is the means to **spread** and **share ideas, thoughts, feelings** and **experiences**. When we listen to the radio or watch television, what we hear or see can affect our thoughts and actions. This is known as **media influence**. Communication is a process, and media serves as the means to spread and share ideas, thoughts, feelings and experiences.
- Look at common elements in different forms of communication: advertisements on TV, films, news articles, political speeches, classroom instructions, complaints about faulty appliances and online shopping. We find that each example involves a medium used to share different messages or information. For example, when we speak or listen to someone, the air acts as a medium for sound waves because sound cannot travel in a vacuum.
- Mass media primarily uses **modern technology** for communication. However, technology does not always mean mass communication is taking place. Mass media is always meant for large, diverse and anonymous audience groups.
- Media does not only include radio and television. It also includes satellite transmission, computer technology and wireless communication. Media has evolved significantly over time and many modern technologies are now used for communication purposes.

Classification of Media

Media can be classified into two broad categories, **traditional** and **modern media.**

Traditional Media

In most of the rural areas, work was completely dependent on traditional media, such as fairs and radio. Even in today's time also, people of some rural areas use this media.

- **Inter-personal Communication** Media largely remains the most used and effective medium of communication in rural and remote areas. For example; puppetry, folk dances, folk theatre, oral literature, fairs and festivals, rituals and symbols, as well as print media. Some examples are as follows
- **Traditional Folk Theatre or Drama** These include Jatra (Bengal), Ramleela and Nautanki (Uttar Pradesh), Bidesia (Bihar), Tamasha (Maharashtra), Yakshagana and Dashavatar (Karnataka) and Bhavai (Gujarat).
- **Oral Literature-cum-Musical Forms** These include folk or tribal songs and dances such as Baul and Bhatiali (Bengal), Sna and Dadaria (Madhya Pradesh), Duha and Garba (Gujarat), Chakri (Kashmir), Bhangra and Gidda (Punjab), Kajri, Chaiti and Allha (UP and Bihar), Powda and Lavni (Maharashtra), Bihu and Mand (Assam) Panihari and songs sung by Charans and Bhaatt (Rajasthan) as well as drum festivals of the North-Eastern and other tribal communities of the country.
- **Forms of Puppetry** These include string puppets or Sutradharika mainly used in Rajasthan and Gujarat and Chhaya Putli (shadow puppets) common in the South India.
- **Festivals, Fairs and Social Rituals** They are used for **conveying messages,** expressions, feelings and traditions of the various communities all over India. They are held seasonally as well as on particular dates in the religious calendar. For example, Uttarayan (kite flying festival in Gujarat) and Hornbill festival (Nagaland).
- **Traditional Print Media** These include charts, posters, handbills, newspapers, magazines and other local publications. Local and national newspapers have been published for over many centuries and will continue to do so.

With the development of technology, it was observed that traditional communication media were neither sufficient nor well-equipped to meet the diverse information needs of modern audiences, causing modern media to be developed.

Modern Media

With the advent of modern technology, the range of communication media has expanded. Some examples of modern media are FM radio, satellite television, modern print media, films projected though various type of projectors, audio cassette and CD—DVD technology, cable and wireless technology, mobile phones, video films and video conferencing.

Functions of Media

The media has the following functions

- **Information** Media performs the function of both providing information and information exchange radio, TV, magazines, newspaper etc., are the examples, which facilitate the communication.
- **Motivation** Media helps in persuading the audience to accept the idea. This is done by suitable understanding of audience psychology and their socio-cultural background.
- **Entertainment** Both, traditional and modern communication media provide a wide variety of entertainment. In education also, media is used in an entertaining form to make learning easy and interesting.
- **Interpretation** Use of communication media, particularly pictographic presentations and facts and figures, make many difficult and complicated concepts easy to understand.

For example, it is easy to locate and understand a geographical area with the help of cartographic map or model of a globe than merely reading about it in a textbook.

- **Transmission of Values** Development of a **healthy society** by the transmission of wholesome values is a function of media. For example, the use of puppetry, street plays, cartoon films and radio programmes to teach the values of cleanliness through the Swachh Bharat Abhiyaan.
- **Education or Training** New learning experiences using appropriate communication media in local language and focusing on local problems always enrich the teaching-learning experience. These include interactive video and audio cassettes, discs of basic printed teaching-learning material on various concepts.
- **Co-ordination** Pace, scope and accuracy of communication has improved tremendously, the ability to co-ordinate large projects spread over a vast geographical area. Video conferencing is one such media.
- **Behavioural Change** Extension educational activities related to varied fields depend largely on the art and technique of effective communication. Media transmits useful messages which lead to direct and indirect improvements in behaviour in the target group of people.
- **Initiating Development** Media is an important medium for development because it mediates between specialists and ordinary persons. It has accelerated the pace of development and made the world smaller by **bringing people closer** through communication.

Quick Test 2

1. What is used for sharing and disseminating, ideas and thoughts?
2. In how many types media can be classified? Name them.
3. FM, Radio, Satellite are included in what category of media?
4. How is media a tool for development?
5. Give an example of how media helps in transmitting values.

6.3 Communication Technology

- Communication technology plays a crucial role in the communication process. We have used different media and communication technologies for communication in various times, settings and communities, such as rural, urban and tribal areas.

Pij village in Gujarat acquired the first TV transmitter in India. It provided programmes in local language along with common programmes from Delhi via satellite.

- Communication technology includes different technologies which created to manage information and support communication. This includes **modern technologies** used to send data, which can be either analogue (electronic signals) or digital. It also involves hardware, organisational structures and social values that people use to gather, process and share information.

Classification of Communication Technologies

A wide range of communication technologies are available. These fall into two broad groups

- **Cable (land) Based Technologies** These are comparatively cheap and less complicated. Landline telephone or a personal computer without internet are examples of such technology.
- **Wireless Technologies** These generally require less infrastructure, but can be more expensive to use than cable-based technologies. Some examples are radio, microwave and satellite wireless telephony or use of bluetooth technology in mobile phones and computers.

  Two significant communication technologies that acted as media and changed the whole communication scenario are the **radio** and the **television**.

(i) **Radio** Radio reaches a wide audience across different geographical areas, incomes, education levels, ages, genders and religions. It can eliminate barriers of time and space through live broadcasts or simulated broadcasts. The development of small transistors allows communication to be received in even the most remote parts of the country.

(ii) **Television** TV was introduced in India in 1959 mainly to enhance education and support rural development. TV programmes are created using various techniques like visual magnification, sound amplification, superimposition, split-screen processes, fading and zooming. These methods make TV more effective and enhance its impact on viewers.

Modern Communication Technologies

The list of modern communication technologies is extensive, and new innovations emerge regularly. Some types of modern communication technologies used mainly for extension purposes are

- **Micro Computers** (PCs) Computers are categorised into mainframe computers (large and expensive), mini computers (less powerful) and micro-computers (based on microchip technology). This classification is based on their power, speed, memory capacity and connectivity. Micro-computers are useful for extension work as they process and record various types of information, handle accounting tasks, store cases and experiences for research, and publish information cost-effectively. When linked, computers can communicate with each other and access information globally.
- **Video Text** Video text, or view-data, is an **electronic text service** sent from a central computer to home TVs via telephone or cable networks. It is interactive, allowing viewers to access the information they want.
- **Electronic Mail (E-mail)** E-mail is a system that sends information electronically from a sender to a receiver. Similar to surface mail, a message is typed on a computer and sent to another computer using a mobile phone. It is a simple way of communicating between two or more persons through the provision of a mailbox. The message is stored in the computer which acts as a post office, unless the receiver asks for it. The mail can be viewed using a modem connected to the telephone.
- **Interactive Video** Interactive video combines computer and video technologies. It uses a multimedia approach, including text, photographs, video, audio and slides. The messages stored in different forms are received by the users as per their choice. Their responses guide the content they receive.
- **Teleconferencing** Teleconferencing allows for interactive group communication among participants in different locations. Advances in telecommunications make it possible to hold meetings without the need for travel.

Bluetooth Technology

Bluetooth Technology[3] is a low-cost, short-range Radio Frequency (RF) connection. It links mobile PCs, mobile phones and other portable devices. Bluetooth can **transmit voice** and **data at a speed of 1 Mbps** This is **three to eight times** faster than average parallel and serial ports. It can send signals through solid, non-metal objects.

Communication technology greatly enhances communication, with more people around the world using these tools. However, the importance of **human interaction** should not be ignored.

Face-to-face communication remains essential in our daily lives. Therefore, everyone should develop basic skills for effective communication.

Quick Test 3

1 Give an examples of cable communication technology.

2 Which communication technology has a universal audience spread geographically and varying in income, education, etc?

3 Which media passes information electronically from sender to receiver through the internet?

3 Bluetooth technology It is a wireless communication technology that can be used for close-range data transmission from one digital device to another.

Mind Map

MEDIA AND COMMUNICATION

1 Communication

- It involves sharing ideas in a way that both sender and receiver understand.

Types of Interaction

One way communication
- Information is shared but the receiver cannot respond.
- **For example** speeches, lecture, watching T.V. etc.

Two way communication
- Communication happens between two or more people.
  For example conversation between two or more friends.

Levels of Communication

Intra-personal Communication
- Means communicating with oneself.
- **For example** self-talk, self-reflection.

Inter-personal Communication
- Exchange of thoughts between two or more people.
- **For example** interview.

Group Communication
- Means direct and personal communication.
- Involves communication between more than two people.

Mass Communication
- Spreading thoughts, ideas and innovation to the large section of society.
- **For example** radio, T.V. and satellite communication.

Intra-organisational Communication
- Happens in structural environment.
- It could be one way or two way.

Inter-organisational Communication
- One organisation communicate with other organisation.
  For example when a company communicates with its suppliers.

Means and Modes of Communication

Verbal Communication
- Auditory means
- **For example** speaking, singing.

Non-verbal Communication
- Gesture, facial expression, posture and eye contact.
- **For example** smoke signal used by tribal groups.

Types of Communication

Audio
- Radio • Lectures • Mobile phone

Visual
- Symbols • Charts • Posters

Audio-Visual
- T.V. • Video films • Multimedia

2 Media

- It is means to spread and share ideas, feelings and experiences.

Media Classification

Traditional Media
- Traditional folk theater or drama
- Oral Literature-cum musical forms
- Forms of Puppetry etc.

Modern Media
- Radio, Satellite, television, mobile phone and print media.

Functions of Media

• Information	Provide in format and exchange information.
• Motivation	Suitable media motivates audience.
• Entertainment	From Folk media and oral tradition to DTH.
• Transmission of values	Help to develop healthy society.
• Education	Learning could be interactive by the use of media.

3 Communication Technology

Classification of Communication Technology

Cable based Technologies.
- Telephone, personal computer

Wireless Technologies
- Radio, satellite, wireless bluetooth.
  Radio-eliminate barriers of time and space

Television
- Based on audio-visual technology.
- Effective communication.

Modern Communication Technologies

Computers
- Mainframe, mini and micro computers.
- Classification is based on speed, memory, power.

Video text
- View data in electronic form.

Email
- Send or receive information electronically.

Bluetooth Technology
- Lowcost Short Range Radio Frequency.
- Speed 1 Mbps.

Process of Communication
- Allows the exchange of information.
- Feedback for future planning.
- Can be explained as who says what to whom etc.

SMRCE Model

Source
- Communication • Originator • Sender

Message
- Information • Ideas
- Content

Receiver
- Audience

Channel
- Tools • Medium

Effect of Communication
- Feedback from audience

Communication Media

NCERT Folder

Intext Questions

1. What do you understand by the term communication? What are the various modes of verbal and non-verbal communication?

Ans The term communication is the process of thinking, observing, understanding, analysing, sharing and transmitting or transferring feelings to others. This happens through a variety of mediums in diverse settings so that they understand the exact meaning of the content.

(i) **Verbal Communication** The modes of verbal communication are normal talking to people face-to-face, on the telephone and in a meeting or conference.

(ii) **Non-verbal Communication** The modes of non-verbal communication includes gestures, facial expressions, posture, sign, language and smoke signals, etc.

2. Explain the process of communication with the help of an example.

Ans. The process of communication consists of transferring information or content from a sender to a receiver using a medium so that it is correctly, clearly and completely understood by the receiver.

The process is completed with the feedback of the receiver to the message sent.

For example, when you are talking to your friend about difficulties faced while studying and he/she gives you some suggestions related to it, it is a process of communication.

3. "The more the number of senses involved in the communication process, the more effective and sustainable is the communication." Write your comments with justification.

Ans. This statement is correct because research has found that people retain only 10% of what they read, in which only one sense, the eye or visual, is involved. However, they remember 50% and more of what they see and hear, in which two senses are involved. Further, they remember 90% and more of what they see, hear and do, in which three senses are involved.

Thus, involvement of more number of senses makes the learning more clearly understandable and permanent.

For example; watching a dance performance live or on TV makes it easier to understand and more enjoyable than reading about it in a newspaper afterwards.

4. How does media affect our day-to-day life? Enumerate the different types of media.

Ans Media affects our day-to-day life because it has the power to influence our thoughts. This influence is sometimes positive and sometimes negative. It is considered as the best source to know about the happenings of the world. Newspapers, magazines, radio, television and internet are the different types of media which affect our day-to-day life.

The different types of media can be classified into two broad categories, traditional and modern.

(i) **Traditional media** includes puppetry, folk dances and theatre, oral literature, fairs and festivals, rituals and symbols, print media (charts, posters, newspapers, magazines and other local publications).

(ii) **Modern media** includes FM radio, satellite television, modern print media, films projected though various type of projectors, audio cassette and CD—DVD technology, cable and wireless technology, mobile phones, video films and video conferencing.

5. How is the term communication technologies defined? Discuss two important communication technologies that have brought a revolution in the communication arena, giving justification for your answer.

Ans. Communication technologies can be defined as various technologies developed and used to handle information and aid communication.

Two important communication technologies that have brought a revolution in the communication arena are radio and television.

Radio has a universal audience spread geographically and varying in income, education, age, sex and religion. Through on the spot broadcasts or simulated broadcasts, radio has overcome the barriers of time and space. It is now possible to receive communication in the remotest parts of the country through it.

On the other hand, television uses various techniques for making TV programmes more effective and strengthening their impact on the viewer.

Thus, both these have justifiably brought a revolution in the communication arena.

Exercise

1. List the various means or modes, types and levels of communication involved in the following experience. Pen down your observations, Did you have the opportunity to live or visit a rural area or a village or a small town in the country? What was your experience? Did you observe symbols of advanced technology and communication like mobile phones, fax machines and other equipments, electricity poles and other similar things? How was the experience of meeting and interacting with people-young, women and older persons? Discuss this in your class. (Pg 80)

Ans. Yes, Last summer, I visited my grandparents' village in rural Punjab. It was an eye-opening experience for me showcasing the contrast between urban and rural communication. I observed the following means/modes of communication there

- **Verbal** Face-to-face conversations with locals
- **Non-verbal** Body language, gestures and facial expressions
- **Written** Signboards, posters and handwritten notes
- **Visual** Television, mobile phones and printed materials
- **Electronic** Mobile phones and limited internet access

I observed that there was widespread use of mobile phones, even among older adults and limited access to internet, fax machines and other advanced technology. There were Electricity poles and connection, but occasional power outages. I had a wonderful experience of meeting and interacting with people there

- Young people were energetic, curious and open to new ideas.
- Women were warm, hospitable and eager to share experiences.
- Older persons were respected, wise and storytelling-oriented.

This experience has broadened my perspective on communication and community dynamics in rural India, enriching my understanding of Home Science principles in action.

2. Identify the possible sources of information in villages/rural areas (Pg. 81)

Ans. The possible sources of information in villages/rural areas are as follows

- **Traditional Sources** such as village elders, community gatherings (Chaupal), local folklore and stories, traditional festivals and events.
- Print media such as local newspapers, regional language newspapers, magazines (e.g., agricultural, health), posters and pamphlets, government publications (e.g., rural development schemes)
- Electronic media such as television (local channels), radio (local stations), mobile phones (SMS, WhatsApp), internet (limited access), community radio stations.
- Government sources such as village panchayat (local governance), block development office, district administration, government health centers, agricultural extension offices.

3. Collect one news story or a campaign or a social message from any two media such as radio, print or TV. (Pg. 81)

Ans. (i) News campaign from radio

"Beti Bachao, Beti Padhao" (Save the Girl Child, Educate the Girl Child) campaign

- **Radio Channel** All India Radio (AIR)
- **Aim** The campaign aims to promote girls' education and combat female foeticide. The radio ads feature inspiring stories of women achievers and emphasise the importance of educating girls.
- **Key Message** Educate girls, empower society.

(ii) News story from print media

"Swachh Bharat Abhiyan" (Clean India Mission) campaign

- **Newspaper** The Times of India
- **Date** October 2, 2022
- **Aim** The campaign aims to promote cleanliness and sanitation across India. The newspaper article highlights the progress made since the campaign's launch and encourages citizens to participate.
- **Key Message** Let's work together for a cleaner India.

4. Find out any one traditional method which tribal and/or rural people in the country use to make important announcements in their areas. (Pg. 81)

Ans. One traditional method used by tribal and rural people in India to make important announcements is beat of the Dhol (drum) or "Dhol Nagada".

In many rural and tribal areas, especially in states like Madhya Pradesh, Chhattisgarh, Jharkhand and Odisha, the beat of the Dhol (drum) is used to convey important messages, announcements and warnings.

It works in the following manner

- Village drummers (known as "Dholi" or "Nagada player") beat the drum in a specific rhythm to convey different messages.

- The drumbeat is loud enough to be heard across the village or community.
- People recognise the distinct rhythms and gather to listen to the announcement.

5. As a receiver of information write down the type and quality of information you tend to get from your school. (Pg. 82)

Ans. As a Class 11th student, I receive various types of information from my school such as follows

(i) **Academic**
- Syllabus and curriculum updates
- Exam schedules and results
- Assignment and project guidelines
- Study materials and resources

(ii) **Co-curricular**
- Sports and extra curricular activity schedules
- Club and society updates
- Event invitations (e.g., cultural festivals, seminars)

(iii) **Administrative**
- School policies and rules
- Fee payment deadlines
- Attendance and leave regulations

(iv) **News and Updates**
- School achievements and awards
- Alumni updates
- Local and national news relevant to students

The quality of Information provided by my school is as follows

(i) **Accuracy** Generally accurate, but occasional errors or outdated information.
(ii) **Relevance** Mostly relevant to academic and school life.
(iii) **Timeliness** Usually timely, but occasional delays.
(iv) **Clarity** Clear and concise, but sometimes ambiguous.
(v) **Reliability** Trustworthy sources, mostly from teachers and school administrators.

6. Collect information on different folk media used in your state in both urban and rural areas. If there are tribal areas in your state, collect the folk media relevant there. (Pg. 84)

Ans. Different folk media used in my state (Uttar Pradesh) are as follows

(i) **Folk media in urban areas**
- Street plays (Nukkad Natak)
- Puppet shows (Kathputli)
- Folk songs and dances (e.g., Rasiya, Holi Geet)
- Storytelling (Kissa Gothi)
- Community radio

(ii) **Folk media in rural areas**
- Folk theater (e.g., Swang, Raasleela)
- Folk music and dance (e.g., Brij Holi, Kajri)
- Oral storytelling (e.g., Panchatantra tales)
- Village fairs and festivals (e.g., Kumbh Mela)

(iii) **Folk media in tribal areas of the state (Bundelkhand, Vindhya regions)**
- Tribal folk dances (e.g., Dhurwa, Pardhi)
- Tribal music and instruments (e.g., Dhol, Nagada)
- Storytelling through tribal art (e.g., Pithora painting)
- Traditional tribal festivals (e.g., Navratra, Sarhul)

7. Write any two messages that you remember from the hoardings displayed on road sides. Also write your interpretation of the messages. (Pg. 89)

(i) Message :..........
Interpretation:.........
(ii) Message :..........
Interpretation:..............

Ans. (i) **Message 1** "Betiyon ko padhao, desh ko badhao" ("Educate daughters, empower the nation")

Interpretation This message emphasises the importance of educating girls to contribute to the country's growth and development.

It highlights the significance of women's empowerment through education, encouraging parents to prioritise their daughters' education.

(ii) **Message 2** "Road safety is in your hands, wear helmet, save life".

Interpretation This message stresses the importance of road safety, specifically emphasising the need to wear helmets while riding two-wheelers. It appeals to individuals to take personal responsibility for their safety, highlighting the potentially life-saving consequences of wearing a helmet.

Exam Pattern Questions

Objective Type Questions

Multiple Choice Questions (MCQs)

1. The word 'communication' comes from the Latin word communis. In the given statement, what is the meaning of the word communis?

(a) Sharing (b) Commuting
(c) Common (d) Transmitting

2. The process of thinking, observing, understanding, analysing, sharing and transmitting feelings to other is known as ....

(a) interactions (b) communication
(c) media (d) feedback

3. How many types of interactions can be there in a communication?

(a) 1 (b) 2 (c) 3 (d) 4

4. 'The receiver of the communication is unable to reciprocate to the sender'. Which type of communication is being referred to in the statement? Competency Based Que

(a) One-way communication (b) Two-way communication
(c) Mass communication (d) Group communication

5. 'This type of communication includes normal talking to people face-to-face, in the telephone, in a meeting or conference, etc'. The statement is referring to which type of communication? Competency Based Que

(a) Inter-personal communication
(b) Verbal communication
(c) Non-verbal communication
(d) Organisational communication

6. Non-verbal communication involves Competency Based Que

I. Normal talking
II. Gestures
III. Face-to-face conversation
IV. Eye contact

Codes

(a) I and II (b) II and III (c) III and IV (d) II and IV

7. The basic elements of any communication process in general are arranged in a definite order to complete the cycle of communication. Which model is used for communication?

(a) SCMRE (b) SMRCE
(c) SEMCR (d) SMCRE

8. In the SMCRE model of communications, 'M' stands for?

(a) Media (b) Mass (c) Message (d) Money

9. The teacher told Satyam to go to the staffroom and ask Nitin Sir for the cupboard keys. What is Satyam in this process of communication? Competency Based Que

(a) Source (b) Channel
(c) Receiver (d) Feedback

10. What kind of communication medium should be used to spread the methods of prevention of dengue to as many people as possible?

(a) Group Communication
(b) Mass Communication
(c) Interpersonal Communication
(d) Intrapersonal Communication

11. Video call is an example of which communication medium?

(a) Distant Conference
(b) Interactive Video
(c) General Message Broadcasting
(d) Mutual Message Broadcasting

12. Match the following. Competency Based Que

List I		List II	
A.	Nautanki	1.	Bengal
B.	Tamasha	2.	Gujarat
C.	Jatra	3.	Uttar Pradesh
D.	Bhavai	4.	Maharashtra

Codes

	A	B	C	D		A	B	C	D
(a)	1	2	3	4	(b)	2	3	4	1
(c)	3	4	1	2	(d)	4	1	2	3

Assertion-Reason Questions

Direction (Q. Nos. 13-17) In the questions given below, there are two statements marked as Assertion (A) and Reason (R). Read the statements and choose the correct option.

Codes

(a) Both A and R are true and R is the correct explanation of A.
(b) Both A and R are true, but R is not the correct explanation of A.
(c) A is true, but R is false.
(d) A is false, but R is true.

13. **Assertion** (A) Two-way communication takes place when the receiver receives the information but is not able to reciprocate it to the sender.

Reason (R) Two-way communication creates a more democratic environment, whereby people can share their thoughts, ideas and opinions, regardless of the hierarchy and improve relationships right across the structure.

14. **Assertion** (A) Inter-personal communication is the most effective type of communication.

Reason (R) There is always proximity and direct contact between the sender and receiver of the communication.

15. **Assertion** (A) Intra-organisational communication takes place in highly structured settings.

Reason (R) They use various levels of communication within their environment and amongst their departments or sections.

16. **Assertion** (A) To be effective in the classroom, a teacher should minimise the communication barriers.

Reason (R) Since communication is a complex process, regular feedback analysis is essential for this purpose.

17. **Assertion** (A) Bluetooth can transmit even through solid and non-metal objects.

Reason (R) Bluetooth technology is a high cost, short range radio frequency (RF) link between devices.

Case Based Questions

18. **Read the passage given below and answer the following questions.**

When Preeti was studying in Class XI, she used to watch the episodes of the Mahabharata, the epic which were being shown on the TV every Sunday. She was much impressed with the production of the episodes because they revealed many facts about the epic which she had not known when she read the story as a comic book during her childhood. She learnt about moral values being illustrated in the episodes and was thoroughly entertained by the action sequences and dialogue delivery of the artists.

The case described above brings out three functions of media.

(i) What are the three functions of media?

(a) Informing
(b) Motivating
(c) Entertaining
(d) All of the above

(ii) What kind of communication takes place while watching TV?

(a) One-way communication
(b) Two-way communication
(c) Inter-organisational
(d) Mass communication

(iii) Television is classified under ....

(a) traditional media
(b) modern media
(c) print media
(d) None of these

(iv) **Assertion** (A) Media is used in an entertaining form to make learning easy and interesting.

Reason (R) Both traditional and modern media provide a wide variety of entertainment. **Competency Based Que**

Codes

(a) Both A and R are true and R is the correct explanation of A.
(b) Both A and R are true, but R is not the correct explanation of A.
(c) A is true, but R is false.
(d) A is false, but R is true.

19. **Read the passage given below and answer the following questions.**

We have been using different mediums and communication technologies for communicating in different times (in the past and at present), in different settings, for example rural, urban and tribal. You may have observed that many new technologies related to electronic media have revolutionised communication media. A wide range of communication technologies are available. They are cable based and wireless technologies.

(i) .... commands a universal audience by geographical spread, income, education, age, sex and religion.

(a) Radio
(b) Television
(c) Computer
(d) None of these

(ii) Which of the following uses wireless technology?

(a) Radio
(b) Landline telephone
(c) Personal computer without internet
(d) None of the above

(iii) .... allows wireless control of and communication between a cell phone and a hands free set or a car kit.

(a) Bluetooth
(b) Radio
(c) Television
(d) Video text

(iv) Micro computers are classified under ....

(a) traditional media
(b) cable
(c) modern communication technology
(d) bluetooth

Answers

1. (c) Common
2. (b) communication
3. (b) 2
4. (a) One-way communication
5. (b) Verbal communication
6. (d) II and IV
7. (d) SMCRE
8. (c) Message
9. (b) Channel
10. (b) Mass Communication
11. (a) Distant Conference
12. (c) 3 4 1 2
13. (d) A is false, but R is true
14. (a) Both A and R are true and R is the correct explanation of A.
15. (a) Both A and R are true and R is the correct explanation of A.
16. (a) Both A and R are true and R is the correct explanation of A.
17. (c) A is true but R is false.
18. (i) (d) All of these
    (ii) (a) One-way communication
    (iii) (b) modern media
    (iv) (b) Both A and R are true, but R is not the correct explanation of A.
19. (i) (a) Radio
    (ii) (a) Radio
    (iii) (a) Bluetooth
    (iv) (c) modern communication technology

Subjective Questions

Very Short Answer Type Questions

1. Why have the gadgets used for communication, for instance smartphones, become popular?

Ans. New gadgets used for communication have become popular because of their cost effectiveness and utility.

2. What are two examples of one-way communication?

Ans. Two examples of one-way communication are speeches and listening to music on the radio.

3. During an exam, Ravi mentally rehearses his answer. What type of communication is this? **Competency Based Que**

Ans. This is an example of intra-personal communication.

4. In a company, e-mails are sent from the manager to the employees. Identify the type of communication involved in this? **Competency Based Que**

Ans. Intra-organisational communication is involved in this.

5. What is mass media? Which kind of audience is mass media catering to?

Ans. Mass media is the process of multiplying a message with the help of any mechanical or electronic device and spreading it to a large number of people at the same time. Mass media is catering to a heterogeneous, anonymous and large audience.

6. On an average, how much of his/ her active time does a person spend in communicating verbally?

Ans. Research has established that an average person spends about 70 per cent of his/her active time in communicating verbally.

7. How many of our senses are involved in watching a film in a cinema hall? Which are these senses?

Ans. While watching a film in a cinema hall, two of our senses are involved. These are visual (seeing) and auditory (hearing).

8. What is the last stage in the SMCRE model of communication, without which the communication is incomplete?

Ans. The last stage in the SMCRE model of communication, without which the communication is incomplete, is the effect of communication or feedback or audience response, which the receiver gives to the sender of the communication.

9. How can media serve for the transmission of values? What are two examples of traditional media used in rural areas?

Ans. Media can serve for the transmission of values by teaching values through stories shown in cartoon films or through puppetry.

Two examples of traditional media used in rural areas are traditional folk theatre, also known as drama and puppetry.

10. How are cable based technologies better or worse than wireless technologies?

Ans. Cable based technologies are comparatively cheap and less complicated than wireless technologies, the wireless technologies require minimum infrastructure, but can be more expensive to use than the former.

11. What is Teleconferencing?

Ans. Teleconferencing is a form of interactive group communication which creates a dialogue between geographically distant participants.

Short Answers Type Questions

1. Briefly describe two differences between one-way and two-way communication, giving the reasons for these differences.

Ans. Two differences between one-way and two-way communication are

One-way Communication	Two-way Communication
A channel carries a message from the sender to the receiver. No feedback is given. Thus it is not interactive.	A channel carries a message from the sender to the receiver. Then, the receiver gives a feedback to the sender. Thus, it is interactive.
It is harder to understand because no clarification is asked from the sender of the communication.	It is easier to understand because clarification can be asked from the sender of the communication.

2. How is interpersonal communication the most effective type of communication?

Ans. Interpersonal communication is the sharing of thoughts and ideas with one or more people in a face-to-face situation.

It is the most effective type of communication because there is always proximity and direct contact between the sender and receiver of the communication. It also provides instantaneous and strong feedback directly by the receiver to the sender.

3. What are the advantages of group communication?

Ans. The advantages of group communication are

- That it helps to facilitate a participatory approach and collective decision-making.
- Gives an opportunity for self-expression to all group members.
- Increases the individual's impact in a group setting, thus, helping in raising the status of individuals in the group.
- It also helps in recreation and relaxation, socialising and motivating the group members.

4. During a community health meeting, Anjali, a health worker, presents important information about vaccination to the villagers. However, she notices that some attendees look confused and unsure. How can Anjali make her communication more effective?

Competency Based Que

Ans. To make her communication effective, Anjali should focus on ensuring that the villagers understand her message as intended. She can simplify her language and use visual aids to clarify information about vaccination. Actively encouraging questions will help identify areas of confusion.

Additionally, Anjali should seek specific feedback from the attendees, asking them to summarise what they've learned.

This two-way interaction will lead to a shared understanding, confirming that the communication process is successful.

5. How many of our senses are involved in (a) talking on the phone (b) carrying out yoga exercises by watching a video on these exercises? Which senses are involved in each case?

Ans. (a) In talking on the phone, only one sense is involved which is the auditory sense.

(b) In carrying out yoga exercises by watching a video on these exercises, three senses are involved. These are the visual, auditory and motor senses.

6. How can communication be made effective?

Ans. A communication is sharing of thoughts or information in such a way that it is understood by the receiver in the same way as the sender intended. Thus, to make a communication effective, the sender must make a conscious effort to create a shared understanding about its intended meaning among the persons involved in the communication.

This can be verified by the sender receiving an appropriate feedback from the receiver.

7. During a group discussion on environmental conservation, Priya and her classmates gather in the college courtyard to share their views. As they engage in a lively debate, how do the key elements of interpersonal communication enhance their collective understanding and support effective decision-making throughout the discussion? **Competency Based Que**

Ans. Interpersonal communication involves sharing thoughts and ideas directly with one or more individuals in a face-to-face setting.

- This form of communication is particularly effective due to the close proximity and direct contact between the sender and receiver.
- It allows for immediate and strong feedback, enabling participants to clarify misunderstandings and adjust their messages in real-time.
- This leads to better understanding and collaboration.

8. Why is traditional media being gradually replaced by modern media even in rural areas?

Ans. Traditional media is being gradually replaced by modern media as like folk theatre, puppetry, fairs and festivals were largely designed for an illiterate population.

In earlier times, most of the persons living in villages were illiterate. With the sharp increase of literacy in the rural areas during the last few years, traditional communication media were neither sufficient nor well-equipped to meet the multiple information needs of the educated populace.

Hence, modern media of communication like mobile phones, radio, television, modern print media and others have become popular.

Long Answer Type Questions

1. During a community meeting in a small village in Rajasthan, local leaders gathered to discuss various issues affecting their residents. As they navigate their discussions, each leader uses different forms of communication. Can you identify the classes of communication demonstrated in each scenario given below, providing an example for each?

(i) Ramesh, the village head, reflects silently on his own experiences to prepare his thoughts.

(ii) Meena engages in a face-to-face discussion with a fellow leader, using gestures to emphasise her points.

(iii) A group of villagers listens as Priya presents her ideas to the entire assembly, encouraging feedback.

(iv) Rajesh broadcasts a message about the meeting through local radio, reaching many villagers at once. **Competency Based Que**

Ans. Classes of communication based on the levels of communication in each scenario are

(i) **Intra-personal Communication** It means communicating with oneself.

An example is thinking which is a mental process involving, observation, analysis and working out meaningful conclusions about the past, present or future.

(ii) **Inter-personal Communication** It means sharing of thoughts and ideas with one or more people in a face-to-face situation in a formal or informal setting.

An example is talking to another person, in which body movements, facial expressions, gestures and postures are used to indicate or emphasise what is being said.

(iii) **Group Communication** This form of communication is between an individual and a group. It helps to facilitate a participatory approach and collective decision-making, gives an opportunity for self-expression and increases the individual's impact in a gathering.

A class lecture is an example of group communication.

(iv) **Mass Media Communication** It is the process of multiplying a message with the help of any mechanical or electronic device and disseminating it to a large number of people at the same time.

An example is a daily newspaper. The receiver of the communication (newspaper readers) are spread over a large area and separated from the communicator in time and space. In this class of communication, feedback is slow, incomplete and delayed.

2. Rahul, a Class 11 Home Science student, is assigned a project on effective communication and media. He needs to understand the concepts of communication, classification of communication and communication technologies to complete his project.

(i) Explain the classification of communication based on the type of interaction, levels of communication, and involvement of number of senses.

(ii) Discuss the role of media in communication, classification of media, and examples of traditional and modern media. **Competency Based Que**

Ans. (i) Communication can be classified into various categories such as the following

Based on type of interaction

- One-way communication (e.g., speeches, lectures)
- Two-way communication (e.g., discussions, phone calls)

Based on levels of communication

- Intra-personal communication (self-reflection)
- Inter-personal communication (face-to-face interaction)
- Group communication (small group discussions)
- Mass communication (large audience, e.g., TV, radio)
- Intra-organisational communication (within an organisation)
- Inter-organisational communication (between organisations)

Based on involvement of number of senses

- Visual (reading)
- Audio (listening)
- Audio-visual (watching TV)

(ii) Media plays a significant role in communication, serving as the means to spread and share ideas, thoughts, feelings and experiences.

Classification of media

- Traditional media (e.g., folk theatre, oral literature, print media puppetry)
- Modern media (e.g., FM radio, satellite TV, internet, mobile phones)

For examples of traditional media are

- Puppetry
- Folk dances
- Fairs and festivals
- Print media (newspapers, magazines)

For examples of modern media are

- Satellite television
- Internet
- Mobile phones
- Video conferencing
- Social media platforms

3. Describe the SMCRE model of communication by drawing a diagram of the process?

Ans. A diagram of the SMCRE model of communication is given below

The SMCRE Model of Communication

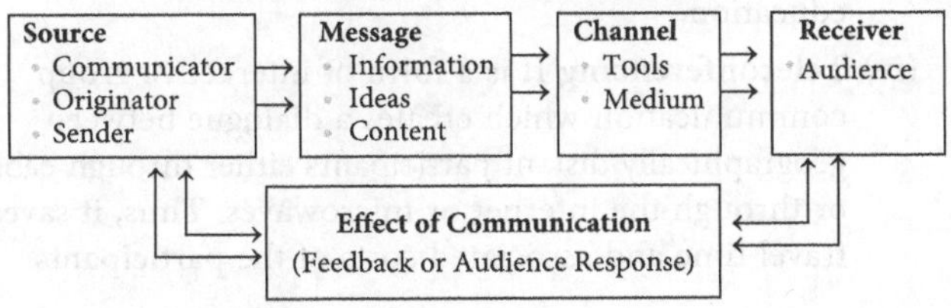

The Process of Communication

Communication is the way we share information and ideas with others. It involves several steps and key elements that help ensure the message is understood clearly.

The process of communication is given below

(i) **Source** This is the person or group who starts the communication. The source is responsible for creating and sending the message. For example, a teacher, a friend, or a community leader can be a source.

(ii) **Message** The message is the information or content that the source wants to share. It can be anything from a simple idea to complex information. A good message should be clear, specific, and relevant to the audience.

(iii) **Channel** The channel is the medium through which the message is sent. This can include face-to-face conversations, phone calls, emails, or social media. Different channels can affect how well the message is received.

(iv) **Receiver** The receiver is the person or group who gets the message. Understanding the audience is important because it helps tailor the message to their needs and preferences.

(v) **Effect (Feedback)** Feedback is the response from the receiver back to the source. It shows whether the message was understood correctly and if it had the desired effect. For instance, if a teacher asks students questions after a lesson, their answers provide feedback on how well they understood.

4. In a team meeting, Rohan shares his innovative marketing strategy for a local bakery in Delhi. However, the team seems confused about the details. What completes the communication process in this situation, and why is the process incomplete without it? **Competency Based Que**

Ans. In the team meeting, the communication process is completed when the team provides feedback on Rohan's innovative marketing strategy.

This response is crucial because it helps Rohan understand whether his message was clear and effective. Without feedback, the process remains incomplete, as Rohan will not be able to know the team's comprehension or address any confusion. If the team's feedback does not align with his expectations, it indicates that his message may need rethinking or clarification.

Thus, the communication cycle may need to be repeated until the team fully understands the strategy. This will ensure that Rohan's objectives are achieved and everyone is on the same page regarding the marketing plan.

5. Explain five functions of media which can lead to changes in behaviour in the receivers of the communication. What benefits can each of these changes give to the senders of the communication? **Competency Based Que**

Ans. Five functions of media which can lead to changes in behaviour in the receivers of the communication are

(i) **Persuasion/Motivation** Suitable communication media can be used to persuade an audience to accept an idea. This needs a deeper understanding of audience psychology and their socio-cultural background.
The sender will benefit due to the acceptance of the idea, as it can then be exploited for commercial gains if required.

(ii) **Interpretation** Use of communication media, particularly pictographic presentations and facts and figures make many difficult and complicated concepts easy to understand.
The sender will benefit with increased consumption of the products due to the receivers of communication better understanding the benefits of consuming the product.

(iii) **Transmission of Values** Development of a healthy society by the transmission of wholesome values is a function of media. An instance is the use of puppetry, street plays, cartoon films and radio programmes to teach the values of cleanliness through the Swachh Bharat Abhiyaan.
The sender will benefit by improving its image in the eyes of the people receiving the communication.

(iv) **Education or Training** New learning experiences using appropriate communication media enrich the teaching-learning experience. These include interactive video and audio cassettes, discs of basic printed teaching-learning material, etc. The senders in this case are usually educational institutions.
They will benefit by their students getting better results in examinations, thus enhancing the reputation of the concerned institutions.

(v) **Improvement in Behaviour** Extension education activities in any field depends largely on the art and technique of effective communication. Media transmits useful messages which lead to direct and indirect behavioural changes in the target group of people.

6. Name the four forms of traditional media used for mass communication and give two examples of each form specific to a state or region of India.

Ans. Four forms of traditional media used for mass communication (with examples) are as follows

(i) Traditional folk theatre or drama examples are Ramleela and Nautanki (Uttar Pradesh).

(ii) Oral literature-cum-musical forms examples are Bhangra and Gidda (Punjab).

(iii) Forms of puppetry examples are Sutradharika (Rajasthan and Gujarat) and Chhaya Putli (South India).

(iv) Festivals, fairs and social rituals examples are Uttarayan (Gujarat) and Hornbill Festival (Nagaland).

7. Describe any four types of major communication technologies in two or three sentences each to bring out their uses. **Competency Based Que**

Ans. Four types of major communication technologies are

(i) **Micro-computers** (PCs) These types of computers are based on microchip technology. They are used for processing data, keeping records, performing accounting work, acting as a repository of various cases and experiences to be used for research and for publishing information or material at reasonable cost.

(ii) **Electronic Mail** (E-mail) It passes information electronically from sender to receiver through the internet. In it, a message is typed on one computer and sent to another computer connected to the internet. It can also be done through smartphones (mobiles phones with internet connection).

(iii) **Interactive/Video** It refers to a video system which is a combination of computer and video. It uses a multimedia approach, i.e. text, still photographs, video, audio, slides, overhead slides, etc.
The messages stored in different forms are received by the users as per their choice. The user response to the system determines the path to be followed for completing the cycle. It is used extensively in online education.

(iv) **Teleconferencing** It is a form of interactive group communication which creates a dialogue between geographically distant participants either through cable or through the internet or microwaves. Thus, it saves travel time and associated costs of the participants.

SELF ASSESSMENT TEST

Objective Type Questions

1. During a panel discussion, participants engage in dialogue and respond to questions. This scenario best exemplifies.
   (a) Intra-personal communication
   (b) Inter-personal communication
   (c) Group communication
   (d) Mass communication
2. What is the source in SMCRE model of communication.
   (a) Content
   (b) Audience
   (c) Sender
   (d) Ideas
3. Video call is an example of which communication medium?
   (a) Distant Conference
   (b) Interactive Video
   (c) General Meassage Broadcasting
   (d) Mutual Message Casting

Very Short Answer Type Questions

4. Why are communication methods and equipment being replaced on a regular basis?
5. Mention two drawbacks of mass communication.
6. What kind of feedback makes the sender of the communication rethink and recast the message?
7. List two forms of oral literature-cum-musical forms of communication, indicating the states or regions where they are popular.

Short Answer Type Questions

8. What are the two types of channels of communication? Explain them.
9. Explain two disadvantages of one-way interaction.
10. What is inter-organisational communication? Give two examples of this form of communication.

Long Answer Type Questions

11. Explain the meaning of the term 'Group communication'. How is it different from 'mass communication'? **Competency Based Que**
12. What are four examples of modern media which have drastically changed people's behaviour in recent times? Explain how they have done so in each case?
13. Explain how communication may be classified on the basis of involvement of the number of senses? Give an example of each type of classification. **Competency Based Que**

07A

CHAPTER

Nutrition, Health and Hygiene

Health is a fundamental human right. All persons, irrespective of age, gender, caste, religion, through out their lives should have the opportunity to achieve a good and healthy life style.

YOUR STUDY GOALS

YOUR PRACTICE GOAL

- Objective Type Questions (15 Qs ; MCQs, A-R, Matching, Case Based)
- Subjective Questions (14 VSAs, 5 SAs, 5 LAs)

7A.1 Introduction

- **WHO (World Health Organisation)** defined health as "A state of complete mental, physical and social well-being and not merely the absence of disease".
- Various environmental conditions and personal lifestyle can impact our health by causing various diseases.
- **Disease** is defined as an impairment of body health. It is an alteration, disruption or derangement in the function of some part or organ of the body which affects normal functions and moves away from a state of complete well-being.

It is the aim of every health professional (persons who deal with various aspects of health) to promote good health; in other words, to promote maintenance of well-being or wellness or quality of life.

7A.2 Health and its Dimensions

The definition of health includes various dimensions: social, mental and physical. Let us briefly discuss all three dimensions before exploring physical health in more detail.

Social Health

- Social health refers to the well-being of individuals and society. For society, it means ensuring equal opportunity and access of essential goods and services for good health to all citizens.
- On an individual level, it refers to each person's well being. It relates to how well a person interacts with others and social institutions. This includes social skills and the ability to function as a member of society.
- When facing problems and stress, social support helps the individuals to cope up with them and solve issues. Social support contributes to **positive adjustment** in both children and adults and encourages personal growth.
- Emphasising social health is becoming increasingly important. Scientific studies show that **socially well-adjusted individuals** tend to live longer and recover faster from illness.
- A few social determinants of health include
  - Employment status
  - Access to health services
  - Socio-economic and environmental conditions[1]
  - Safety in workplaces
  - Cultural and religious beliefs, taboos and value systems

Mental Health

- Mental health refers to emotional and psychological well-being.
- An individual who feels a sense of well-being can use their cognitive[2] and emotional abilities effectively. Such individuals function well in society and meet the everyday demands of life.

A Person Who Has Positive Mental Health

- feels that he/she is capable and competent.
- can handle normal levels of stress he/she faces in daily life.
- has satisfying relationships.
- can lead an independent life.
- if faced with any mental or emotional stress or events, he/she can cope with them and recover from them.
- does not feel defeated or depressed for unusually long periods of time when small difficulties/problems are encountered.

Physical Health

- It encompasses physical **fitness** and **the functioning of the body**.
- A physically healthy person can perform normal activities without feeling unusually fatigued. They also have adequate resistance to infection and disease.

7A.3 Health Care

- Every individual is responsible for his/her own health. However, health is also a major public concern. Therefore, the government takes on significant responsibility for providing health services at various levels to its citizens.
- Health care consists of all the services provided to individuals or communities by health service agents or professionals. These services aim to promote, maintain, monitor or restore health. Health care includes **preventive, promotive** and **therapeutic care**.

  Health care services are delivered at three levels

  (i) **Primary Health Care** This is the first level of contact between individuals and the health care system.

1 Environmental condition It means surroundings affecting health, including physical, biological and social factors.

2 Cognitive It is related to mental processes of understanding, reasoning and learning.

(ii) **Secondary Health Care** This level occurs when patients from primary health care are referred to specialised hospitals, such as district hospitals.

(iii) **Tertiary Health Care** When patients are referred from primary and secondary health systems for specialised intensive care, advanced diagnostic support and medical care then it is called as tertiary health care.

Indicators of Health

Health is multi-dimensional, each dimension is influenced by several factors. Therefore, various indicators are used to assess health.

These indicators include

- Mortality rates
- Disability rates
- Health care delivery
- Environmental factors
- Quality of life
- Morbidity (illness or disease) rates
- Nutritional status
- Health care utilisation
- Health policy

Quick Test 1

1 Name the leading organisation in health matters?
2 Which dimension of health is related to emotional and psychological well-being?
3 What is the first level of contact between the individuals and the health care system called?
4 Mention two indicators used to assess health.

7A.4 Nutrition and Health

- Nutrition and health are closely linked. In the global campaign of **'Health for All,'** promoting nutrition is a primary element. Nutrition focuses on maintaining the structure and function of body organs and tissues. It also supports growth and development.
- Good nutrition allows individuals to enjoy good health. It helps them to resist infections, maintain adequate energy levels and perform daily tasks without fatigue.
  - For children and adolescents, nutrition is vital for growth, mental development and achieving their potential.
  - For adults, adequate nutrition is essential for leading a socially and economically productive and healthy life.
- Additionally, an individual's health status determines their nutrient requirements and food intake. During illness, nutrient requirements increase as the breakdown of nutrients is higher. Therefore, illness and disease can negatively impact nutritional status.
- Hence, nutrition is a 'fundamental pillar' of human life health and developments.

Nutrients

Nutrients are the substances which are essential for the growth, maintenance and repair of the body. They provide energy, support immune function and regulate various bodily processes.

Classification of Nutrients

There are more than 50 nutrients in our food. Nutrients are categorised into two main types **macro-nutrients** and **micro-nutrients.**

- **Macro-nutrients** They are required in large amounts. They include fats, proteins, carbohydrates and fiber.

- **Micro-nutrients** They are required in small amounts. They include minerals (e.g., iron, zinc, selenium) and vitamins (both fat-soluble and water-soluble).

Functions of Nutrients

- Nutrients play crucial roles in various bodily functions.
- Some act as Co-factors and Co-enzymes in metabolic reactions.
- They can influence gene expression and transcription.

Digestion and Metabolism

- Different organs and systems are involved in the digestion, absorption, metabolism, storage and excretion of nutrients and their metabolic products.
- Every cell in the body requires nutrients to function.

Nutrient Requirements

- Nutrient requirements in normal healthy state vary according to age, sex and physiological state (e.g., growth periods like infancy, childhood, adolescence, pregnancy and lactation).
- Physical activity levels also influence the requirements for energy and specific nutrients, such as vitamins.
- It is essential to consume a balanced diet that provides all necessary nutrients in appropriate amounts.
- Understanding nutrients, their metabolism, and sources is crucial for maintaining health.

Role of Nutritionists

- Nutritionists study various aspects of nutrition, including biological, metabolic and clinical nutrition.
- They focus on the nutritional needs of populations and their nutritional problems, including health problems caused by **lack of nutrients** (public health nutrition) and **prevention of diseases** such as heart disease, diabetes, cancer, hypertension, etc.

7A.5 Influences on Food Choice

When a person is ill, they often lose their appetite and may not feel like eating. The quantity and type of food consumed depend not only on taste but also on food availability. This is known as **food security**. Food security is influenced by several factors, including

- **Purchasing Power** Economic factors determine how much food a person can afford.
- **Environment Conditions** such as water supply and irrigation, impact food production.
- **Policies** National and International policies can affect food access.

In addition, cultural influences play a significant role in food choices. Factors such as religion, social status, personal beliefs and taboos can shape what people eat.

Impact of Good Health and Nutrition

- Good health and nutrition contribute to a happier and more productive life.
- Healthy parents are able to take adequate care of their children and healthy children are generally happy and do well in school.
- When one is healthy, one is more constructive for one-self and can take active part in activities at the community level.

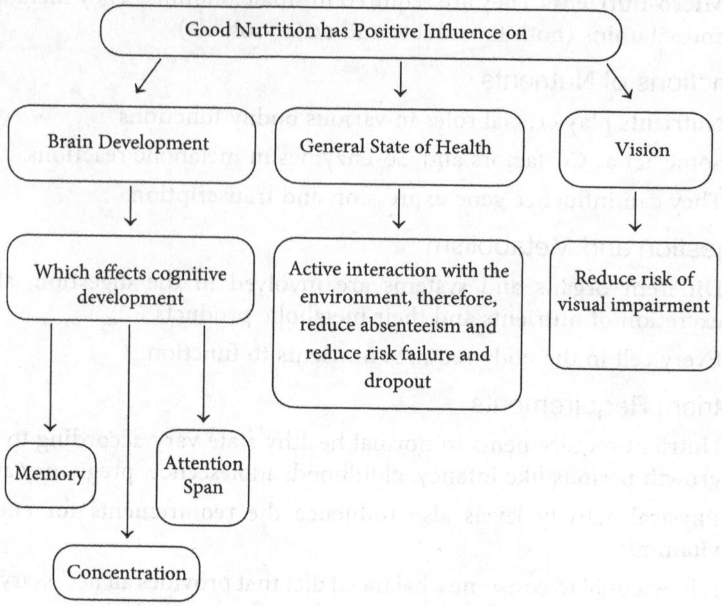

▲ *Benefits of Good Nutritional Status for Children's Education*

- Under-nourishment can hinder one's ability to achieve good health and engage socially.

Optimum nutritional status is important because it

maintains body weight	provides resistance to infection
maintains muscle mass	helps to cope with physical and mental stress
decreases risk of disability	improves productivity

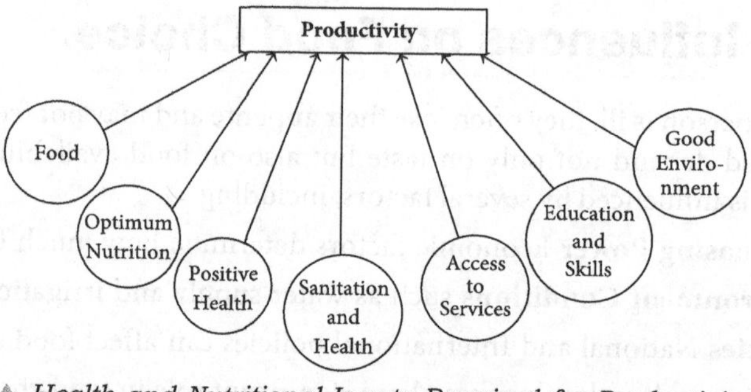

▲ *Health and Nutritional Inputs Required for Productivity*

7A.6 Factors Affecting Nutritional Well-Being

The **World Health Organisation** has listed four main factors that are important for nutritional well-being.

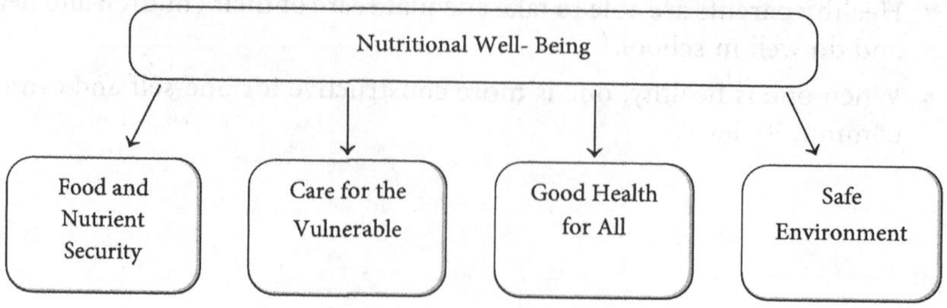

(i) **Food and Nutrient Security** Everyone should have access to adequate food and nutrients year-round. This access is essential for leading a healthy life.

(ii) **Care for Vulnerable Individuals** Care for vulnerable individuals is important. Each person requires loving care, attention and support.
- For babies, this includes receiving the correct type and amount of food along with proper care.
- Expectant mothers need support from their families, communities and employers.
- Sick individuals require assistance through food, nourishment and medication.

(iii) **Health for all** It includes prevention of disease and curing disease when it occurs.
- Special attention needs to be paid to infectious diseases since they can deplete the nutrients and lead to poor health and poor nutritional status.
- Every citizen should get a minimum amount of health care.
- Some of the diseases that take their toll in India, especially among young children are diarrhoea, respiratory infections, measles, malaria, tuberculosis among others.

(iv) **Safe environment** encompasses physical, biological and chemical factors that influence health. This includes access to safe drinking water, hygienic food and efforts to prevent pollution and environmental degradation.

Nutritional Problems and their Consequences

- In India, there exist several nutritional problems in the population.
- We have two main nutritional problems: under-nutrition (nutritional deficiencies) and over-nutrition (diet-related chronic, non-communicable diseases). This situation is called the **'double burden of malnutrition.'** According to the **fourth National Family Health Survey** (NFHS-4), 26.6% of men and 31.3% of women in urban areas are over-weight or obese. In rural areas, only 15.0% of men and 14.3% of women are in the same category.

Malnutrition

- Malnutrition refers to a condition that arises from an imbalance in nutrition. It occurs when nutrient intake is either insufficient or excessive compared to what the body needs.
- Malnutrition can manifest in two main forms
  (i) **Under-nutrition** It results from in-adequate nutrient intake.
  (ii) **Over-nutrition** It arises from consuming too many nutrients.
- In adolescents, poor food choices and improper food combinations are significant contributors to malnutrition.

Under-nutrition

- Under-nutrition is a major problem which is reflected in the high numbers of pregnant women who are under-nourished and have small babies with low birth weight. It is also found in young children (below 3 years of age) who are under-weight and stunted. One-third of the babies born in India are low birth weight, i.e., less than 2500 gms.
- There are other nutrition-related deficiencies such as iron deficiency, anaemia, vitamin A deficiency and consequent blindness and iodine deficiency. Under-nutrition has several **negative effects** on the individual.

- Under-nutrition not only reduces body weight but has devastating effects on children's cognitive development and immunity[3].
- It may also result in other nutrient related deficiencies such as
    - **Iron deficiency** It has a negative impact on health and well-being. In infants and young children, impairs **psychomotor** and cognitive development and thus adversely affects academic performance. It also decreases physical activity. Iron deficiency during pregnancy affects the growth of the foetus and increases risk of morbidity[4] and **mortality** for the pregnant women.
    - **Vitamin A deficiency** It can cause blindness.
    - **Iodine deficiency** It is a threat to health and development, specially for young children and pregnant women. This is because it results in goitre, still birth and miscarriage in women and deaf-mutism, mental retardation and cretinism in children.

Over-nutrition

- It occurs when there is an excess of nutrients than what is required by the body.
- Obesity increases the risk of several diseases such as diabetes, heart disease and hypertension.
- Excess intake of certain nutrients can lead to toxicity, which may cause health problems. This can result in a person becoming over-weight or even obese.

Nutrition and Infection

- Nutrition and infection are closely linked. Providing enough food to fulfill nutritional requirements is not adequate. The **influence of the environment** is also important.
- Nutritional status does not depend only on sufficient supply of food and nutrients but also on the person's health status.
- Poor nutrition weakens the immune system, which increases the risk of infections. During infections, the body loses nutrients through vomiting and diarrhea, while the nutrient requirements are actually increased.
- If a person doesn't get enough nutrients because they have a reduced appetite or can't eat due to nausea or vomiting, their nutrition worsens. This makes them more likely to get another infection. This is especially risky for children, the elderly and those who are already under-nourished.
- In developing countries, **food-borne illnesses** such as diarrhea and dysentery are major problems since they can lead to de-hydration and death.
- Many of the infectious and communicable diseases are due to poor environmental sanitation, poor household, personal and food hygiene. It is therefore important to prevent these diseases.

Quick Test 2

1. Nutrients have been categorised into how many groups?
2. What is condition caused by imbalance in nutrition called?
3. What does Vitamin A deficiency leads to?
4. Name the disease an over-weight person suffers from.

3 Immunity It refers to body's ability to resist infections and diseases through defense mechanisms.
4 Morbidity It is the state of being unhealthy or having symptoms of a disease or condition.

7A.7 Hygiene and Sanitation

To prevent and control diseases, we must consider both internal and external factors. Key elements include sanitation[5], hygiene, nutrition and immunisation.

Intrinsic/Host Factors	Extrinsic/Environmental Factors
Demographic factors such as age, sex ethnicity and race.	Physical environment i.e. air, water, soil, housing, climate, geography, heat, light, noise and radiation.
Biological factors such as heredity, blood groups, enzymes, levels of various substances in blood, e.g. cholesterol and functioning of various organs and systems.	Biological environment includes human being and all other living beings such as animals, rodents, insects, plants viruses and micro-organisms. Some of these act as disease-producing agents, some as reservoirs of infection and others as intermediate hosts and vectors of disease.
Social and economic characteristics such as occupation, marital status, housing, etc.	Psycho-social factors such as emotional well-being, cultural values, customs, habits, beliefs, attitudes, religion, lifestyle, health services, etc.
Lifestyle factors, e.g. nutrition, diet, physical activity, living habits, use of addictive substances such as drugs, alcohol, etc.	

Hygiene

- Hygiene refer to the conditions and practices that help in the maintain of health and prevention of spread of diseases.
- Hygiene focuses on two main areas **Personal Hygiene** and **Environmental Hygiene.**

Personal Hygiene

- Good health relies on the social environment, lifestyle and individual behaviours, including food intake and hygiene practices.
- Poor hygiene can lead to infections, such as worm infestations.

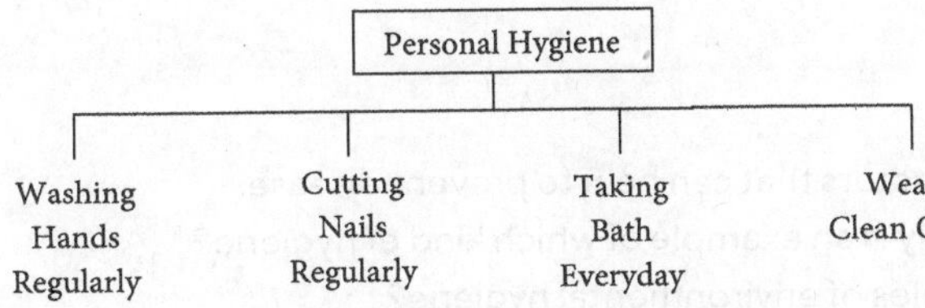

▲ *Personal Aspects of Hygiene*

Environmental Hygiene

- It comprises both **organic and in-organic** materials found in our homes and communities. This includes physical factors such as water, air, housing, radiation, etc., as well as biological factors such as plants, bacteria, viruses, insects, rodents and animals.
- Environmental health is important to create conditions that support good health and prevent disease.
- Safe drinking water and proper sanitation, especially for waste (faeces) disposal are crucial.
- Air and water pollution are also concerns. Contaminated water can cause many illnesses, including diarrhoea, worm infestations and skin infections.

5 **Sanitation** It means to maintain health through proper disposal of waste and cleanliness.

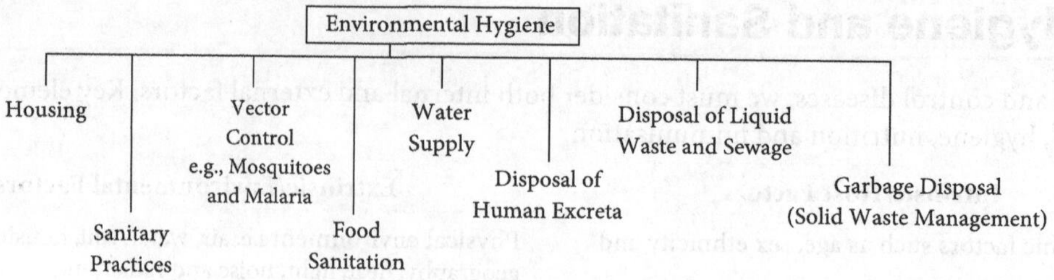

▲ *Environmental Aspects of Hygiene*

Food Hygiene

- Food-borne illnesses arise from eating **contaminated**[6] food with harmful micro-organisms (pathogens). For a food borne illness to occur, several conditions must be met
  - Pathogens or their toxins must be present in the food.
  - There must be enough harmful micro-organisms.
  - The contaminated food must be consumed in a sufficient amount.
- Common illnesses include diarrhoea, dysentery, amoebiasis, infective hepatitis, typhoid, listeriosis, botulism, cholera and gastro-enteritis. These are often linked to poor food handling practices, such as
  - Using spoiled or unsafe food and water.
  - Improper storage, which allows **micro-organisms** to grow.
  - Lack of insect and vermin control.
  - In-adequate cooking or re-heating.
  - Improper heating
  - Leaving food uncovered.
  - Using dirty utensils or equipment.
  - Improper cooling
  - Cross-contamination between foods.
  - Use of contaminated substances for garnishing.
  - Storage of foods at temperatures favourable to growth of micro-organisms (4 to 600C).
  - Poor hygiene among those preparing food such as unclean clothes, not washing of hands, dirt and grime under the nails.
  - Effective practices in nutrition, health and hygiene are important for productivity both at home and at work.

Quick Test 3

1. Name two Intrinsic factors that can help to prevent disease.
2. Cutting nails regularly is an example of which kind of hygiene?
3. What are two examples of environmental hygiene?
4. Mention one disease that can occur due to contaminated food.

6 **Contaminated** It means polluted or infected with harmful substances or micro-organisms, unsafe for consumption.

Mind Map

NUTRITION, HEALTH AND HYGIENE

1 Health and its Dimensions

Social Health
- Well-being of individual and society
- It includes
  - Employment status
  - Socio-economic status
  - Environmental conditions

Mental Health
- Emotional and psychological well-being.
- Positive mental health Feels capable, cope with stress, live an independent life.

Physical Health
- Physical fitness
- Functioning of body

2 Health Care

Indicators of Health
- Mortality rates
- Disability rates
- Environmental factors
- Quality of life, etc.

Three levels of Health Care Services

Primary Health Care
- Between individual and health care system.

Secondary Health Care
- Patient refer to specialised hospital.

Tertiary Health Care
- Patient refer to ICU and advance medical care.

3 Nutrition and Health

Nutrients

Role of Nutritionists
- Study biological, metabolic and clinical aspects of nutrition.
- Focus on
  - Nutritional problems
  - Nutritional needs
  - Plan food/ Diet chart

Nutrient Requirements
- Nutrient needs based on age, sex, physiological state.
- Essential to consume balanced diet.

Functions of Nutrients
- Play crucial role in bodily functions.
- Influence gene expression and transcription.

Classification of Nutrients

Macro-nutrients
- Required in large amount.
- It includes fats, proteins, fibre etc.

Micro-nutrients
- Required in small amount.
- It includes minerals and vitamins.

Influences on Food Choice

Purchasing Power
- Economic factor determine purchasing power.

Environment
- Water supply and irrigation impact food production.

Policies
- National and international policies affects food choices.

4 Factors Affecting Nutritional Well-being

Nutritional Well-Bing
- Food and nutrient security
- Health for all
- Care for those who are vulnerable
- Safe environment

Nutritional Problems and their Consequences

Under-nutrition
- Major problem in pregnant women, who have small babies with Low birth rates.
- **Consequences** Iron deficiency, Vitamin A deficiency, blindness etc.

Over-nutrition
- Excess of nutrients in body.
- **Consequences** diabetes, heart disease, hypertension etc.

Impact of Good Health and Nutrition
- Happier and more productive life.
- Actively participates in activities.
- Increase attention span.
- reduce risk of diseases.

Malnutrition

Under-nutrition
- Results from inadequate nutrients intake.

Over-nutrition
- Arises from consuming too many nutrients.

Nutrition and Infection
- Poor nutrition weakens the immune system.
- Increase risk of infection.
- Body loses nutrients through vomiting and diarrhea.
- Infections are due to
  - Poor sanitation
  - Poor environment
  - Poor food hygiene
  - Poor household

5 Hygiene and Sanitation

Hygiene

Personal Hygiene
- Bath daily
- Keep hair clean
- Wear clean clothes
- Wash hands with soap

Environmental Hygiene
- Keep house clean
- Limited use of hazardous chemicals
- Put garbage in dustbin

Food Hygiene
- Use clean utensils
- Not to leave food uncovered
- Proper cooling and heating of food
- Proper storage of food

Factors

Intrinsic/Host Factors

Demographic Factors
- Age, sex, race, etc.

Biological Factors
- Heredity, blood groups, enzymes etc.

Social and Economic Factors
- Occupation, marital status etc.

Lifestyle Factors
- Nutrition, diet, physical activity etc.

Extrinsic/Enviromental Factors

Physical Environment
- Air, water, soil, climate, radiation etc.

Biological Environment
- Animals, insects, plants, viruses, micro-organism etc.

Psycho-Social Factors
- Emotional well-being, cultural values, beliefs, lifestyles etc.

NCERT Folder

Intext Questions

1. Identify at least 5-6 key indicators that you think are important for health and see how India ranks among the various countries in the world. (Pg. 103)

Ans. As a student, I've learned that health is a multifaceted concept. The following are 6 key indicators to measure a country's health

(i) Life Expectancy at Birth
(ii) Infant Mortality Rate (IMR)
(iii) Maternal Mortality Ratio (MMR)
(iv) Healthcare Access and Quality (HAQ) Index
(v) Prevalence of Malnutrition

According to various sources (WHO, World Bank, and OECD), India's rankings are

- **Life Expectancy at Birth** 69.8 years (ranked 123rd out of 194 countries)
- **Infant Mortality Rate (IMR)** 32.7 deaths per 1000 live births (ranked 131st out of 194 countries)
- **Maternal Mortality Ratio (MMR)** 145 deaths per 100,000 live births (ranked 136th out of 194 countries)
- **Healthcare Access and Quality (HAQ) Index** 41.2 (ranked 145th out of 195 countries)
- **Prevalence of Malnutrition** 38.4% of children under 5 are stunted (ranked 114th out of 132 countries)

These rankings indicate that India still faces significant health challenges.

2. There are so many dimensions of health. List the various occupations or professions which are involved in providing services for health and nutrition-including prevention of health problems, promotion of good health and therapeutic services. (Pg. 103)

Ans. The health care sector employs various professionals to provide services for health, nutrition, prevention, promotion, and therapy. Some key occupations in this field include

(i) **Medical Professionals**
- Doctors (specialists and general practitioners)
- Nurses
- Dentists
- Pharmacists

(ii) **Allied Healthcare Professionals**
- Physiotherapists
- Dietitians
- Nutritionists

(iii) **Mental Health Professionals**
- Psychologists
- Psychiatrists
- Counselors
- Social workers

(iv) **Alternative Medicine Professionals**
- Ayurvedic doctors
- Homeopathic doctors
- Yoga therapists
- Naturopaths

(v) **Healthcare Support Staff**
- Lab technicians
- Radiologists
- Healthcare assistants

These professionals work together to provide comprehensive healthcare services, address health disparities, and promote overall well-being.

Execrcise

1. 'Nutrition affects productivity, income and quality of life'. Write your opinion about this statement.

Ans. Nutrition affects productivity, income and quality of life. Good nutrition results in healthy individuals. Healthy individuals are able to work hard and their productivity is more than an unhealthy individual. They regularly go to office and live a good quality of life.

When the nutrition and nutritional status of an individual is not optimum, it affects their health. Unhealthy individuals have an increased risk of illness due to decreased immunity, which leads to increased absenteeism from office, thereby resulting in loss of income.

Additionally, infections can cause various other diseases that affect the quality of life negatively.

Thus, optimum nutrition is required to have greater productivity, income and better quality of life.

2. How is nutrition linked to mental and visual disability and quality of life?

Ans. Nutrition is closely linked to mental and visual disability and quality of life. Nutrition is important for the physical and mental growth of children and adolescents. They require adequate amounts of nutrition to achieve their full potential.

Adults also require good nutrition to have a productive and healthy life. If the body lacks vitamin A, iron or iodine, it may lead to various consequences such as

(i) Vitamin A deficiency may lead to blindness if not corrected and reduced immunity to infections.
(ii) Iron deficiency, anaemia results in poor fetal growth, poor cognitive and mental development.

(iii) Iodine deficiency also results in poor mental and cognitive development, cretinism in children and deaf-mutism.

3. Divide the class into groups. Each group should visit a food service establisment, e.g. canteen/cafeteria, restaurant, street food vendor. Identify the poor hygiene practices related to
(i) Food hygiene (ii) Personal hygiene

Ans. (i) For poor food hygiene refer to text under the heading 'Poor Food Hygiene'.

(ii) Personal hygiene practices include
- Not washing hands with soap and water before touching food and after using toilet.
- Wearing dirty or soiled clothes.
- Nails are not cut and cleaned properly.
- Not taking bath everyday.
- Not covering hair while cooking.
- Not covering mouth while coughing and sneezing and not washing hands afterwards.

Exam Pattern Questions

Objective Type Questions

Multiple Choice Questions (MCQs)

1. Which of the following is not a determinant of health?
(a) Employment status (b) Safety in workplace
(c) Access to health service (d) Access to good housing

2. What includes preventive, promotive and therapeutic care?
(a) Government schemes (b) PHC
(c) Health care (d) Nutrition

3. Which among the following is the indicator of health?
(a) Morbidity (b) Environment
(c) Nutritional status (d) All of these

4. Which deficiency results in goitre?
(a) Vitamin A (b) Vitamin B
(c) Iodine deficiency (d) Iron deficiency

5. Which among the following is not an environmental aspect of hygiene?
(a) Sanitary practice (b) Water supply
(c) Food sanitation (d) Facial care

6. Optimum nutritional status is important because it...... .
(a) maintain muscle mass.
(b) helps to cope with physical and mental stress.
(c) improve productivity.
(d) All of the above

7. Find the incorrect statement regarding under-nutrition among the following **Competency Based Que**
(a) Under-nutrition reduces immunity and increases susceptibility to infections.
(b) Under-nutrition increases weight thereby decreasing immunity.
(c) Nutrient deficiency in children negatively affect the cognitive development.
(d) Nutrient deficiency has negligible effect on immunity.

8. Kartik is a 10 years old boy. One day, after having his breakfast, he felt sick and vomited everything he ate and fell unconscious. When the doctor visited him, he informed that Kartik was suffering from a food-borne illness. He also stated some possible reasons for this.
Choose the option which could be a possible reason as told by the doctor. **Competency Based Que**
(a) Not wearing new and clean clothes
(b) Not using new utensils to eat food
(c) Not washing hands after throwing garbage
(d) Not having freshly cooked meals

9. Which disease increases the chances of obesity?
(a) Mental retardation
(b) Anaemic
(c) Night blindness
(d) Heart disease, high blood pressure

10. Read the following statements.
I. There are less than 50 nutrients in food.
II. Health is a fundamental human right.
III. Health is multi-dimensional.
IV. One-fifth of the babies born in India are low birth weight. **Competency Based Que**

Codes
(a) I and II
(b) II and III
(c) I and IV
(d) III and IV

11. Match the following.

	List-I		List-II
A.	Intrinsic factor	1.	All nutrients in appropriate amounts
B.	Balanced diet	2.	Carbohydrates
C.	Macro-nutrient	3.	Over-nutrition and under-nutrition
D.	Malnutrition	4.	Heredity, blood group, enzymes

Codes

	A	B	C	D
(a)	1	3	2	4
(b)	4	1	2	3
(c)	2	4	1	3
(d)	3	2	1	4

Assertion-Reason Questions

Direction (Q. Nos.12-14) In the questions given below, there are two statements marked as Assertion (A) and Reason (R). Read the statements and choose the correct option.

Codes

(a) Both A and R are true and R is the correct explanation of A.

(b) Both A and R are true, but R is not the correct explanation of A.

(c) A is true, but R is false.

(d) A is false, but R is true.

12. **Assertion** (A) Chances of heart diseases are higher in a village.

Reason (R) Community health is essential for good individual health.

13. **Assertion** (A) Some children fall ill more frequently than others.

Reason (R) Malnutrition makes children more susceptible to diseases.

14. **Assertion** (A) In developing countries, food-borne illnesses such as diarrhea and dysentery are major problems.

Reason (R) Poor personal and food handling practices result in food-borne illnesses.

Case Based Questions

15. **Read the passage given below and answer the following questions.**

Every individual is responsible for his/her own health, but it is also a major public concern. Thus the government assumes considerable responsibility and provides health services at various levels to the citizens of the country. This is because good health is the foundation for good quality of life and standard of living for the individual and the family, and is the key for ensuring social, economic and human development of a community and a nation.

(i) **Health may be defined as ....**

(a) absence of disease.

(b) mental, social and psychological well-being.

(c) healthy individuals living a healthy productive life.

(d) All of the above

(ii) **Primary health care level is ....**

(a) first level of contact between individuals with the health care system.

(b) when patients are referred to district hospitals.

(c) when patients are referred for specialised intensive care, advanced diagnostic support medical care.

(d) None of the above

(iii) **What does healthcare include?** **Competency Based Que**

I. Preventive care
II. Economic care
III. Therapeutic care
IV. Social care

Choose the correct option.

(a) I and II
(b) II and III
(c) I and III
(d) III and IV

(iv) **Assertion** (A) The government assumes considerable responsibility and provides health services at various levels to the citizens of the country.

Reason (R) Every citizen has a right to health care at all stages of life irrespective of age, class, gender, etc.

Codes **Competency Based Que**

(a) Both A and R are true and R is the correct explanation of A

(b) Both A and R are true, but R is not the correct explanation of A

(c) A is true, but R is false

(d) A is false, but R is true

Answers

1. (d) Access to good housing
2. (c) Health care
3. (d) All of these
4. (c) Iodine deficiency
5. (d) Facial care
6. (d) All of the above
7. (d) Nutrient deficiency has negligible effect on immunity.
8. (d) Not having freshly cooked meals
9. (d) Heart disease, high blood pressure

10. (c) I and IV 11. (b) 4 1 2 3
12. (d) A is false, but R is true
13. (a) Both A and R are true and R is the correct explanation of A
14. (a) Both A and R are true and R is the correct explanation of A
15. (i) (d) All of the above
(ii) (a) first level of contact between individuals with the health care system.
(iii) (c) I and III
(iv) (a) Both A and R are true and R is the correct explanation of A

Subjective Questions

Very Short Answer Type Questions

1. What does the Universal Declaration of Human Rights state?

Ans. The Universal Declaration of Human Rights states, "Everyone has the right to a standard of living adequate for the health and well-being of one-self and one's family including food".

2. What should be the aim of every health professional?

Ans. The aim of every health professional should be to promote good health, meaning that they should promote maintenance of well-being or wellness and quality of life.

3. Name any two determinants of social health?

Ans. Two determinants of social health are
(i) Employment status
(ii) Cultural/religious beliefs, taboos and values systems

4. What is the role of social support during illness?

Ans. The role of social support during illness is to help all citizens to cope with the illness. It helps by providing better socio-economic and environmental conditions, safety in workplace and access to health services, so that ill persons recover quickly from their illness.

5. Why does the government provide health services?

Ans. The government provides health services at three different levels to the citizens of the country because good health is the foundation for good quality of life and standard of living.

Further, the government wants to ensure social, economic and human development of the community and the nation.

6. What does nutritional status depends on?

Ans. Nutritional status depends both on a sufficient supply of food and nutrients as well as on the person's health status.

7. Aryan is a 17 year old high school student going through a growth sport and priya is a 30 years old new mother recovering from a severe case of pneumonia. What two conditions do Aryan and priya have in common that requires a person to consume a higher level of nutrition than normal? Competency Based Que

Ans. The two conditions under which a person may require a higher level of nutrition than normal are
(i) During periods of growth such as infancy, childhood and adolescence, as well as during pregnancy and lactation in women.
(ii) During infections and illness period serving this time an individual requires increased amount of nutrient to compensate for the losses occured due to illness and to repair and recover the damaged cells and tissues.

8. What are the two types of nutritionists? Describe their nature of work.

Ans. The two types of nutritionists are
(i) **Clinical Nutritionists** Their work is concerned with the biological and metabolic aspects of what happens during a disease state and how the body is nourished.
(ii) **Public Health Nutritionists** Their work is to study the nutritional needs of populations and their nutritional problems, including health problems caused by lack of nutrients.

9. What does food and nutrient security imply?

Ans. Food and nutrient security implies that every person has access to and can obtain adequate food and nutrients throughout the year as per his/her requirement to enable him/her to lead a healthy life.

10. What do you understand by the term 'low birth weight'?

Ans. The term 'low birth weight' means a baby born with a body weight less than 2.5 kg.

11. What are the adverse effects of over-nutrition?

Ans. The adverse effects of over-nutrition are that it leads to diet-related chronic and non-communicable diseases.

A person may become over-weight and obese. Obesity further increases the risk of several diseases such as type II diabetes, heart disease and hypertension. It can also lead to toxicity in the body.

12. What problems result in women and children if their diet is deficient in Iodine?

Ans. If diet of women and children is deficient in Iodine, it results in goitre, still birth and miscarriage in women. In the case of children, it can cause deaf-mutism, mental retardation and cretinism.

13. Which diseases are termed as food-borne illnesses?

Ans. The diseases which are termed as food-borne illnesses are diarrhoea, dysentery, amoebiasis, infective hepatitis, typhoid, listeriosis, botulism, cholera and gastroenteritis.

14. What are two examples of poor hygiene and sanitation of persons handling food?

Ans. (i) The person handling food may not be washing hands with soap and water after using toilet and before touching food.

(ii) The person may not have clean nails or clothes.

Short Answer Type Questions

1. How does WHO define health? What are three conditions under which we can say that a person is diseased?

Ans. WHO defines health as "A state of complete mental, physical and social well being and not merely the absence of disease". The three conditions under which we can say that a person is suffering from a disease are

(i) The person's health is impaired.

(ii) The functioning of some part or organ of the body of the person is altered, disrupted or deranged, thus interrupting normal functions of the part.

(iii) The person's body health has deviated from a state of complete well-being.

2. Neha, a 28 years old woman from Delhi, has been experiencing persistent abdominal pain. After visiting her local Primary Health Care center, where she receives dietary advice and pain relief medication, her symptoms worsen after a week. What should Neha do next in terms of seeking care? How will her treatment transition through Secondary and Tertiary Health Care levels? Consider the roles and responsibilities of the healthcare system at each level. **Competency Based Que**

Ans. Neha should return to her Primary Health Care center to discuss her worsening symptoms.

If the healthcare provider determines her condition requires further evaluation, she will be referred to a Secondary Health Care facility, such as a district hospital, for specialised tests and treatment.

If her condition is serious and requires advanced care, she may then be referred to a Tertiary Health Care center, where she can receive intensive care and comprehensive diagnostic support.

This structured approach ensures Neha receives appropriate care at each level of the health care system, promoting her overall health and recovery.

3. What is food security? What factors does it depend on?

Ans. Food security is the state of having reliable access to a sufficient quantity of affordable, nutritious food. It depends on the following factors

(i) Purchasing power of the person concerned i.e. economic factors.

(ii) Environmental factors (water and irrigation)

(iii) The policies of the government at the national and international levels.

4. What happens to a person with poor nutritional status?

Ans. A person with poor nutritional status has a decreased level of resistance and immunity to diseases and thus, has an increased risk of infection.

If nutrient intake of such a person is insufficient compared to the requirement due to loss of appetite or inability to eat (if there is nauesa and/or vomiting), infections will affect the nutritional status adversely, thus leaving the person vulnerable to another infection.

5. Safe environment encompasses physical, biological and chemical factors that influence health.

(i) What is the function of environmental health?

(ii) Which two factors affect environmental health significantly? **Competency Based Que**

Ans. (i) The function of environmental health is to create and maintain ecological conditions that will promote health and prevent disease.

(ii) Two factors affecting environmental health significantly are

(a) Availability of safe drinking water, as contaminated water is the cause of many diseases such as diarrhea, worm infestations, skin and eye infections, guinea worm, etc.

(b) Proper sanitation, especially proper disposal of faeces, as it may lead to diseases related to fecal-oral route such as typhoid, cholera, worm infections, etc.

Long Answer Type Questions

1. Explain by giving four reasons how nutrition is a fundamental pillar of human life, health and development? **Competency Based Que**

Ans. Nutrition is a fundamental pillar of human life, health and development because

(i) Good nutrition enables a person to enjoy good health, resist infection, have adequate energy levels and perform daily tasks without feeling fatigued.

(ii) For children and adolescents, nutrition is vital for their growth, mental development and achieving their potential.

(iii) For adults, adequate nutrition is crucial to lead a socially and economically productive and healthy life.

(iv) The health status of an individual determines the nutrient requirements of that person and its food intake; however, illness and disease adversely affect nutritional status.

2. What do you understand by social health? Describe four determinants of social health in one sentence each?

Ans. The social health can be understood as the health of individuals and of a society. At the individual level, social health includes an individuals well being, his/her social skills and the ability to function as a member of a society. This also comprises how well an individual gets along with other people and with social institution.

At the society level, it refers to a society where there is equal opportunity as well as access for all citizens to the goods and services essential for good health. When the citizens face problems and stress, social support helps them to cope with these issues.

Social support measures contribute to positive adjustment in children and adults and encourage personal growth. Persons who are socially well-adjusted tend to live longer and recover faster from disease.

Four determinants of social health are

(i) **Employment Status** It means whether the person is employed or not employed.

(ii) **Workplace Safety** It means that the place where the person works, either in the office/factory or at the home (in the case of a homemaker) is safe to work in.

(iii) **Health Services Accessibility** It means that all health services including hospitalisation, are easily available.

(iv) **Cultural/Religious Beliefs/Value Systems** It means that values and beliefs held in the society in which the person lives.

3. Meera, a 28-years-old woman from Delhi, often feels overwhelmed by stress and anxiety.
She wants to improve her mental health and seeks to understand what it means.

(i) What is meant by mental health?

(ii) What qualities should she look for in herself and others to identify positive mental health? **Competency Based Que**

Ans. (i) Mental health refers to emotional, psychological, and social well-being, affecting how individuals think, feel and act.

(ii) For Meera, six qualities of positive mental health include-

- Resilience
- The ability to cope with stress
- Self-awareness
- Good emotional regulation
- Healthy relationships
- A sense of purpose

By cultivating these qualities, she can enhance her mental well-being, manage stress effectively and build positive interactions in her life.

Seeking support from friends or professionals can further aid her journey toward better mental health.

4. How is under-nutrition a major problem in India? What are three major nutrition-related deficiencies existing in the population?

Ans. For answer refer to text under the heading 'Under-nutrition' on pg no. 119 and 120.

5. Shikha is a 5-years-old girl who had low birth weight. She is suffering from delayed psychomotor and cognitive development and does not indulge in physical activity. **Competency Based Que**

(i) Which nutrient deficiency disorder is she suffering from? Discuss.

(ii) What do you understand by under-nutrition?

(iii) Differentiate between under-nutrition and over-nutrition.

Ans. (i) Shikha is suffering from iron deficiency. It affects the growth of the foetus and increases risk of morbidity and mortality for the mother. In infants and young children, if affects psychomotor and cognitive development.

(ii) When the intake of nutrients is less than the amount required by the body, then an individual suffers from under-nutrition. It is a major problem reflected in the high numbers of under-nourished pregnant women in India.

(iii) When the intake of nutrient is less than the amount required by the body, then it leads to under-nutrition and when there is an excess of nutrient then what is required by the body it leads to over-nutrition.

SELF ASSESSMENT TEST

Objective Type Questions

1. When patients are transferred for specialised intensive care, it is known as ....
   (a) Primary Health Care
   (b) Secondary Health Care
   (c) Tertiary Health Care
   (d) District Hospitals
2. Which among the following is not an indicator of health?
   (a) Disability Rates
   (b) Health Policy
   (c) Morbidity
   (d) Employment Status
3. Availability of food is also known as ....
   (a) plenty of resources
   (b) food security
   (c) food warehouse
   (d) productivity

Very Short Answer Type Questions

4. How are nutrients broadly classified?
5. Briefly explain the dimensions of health.
6. Briefly describe the two types of nutritionists.
7. Why is a balanced diet important?
8. How does environmental hygiene affect nutritional status?

Short Answer Type Questions

9. What is dual burden of malnutrition? Explain briefly.
10. How are nutrition and health interlinked?

Long Answer Type Questions

11. Explain how an infection affects the nutritional status of a person? Why is the requirement of nutrients increase during illness?
    Competency Based Que
12. Explain four important aspects of environmental hygiene which need to be followed to ensure good health among the population.
    Competency Based Que

07B

CHAPTER

Resources availability and management focuses on effectively using resources to achieve goals, emphasising time management, planning and organisation for success.

YOUR STUDY GOALS

YOUR PRACTICE GOAL

- Objective Type Questions (11 Qs ; MCQs, A-R, Matching, Case Based)
- Subjective Questions (12 VSAs, 6 SAs, 2 LAs)

Resource Availability and Management

Resources are materials, possessions or funds used to achieve goals. Examples of resources include money, time, space and energy. These **valuable assets** are often limited and not equally accessible to everyone.

If resources are wasted or mismanaged, we may struggle to achieve our objectives. Therefore, effective management of available resources is essential for reaching our goals. Timely and efficient management enhances resource utilisation.

7B.1 Time Management

- To be successful it is essential to develop time management skills. Developing these skills leads to success in various areas, including business, sports and personal life. It helps to balance work with rest and recreation.
- Effective time management means **focusing on getting results** instead of just staying busy. Many people feel anxious about unfinished tasks but accomplish little because they don't prioritise what's truly important i.e. time.
  - For example, some students may spend their time worrying about examinations rather than actually studying for them.
- Time management starts with planning. A **time plan** is necessary. It can be defined as an advance **schedule**[1] of activities to be performed in a given time period.

1 **Schedule** A planned timetable for activities and tasks, facilitating better time management.

Activity : Identify Your Own Time Management Skill

- Score the questions given below and determine how well these statements describe you. The following are the ratings for your answer.
- Not at all = 1, Rarely = 2, Sometime = 3, often = 4, very often = 5
- After answering all the questions add your scares across all the questions to get the final total.

The questions to be scored are

Question	Not at all	Rarely	Sometimes	Often	Very often
1. Are you able to complete your highest priority tasks during the day?					
2. Are you able to place all your tasks according to their priority?					
3. Are you able to perform your tasks in the given time period?					
4. Do you keep separate time for planning and scheduling?					
5. Do you keep track of the time spent on the jobs done by you?					
6. How often are you able to work without distractions and interruptions?					
7. Do you do goal setting to help you decide the various tasks you would work on?					
8. Do you keep extra time margin in your schedule to deal with 'the unexpected'?					
9. Do you prioritise the importance of any new assignment given?					
10. Are you able to complete your task without being pressured by deadlines and commitments?					
11. Are you able to work effectively on important tasks because of distractions?					
12. Are you able to complete your work at the work place instead of taking it home?					
13. Do you prepare a "To do" list or an action programme before carrying out the tasks?					
14. Do you consult persons with experience before setting priorities for a given task?					
15. Do you consider whether the task would be worth the time put in, before you start your task?					

Total =

Score Interpretation

Score	Comment
46-75	You are managing your time very effectively! However, check the section below to make it even better.
31-45	You are good at some aspects, but there is scope for improvement elsewhere. Focus on the key issues in the section below and you will most likely find that work becomes less stressful.
15-30	The good news is that you have a great opportunity to improve your effectiveness at work for long term success. However, to realise this you have to improve your time management skills.

After knowing your score, you can follow the given step further improve your time management skills.

Steps for Time and Activity Planning

Step I Start your work quickly as possible. Don't delay tasks. When you get home, relax a bit, eat and then start your school work without postponing.

Step II Create a **daily routine**. Set specific times for school work and household chores and stick to them. This helps you finish tasks on time.

Step III **Prioritise your tasks**. Before picking up any new task make sure it does not impact the already existing activities. Do not undertake too many activities at a particular time. Focus on important tasks first, like studying for a test before doing homework.

Step IV Avoid unimportant tasks. **Learn to say 'No'.** If you're busy, skip low-priority activities, like watching TV, if you have assignments due.

Step V **Divide the big tasks** into a series of small manageable activities. The day's school work (big task) can be divided into smaller tasks by dividing the work as per different subjects.

Step VI Don't waste **time and energy** on tasks that don't need much attention.

Step VII Focus on **one task** at a time until it's done. Don't leave tasks unfinished.

Step VIII Set specific **'start'** and **'stop'** times for your activities. Allocate time for each subject without spending too long on any one of them.

Step IX **Make a schedule** of your activities and tasks. This will help to effectively manage time allocated to each task. A proper time schedule should be prepared for the entire day, which must always include leisure time.

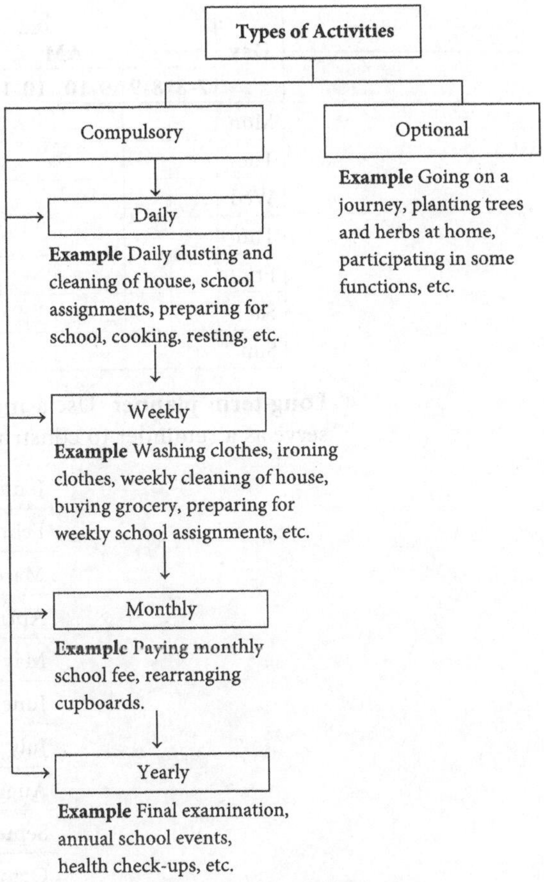

▲ *Types of Time Schedules*

7B.2 Time Plan

Time plans are made according to the individual needs of a person. Every individual has different goals and requirements and therefore, a different routine. For example a time plan for a student is very different from a time plan of a person who goes out to work.

Tips for effective time management

- **Create a simple 'To Do' list** It helps you to identify the activities, reasons for doing them and a timeline for completing them.

S. No.	Activity	Day/Date of completion	Reason for carrying out the activity
1			
2			
3			

- **Daily/weekly planner**

Day	Hours														
	AM					PM									
	7-8	8-9	9-10	10-11	11-12	12-1	1-2	2-3	3-4	4-5	5-6	6-7	7-8	9-10	10-11
Mon															
Tue															
Wed															
Thu															
Fri															
Sat															
Sun															

- **Long term planner** Use a **monthly chart** so, that you can plan ahead. Long-term planners will also serve as a reminder to constructively plan time for oneself.

January
February
March
April
May
June
July
August
September
October
November
December

Tools in Time Management

Following are the tools which help in managing time effectively.

- **Peak Load Period** It is the **maximum load** of work during a specified period of time. For example, early morning time or dinner time.
- **Work Curve** This shows how work varies over time. The curve has different phases
  - **a to b** Warming up.
  - **c** Maximum ability to work.
  - **d** Drop in performance due to fatigue.

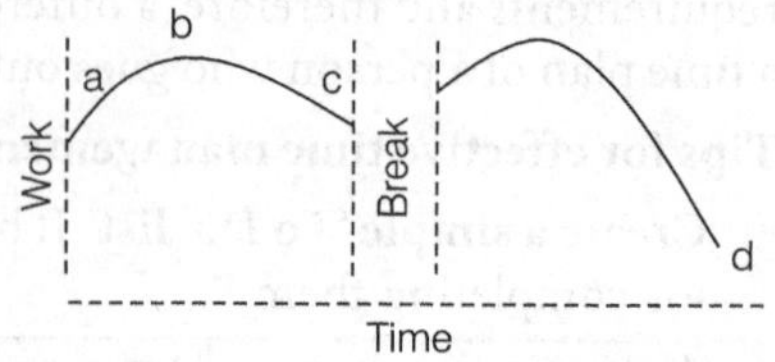

- **Rest Periods** These are **unproductive interruptions** of working time, i.e. breaks from work.

  The timing and length of breaks are important. They should be neither too long nor too short.
- **Work Simplification** This means finding the easiest, simplest and quickest ways to do tasks. It combines time and energy to achieve more work or reduce effort.

  Effective time management seeks to achieve more with the same time and energy, or to reduce both to complete a set amount of work.

To improve work processes and simplify tasks, three levels of change are crucial

- **Changes in Hand and Body Motions** This involves adjusting how we use our hands and body while keeping the same tools and products. We can reduce effort by
  - **Eliminating Steps** For example, letting dishes air dry instead of wiping them, or making a shopping list to buy all items at once instead of separately.
  - **Improving Sequence** Grouping similar tasks together, like dusting, sweeping and mopping all at once in each room, helps maintain rhythm or smooth workflow.
  - **Skill Development** Mastering a task helps eliminate unnecessary movements, saving time and energy.
  - **Better Posture** Maintaining good posture[1] is important for using muscles effectively and keeping the body aligned.
  - This allows us to support weight using our bones, reducing strain on the muscles.
  - For example, using a long-handled broom instead of bending down to sweep helps maintain a stable posture.

Good Standing Posture A good standing posture keeps the head, neck, chest and abdomen aligned so that weight is mainly supported by the bones. This **minimises strain** on muscles and ligaments.

Good Sitting Posture A good sitting posture for work is balanced and well-aligned(poised). It allows the skeleton to support the weight and relieve strain on muscles and nerves. Adjustments are made as needed to carry out the work.

▲ *Alignment of Body Parts in Line With Gravity*

- **Changes in Workspaces and Equipment** This involves organising storage areas, rearranging kitchen tools and adjusting work surfaces to the right height. Using labour-saving devices like pressure cookers and microwaves can also save time and effort.
- **Changes in End Products** These changes can occur by
  - **Using different raw materials** For example, opting for ready-made ground spices instead of whole spices.
  - **Creating different products from the same raw material** Making kulfi instead of ice cream or lauki paranthas instead of kofta curry.
  - **Changes in both the raw material and finished product** For example, using ball pen instead of ink pen, etc.

Quick Test 1

1. Define valuable assets?
2. Why is time management crucial?
3. Time management starts with which activity?
4. What does point 'c' in work curve denotes?

1 **Posture** The position of the body while sitting or standing, affecting comfort and health.

7B.3 Space Management

- Space is used for various activities at home, outdoors and in the workplace.
- A well-designed room feels spacious, while a room of the same size can look cramped or cluttered if not organised well.
- Space management involves- planning of space, organising it as per the plan, implementing the plan in terms of its utilisation and evaluating it in terms of achieving functionality and aesthetic[2] look.
- A well-managed space provides comfort while working and looks attractive.

Space and the Home

- Major home activities include sitting, sleeping, studying, cooking, bathing, washing and entertainment.
- Wherever there is space available, specified rooms are built to carry out such activities.
- Most urban middle **Socio Economic Status (SES) homes** typically have a sitting room, bedrooms, kitchen, store room, bathroom, toilet and optional verandah/courtyard.
- Additional rooms may include a dining room, study room, entertainment room, dressing room, guest room, children's room, garage, stairs, passages, puja room, garden and terrace.

Principles of Space Planning

- **Aspect** This refers to the placement of doors and windows in a building. It allows occupants to enjoy natural light, fresh air and views of nature.
- **Prospect** This is the overall appearance of a house from the outside. It focuses on its **visual appeal** using natural beauty, the arrangement of doors and windows and hiding unattractive views.
- **Privacy** Privacy is crucial in space planning and includes
  - **Internal Privacy** Internal privacy refers to keeping one room separate from another. This is achieved through careful planning, including how rooms are grouped, where doors are placed and adding small corridors or lobbies. Screens and curtains can also help provide privacy. In larger families, separate sitting areas for women may be created to ensure their privacy.
  - **External Privacy** External privacy means keeping all parts of a house private from neighbouring buildings, public streets and pathways. This can be achieved by thoughtfully planning such as using trees or climbing plants for covering the entrance.
- **Grouping** This refers to how rooms are positioned in relation to each other. For example, the dining area should be near the kitchen, while the kitchen should be far from the toilet.
- **Roominess** This refers to the spacious feel of a room. To maximise space, use built-in cupboards, shelves and storage areas to keep the floor clear for activities. The room's size, shape, furniture arrangement and colour scheme affect its spaciousness.

  For example, a well-proportioned rectangular room feels larger than a square room of the same size and light colours make a room look more open than dark colours.
- **Furniture Requirements** Rooms should be planned with the necessary furniture in mind. Only essential pieces should be placed and furniture should be arranged to allow for easy movement and circulation.
- **Sanitation**[3] This includes providing adequate light, ventilation, cleaning facilities and sanitary conveniences.
  - **Light** It is essential for **illumination and hygiene**. It may be provided by natural or artificial sources. Windows, bulbs, tubelights are some sources of light.

---

2 Aesthetics The visual appeal and beauty of a space or design.

3 Sanitation Maintaining cleanliness and hygiene to prevent disease and promote health.

- **Ventilation** Ventilation is the supply of outside air into the building. This is an essential factor for comfort. Good ventilation is achieved by placing windows, doors and ventilators to allow maximum airflow. Windows opposite each other provide good ventilation. Without fresh air, people may experience headaches, sleepiness and difficulty in concentration. Ventilation can be natural or mechanical (such as using an exhaust fan).
- **Cleanliness and Sanitary Conveniences** Occupants are responsible for general cleaning and up-keep of the building, but planning should include features that make cleaning easier and reduce dust. Sanitary conveniences must include bathrooms, toilets and lavatories. In rural homes, these are often built as separate units in the backyard or front yard to maintain hygiene and keep them away from other rooms.

- **Circulation** Air circulation between rooms is important. To ensure good circulation, each living space should have its own entry through a shared area. This also ensures privacy for the occupants.
- **Practical Considerations** When planning spaces, consider practical factors like the strength and stability of the structure, the comfort and convenience for the family, simplicity, aesthetics and plans for future expansion. Don't compromise on building's strength to reduce costs.
- **Elegance** It refers to the overall effect of the space layout. A good space plan should be visually appealing while still being economical.

Quick Test 2

1. State two pinciples of space planning?
2. Mention one step that help ensure internal privacy?
3. How is good ventilation achieved?
4. What helps in maintaining hygiene in the house?

Mind Map

RESOURCE AVAILABILITY AND MANAGEMENT

1 Time

Time Management
- Time is limited and irreversible, So, it is important to manage it properly.
- To be successful it is essential to develop time management skills.
- Effective time management means focusing on getting results instead of just staying busy.
- Time management starts with planning.

Steps of Time and Activity Plan
- Start your work as quickly as possible.
- Get into a routine every day.
- Prioritise your tasks.
- Do not take responsibility for low priority tasks.
- Divide big tasks into a series of activities.
- Do not waste energy and time.
- Do one thing at a time.
- Set start and end times.

Tips for Effective Time Management
- Create a simple "To Do" List.
- Daily/weekly planner.
- Long term planner.

Tools in Time Management

Peak Load Period
- Maximum load of work during a specific period of time.
- **For example** morning time.

Work Curve
- Graphical representation of work.
- This shows how work varies over time.

Rest Period
- These are unproductive interruption of working time.
- Neither too long nor too short.

Work Simplification
- Means finding the easiest way to do tasks.

Levels to Improve Work Processes and Simplify Task
- **Changes to improve hand and body motions**
  - Eliminating steps
  - Improving sequences
  - Skill development
  - Better posture
- **Changes in Work Spaces and Equipment**
  - Organise storage area
  - Rearrange tools
- **Changes in End Products**
  - Use different row materials
  - Changes in both the raw materials and finished products.

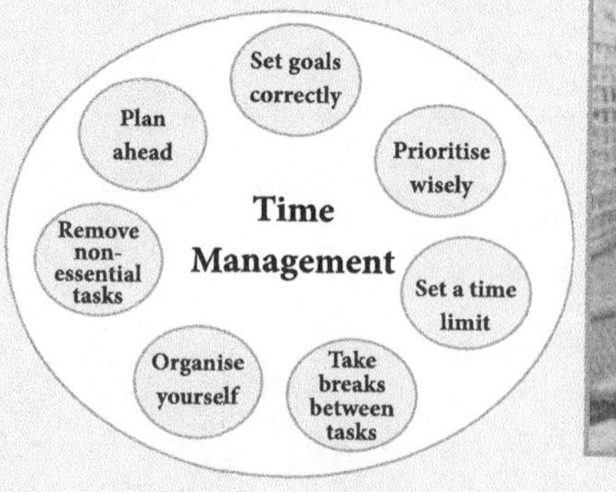

Time Management

2 Space Management

It involves
- Planning of Space
- Organising it as per the plan
- Implement the plan
- Evaluate the plan

Well managed space provides comfort and looks attractive.

Principles of Space Planning

Aspect
- Proper placement of doors and windows for light and air.

Prospect
- Focuses on visual appeal of house.

Privacy
- **Internal** Separate rooms with doors.
- **External** Use trees, plants for privacy.

Grouping
- Place related rooms near each other.

Roominess
- Means the spacious feel of a room.

Furniture Requirements
- Room should be planned with necessary furniture only.

Sanitation
- It provides adequate light, ventilation etc.

Circulation
- Air circulation is important.

Practical Considerations
- While planning space, consider practical factors like strength and stability.

Elegance
- Overall effect of the space layout.
- Good space plan should be visually appealing.

External Privacy- A House Secured by Fence and shrubs.

NCERT Folder

1. Describe time and space resources.

Ans. Both time and space resources can be used to achieve goals. They are assets for everyone to utilise. These resources are rarely in abundant supply and are also not equally available to everyone.

While time is limited and irreversible, space is limited by financial and other constraints. We cannot stop time or change its speed of passing. Once passed, time can never be regained.

On the other hand, space is used to carry out various activities at home, outside the home and at the workplace.

2. Why is time management necessary?

Ans. An effective time management is crucial as in today's fast changing world, our responsibilities at home, school and work has increased. People who use time management techniques are not only successful but also high achievers at all stages of life.

All aspects of personal and professional life require one to possess time management skills. These skills not only increase productivity but also ensure that one takes adequate rest and recreation along with work.

3. Discuss the steps in a time and activity plan.

Ans. The steps to be followed in a time and activity plan are

(i) Starting work as quickly as possible without wasting time in avoiding or delaying task.

(ii) Getting into a routine everyday. A time must be chosen to accomplish certain tasks, and then an individual should stick to the routine activities.

(iii) Prioritising your tasks. Any new task should not impact the already existing activities. Do not take too many activities at a particular time. Complete compulsory activities first and keep the optional tasks for a later time.

(iv) Do not commit yourself to unimportant and low priority tasks. Learn to say 'No'.

(v) Dividing the big tasks into a series of small manageable activities.

(vi) Energy and time should not be wasted on tasks which do not need much attention.

(vii) Completing one task at a time. Do not put it aside before completion.

(viii) Allot appropriate time to each subject. Arrange 'start' and 'stop' times to schedule activities.

(ix) Making a schedule of activities and tasks helps in effectively managing time allocated to each task. A proper time schedule should be prepared for the entire day, and must include leisure time.

4. What are the tools in time management?

Ans. For answer refer to text under the heading 'Tools in Time Management' on page no. 134 and 135.

5. Define space management. Discuss the principles of planning space inside the home.

Ans. Space management is the planning of space, organising it as per the plan, implementing the plan in terms of its utilisatioin and evaluating it in terms of achieving functionality and aesthetic appeal. The principles of planning space inside the home are

(i) **Aspect** The arrangement of doors and windows in the external walls of a building to allow the occupants to enjoy sunshine, breeze, etc.

(ii) **Prospect** The outside appearance of home and its impression on an onlooker. It includes its natural beauty, positioning of door and windows, etc.

(iii) **Privacy** Internal privacy is privacy of one room from another. External privacy means privacy of the entire house from the neighbouring buildings or houses, public streets, lanes, etc.

(iv) **Grouping** It is the placement of the rooms within the house in relation to each other.

(v) **Roominess** It is the effect of spaciousness that a room gives to those who live in it. It can be created by fully utilising the available space or changing the size and shape of the room, the furniture arrangement and the colour scheme used.

(vi) **Requirement of Furniture** Rooms should be planned keeping in mind the furniture to be placed in them. Only the required furniture should be placed to allow free space for movement.

(vii) **Sanitation** It means providing the conveniences of light, ventilation, cleanliness and sanitary conveniences like provision of bathrooms, water closets and lavatories in a house to maintain hygiene.

(viii) **Circulation** Good air circulation can be ensured by providing an independent entry to each living space through a common space like a lobby or passage. It gives privacy to members.

(ix) **Practical Considerations** While planning the house, one should consider strength and stability of the structure, convenience and comfort for the family, simplicity, beauty and provision for expansion in future.

(x) **Elegance** The effect produced by the general layout of the plan. So, the space plan should be aesthetically appealing.

Exam Pattern Questions

Objective Type Questions

Multiple Choice Questions (MCQs)

1. Find the incorrect statement. **Competency Based Que**

(a) We should create a daily routine and set specific times for school work and household tasks.
(b) Dividing big tasks into a series of small manageable activities is helpful in time planning.
(c) Giving proper time to low priority activities helps manage our time well.
(d) Preparing a schedule for activities and tasks help in effectively managing time allocated to each tasks.

2. Zeenath is following the time management steps. She just made a list of her tasks and estimated how much time they will take. What should she do next? **Competency Based Que**

(a) She should take a break and eat a snack.
(b) She should organise her tasks alphabetically.
(c) She should cross off tasks that she doesn't want to do right away.
(d) She should prioritise her tasks, or put them in order of importance.

3. Time plans are made according to the individual needs of a person. This is because ....

(a) every individual has different time planners.
(b) every individual has different week planners.
(c) every individual has different thinking.
(d) every individual has different goals and requirements, and different routines.

4. Space must be planned for its optimal utilisation. Choose the correct reason for the given statement.

(a) To make it look cluttered
(b) To make it comfortable
(c) To make it look attractive
(d) Both (b) and (c)

5. Which of the following would help a small room feel larger?

(a) Use cool light colours
(b) Use large furniture, patterns and textures
(c) Use rough textures
(d) Place lighting as one chandelier

6. Read the following statements and identify the true one(s)? **Competency Based Que**

I. Time management means always doing more than one task at the same time.
II. Good time management means never taking breaks.
III. Time management is about planning to get tasks done and doing them.
IV. One way to manage your time well is to ignore deadlines and focus on doing the most fun activities.

Codes

(a) I and II (b) Only III
(c) II and IV (d) Only I

7. Which of the following shows the steps for time management in the correct order?

I. Make a schedule; Estimate how long each task will take; Prioritise; Make a list of everything that you have to do and want to do.
II. Make a list of everything that you have to do and want to do; Estimate how long each task will take; Prioritise: Make a schedule. **Competency Based Que**

Codes

(a) Only II
(b) Only I
(c) Both I and II
(d) Neither I nor II

8. Match the following.

	Principles of space planning		Meaning
A.	Aspect	1.	Placement of the rooms within house
B.	Prospect	2.	It includes light, cleanliness, ventilation
C.	Sanitation	3.	It is the look of house from outside
D.	Grouping	4.	Arrangement of doors/windows.

Codes

	A	B	C	D		A	B	C	D
(a)	1	2	3	4	(b)	2	3	4	1
(c)	4	3	2	1	(d)	3	1	4	2

Assertion-Reason Questions

Direction (Q. Nos.9-10) In the questions given below, there are two statements marked as Assertion (A) and Reason (R). Read the statements and choose the correct option.

Codes

(a) Both A and R are true and R is the correct explanation of A.
(b) Both A and R are true, but R is not the correct explanation of A.
(c) A is true, but R is false.
(d) A is false, but R is true.

9. Assertion (A) Managing time is a specialised skill required by everyone.
Reason (R) Time management is necessary to achieve goals in professional and personal lives.

10. Assertion (A) The house should be designed in such a way that it is hidden from neighbouring buildings, houses, lanes and streets.
Reason (R) Privacy of one room from another is referred to as internal privacy.

Case Based Questions

11. Read the passage given below and answer the following questions.

It is the spacious effect a room gives to those who live in it. The available space should be fully used. For example, one can have built-in wall cupboard, shelves and storage area so that the floor of the room is left free for various activities. In addition, the size and shape of the room, the furniture arrangement as well as the colour scheme used have a bearing on its roominess. Well proportionate rectangular room looks spacious compared to a square room of similar dimensions. Light colours make a room look more spacious than dark ones.

(i) If the room is painted dark violet colour with a sofa set, one chair, one dressing table, two wardrobes, what impression will the room give?

(a) Spacious (b) Elegant
(c) Well-designed (d) Cluttered

(ii) When designing the layout of rooms, the kitchen should be ....

(a) near the toilet
(b) near the dining table
(c) near the drawing room
(d) near the bedroom

(iii) The size and shape of the room has a bearing on its roominess. Which type of rooms look bigger?

(a) Rectangular shaped
(b) Square shaped
(c) Taper from inside
(d) Broad from inside

(iv) Assertion (A) The room should look bigger and well-designed even if it is small in size.
Reason (R) Only dark colour schemes should be used in bedrooms.

Codes

(a) Both A and R are true and R is the correct explanation of A.
(b) Both A and R are true, but R is not the correct explanation of A.
(c) A is true, but R is false.
(d) A is false, but R is true.

Answers

1. (c) Giving proper time to low priority activities helps manage our time well.
2. (d) She should prioritise her tasks, or put them in order of importance.
3. (d) every individual has different goals and requirements, and different routines
4. (d) Both (b) and (c)
5. (a) Use cool light colours
6. (b) Only III
7. (a) Only II
8. (c) 4 3 2 1
9. (a) Both A and R are true and R is the correct explanation of A
10. (d) A is false, but R is true
11. (i) (d) Cluttered
(ii) (b) near the dining table
(iii) (a) Rectangular shaped
(iv) (c) A is true, but R is false

Subjective Questions

Very Short Answer Type Questions

1. What happens if we do not properly manage the time available to us?

Ans. If we do not manage the time properly, we won't be able to complete all the tasks to be done in a day, we will feel fatigued and stressed.

2. Why should we develop time management skills?

Ans. We should develop time management skills because, in today's fast changing lifestyle, our demands and responsibilities at home, at school and at work have increased.

By using these skills, we can become high achievers in both our professions and our personal lives, besides having adequate time for rest and recreation.

3. How do we prioritise our tasks in a time and activity plan?

Ans. In a time and activity plan, we prioritise our tasks by first grouping them into compulsory activities and optional activities. First, we complete the compulsory activities. Then, if time permits, we take up the optional activities for completion.

4. Why and how should we control the break periods while performing tasks?

Ans. We should control the break periods while performing tasks because they are unproductive interruptions of working time.

We can control them by ensuring that their frequency is less and their duration is neither too long nor too short.

5. What is the objective of work simplification?

Ans. The objective of work simplification is either accomplishing more work in a given amount of time and energy, or reducing the amount of time and/or energy used to accomplish a given amount of work.

6. What kind of posture should we adopt for doing domestic tasks to ensure that our muscles get less strained?

Ans. The kind of posture we should adopt for doing domestic tasks to ensure that our muscles get less strained is one in which we keep our body parts in alignment and carry the maximum weight on our bony framework.

7. Give one example each of eliminating work processes and combining them.

Ans. The examples are

(i) **Eliminating** Allowing washed dishes to dry on utensil racks eliminates the process of drying them by wiping.

(ii) **Combining** Listing all the items required from the market and buying them together combines the processes of buying each item separately as and when its requirement occurs.

8. What is the difference between external and internal privacy as a principle of space planning?

Ans. Internal privacy means maintaining privacy of one room from another through suitable grouping, positioning of doors, provision of a small corridor or lobby, or by installing screens and curtains.

However, external privacy means privacy of the entire house from the neighbouring buildings or houses, public streets, lanes, etc. which can be achieved through suitably locating the entrance to the house and covering it suitably.

9. What are the important things to be kept in mind while explaining the following?

(i) Kitchen **(ii) Bedroom**
(iii) Meeting

Ans. The following essential things should be kept in mind while explaining.

(i) Kitchen-Lighting and ventilation.

(ii) Bedroom-Privacy and furniture as required.

(iii) Meeting-Furniture and openness.

10. How can good air circulation in the design of a house be ensured?

Ans. Good air circulation in the design of a house can be ensured by providing an independent entry to each living space through a common space like a lobby or passage.

11. What is ventilation as a principle of space planning? What difficulties will the occupants of a house face if the house is not well-ventilated?

Ans. Ventilation as a principle of space planning is the supply of the outside air into the rooms.

It affects the comfort of the occupants in the house; so if the house is not well-ventilated, the occupants will experience headaches, sleepiness, inability to focus attention, etc.

12. What practical considerations should be there in planning a house?

Ans. The practical considerations which should be there in planning a house are strength and stability of the structure, convenience and comfort for the family, simplicity, beauty and provision for expansion in future.

Short Answer Type Questions

1. Effective time management enhances resource utilisation. **Competency Based Que**

(i) What is the primary goal of effective time management?

(ii) Why is effective time management crucial?

Ans. (i) The primary goal of effective time management is to achieve more with the same time and energy. This involves prioritising tasks, minimising waste, and maximising productivity. By doing so, individuals can optimise their resources, reduce stress, and accomplish their objectives efficiently.

(ii) Effective time management is crucial because it enables individuals to prioritise tasks, manage stress, and increase productivity. Proper time management helps allocate sufficient time for tasks, avoids procrastination and enhances focus. This leads to better work quality, improved work-life balance and increased overall well-being.

2. Rohan, a Class 11 student, has multiple assignments due soon and wants to manage his time efficiently. **Competency Based Que**

(i) What tool can Rohan use to prioritise his tasks?

(ii) How can Rohan ensure he completes his tasks on time?

(iii) What benefits will Rohan gain from effective time management?

Ans. (i) Rohan can use a 'To-Do' list to prioritise his tasks effectively. This involves listing all tasks, ranking them based on importance and urgency, and breaking down larger tasks into manageable chunks. By doing so, Rohan can visualise his workload, focus on critical tasks, and make timely progress.

(ii) Rohan can create a daily/weekly planner to schedule his tasks and allocate sufficient time for each. This planner should account for task duration, breaks and contingencies. By scheduling tasks and setting realistic deadlines, Rohan can stay organised, avoid last-minute rushes and maintain consistent productivity.

(iii) Rohan will gain numerous benefits from effective time management, including reduced stress, increased productivity and improved academic performance.

Effective time management will also enable Rohan to develop essential life skills, such as prioritisation, organisation and self-discipline.

3. Arjun, a graduate student in Chennai, juggles coursework, part-time work and family responsibilities. He often feels stressed about managing his time effectively. Suggest him tips for effective time management. **Competency Based Que**

Ans. Some tips for effective time management that Arjun can implement are as follows

(i) **Create a 'To Do' List** Arjun should start each day by listing all his tasks. This helps him prioritise activities based on deadlines and importance, providing clarity on what needs to be done.

(ii) **Use a Daily/Weekly Planner** He can allocate specific time slots for studying, work and family activities. This structured approach allows him to visualise his day and manage his time effectively.

(iii) **Implement a Long-Term Planner** By maintaining a monthly chart, Arjun can track important deadlines, exams and personal commitments. This will remind him to plan ahead and ensure he dedicates time for relaxation and self-care.

4. What is time management? Give examples of following compulsory activities: daily, weekly, monthly and annual. List the tools required in time management.

Ans. The ability to use one's time effectively or productively, at work, home or other places is called time management.

Examples of compulsory activities are

(i) **Daily Activities** Dusting and cleaning of house, school assignments, cooking, resting, etc.

(ii) **Weekly Activities** Washing clothes, ironing clothes, buying grocery, etc.

(iii) **Monthly Activities** Paying bills (electricity, water, etc.), rearranging cupboards.

(iv) **Annual Activities** Final examination, annual school events, health check-ups, etc.

The tools required in time management are

(i) Peak load (ii) Work curve

(iii) Rest periods (iv) Work simplifications

5. Briefly explain the three levels of changes important in work simplification.

Ans. The three levels of changes important in work simplification are

(i) **Change in Hand and Body Motions** While keeping the same work tools and product. This can be done by eliminating and combining certain process, by improving the sequence and rhythm of work, by developing skills at work and by improving body posture.

(ii) **Change in Work, Storage Space and Equipment** It involves organising storage spaces, rearranging kitchen equipment, planning work surfaces with proper height and width according to the user, using labour-saving devices like pressure cookers, washing machines, etc., which help in saving time as well as hand motions.

(iii) **Change in the End Product** These changes result from the use of different raw materials, making different products from same raw materials and changes in both the raw material and finished product.

6. How do good standing and sitting postures help in work simplification?

Ans. Both good standing and sitting postures help in work simplification in the following manner

(i) Good standing posture is one in which the head, neck, chest and abdomen are balanced one upon the other, so that the weight is carried mainly by the bony framework and minimum effort and strain is placed upon the muscles and ligaments. Thus, work can be done easily and effectively. For example, using a long-handled mop instead of sitting and mopping the floor.

(ii) Good sitting posture for work is a well-balanced and poised position. The weight is carried by the bony support of the skeleton thus releasing the muscles and nerves of all strain. The poise is such that as much adjustment is done as is necessary to carry out the work. Sitting in an upright position prevents back pain and helps in working efficiently.

Long Answer Type Questions

1. Ria, a Class 11 student, wants to excel in her studies while also participating in extracurricular activities. She has limited time and space to manage her study materials, assignments and personal belongings. Ria's room is small and she shares it with her younger sister.

Competency Based Que

(i) How can Ria effectively manage her time to balance studies and extracurricular activities?

(ii) What space management principles can Ria apply to optimize her small room?

Ans. (i) Ria can effectively manage her time by

- Creating a daily/weekly planner to schedule study sessions, assignments, and extracurricular activities.
- Prioritising tasks based on importance and urgency.
- Allocating specific times for studying, relaxation, and leisure activities.
- Setting realistic goals and deadlines.
- Avoiding procrastination and minimising distractions.

(ii) Ria can apply the following space management principles

- **Grouping** Organise study materials, books and personal belongings into categories.
- **Roominess** Use built-in cupboards, shelves and storage areas to keep the floor clear.
- **Furniture Requirements** Arrange essential furniture to allow for easy movement and circulation.
- **Sanitation** Ensure adequate light, ventilation and cleanliness.
- **Practical Considerations** Consider comfort, convenience, simplicity and future expansion.

By implementing these time and space management strategies, Ria can efficiently utilise her resources, achieve her goals and maintain a comfortable and organised living space.

2. Explain four changes we should make in work, storage space and equipment to improve our time management in the kitchen.

Ans. Four changes we should make in work, storage space and equipment in the kitchen are

(i) **Organising Storage Spaces** All ingredients commonly used in cooking any dish should be placed near to the cooking area so that they can be reached without effort. Other items used in larger quantities like flour, various dals and rice may be stored farther away, as they are needed only once in a cooking cycle.

(ii) **Rearranging Kitchen Equipment** The utensils and cutlery used for cooking should be stored near the cooking area.
Other equipment not used frequently like mixers, ovens refrigerators, etc. may be placed farther away.

(iii) **Planning Work Surfaces** All work surfaces should be according to their function. Thus, a surface used for cutting vegetables and other ingredients must be hard and should not get easily damaged by knife marks.

(iv) **Using Labour-saving Devices** We should use items like mixer-grinder, microwave oven and other similar equipment to save time and manual labour.

SELF ASSESSMENT TEST

Objective Type Questions

1. .... is/are an assets for an individual.
   (a) Time
   (b) Space
   (c) Resources
   (d) Both (a) and (b)
2. What is useful to plan monthly chart?
   (a) 'To Do' List
   (b) Daily/weekly planner
   (c) Time Schedules
   (d) Long term planner
3. Unproductive interruptions of working time is defined as?
   (a) Work Curve
   (b) Break Period
   (c) Peak Period
   (d) Work Simplification

Very Short Answer Type Questions

4. How can we ensure optimum utilisation of resources?
5. What is the basic concept in time management?

Short Answer Type Questions

6. Suggest a format for a 'To Do' list, explaining how each column of the list is to be filled up.
7. Define the term 'work simplification'. What does it imply?
8. Describe three principles of space planning.

Long Answer Type Questions

9. Explain each of the four tools used in time management in one or two sentences each.
10. You are a Class XI student in a city who wants to improve her/his time management skills so that you get more time to study besides doing your homework. What are five important questions you should ask yourself so that you can modify your activities based on the answers to these questions? Write all the steps involved in planning time and activity. **Competency Based Que**

08

CHAPTER

Survival means to stay alive, in spite of difficult situations. It is important to maintain life functions for growth and development.

▼ YOUR STUDY GOALS

8.1 Meaning fo Survival
8.2 Growth and Development
8.3 Good Nutrition
8.4 Stages in Development
8.5 Development Across Stages

▼ YOUR PRACTICE GOAL

- Objective Type Questions (20 Qs ; MCQs, A-R, Matching, Case Based)
- Subjective Questions (11 VSAs, 7 SAs, 7 LAs)

Survival Growth and Development

8.1 Meaning of Survival

Survival primarily means remaining alive and maintaining essential life functions. It includes the ability to remain alive in various situations.

For children, survival is closely linked to access to proper care, adequate nutrition and protection from diseases. While many children may survive under basic conditions, their well-being requires more comprehensive support.

Challenges in Low-Income Families

- Children from low-income families face more survival challenges. They require sufficient nutritious food to support their growth and development.
- **Immunisation**[1] against common childhood diseases such as tuberculosis, whooping cough, diphtheria, polio, tetanus, malaria and pneumonia is essential to ensure their health and survival.
- According to a **UNICEF report (2007)**, approximately 9.2 million children worldwide may die before reaching five years of age, with three million of these children located in South Asia. Many of these deaths occur from preventable or treatable conditions, including pneumonia and **diarrhea**[2] diseases.

1 Immunisation The process of becoming immune to a disease through vaccines.

2 Diarrhea Relating to the frequent discharge of watery feces.

- Malnutrition contributes to over a third of these deaths, while diarrheal diseases account for 17 per cent (2 million) of deaths among children under five years of age worldwide. Thus, it is becoming the second most common **cause of child deaths** worldwide.
- Child mortality[3] is intricately linked to poverty. Inadequate income often leads to a lack of essential services, compromising children's health and survival. This issue is prevalent not only in developing countries but also among marginalised communities in more advanced nations.
- Addressing these challenges requires improvements in public health services, including access to safe water and better sanitation. Education, particularly for girls and mothers, plays a crucial role in enhancing child survival rates.
- It's essential to recognise that just survival is not enough; growth and development are also important for a child's overall well-being. A child can only grow properly when they have enough important resources around them. If a child doesn't grow as expected, it is called **growth failure.**

8.2 Growth and Development

- Development can be defined as the **gradual and organised** emergence of physical structures, psychological[4] traits, behaviours and ways of thinking that help a child adapt to life's demands.
- Growth focuses mainly on physical changes, development occurs across various dimensions simultaneously. For example, an infant's cognitive abilities develop as they learn to form relationships, understand emotions and communicate with increasingly complex sentences.
- While the terms 'growth' and 'development' are often used interchangeably, they refer to different processes.
  - **Growth** Specifically means changes in size or quantity. It is only a **quantitative change,** such as increases in weight, height and the size of internal organs. It is primarily about measurable physical changes. For example, a child grows in height and weight, which can be easily observed and quantified.
  - **Development** It is qualitative and quantitative change and it refers to changes in form, complexity and function of body parts. For instance, an infant progresses from raising their head to rolling over, sitting up, crawling, walking and eventually running. These changes indicate development.

The following characteristics of development are

- **Progressive Development** leads to the acquisition of more complex and refined skills over time.
- **Orderly Development** follows a specific sequence, where each stage builds on the previous one. No stage can occur before the earlier one is established.
- **Multifaceted Development** takes place in many areen at the same time period. For example physical development, cognitive development, psychological development etc.

Simultaneous Nature of Growth and Development

- Growth and development occur together and continue over many years.
- As a child grows, their organs increase in size and improve in function.
- This process continues through the school years and into adolescence until they reach full adult size and capability.

Areas of Development

Development is categorised in different fields that is why we call it **multi-dimensional**

- **Physical Development** This refers to the changes in size, structure and proportion of the body that occur from conception onward. It encompasses overall physical growth.

3 Mortality The state of being subject to death; death rate.
4 Psychological Relating to the mind; affecting mental processes and behaviour.

- **Motor Development** This involves gaining control over body movements, leading to improved co-ordination among various body parts. While physical growth increases body size, motor development focuses on achieving **smooth and effective movements.** The control over movements is brought about by control over the movement of the muscles of the body. Motor development is of two types depending upon the muscles involved in the movement. They are
  - **Gross Motor Development** This deals with the control of large muscle groups, such as those in the shoulders and thighs. It enables actions like sitting, bending, walking and moving the arms.
  - **Fine Motor Development** This refers to the control of smaller and fine muscles, such as those in the wrists and fingers. It facilitates skills like writing, turning pages and other precise tasks.
- **Cognitive Development** It refers to **emergence of thinking capabilities** in a child at the time of his/her birth.
  - As a person grows, his/her ways of thinking changes due to the changes in mental structures and understanding of experiences.
  - For example, when an object is taken away from an infant's view, the infant acts as though the object no longer exists. It is only during the second half of the second year of life that the infant begins to understand that objects continue to exist even when they are not visible.
- **Sensory Development** This refers to the development of the **five senses:** vision, hearing, smell, touch and taste in a child.
  - Infants are born with relatively well-developed sensory abilities, which refine and improve as they grow.
  - For example, a newborn can best focus on faces and objects that are about eight inches away. Over time, a child's visual skills develop, allowing them to focus on objects regardless of their distance.
- **Language Development** It refers to the changes which enables a child to understand what others are saying and to form and speak complex sentences on his or her own.
- **Social Development** This area focuses on the skills that help individuals behave in accordance with **societal expectations** and **maintain relationships** with others. It involves understanding social norms and interactions.
- **Emotional Development** This refers to the development of emotions and learning socially acceptable ways to express them. It is important to recognise that all areas of development are simply different aspects of personal development.
- Personal development involves understanding oneself, including one's talents, skills and future ambitions.

  For example, when a child learns to ride a bicycle, there is a physical skill involved, but there is also an emotional aspect, such as fear or excitement, that should be taken into account during the teaching process.

Quick Test 1

1. What is the second most common cause of child deaths?
2. Define development.
3. Give two examples of fine motor skill.
4. Which five senses are involved in sensory development?

8.3 Good Nutrition

Good nutrition is essential for children's growth and development. The nutritional needs increase as children reach school age. From around age 10, boys and girls have different nutrient requirements.

Stages of Childhood Development

According to the **Indian Council of Medical Research (ICMR),** childhood can be divided into different stages based on nutrient needs. Stuges of child development is as follows

Stage I **Infancy** Birth to 6 months and 6 to 12 months

Stage II **Preschool Years** 1 to 3 years and 4 to 6 years

Stage III **School Years** 7 to 9 years and 10 to 12 years

Indicators of Health

- Normal growth is often seen as a sign of good health, but it alone is not enough to guarantee a child's overall well-being.
- To ensure children meet their development milestones, they need a variety of resources and conditions, including
  - A stimulating environment
  - Adequate breast milk
  - A safe and hygienic living space
  - Access to proper healthcare
  - Avoidance by the mother of habits such as smoking or drinking.
- When children's physical needs are met and their surroundings support healthy development, they tend to grow similarly during the first five years. In India, children from wealthy families often grow similarly to those in developed countries, especially if their parents are well-educated.
- However, problems like diseases, infections and insufficient food can hinder growth.

Growth Monitoring

- Growth charts are commonly used worldwide to track children's growth. A normal growth curve should **move upward**. If conditions like giving a safe and healthy environment, providing nutritious food etc are fulfilled on time then the growth of a child will happen normally and he will learn new skills and live a healthy life and on the other hand if there are issues, the growth curve may
  - **Flatten**- indicating growth has stopped.
  - **Move downward**- showing declining growth.
  - **Move upwards** - shows that growth is taking place.

With extra food and treatment for infections, growth can start to improve again. This is known as catch-up growth.

▲ *Growth Charts*

8.4 Stages in Development

- In child development, the lifespan is divided into stages based on developmental milestones. These milestones are specific skills or tasks that most children are expected to achieve within certain age ranges.
- Development can be measured against these milestones to see if a child's growth is on track for their age.
- The five stages of the human lifespan are
  - (i) **Infancy** Birth to 2 years
  - (ii) **Early Childhood (Pre-school Years)** 2 to 6 years
  - (iii) **Middle Childhood** 6 to 11 years
  - (iv) **Adolescence** 11 to 18 years
  - (v) **Adulthood** 18 years and older

Neonate

The term 'neonate' refers to a newborn baby in the first month of life. Although neonates are completely helpless and dependent on adults, they possess several capabilities that help them adapt to their environment. Their awareness can be seen in two ways

(i) Reflexes

- Newborns are born with certain actions that assist in their survival until; they develop motor skills.
- Reflexes are simple, automatic responses to specific types of stimulation and do not require higher brain functions.
- Examples of reflexes include
  - **Eye Blink Reflex** When something is near to the eye then, our eyelid automatically blinks.
  - **Sucking Reflex** Helps in feeding.
  - **Elimination Reflex** Aids in urination and bowel movements.

(ii) Sensory Capabilities

- **Vision** It is the most developed sense at birth. A neonate can distinguish between light and dark and actively seeks light. If we show any thing to a child he can move his eyes very fast
  - They can follow moving objects with their eyes and focus best on objects about 8 inches away.
  - Newborns are especially inclined to focus on human faces.
- **Hearing** Newborns are very responsive to sounds, particularly human voices, more than any other sounds.
- **Touch** They respond well to touch and can differentiate between pleasant and unpleasant smells.
- **Taste** Neonates can distinguish between basic tastes: sweet, sour, salty, and bitter.
- **Sleep Patterns** Newborns sleep for about 16 to 18 hours a day in phases. They often enjoy interaction with caregivers.
- **Communication** Crying is the primary way for newborns to communicate. There are different types of cries indicate various needs, such as hunger, anger, pain or discomfort. Caregivers typically learn to recognise the reasons behind the infant's cries.

Quick Test 2

1. Which age group is included in the pre-school years?
2. What does flattening in growth curve indicate?
3. Define the term 'neonate'.
4. Give one example by reflexes.

8.5 Development Across Stages

Development occurs across various domains. There are infancy, early childhood, middle childhood and adolescence.

Physical and Motor Development

Increase in Height and Weight

The most significant growth in height and weight happens during the **prenatal period** when a single cell develops into a fetus, reaching about 20 inches in length and weighing around 2.5 to 3 kg.

- By six months of age, an infant typically doubles their birth weight. By their first birthday, an infant's weight is usually three times what it was at birth.

- The next period of rapid growth occurs during infancy, with most infants weighing between 8 to 9 kg by the time they turn one year old.

Weight for Age

Age Range	Girls (kg)	Boys (kg)
0-2 years	3.2-11.5	3.3 - 12.2
2-5 years	11.7-18.2	12.4-18.3
5-6 years	18.3-20.2	18.5-20.5
6-7 years	20.3-22.4	20.7-22.9
7-8 years	22.6-25.0	23.1-25.4
8-9 years	25.3-28.2	25.6-28.1
9-10 years	28.5-31.9	28.3-31.2

Height for Age

Age Range	Girls (cms)	Boys (cms)
2.5 years	85.7-109.4	87.1- 110.0
5-8 years	109.6-126.6	110.3 -127.3
8-11 years	127.0-145.0	127.7 -143.1
11-14 years	145.5-159.8	143.6-163.2
14-17 years	160.0-162.9	163.7-175.2
17-19 years	162.9-163.2	175.3-176.5

Motor Development

- Motor development refers to the changes in a child's ability to control their body movements. Gross motor development (e.g., use of arms and legs) precedes the development of fine motor skills (e.g., holding a glass in one hand).
- Progress in motor development occurs within a certain age range rather than during specific months. If a child does not achieve multiple milestones within the expected age range, it may be a cause for concern. A table of important motor milestones in the first 10 years of childhood is typically used to track progress.

Motor Development Milestones

Age	Nature of Milestone
Birth-3 months	▪ Lifting and holding the head
Newborn	▪ Newborns can move their head from side to side slightly
1 month	▪ They can raise their head
2 months	▪ They can also lift their chest while lying on stomach (prone position)
3 months	▪ The infant begins to hold her/his head, and this is a major milestone in development. If the child is unable to do this even by the age of 6 months. It shows that there is delay in development
4-6 months	▪ Can roll over from back to stomach and stomach to back
6-8 months	▪ Sitting with adult support or in a seat with straps ▪ Sitting without support
8-9 months	▪ **Crawling** However, some children do not crawl and directly learn to stand after being able to sit ▪ **Standing** If supported or by holding on to something
10 - 11 months	▪ Can pull up from sitting position to standing; standing independently briefly

12 - 18 months	▪ Walking; initially the child's walk is unsteady but gradually it becomes steady ▪ Running; after the child learns to walk, she/he begins to run, failing down often. As the balance improves, she/he is able to run in a more co-ordinated manner without falling frequently by the age of 2 years
18 - 24 months	▪ Climbing stairs/steps by placing both feet on each step, if hand held by someone
2 years	▪ Walking backwards, goes down slide, climbs ladder ▪ Jumping from low platform with both feet
3 years	▪ Can balance on one foot ▪ Can kick large ball ▪ Can throw and catch a ball
3 - 4 years	▪ Can walk upstairs with alternating feet as adults do, by holding onto something
5 years	▪ Skipping and pedalling a tricycle
6 years	▪ Well co-ordinated hopping, jumping and climbing
7 years	▪ Balancing and pedalling a bicycle
8-10 years	▪ Has balance, co-ordination and strength that allows child to participate in various games and gymnastic

Language Development

- Almost every species on Earth has a way to communicate. **Honey Bees** perform dances to show other bees the direction and distance of food and threats. **Birds** use special chirps and shrieks to communicate the location of their nests.
- Human communication differs from that of other species.
  - Animals primarily have **inborn communication patterns** that are not influenced by experience.
  - Human infants are born with the ability to learn language, but their learning is influenced by their environment.
  - As they grow, humans can create an infinite number of original sentences.
  - Humans can discuss events and objects from different times and places, which is not possible for animals.
- The sounds made by the children in the first year of life, before they are able to speak words, are called **pre-linguistic sounds**. These noises include crying, cooing and babbling.
- As they reach the first year of age, most children acquire their first words and their language continues to develop rapidly. By the time they reach adolescence, their language becomes sophisticated and then vocabulary continues to develop throughout life. A key point is that children can understand more than they can express from day one. Comprehension **(receptive language)** comes before production **(expressive language)**.

Stages in Development of Language

- **Crying** It is the first form of a child's communication that is **innate or in-born**. This means that the child is not taught to cry, it is a sound an infant makes on his/her own.
- **Cooing** By the second month, children start cooing, making **vowel-like sounds** such as 'oooh' and 'aaah.' They make these sounds when they feel happy or content.
  - When the infant coos, parents respond by talking, smiling or imitating the sounds, then wait for the child to coo again. This creates the impression that the infant and the parents are 'talking' to each other.
  - Cooing decreases significantly by around 8 months.
- **Babbling** It consists of **consonant-vowel combinations** that create sounds like 'dadada' and 'mamama,' which infants start making around 6 months.

- These sounds resemble human speech, as infants can produce all the sounds found in different languages.
- Even deaf children, who cannot hear others speak, still babble. This indicates that this behaviour is innate.
- However, as children grow, they gradually drop sounds they do not hear in their environment. This shows that the environment plays a significant role in language learning.

- As the child reaches the age of one, he/she starts forming words. Around his/her first birthday, the child speaks out first word. By their first birthday, they typically say their first word, which they use consistently to refer to the same meaning. First words are usually brief, **consisting of one or two syllables,** such as 'papa,' 'amma,' or 'tata.'
- **The child's first words usually include** Names of people, animals and things (nouns), action words, like 'bye-bye' and expressive words, such as 'no' or 'namaste'. Sometimes, children use a word to refer to things or actions for which they do not yet have specific words.
- By 18 months, children typically produce around two dozen words. By the age of two, their vocabulary may expand to about 250 words and they continue to add hundreds of words each year.
- One or two word utterances from a child can express complete meanings. For example, if a child sees their mother and says 'mamma,' it may indicate that their mother is present or that they want to go to her. This type of simple speech, consisting of one or two words that convey full meanings, is known as **telegraphic speech.**
  - Between the ages of 2 and 3, children begin to learn grammatical forms. Their sentence structure expands to include words that were previously missing in telegraphic speech, such as articles, conjunctions and possessives.
  - By the age of 4, a child's language skills are well established.
  - By age 6, a child's vocabulary can reach around 10,000 words.
  - Between ages 7 and 9, children start to understand that words can have multiple meanings. They also begin to enjoy language-based jokes and riddles.

Quick Test 3

1. Give one example of gross motor development.
2. What milestone of development is achieved in 8-9 months of age?
3. Define the first stage of language development.
4. Which stage of language development consist consonant-vowel combination?

Social and Emotional Development

Early Relationships and Emotions

- From the very first day, infants show behaviours that lead to social and emotional responses from caregivers.
- Adults also show specific behaviour towards which the infants are attracted. Thus, both the caregivers and the children have behaviour that helps them interact with each other and develop attachment.

(i) Forming attachments

- The caregivers provide a lot of physical contact to the infant. Infants have the inborn need of physical contact and when the caregivers pick up the child, this need is fulfilled.
- Adults and older children use a special type of speech when talking to infants known as **motherese**. Such speech delights the infant and she/he responds by cooing and babbling.

- We smile at the infant and seeing us smile, the infant smiles back, coos and babbles. The mutual gazing between caregivers and infants helps in establishing a link between the two and is one of the first forms of socio-emotional interactions.
- Caregivers make facial expressions and also make rhythmic movements, while talking to an infant. This helps the baby to learn about various emotional expressions.
- Caregivers also play simple games with the infant when she/he is a little older, e.g. peek-a-boo is common in all cultures.
- Infants also initiate behaviours to make social contact. When infants cry in discomfort, the mother rushes towards him/her. When infants coo, babble, smile and gaze on their own initiative and these behaviours develop the sense of protection in caregivers.
- Frequent interactions between caregivers and infants help develop a strong bond of attachment.
- Usually, the mother primarily cares for the child, leading to the infant forming an attachment to her first, making this the **first social relationship**. If the interactions with the mother are not warm and pleasant, the infant may become irritable and anxious, making it hard to form a proper attachment.
- People can recover from early social deprivation if their environment improves and they find loving caregivers.
- Forming a secure attachment is a crucial developmental task in the first year of life, as it helps the child build trust in adults.
- In many families, due to the division of labour, the father often works outside the home and earn i.e. he is the breadwinner, while the mother spends more time with the children. This does not hurt the relationship between the child and the father.
- Research shows that the **quality of time** caregivers spend with children is more important than the quantity. Positive interactions help build a strong bond between caregivers and children.
- **A secure infant**
  - Cries less and is more co-operative with caregivers.
  - Does not cling to the caregiver out of fear and is willing to explore their surroundings.
  - As a pre-schooler, the secure child is emotionally warm, socially mature, popular with peers, curious and self-reliant.

(ii) Children's Emotions

- Infants experience various emotions like joy, distress, anger and rage. However, it can be difficult to understand their exact feelings just by looking at their facial expressions. Over time, these emotions become more specific, such as happiness, interest, excitement, sadness and fear.
- Around six months old, infants often develop a fear of strangers, which can make them cry when someone unfamiliar approaches. This is known as **stranger anxiety**.
  - Stranger anxiety peaks between 8 to 12 months and usually goes away by 15 to 18 months.
- Shortly after stranger anxiety, infants also develop a fear of being separated from their caregivers, known as **separation anxiety**. They may become upset when their mother is out of sight.
  - Separation anxiety peaks around 12 to 18 months and generally fades by 20 to 24 months.
- It's important to remember that not all children show the same emotions. Their feelings can vary based on past experiences, **temperament**[5], and the people around them.

Parents' Child Rearing Practices

- Parents' child-rearing practices refer to how they raise their children (upbringing). These practices have a significant impact on a child's personality. Children learn appropriate behaviours in their community through direct teaching or instructions from parents and by observing others.

5 Temperament It refers to an aspect of personality concerned with emotional reactions and their speed and intensity.

- This learning process by which children acquire behaviours, skills, values and beliefs that are important in their culture is known as **Socialisation**. The goals of socialisation can differ between cultures and families.
- Parents differ in how much warmth and affection they show to their children, with some being very warm and others more distant or cold. **'Warmth'** and **'coldness'** can be seen as two ends of a continuum, with most parents positioned at various points along this continuum.
- Parents also differ in **strict/permissive** or **lenient/restrictive**. Restrictive parents set many rules and closely monitor their child, while permissive parents set fewer rules and allow their child to make their own choices.
- Child-rearing practices can also be categorised by the type of discipline used. Some parents explain the consequences of actions and reason to their children. This affectionate and gentle approach is known as **affection-oriented disciplining**.
- Other parents may use commands to stop their child from behaving in a particular way and use threats, or physical punishment to discipline their children. This is referred to as **power-oriented disciplining.**
- Generally, when parents show the qualities they want their children to have and use explanations to point out desirable behaviour rather than punishment, it helps shape well-rounded personalities in children.

Relationship with Siblings and Peers

- Siblings play a significant role in each other's development. The responsibility of the younger child is often put on the elder sibling. As siblings are near in age to each other, the relationship between them is more equal, friendly and democratic as compared to that with parents. They often provide emotional support by playing, sharing and confiding in each other.
- Sibling relationships can also involve conflicts, competition and jealousy. It's important for parents to encourage a positive bond between siblings.
- As children grow, their friends or peers become more important. These friends can be close or not-so-close, but they play a key role in social development.
- Friendships with peers allow children to play, argue and share secrets, all of which contribute to their social and emotional growth.

Cognitive Development

- Cognitive development refers to how children's thinking or thought processes develop. It involves understanding, observation, language, concepts, memory, imagination, reasoning and judgment.
- Cognition is about how we understand the world around us. It involves how we receive, interpret and mentally represent information.
- Various mental processes involved in thinking are
  - **Discrimination** Recognising differences between things like tastes, colours, shapes and living and non-living things.
  - **Association** We associate certain emotions with certain experiences, certain people with a certain type of behaviour and certain behaviour with certain persons.
  - **Cause-Effect Relationships** Understanding that our actions have intentions and consequences.
  - **Problem Solving** Developing creativity and the ability to solve problems with time and age .
- Other cognitive processes include understanding relationships between objects, thinking about hypothetical situations and thinking abstractly about ideas and emotions.
- The study of cognitive development looks at how these mental processes grow from birth to maturity. **Jean Piaget** described different stages of cognitive development, noting that while some children may develop faster than others, the sequence of stages remains the same for all.

Stages of Cognitive Development

According to Piaget, there are four stages through which cognitive development proceeds.

(i) The Sensory Motor Stage (Birth Till 2 Years)

- During this period infants try to understand the world through their senses and through their motor capacities (i.e. actions). Therefore, the name sensori-motor period of development. Thus, infants understand the world on the basis of their actions on objects and people and how they appear to them.
- An infant knows a toy in terms of how it appears to his/her eyes and feels to his/her touch (sensory information) and that he/she can throw it, kick it, push it and bang it (motor actions). The infant does not yet understand the toy in terms of its properties as hard or soft, made of wood or metal, big or small, light or heavy. At this stage the child has many reflexes, including the sucking reflex.
- **By 2 Months** They start showing interest in their surroundings.
- **By 3 Months** Babies begin to understand what other people's actions mean. For example, a child understands that the mother will feed her/him by the specific gestures and actions the mother makes at the time of feeding.
- **4 to 8 Months** They learn that their actions can cause **things to happen**. For example, kicking a ball makes it move or dropping a toy makes a noise. This is the beginning of a cause and effect relationship.
- **8 to 12 Months** Babies start to intentionally perform actions. This means that she/he understands which action will have what effect and will be appropriate in a given situation.
- **12 to 18 Months** They experiment with different ways of doing things. He/she changes his/her actions to produce different results. For example, throwing a toy from different heights to see how it moves or sounds.
- **18 to 24 Months** An important development takes place the infant begins to form **mental images** of events, objects and people. An infant is able to form an idea in mind like a mental picture. This is called mental representation.

(ii) The Pre-operational Period (2-7 Years)

- During this age, children begin to develop concepts related to shape, space, size, time, distance, speed and number based on their environment.
- The term **'operation'** refers to mental acts in which objects are changed or transformed and can then be returned to their original states. This means that an action is **reversible**.
- For example, an individual can flatten a piece of clay and imagine it as a ball of clay to know that the amount of clay is the same in both. Such an activity is not possible for a child in this age group as he/she cannot yet mentally reverse an action and can only react to what he/she sees.

The key characteristics of pre-operational stage are as follow

- **Conservation** This refers to understanding that the amount of a substance remains the same, even if its shape changes or it is moved to a different container.
- **Seriation** It means performing the task of placing things in a serial order.
- **Taking Another Person's Perspective** Child focus on one aspect of a situation and can only understand it from their own viewpoint. They cannot grasp that others may see things differently.
- **Animism** When children believe everything has life in it, it is referred to as animism. They tend to believe the stories told to them as true.

(iii) The Concrete Operational Stage (7-11 Years)

- During middle childhood, children can now **mentally reverse actions** they've performed and can focus on multiple aspects of a problem at the same time. This means they can **conserve and seriate** with any materials or in any situation. At this stage, children become **less egocentric**. They start to understand that different people can see the same event in different ways based on their situations and values. This awareness helps them develop feelings of sympathy and empathy.
- Children also develop a stable understanding of numbers. They know what a specific number means and can count accurately without mistakes. Additionally, they understand that an object can belong to different categories depending on various criteria. This ability to classify things helps them develop logic as they grow into adulthood.

(iv) The Stage of Formal Operations (11-18 Years)

When a child reaches around 11 or 12 years old, they enter the adolescent stage. The main characteristics of this stage are

- **Abstract Thinking** Adolescents can think about abstract ideas, not just concrete things. They can understand complex concepts.
- **Reversible Thinking** They can apply their ability to think, reversible the ideas, allowing them to follow arguments from start to finish and back again.
- **Hypothetical Thinking** Adolescents start to explore hypothetical questions, like 'What would happen if...?' This ability leads them to **imagine** different possibilities and engage in elaborate fantasies, including ideas about changing the world. Their thinking can become **idealistic and utopian**. They become restless with the 'slow' pace they believe the older are moving with.
- **Logical Reasoning** Their thinking becomes more logical and systematic. Instead of just trying things out (trial and error), they consider different possible actions before deciding how to solve problems. This way of thinking is called **hypothetico-deductive reasoning**.
- **Meta-Thinking** Adolescents can reflect on their own thoughts and think about their thinking process. This is known as meta thinking.
- **Imaginary Audience** They often believe that others are watching them closely (imaginary audience), leading to a strong concern about their physical appearance.
- **Personal Fable** Adolescents may feel that they are unique and that no one else can truly understand what they are going through. This belief can make them feel special but also **isolated**[6].

Quick Test 4

1. What is the special type of speech used while talking to infants?
2. At what age the separation anxiety in children fades away?
3. Name the person who described four stages of cognitive development.
4. Mention two characteristics of the concrete operational stage.

6 **Isolated** Separated from others; alone, remote or lacking connection or support.

Mind Map

SURVIVAL GROWTH AND DEVELOPMENT

1 Survival

- Ability to remain alive in various situations.
- For children, it means proper care, nutrition and protection.

Challenges in Low - Income Families

- Children from low-income families face more survival challenges.
- Malnutrition is the second most cause of child death.
- Newborns are affected by some diseases like-Diphteria, Polio etc.

2 Growth and Development

Areas of Development

Physical Development

- Increase in height, weight and size of different organs.

Motor Development

- Grass motor development
- Fine motor development

Sensory Motor Development

- Development of senses like hearing, listening etc.

Cognitive Development

- Ability to think and understand

Language Development

- From crying to create sound and develop language.

Emotional Development

- Emotions like crying, smiling etc.

Social Development

- Behave as per the societal norms.

Nature of Growth and Development

Growth is Quantitative

- Increase height and weight
- Increase the size of internal organs.

Development is Qualitative

- From raising their head to rolling over, sitting then walking etc.

They both occur together and continue over many years.

3 Good Nutrition

Good Nutrition

- Essential for childrens growth and development.
- From age 10 boys and girls have different nutrient requirements.

Growth Monitoring

Flatten

- Indicate growth has stopped.

Move downward

- Showing declining growth.

Move upwards

- Showing growth is taking place.

Indicators of Health

- Stimulating environment
- Adequate breast milk
- Hygienic living space
- Access to health care

4 Stages of Development

- Infancy (Birth- 2 years)
- Early childhood (2-6 years)
- Middle childhood (7-11 years)
- Adolescence (11-18 years)
- Adulthood (18 years and above)

5 Development Across Stages

Physical and Motor Development

Increase in Height and Weight

- Significant growth happens in pre-natal period.
- Next period of rapid growth occurs in infancy.

Motor Development

- Gross motor development - use of legs and hands.
- Fine motor development - use of fingers.

Language Development

- In early stages child produces some sounds like crying, cooing and bubbling.
- From these sounds language development starts.
- From one word, two words sentences, they develop language.

Social and Emotional Development

- Child's social development starts with his/her mother.
- Emotional development starts when mother feeds child and changes clothes.
- Parent's care of child affects their personality.

Cognitive Development

- Jean Piaget gives 4 steps of cognitive developments
  - Sensory Motor Stage (Birth - 2 years)
- Children learn through senses and actions
  - Pre-operational Stage (2 -7 years)
- Children develop basic concept
- Think ego centrically
- Struggle with logic
  - Concrete Operational Stage (7 - 11 years)
- Children's think logically
- Understand others perspectives
  - Formal Operational Stage (11 - 18 years)
- Adolescents think abstractly
- Explore complex ideas
- Solve problem logically

Growth Chart

NCERT Folder

1. Differentiate between growth and development. Giving examples, define the various areas of development.

Ans. The differences between growth and development are

Growth	Development
Growth means to grow i.e. increase in physical body dimensions.	Development is a progressive change. A child undergoes which increases its physical, social, mental and emotional capabilities.
Growth is quantitative.	Development is qualitative and quantitative both.
Growth is for limited period. It can be measured.	Development happens till death and can only be observed.
Growth explains one aspect of personality at a time.	Development deals with all the aspects of personality altogether.

For various areas of development refer to the text under the heading 'Areas of Development'.

2. What conditions and resources are required to promote the healthy growth of a child from the time she/he is born till she/he completes adolescence?

Ans. Adequate educational and physical stimulation within the home are necessary to promote the healthy growth of a child.

Additionally, a stimulating, safe and hygienic environment, proper healthcare services access to adequate breast milk, etc. can be ensured so that a child can grows optimally till the time he/she completes adolescence.

3. Would you say that the neonate is helpless? Give reasons in support of your answers.

Ans. No, neonates are not entirely helpless. While it is true that they are completely dependent on adults, it is also true that they have many capabilities that help them adapt to their surroundings. They are more aware than we can imagine.

The reason for this are

- They are born with certain reflex actions which help them survive and adapt.
- Vision is the most well developed sense at birth. A neonate can distinguish between light and dark and it actively searches for light. She/he can follow a moving object with her/his eyes and can focus best when the object/ person is about 8 inches from her/ his face.

4. Describe the sequence of motor development from birth till 10 years of age.

Ans. The sequence of motor development from birth till 10 years of age is

Age	Nature of Milestone
Birth-3 months	Lifting and holding the head
Newborn	Newborns can move their head from side to side slightly
1 month	They can raise their head
2 months	They can also lift their chest while lying on stomach (prone position)
3 months	The infant begins to hold her/his head, and this is a major milestone in development. If the child is unable to do this even by the age of 6 months, it shows that there is delay in development
4 - 6 months	Can roll over from back to stomach and stomach to back
6 - 8 months	Sitting with adult support or in a seat with straps, sitting without support
8 - 9 months	Crawling; however, some children do not crawl and directly learn to stand after being able to sit, standing if supported or by holding on to something
10 - 11 months	Can pull up from sitting position to standing; standing independently briefly
12 - 18 months	Walking; initially the child's walk is unsteady but gradually it becomes steady, running; after the child learns to walk, she/he begins to run, falling down often. As the balance improves, she/he is able to run in a more co-ordinated manner without falling frequently by the age of 2 years
18 - 24 months	Climbing stairs/steps by placing both feet on each step, if hand held by someone
2 years	Walking backwards, goes down slide, climbs ladder, jumping from low platform with both feet
3 - 4 years	Can walk upstairs with alternating feet as adults do, by holding onto something
5 years	Skipping and pedalling a tricycle
6 years	Well co-ordinated hopping, jumping and climbing
7 years	Balancing and pedalling a bicycle
8 - 10 years	Has balance, co-ordination and strength that allows child to participate in various games and gymnastic

5. Explain how infants form attachment with the caregivers in the first year of life.

Ans. Infants form attachment with their caregivers in the following manners

- The caregivers provide a lot of physical contact to the infant. Infants have an inborn need of physical contact and when the caregivers pick up the child, they fulfil this need is fulfilled.
- Adults and older children use a special type of speech when talking to infants known as motherese. Such speech delights the infant and she/he responds by cooing and babbling.
- We smile at the infant and seeing us smile, the infant smiles back, coos and babbles.
- The mutual gazing between caregivers and infants helps in establishing a link between the two and is one of the first forms of socio-emotional interactions.
- Caregivers make exaggerated facial expressions and also make rhythmic movements, while talking to an infant.
- Caregivers also play simple games with the infant when she/he is a little older, e.g. peek-a-boo is common in all cultures.

6. Differentiate between the power-oriented and affection-oriented approach to disciplining. In your opinion, which is a better approach and why?

Or **Describe the child rearing practices that will contribute to shaping an all round personality in children.**

Ans. On the basis of the type of disciplinary techniques used by the parents. Child rearing practices can be classified as two types

- In order to discipline their children, some parents explain to them the consequence of their actions and reason with them and in order to prevent them from doing unsuitable actions. They are firm in their discipline but are also affectionate and gentle with the child. This is called the affection oriented disciplining approach.
- Some parents use commands to stop their children from behaving in a particular way, without giving them any reason. They may also threaten the child and use physical punishment. This is a power-oriented approach of disciplining.
- A combination of both these practices as per situations would be a better approach. This would ensure, the child understands that certain behaviour can be improved and certain behaviours are un-acceptable.

7. Describe the major characteristics of each of the following stages of cognitive development.

(i) Sensori-motor stage

(ii) Pre-operational stage

(iii) Concrete operational stage

(iv) Formal operations stage

Ans. According to Piaget, there are four stages through which cognitive development proceeds. These are discussed below

(i) **The SensoryMotor Stage** (Birth Till 2 Years) During this period infants try to understand the world through their senses and through their motor capacities (i.e. actions) – therefore, the name sensori-motor period of development. Thus, infants understand the world on the basis of their actions on objects and people and how they appear to them.

(ii) **The Pre-operational Period** (2-7 Years) A child, in this age group, begins to develop concepts of shape, space, size, time, distance, speed, number, etc. that she/he sees in her environment.

The characteristics of this period is best understood by the term 'pre-operational'. The term 'operation' refers to mental acts in which objects are changed or transformed and can then be returned to their original states. This means that an action is reversible.

(iii) **The Concrete Operational Stage** (7-11 Years) It corresponds with the middle childhood stage. The child can now mentally reverse performed actions and child can focus on multiple dimensions or aspects of a problem at the same time. In other words, children at this stage will conserve and seriate under any situations or with any material. The children at this stage are less egocentric.

They see that different people can see the same event in different ways because of different situations and different sets of values. This helps in developing emotions of sympathy and empathy.

(iv) **The Stage of Formal Operations** (11-18 Years) A child enters this stage by the age of 11/12 years and transforms into an adolescent. Following are the characteristics of this stage

- The child can think in terms of abstract ideas.
- A child can apply the acquired reversibility of thinking to ideas and think of multiple possibilities, which allows her/him to follow an argument from its start to end and back again.
- The adolescent's thinking becomes more logical, their reasoning becomes more systematic and they become more effective in solving problems.
- Adolescents become more capable of examining their own thoughts and think about thinking also known as meta-thinking.
- This leads the adolescent to be very concerned about her/his physical appearance.

Exam Pattern Questions

Objective Type Questions

Multiple Choice Questions (MCQs)

1. Children remain healthy and alive when they are provided with which of the following?

(a) Proper care (b) Adequate food
(c) Medical facility (d) All of these

2. What is the main cause of child mortality rate?

(a) Poverty (b) Ignorance
(c) Lack of medical facilities (d) Both (a) and (c)

3. Which of the following can be defined as a progressive change in a person starting from conception till death?

(a) Growth (b) Development
(c) Recognition (d) Real-self

4. Which of the following factors affects has effect on our physical development? **Competency Based Que**

I. Nutrition II. Number of friends
III. Immunisation IV. Heredity

Choose the correct option

(a) I and IV (b) I, II and IV
(c) I and III (d) I, III and IV

5. For doing any activity using fingers and thumb we call it?

(a) Gross motor skills (b) Fine Motor skills
(c) Emotional development (d) Social development

6. "The development of abilities that enable a person to behave in accordance with the expectations of society and maintain relationship with others".
Which of the following is being referred to in the above statement? **Competency Based Que**

(a) Social development (b) Sensory development
(c) Emotional development (d) Cognitive development

7. Which of the following growth curves means that a child is lagging behind in normal growth pattern?

(a) Flattening (b) An upward direction
(c) A downward direction (d) None of these

8. Find the incorrect statement **Competency Based Que**

(a) Crawling starts at the age of 4-6 months.
(b) One-month old babies can raise their head.
(c) 8–9-month babies can stand if supported or by holding on to something.
(d) At 3 months the infant begins to hold her/his head.

9. How does a parent respond to a child's cooing?

(a) By talking to them
(b) By smiling
(c) By imitating the cooing sound
(d) All of the above

10. Prerna is three months old. She often cries when she is hungry or for other reasons.
Crying is considered as very important in the language development of a child. How is crying considered as important in the language development of a child? **Competency Based Que**

(a) The child cries differently for different reasons
(b) Crying is the first form of communication
(c) Crying also reveals the urgency of the needs
(d) All of the above

11. At which age, does a child acquire grammatical forms including articles, conjunctions and possessives in their speech?

(a) Between 18-24 months
(b) Between 2-3 years
(c) Between 12-24 months
(d) Between 3-5 years

12. What do you understand by motherese?

(a) Special type of speech used by adults to talk to infants
(b) Special type of care provided by adult caregivers to children
(c) It refers to the process of communication between a mother and a child
(d) It refers to the bond between a mother and a child

13. Three year old Bunty is feeling shy of his uncle. He starts feeling conscious of unfamiliar face around him. Bunty feels extremely comfortable in the presence of his mother. But he feels shy whenever his uncle comes to their place.
What are the ways in which Bunty could react? **Competency Based Que**

(a) He runs and hides himself behind his mother
(b) He gets irritated and it appears on his face
(c) Both (a) and (b)
(d) Neither (a) nor (b)

14. Match the following.

	Areas of Development		Features
A.	Motor development	1.	Development of five senses
B.	Cognitive development	2.	Gaining control over body movements
C.	Sensory development	3.	Maintaining relationships with others
D.	Social development	4.	Emergence of thinking capabilities

Codes

	A	B	C	D
(a)	2	3	4	1
(b)	2	4	1	3
(c)	1	3	4	2
(d)	4	3	1	2

Competency Based Que

Assertion-Reason Questions

Direction (Q. Nos.15-18) In the questions given below, there are two statements marked as Assertion (A) and Reason (R). Read the statements and choose the correct option.

Codes

(a) Both A and R are true and R is the correct explanation of A.
(b) Both A and R are true, but R is not the correct explanation of A.
(c) A is true, but R is false.
(d) A is false, but R is true.

15. Assertion (A) Diarrheal diseases are a significant cause of child mortality worldwide.

Reason (R) Vaccination is the primary prevention strategy against diarrheal diseases.

16. Assertion (A) Motor development results in smooth, controlled and effective body movements.

Reason (R) Motor development includes physical growth of a person's body.

17. Assertion (A) Children's language development is influenced by their environment.

Reason (R) Children born to deaf parents will never learn to speak.

18. Assertion (A) All children grow very similarly over the first five years of their lives.

Reason (R) Children receive proper care from their caregivers in the same manner.

Case Based Questions

19. Read the passage given below and answer the following questions.

During this period infants try to understand the world through their senses and through their motor Capacities (i.e. actions). Therefore, the name sensoriy-motor period of development. Thus, infants understand the world on the basis of their actions on objects and people and how they appears to them. An infant knows a toy in terms of how it appears to his/her eyes and feels to his/her touch (Sensory Information) and that he/she can throw it, kick it, push it and bang it (motor actions). The infant does not yet understand the toy in terms of its properties as hard or soft, made of wood or metal, big or small, Light or heavy. At this stage the child has many reflexes, including the sucking reflex.

(i) What is the primary way infants understand the world during the sensory motor period?

(a) Through language and communication
(b) Through senses and motor actions
(c) Through social interactions
(d) Through problem-solving

(ii) During the sensory motor period, how does an infant understand a toy?

(a) By its color and shape
(b) By its properties (hard/soft, big/small)
(c) By how it appears and feels, and how they can act on it
(d) By its price and brand

(iii) What is a characteristic of infants during the sensory motor period?

(a) They have few reflexes
(b) They understand objects' properties (e.g., hard/soft)
(c) They rely heavily on language
(d) They have many reflexes, including sucking

(iv) Assertion (A) Infants during the sensory motor period do not understand object's properties.

Reason (R) Infants understanding is limited to sensory information and motor actions.

(a) Both A and R are true and R is the correct explanation of A.
(b) Both A and R are true, but R is not the correct explanation of A.
(c) A is true, but R is false.
(d) A is false, but R is true.

20. Read the passage given below and answer the following questions.

This stage corresponds to the stage of middle childhood. The child can now mentally reverse performed actions.

Also, unlike the pre-operational child who can focus on only one dimension of a problem at a time, the concrete operational child can focus on multiple dimensions or aspects of a problem at the same time. Thus, the child will conserve or seriate under any situation or with any material.

(i) Which stage is being described in the above passage?
(a) Pre-operational stage
(b) Concrete-operational stage
(c) Formal operational stage
(d) Sensory motor stage

(ii) Which of the following does a child develop during this stage?
(a) The ability to understand the quantity a particular number signifies
(b) The ability to multiply numbers in tens
(c) The ability to not make counting errors
(d) Both (a) and (c)

(iii) Which quality do you think, a child at this stage would exhibit?
(a) Develop emotions of sympathy
(b) Problem-solving
(c) Abstract thinking
(d) The ability to follow an argument

(iv) Given below are two statements labelled as Assertion (A) and Reason (R).

Assertion (A) The children at this stage is more egocentric than those at the previous stage.

Reason (R) They see that different people can see the same event in different ways.

Codes
(a) Both A and R are true and R is the correct explanation of A
(b) Both A and R are true, but R is not the correct explanation of A
(c) A is true, but R is false
(d) A is false, but R is true

Answers

1. (d) All of these
2. (a) Poverty
3. (b) Development
4. (d) I, III and IV
5. (b) Fine motor skills
6. (a) Social development
7. (c) A downward direction
8. (a) Crawling starts at the age of 4-6 months.
9. (d) All of the above
10. (d) All of the above
11. (b) Between 2-3 years
12. (a) Special type of speech used by adults to talk to infants
13. (c) Both (a) and (b)
14. (b) 2 4 1 3
15. (c) A is true, but R is false
16. (c) A is true, but R is false
17. (c) A is true, but R is false
18. (c) A is true and R is false
19. (i) (b) Through senses and motor actions
(ii) (c) By how it appears and feels, and how they can act on it
(iii) (d) They have many reflexes, including sucking
(iv) (a) Both A and R are true and R is the correct explanation of A.
20. (i) (b) Concrete operational period
(ii) (d) Both (a) and (c)
(iii) (a) Develop emotions of sympathy
(iv) (d) A is false, but R is true

Subjective Questions

Very Short Answer Type Questions

1. Aditi, a one-year-old girl in Ahmedabad, is being introduced to solid foods. What nutritional considerations should her parents keep in mind?
Competency Based Que

Ans. Aditi's parents should ensure her diet includes a variety of fruits, vegetables, grains and proteins while avoiding added sugars and salt. Balanced nutrition is vital for her growth and development.

2. List some factors which badly affect motor development.

Ans. Ill health, hereditary factors, imbalanced food and lack of opportunity are some factors which badly affect motor development.

3. At what age, does a child make small sentences of 2 to 3 words for the first time?

Ans. When a child reaches 2 years of age, he/she can make small sentences of 2 to 3 words.

4. Suggest two examples of motor development in late childhood.

Ans. Two examples of motor development in late childhood are

(i) During late childhood, a child acquires hand skills through which he/she is able to write.

(ii) Leg skills through which he/she can play different types of sports, dancing, skating, etc.

5. Anaya frequently babbles but has not yet formed words. Is this typical behaviour for her age? **Competency Based Que**

Ans. Yes, Anaya's babbling is a normal stage of language development. It signifies her exploration of sounds and prepares her for future language acquisition, leading to meaningful speech.

6. What are the different types of Motor development?

Ans. Motor development is divided into two parts

(i) **Gross Motor Developments** It controls over the movements of the large muscles of the body.

(ii) **Fine Motor Developments** It controls over the fine muscles of the body.

7. How is language developed in the late childhood stage?

Ans. During the late childhood, the pronunciation and dictation of a child improves and he/she can write and read the language easily.

8. List the various emotions which emerge during the first year of a child's life.

Ans. Anger, fear, happiness, affection towards adult develop during the first year of a child's life.

9. Ishaan shows fear of separation from his mother when she leaves the room. What is this known as? **Competency Based Que**

Ans. Ishaan's fear is called separation anxiety, common in infants around his age. It reflects his attachment to his caregiver, indicating a developing bond and a need for security.

10. List any two characteristics of early childhood.

Ans. Two main characteristics of early childhood are

(i) The speed of development in this stage is slower than development in the stage of infancy.

(ii) Mental, social, emotional and language development are rapid.

11. What is 'egocentrism' of a child?

Ans. A pre-school child assumes that others see a situation as he/she does and this quality is known as egocentrism.

Short Answer Type Questions

1. In the case of Aarav, a 2-year-old child who has grown taller but struggles to express his needs verbally, how can we differentiate between his growth and development? **Competency Based Que**

Ans. Aarav's physical growth is evident in his increased height, which can be measured. However, his verbal skills indicate a developmental delay, as he is not yet able to express his needs effectively.

Growth focuses solely on quantifiable changes, such as size, while development encompasses the acquisition of skills and abilities. In this context, Aarav's situation illustrates that despite physical growth, his cognitive and linguistic development is still progressing.

It highlights the importance of understanding that a child may experience growth in one area while needing further support in another, such as communication.

2. "Child development is a multi-dimensional process that encompasses physical, cognitive, language, sensory, social and emotional growth." **Competency Based Que**

(a) What are the different areas of development in children?

(b) What factors contribute to a child's overall development?

Ans. (a) Child development encompasses seven key areas

(i) Physical (growth, body proportions)

(ii) Motor (gross and fine motor skills)

(iii) Cognitive (thinking, problem-solving)

(iv) Sensory (processing sensory information)

(v) Language (verbal and nonverbal communication)

(vi) Social (interactions, relationships)

(vii) Emotional (recognising and managing emotions)

(b) Key factors that contribute to a child's overall development include

(i) Genetics (ii) Nutrition

(iii) Environment (iv) Health Care

(v) Social Interactions (vi) Education

(vii) Parental Influence (viii) Cultural Background

(ix) Economic Factors

3. In the case of little Meera, a two-week-old neonate, how do her reflexes contribute to her survival and interaction with her environment? **Competency Based Que**

Ans. Meera, at two-weeks-old, demonstrates crucial reflexes that aid her survival, such as the sucking reflex, which ensures she can feed effectively. For example her eye blink reflex protects her from potential dangers, while the elimination reflex helps manage bodily functions.

These automatic responses are essential for her adaptation, allowing her to thrive in a world where she is completely dependent on caregivers.

Additionally, these reflexes enable her to engage with her environment and caregivers, fostering early connections that are vital for her emotional development.

4. How do relationships with siblings and peers influence a child's social and emotional development?

Ans. Sibling relationships significantly impact development, as older siblings often take on a caregiving role while providing emotional support through play and sharing. These relationships can also involve conflicts and competition, making it essential for parents to foster positive bonds.

As children grow, friendships with peers become increasingly important, allowing them to engage in play, arguments and secret-sharing. These interactions contribute to their social skills and emotional growth, helping children learn about co-operation, empathy and conflict resolution.

Together, sibling and peer relationships shape a child's overall social development and emotional resilience.

5. Eight-months-old Diya is attending a wedding with her parents. She begins to cry loudly when her uncle, whom she rarely sees, tries to hold her. Identify the kind of anxiety and briefly describe its characteristics. **Competency Based Que**

Ans. Diya's reaction is a typical case of stranger anxiety, which peaks between 8 to 12 months. At this developmental stage, infants often become fearful of unfamiliar people, leading to distress when approached by someone they don't recognise. This response is completely normal and usually fades by 15 to 18 months.

To help Diya feel more comfortable, her parents can gradually introduce her to her uncle and offer re-assurance, creating a safe environment for her to explore new relationships.

6. What is cognitive development in children and what key processes are involved?

Ans. Cognitive development refers to how children's thinking evolves, encompassing processes like understanding, observation, language and reasoning. It involves recognising differences (discrimination), associating emotions with experiences (association), and understanding cause-and-effect relationships. Problem-solving skills also develop with age, fostering creativity.

Other important cognitive processes include understanding relationships between objects, abstract thinking and contemplating hypothetical situations.

7. 2-year-old child is brought to a pediatrician for a regular check-up. **Competency Based Que**

(i) What are the expected physical developments in a 2-year-old child?

(ii) What are the expected language developments in a 2-year-old child?

(iii) What are the key indicators of motor development delay in a 2-year-old child?

Ans. (i) At 2 years old, a child typically demonstrate significant physical growth, including walking independently, running, climbing stairs with support, kicking a ball, throwing objects and improving balance and co-ordination. They also show some refined motor skills like building towers with blocks.

(ii) By 2 years old, children's language skills accelerate rapidly.

- They typically possess a vocabulary of around 250 words
- They start combining two words to form simple sentences
- They understand simple instructions
- They identify body parts and begin using gestures like waving good-bye.

(iii) Key indicators of motor development delay in a 2-year-old child include inability to walk independently, lack of balance, not pointing to objects, difficulty grasping small objects, inability to climb stairs, limited hand-eye co-ordination, and significant delays in achieving milestones like sitting, crawling or standing.

Long Answer Type Questions

1. In the case of little Aisha, whose growth curve has flattened on her growth chart, what factors might be contributing to this issue, and how can her caregivers address them? **Competency Based Que**

Ans. Aisha's flattened growth curve may indicate several underlying issues that need attention.

- Firstly, her caregivers should evaluate her access to a stimulating environment, which is crucial for healthy development.
- Additionally, they must ensure she is receiving adequate breast milk or nutrition appropriate for her age.
- A safe and hygienic living space is essential to prevent infections, which can also hamper growth.
- Regular health care visits are important to monitor her health and identify any diseases.
- If infections are present, timely treatment and increased nutritional support can facilitate catch-up growth, allowing Aisha to resume her normal growth trajectory.

- A holistic approach, including environmental, nutritional and healthcare factors, is vital for Aisha's overall well-being and development.

2. How does human language development differ from animal communication and what are the stages of language acquisition in children?

Ans. Unlike animals, whose communication patterns are largely innate, human infants are born with the capacity to learn language influenced by their environment. They produce pre-linguistic sounds like crying, cooing and babbling in their first year. By around age one, most children say their first words and their language skills develop rapidly thereafter.

While children can understand more than they can express from the start, their comprehension (receptive language) precedes their ability to produce language (expressive language).

By adolescence, their language becomes sophisticated, with vocabulary continuing to grow throughout life.

3. Rahul, a concerned parent, notices that his 2-year-old child, Rohan, is not speaking as clearly as his peers. Rahul wants to understand Rohan's language development stage and how to support his growth.

Competency Based Que

(i) What stage of language development is Rohan likely in and what are some characteristic features of this stage?

(ii) How can Rahul support Rohan's language development, and what milestones should he expect in the next year?

Ans. (i) Rohan is likely in the telegraphic speech stage, characterised by one or two-word utterances that convey complete meanings. At this stage (between 2-3 years), children begin to learn grammatical forms, and their sentence structure expands to include words previously missing in telegraphic speech.

Rohan's vocabulary is expected to expand rapidly, reaching around 250 words by age 2, and continuing to add hundreds of words each year.

(ii) Rahul can support Rohan's language development by engaging in conversations, reading books, singing songs and encouraging imitation. He should expect Rohan's vocabulary to expand significantly, with around 500-1000 words by age 3.

By age 3, Rohan should begin using simple sentences, understanding basic grammar, and identifying objects and people. Rahul should also look for milestones such as using pronouns, forming short sentences and identifying word meanings.

4. Describe the stages in development of language in a child's life.

Ans. Stages in Development of language in a child's life are

I. **Crying**

- It is the first form of a child's communication that is innate or inborn.
- This means that the child is not taught to cry, it is a sound, an infant makes on his/her own.
- An infant's cry produces a physiological response in adults and children which motivates them to run to the baby to try to relieve her/ his distress.
- The reason behind crying can be any, depending on different bodily states –hunger, pain and illness.

II. **Cooing**

- By the second month, children begin 'Cooing' or making vowel like sounds like oooh, aaah etc.
- They make these sounds when they are contended or feeling pleasure. When the infant coos, the parents respond by talking, smiling or imitating the sound and then wait for the child to coo again.

III. **Babbling**

- It is a consonant-vowel combination leading to sounds like 'dadada', 'mamama', etc. which the infant starts making by 6 months.
- It sounds like human speech as the infant is capable of producing all the sounds contained in all human languages.

5. What do you understand by 'child rearing'? What are the two classifications of a parents's child rearing practices?

Ans. For answer refer to the text under the heading 'Parents' Child Rearing Practices'.

6. Explain the pre-operational stage of cognitive development.

Ans. For answer refer to the text under the heading 'The Pre-Operational Period (2-7 years)'.

7. What is the chief characteristic of the adolescent thinking in the stage of formal operation?

Ans. An adolescent enters the stage of formal operations by 11-12 years of age. The chief characteristics of this stage is that the adolescents' thinking is not tied to concrete events, objects and situations.

They can think in terms of ideas i.e. in abstract terms. An adolescent can apply reversibility to ideas and think of multiple possibilities which allows him/her to follow an argument from its inception to conclusion and back again. Due to hypothetical thinking, adolescents are able to engage in elaborate fantasies, for instance, ideas of changing the world.

The adolescents' thinking becomes more-logical, their reasoning becomes more systematic and they become more effective in solving problems.

SELF ASSESSMENT TEST

Objective Type Questions

1. Which of the following is multi-functional and versatile.
   (a) Growth (b) Development
   (c) Actions (d) Activity
2. .... refers to changes in the ability to control ones body movements.
   (a) Increase in weight (b) Increase in height
   (c) Motor development (d) None of these

Very Short Answer Type Questions

3. Explain the term 'development'.
4. What is the average weight gain of a child in early childhood?
5. At what age, does the emotion of anger emerge?
6. When does a child start thinking everything in a more organised way?

Short Answer Type Questions

7. How can a child can improve his/her language?
8. What are the general causes and responses of curiosity in a child?
9. State the role of family in the identity development of the adolescent.
10. Explain the mental processes involved in thinking.

Long Answer Type Questions

11. What do you understand by 'good nutrition'? What is a growth chart and how is it affected by good nutrition?
12. Define the term neonate and also explain the sensory capabilities of neonate.

Competency Based Que

13. Describe the emotional and social development of a child, with examples.
14. Discuss the causes of fear among the children? What are their reactions to these fears?
15. Explain the language development of a child during early childhood.

09

CHAPTER

Nutrition, Health and Well-being are closely related to each others and they are important for a person's overall quality.

Nutrition, Health and Well-being

▼ YOUR STUDY GOALS

▼ YOUR PRACTICE GOAL

- Objective Type Questions (25 Qs ; MCQs, A-R, Matching, Case Based)
- Subjective Questions (10 VSAs, 8 SAs, 5 LAs)

9.1 Introduction

Our diet consists of the foods we eat. Nutrition is how food works in our bodies to provide nutrients for **growth**, **repair** and **overall well-being**. Understanding which foods contain which nutrients is important, especially for children.

- Children grow continuously, so their nutritional needs depend on their growth rate, body weight and how well their bodies use nutrients at each stage of their development.
- Since physical and mental development takes place very rapidly in children, a lack of nutrition can lead to long-term problems. On the other hand, good nutrition helps children to reach their full potential.
- It's essential to balance their food intake and enjoy a variety of foods from all food groups.
- Good nutrition not only reflects in children's height and weight but also improves their overall well-being.
- Adequate nutrition helps with
  - The functioning of organs and body systems.
  - Cognitive performance (thinking and learning).
  - The body's ability to fight diseases and heal.
  - Increased energy levels.
  - A positive and pleasant attitude.

9.2 Nutrition, Health and Well-being During Infancy (Birth-12 Months)

- Infancy is a time of **rapid growth,** especially in the first six months.
- During this period, infants need twice as many calories per kilogram of body weight as adults who do heavy work.
- Meeting this requirement is possible with proper nutrition.
- All the children should get
  - **Protein** For muscular growth.
  - **Calcium** For healthy bones.
  - **Iron** For growth and expansion of blood volume.

In infants,

- Weight doubles in 6 months and triples in 1 year.
- Height, which is normally 50 to 55 cm at birth, increases to 75 cm by one year.
- Both head circumference and chest circumference increases.

Dietary Requirements of Infants

- Infants are able to regulate their needs by consuming more milk or less milk.
- Their nutritional needs are met by **breast-milk** and **complementary** foods.
- The nutrients needed are based on the composition of the mother's milk. A well-nourished mother produces about 850 ml of breast-milk daily, which provides all the necessary nutrients for the first 4.6 months.
- To ensure her baby thrives, the mother should eat a rich diet in protein, calcium, iron and drink enough fluids like milk, soups, fruit juices and water to prevent **malnutrition**[1].

Recommended Dietary Allowances for Infants Recommended by ICMR*

Nutrient	Birth to 6 Months	6 to 12 Months
Energy (Kcal)	108/kg body weight	98/kg body weight
Protein (gm)	2.05/kg body weight	1.65/kg body weight
Calcium (mg)	500	500
Vitamin A Retinol (µg) or Beta Carotene (µg)	350 1200	350 1200
Thiamine (µg)	55/kg body weight	50/kg body weight
Niacin (µg)	710/kg body weight	650/kg body weight
Riboflavin (µg)	65/kg body weight	60/kg body weight
Pyridoxine (µg)	0.1	0.4
Ascorbic Acid (µg)	25	25
Folic Acid (µg)	25	25
Vitamin B12 (µg)	0.2	0.2

1 **Malnutrition** It refers to both under-nutrition and over-nutrition. In under-nutrition the body suffers due to lack of nutrients and in over-nutrition the body suffers due to excess of nutrients.

Breast Feeding

- Mother's milk is nature's gift to the newborn baby. It has all the required nutrients which are easily absorbed.
- **WHO recommends exclusive breastfeeding for six months.**
- During breastfeeding even water is not required.
- Babies should be put on breast-milk soon after birth. During the first 2-3 days a yellow coloured fluid known as **colostrum** is produced. Babies must be fed on it as it is very rich in antibodies and protects a child from infections.

Benefits of Breastfeeding

- It is nutritionally mode to meet infants' nutritional needs.
- It contains all essential nutrients in the right amounts and form (e.g,. the fat present is emulsified, which helps in easier digestion)
- It contains **low protein content** which reduces strain on babies' kidneys and vitamin C remains intact.
- It is a simple, hygienic and convenient method of feeding for both mother and child; milk is always available at the right temperature.
- It provides natural immunity with antibodies, protecting against gastro-intestinal, chest and urinary infections. It is also free from allergens.
- It gives protection to mothers against breast and ovarian cancers and helps prevent weak bones.
- It creates a healthy and happy emotional bond between mother and child.

Babies know when and how much they want to eat, so the **'best clock is baby's hunger'**. However, after a baby is one month old, it's important to try to establish regular feeding times/intervals.

Feeding the Low Birth Weight Infant

- Babies born weighing less than 2.5 kg are considered low birth weight. Low birth weight babies often struggle with sucking and swallowing. Their small stomachs and intestines make it hard for them to absorb nutrients,
- They have a relatively **high calorie requirement.**
- Breast-milk from their mothers contains all the essential nutrients they need, including amino acids, calories, fat and sodium.
- Mother's milk also helps protect them from infections due to its anti-microbial properties.
- Breast-milk is the best food for low birth weight babies.
- These babies also need vitamins, calcium, phosphorus and iron for healthy growth. Dietary supplements should only be considered if the baby isn't gaining weight well.

Complementary Foods

- Complementary feeding means gradually introducing other foods along with breast-milk.
- These additional foods are called complementary foods and can be introduced around 6 months of age.
- It's important to maintain good hygienic conditions when using feeding bottles and utensils to prevent infections.
- Complementary foods should be **high in calories** and provide at least **10 per cent of energy** from proteins to meet infants' nutritional needs.

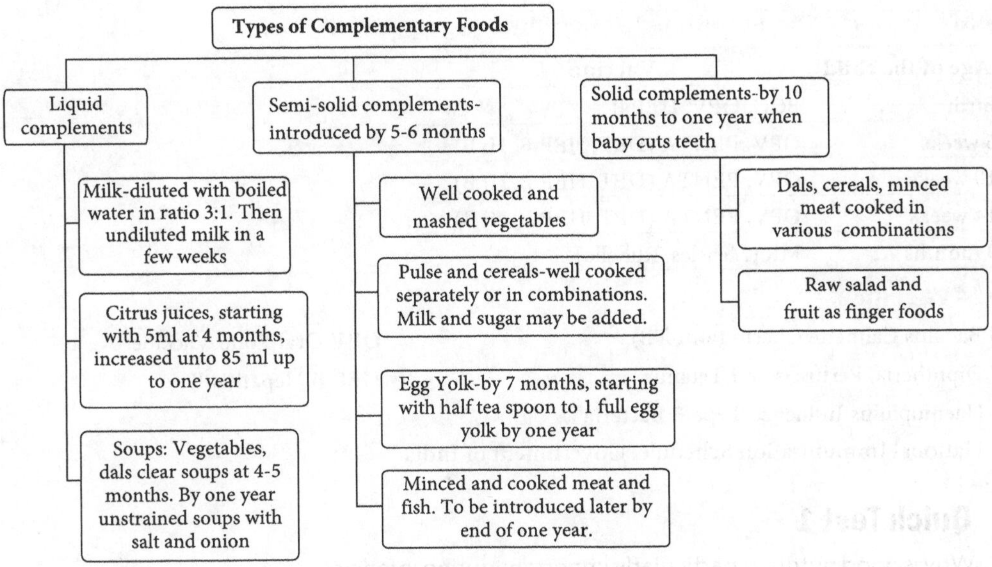

▲ *Types of Complementary Foods*

Some Low Cost Complementary Foods

- **Indian multipurpose flour** Low fat groundnut flour and bengal gram (75:25)
- **Malt food** Cereal mait, low fat groundnut flour and bengal gram (4:4:2)
- **Balahar** Whole wheat, groundnut and bengal gram flours (7:2:2)
- **Win food** Pearl millet, green gram dal, groundnut and jaggery (5:2:2:2)
- **Poshak** Cereal (wheat/maize/rice/jowar) pulse (chana/green gram), groundnut and jaggery (4:2:1:2)
- **Amutham** Rice, ragi, bengal gram and sesame, groundnut flours and jaggery (1.5:1.5:1.5:2.5:2.5)
- **Amritham** Wheat, bengal gram, soya and groundnut flours and beet sugar (4:2:1:1:2)

All these foods are prepared from locally available cereals which are roasted and mixed in relevant proportions as shown, seasoned and fortified with vitamins and calcium. They are very nutritious and can be easily prepared at home.

Guidelines for Complementary Feeding

- Only one food should be introduced at a time.
- Small quantities should be fed in the beginning which can be gradually increased.
- Do not force if the child dislikes any food. Try something else and re-introduce it later.
- Spicy and fried foods should be avoided for small babies.
- All types of food should be encouraged without showing personal dislikes.
- Variety in foods is very important to make new foods acceptable.

Immunisation

- Good health and well-being are not entirely dependent on good nutrition. Immunisation plays important role in protecting children from various diseases.
- A vaccine contains a harmless, **inactive form of a bacterium**, virus or toxin from a germ. When it is injected into a child, it doesn't cause an infection, but it helps the white blood cells in the body to produce antibodies. These antibodies will attack and destroy the germs if they try to infect the child later.

National Immunisation Schedule (Recommended by ICMR)

Age of the child	Vaccine
Birth	BCG, OPV, HEP B
6 weeks	OPV, PENTA (DPT, HEP B, Hi B)
10 weeks	OPV, PENTA (DPT, HEP B, Hi B)
14 weeks	OPV, PENTA (DPT, HEP B, Hi B)
9 months	MR (Measles, Rubella)

Name of Vaccines

- **BCG** Bacillus Calmette Guerin (anti-TB)
- **OPV** Oral Polio Vaccine
- **DPT** Diphtheria, Pertussis and Tetanus
- **HEP B** Hepatitis B
- **Hi B** Haemophilus Influenza Type B Bacteria

Source National Immunisation Schedule, Government of India

Quick Test 1

1. Why is good nutrition particularly important during infancy?
2. Breast-milk helps fight infections in infants due to which property?
3. What is meant by complementary feeding?
4. Mention the name of two Indian complementary foods.

Common Health and Nutrition Problems in Infants and Young Children

- Malnutrition is linked to infections and is a national problem. It is caused by factors like illiteracy, poverty, ignorance about nutrition and limited access to health care, especially in rural and tribal areas.
- Children may become **malnourished** when breast milk is no longer enough and before they can fully benefit from the family diet.
- During this time, **diarrhea** is common, leading to loss of water and electrolytes. This can result in high infant mortality.
- Poor nutrition can contribute to diseases like tuberculosis, especially in areas with food shortages. Malnutrition can also make children more prone to infections like **primary herpes simplex**.
- If infants are not exclusively breastfed or if complementary foods lack necessary nutrients, they may suffer from deficiency diseases, including
  - **Protein Energy Malnutrition (PEM)** Causes growth delays and increases the risk of infections and dehydration.
  - **Anemia** Resulting from iron deficiency.
  - **Nutritional Blindness** Due to a lack of vitamin A.
  - **Rickets and Osteopenia** Bone problems from insufficient vitamin D and calcium.
  - **Goitre** Enlargement of the thyroid gland from iodine deficiency.
- The six dreaded **communicable diseases**[2] like polio, diphtheria, tuberculosis, pertussis, measles and tetanus can lead to high **mortality**[3] and **morbidity**[4], especially in developing countries. The risk is higher when infections and malnutrition occur together. The low age of attack is one more factor responsible for high fatality.
- Vaccinations at different stages in the first year of life provide life-long immunity against many communicable diseases.

2 Communicable disease Diseases which spread from person to person or animals.
3 Mortality It is the incidence of death in a population over time.
4 Morbidity It is the condition of being diseased or the prevalence of illness.

- In rural and tribal areas, factors like limited health care access, climate, local customs and untested traditional treatments make children more vulnerable to infectious diseases.
- It is essential to **educate people** about the health risks of contaminated food, poor sanitation and inadequate hygiene, as these can lead to communicable diseases.

9.3 Nutrition, Health and Well-being of Pre-school Children (1-6 Years)

- Pre-schoolers are full of energy and are very active, even though their rapid growth from infancy slows down. During this time, they continue to grow physically, mentally and emotionally.
- They are still learning to eat and developing their skills in chewing and swallowing. This is a great time to introduce them to healthy meals and snacks.
- Healthy eating habits formed now are likely to influence their food choices and behaviours in the future.

Nutritional Needs of Pre-school Children

- Pre-schoolers have nutritional needs similar to the rest of the family, but the amounts vary based on their age, height, weight, health and activity level.
- They require more energy to support their growth and development.
- It is important to remember that each child's nutritional needs may be slightly different due to **basal losses and extra requirements.**

Recommended Dietary Allowances for Pre-school Children (Recommended by ICMR), 2010

Nutrient	Age in years: 1–3 years	Age in years: 4–6 years
Energy(Kcal)	1240	1690
Protein(g)	22	30
Fat(g)	25	25
Calcium(mg)	400	400
Iron(mg)	12	18
Vitamin: Retinol(μg)	400	400
Beta-carotene(μg)	1600	1600
Thiamine (mg)	0.6	0.9
Riboflavin (mg)	0.7	0.1
Niacin (mg)	8	11
Vitamin C (mg)	40	40
Pyridoxine (mg)	0.9	0.9
Folic Acid (μg)	30	40
Vitamin B-12 (μg)	0.2-1	0.2-1

Guidelines for Healthy Eating for Pre-schoolers

The child should develop good food habits early in life. In order to teach them that **'healthy eating is part of healthy lifestyle'** one can follow the suggestions given below

- **Family Mealtime** Mealtime can be a family time. Eating together in a happy atmosphere helps children to learn by watching others.

- **Variety of Foods** It offers a mix of different foods in small portions. Encourage children to finish what's on their plate but give them enough time to do so.
- **Regular Mealtimes** It is important to keep regular schedules for meals and snacks so, children get hungry at the right times.
- **Introduce New Foods** Add new foods to meals along with the child's favourite food. Include a balance of hard, soft and colourful foods to keep them interested.
- **Easy-to-Eat Foods** Serve meals that are easy to handle, like finger foods such as small sandwiches, chapatti rolls, samosas, whole fruits or hard-boiled eggs.
- **Designated Eating Area** Serve meals in one place, not while the child is walking around. Ensure they have a comfortable seating arrangement.
- **Rest Before Meals** Make sure the child has a chance to rest before mealtime, as a tired child may not want to eat.
- **Avoid Bribing or Punishing** Never **bribe or punish a child to eat certain foods,** as this can harm their development of healthy eating habits.

Planning Balanced Meals for Pre-school Children

- An active pre-school child's energy needs can be similar to those of some adult women, so it's not necessary to track their calorie intake closely.
- If children do not get nutritious and balanced meals, they may not reach their genetic potential for adult height. They can face health issues.
- Children can face these issues if their meals are missing key nutrients
  - **Protein-Energy Malnutrition (PEM)** Occurs when there isn't enough protein or calories in their diet.
  - **Xerophthalmia** Vitamin A deficiency.
  - **Anemia** Occurs due to insufficient intake of iron.
- Using iodised salt is a simple and affordable way to prevent Iodine Deficiency Disorders.

Key Aspects of a Pre-school Child's Diet

- **Variety** Include different textures, tastes, smells and colours to enhance nutritional intake and make eating enjoyable.
- **Balance** Ensure a mix of complex carbohydrates, lean proteins and essential fats in their meals.
- **Moderation** Limit sweets, ice creams and fast foods that are high in fats and refined flours.

Quick Test 2

1. What is protein energy malnutrition?
2. List some common deficiency diseases in infants.
3. How many meals and snacks should be planned for a pre-school children?
4. What nutrient deficiency can lead to anemia in pre-school children?

Food Groups for Balanced Meals

- The five food groups suggested by **ICMR (Indian Council of Medical Research)** permit us to plan balanced meals according to our recommended dietary allowances.
- When planning daily diets, it is important to include foods from all five food groups.
- The ICMR provides specific diet suggestions for different age groups, which can guide the amounts of various food groups to include in a balanced diet for pre-school children.

Balanced Diet for Pre-school Children (Recommended by ICMR) 2010

S. No.	Food groups	1-3 years (gm/day)	4-6 years (gm/day)
1.	Cereals and Millets	60	120
2.	Pulses	30	30
3.	Milk (ml)	500	500
4.	Fruits and vegetables		
	Roots and tubers	50	100
	Green leafy vegetables	50	50
	Other vegetables	50	100
	Fruits	100	100
5.	Sugar	15	25
	Fats/oils (visible)	20	25

- **Three meals and two snacks** should be planned for a pre-school child.
- Pre-schoolers often find it hard to eat enough in just three meals, so healthy snacks provide extra calories and nutrients. They are also a good time to introduce new foods and are convenient for school tiffins.
- For a 6 years old, parents can plan
  - **Breakfast** Wheat porridge cooked in milk or bread/roti with an egg and seasonal fruit.
  - **School Tiffin** A sandwich with vegetable filling and a healthy drink.
  - **Lunch** Vegetable paratha/roti, rice, curd, boiled channa and salad.
  - **Evening Snack** Milk, biscuits or peanuts and fruit.
  - **Dinner** Chapati or rice, dal or chicken, cooked seasonal vegetables and salad.
- Nutritious snacks from different regions like murukku, laddoos, upma, mathi and chana-chur are great options, as they cater to children's energy needs.
- The high activity levels of pre-schoolers increase their energy needs, making these nutritious snacks important for their overall health.

Some examples of Low Cost Snacks

- Equal amounts of soya bean, dal and sunflower seeds are ground, mixed and fermented together.
- Sweet chikki (like traditional peanut chikki) has great acceptability in rural and semi-urban areas of India.
- Indigenous foods such as flours of rice, cow pea, horse grain and amaranths, jaggery are mixed in equal amounts with ground nut oil to prepare various snacks.
- Sundal, Payasam, Dhokla and Upma are popular snacks.
- Vegetable soup prepared from seasonal and locally available vegetables. Even leftover vegetables, dals and cereals can be added.
- Spiced baked potatoes.
- Chiwrha (poha) prepared from rice, wheat or maize flours or other products and stuffed with seasonal vegetables can be served with sauce.

Feeding Children with Special needs

Feeding children with special needs can be tough at mealtimes. When helping them eat and deal with nutrition, there are three key things to consider

(i) **Observations** It's important to closely watch the child's behaviour and progress during mealtimes. Take note of their ability to handle food, food preferences, allergies and any specific conditions. This helps in promoting the skills they need for good nutrition and enjoyable mealtimes.

(ii) **Developing Eating Skills** Children with disabilities may need more time to eat and might struggle with self-feeding. They often make messes.

- Use **positive re-inforcement** to encourage them and keep them motivated.
- Ensure they are seated comfortably and support their self-feeding efforts.
- As the child progresses, allow them to try foods with different textures. Adaptive equipment can be helpful if needed.
- Respect their food preferences and try to establish regular feeding times.

(iii) **Special Diets** Some children may need dietary modifications based on their abilities. For example, spastic[5] children may have trouble with certain textures, so thin liquids might need to be thickened and dry or lumpy foods should be softened. A feeding-tube may be used if necessary.

- Some children with disabilities have a tendency to be overweight making eating difficult.
- Children with autism have an altered sense of taste or smell affecting their acceptance of food.
- Depending on their choices extra fat, limited liquids, special formula or other dietary changes may be needed.
- All foods to which a child with special needs is allergic should immediately be removed from her/his diet as it may cause damage.

Immunisation for Pre-school Children

Pre-school children need more vaccinations to protect against communicable diseases. They are due for the following vaccines

- Measles, Mumps and Rubella (**MMR**) Vaccine
- **Typhoid Vaccine**
- Booster doses of **DPT (Diphtheria, Pertussis, Tetanus)**
- Booster doses of **OPV (Oral Polio Vaccine)**

Make sure to follow up on these vaccinations to keep the child safe.

Immunisation Schedule

Age of Child	Vaccine
15-18 months	MMR (for Measles, Mumps and Rubella)
16 months-2 years	DPT, OPV booster doses
2 years	Typhoid Vaccine
5 years	DT
10-16 years	Tetanus Toxoid (TT)
18, 24, 30, 36 months	Vitamin A (drops)

5 Spastic It is characterised by the lack of control of one's muscles and movements because of cerebral palsy. (Although using this word is considened offen give now)

9.4 Health, Nutrition and Well-being of School-age Children (7-12 Years)

School-age children are very active physically. With fewer communicable diseases because they are generally stronger. Growth may slow down during this period, but changes in the body occur gradually especially between the ages of 9-10, when boys and girls show different growth pattern.

Nutritional requirement of School Children

- Although this is a time of slower growth, children are involved in many activities, so maintaining energy is important.
- Upto age 9, boys and girls have similar nutritional needs. After that, girls need more protein, iron and calcium for bone growth and preparation for menstruation/menarche. Boys, on the other hand, need more calories to support their **growth spurt** during adolescence.

Recommended Dietary Allowances of School-age Children (7-12 years)
(Recommended by ICMR)

Nutrients	Age (in years)		
	7-9	10-12	
		Boys	Girls
Energy (kcal)	1690	2190	2010
Protein (g)	29.5	39.9	40.4
Fat (g)	30	35	35
Calcium (mg)	600	800	800
Iron (mg)	16	21	27
Vitamin A Retinol (μg) or	600	600	600
B Carotene (μg)	4800	4800	4800
Thiamine (mg)	1.0	1.1	1.0
Riboflavin (mg)	1.2	1.3	1.2
Pyridoxine (mg)	1.6	1.6	1.6
Folic acid (μg)	120	140	140
Ascorbic acid (mg)	40	40	40
Vitamin B12 (mg)	0.2-1	0.2-1	0.2-1
Niacin (mg)	13	15	13

Quick Test 3

1. How many meals & snacks should be planned for a pre-school child?
2. Name some common snack option in rural India.
3. What does DPT stands for?
4. Which vaccine is provided to children at 2 years of age?

Planning Diets for School-age Children

- **Aim for Variety** Children need a range of foods to get all necessary nutrients. A varied diet helps them accept new foods.
- **Ensure Good Nutrition** School-age children require more protein, calcium, iron and iodine. Encourage them to eat
  - Vegetables and fruits are essential to improve the macro-nutrient density in their diets.
  - Whole grains requires to reduce the risk of diseases like cardiovascular(heart) and diabetes[6].
  - Iodised salt is essential to prevent iodine deficiency.
- **Limit Intake of Saturated Fat, Salt and Sugar**
  - As the growth of school children slows down, it is important to limit the consumption of calories. Maintain fat calories to 20 per cent of total calories.
  - Diets rich in fats and sugars increase the risk of obesity[7] and its related problems.
  - Foods with added sugars are also a cause of dental caries.
  - A high sodium intake may increase blood pressure leading to major risk factors of stroke, kidney and coronary diseases.
- **Ensure Eating Breakfast**
  - Breakfast is a special meal. It should contain more protein and energy.
  - After a long night's fasting the child should never be allowed to skip breakfast.
  - Skipping breakfast can harm physical and mental performance and the loss of calories and nutrients cannot be made up later in the day.
- **Involve Children in Meal Planning**
  - As they grow, let children help plan their meals. It will make healthy eating interesting for them.
  - Take them shopping and teach them how to choose healthy ingredients.
  - Encourage them to help cook and serve meals, making healthy eating fun and engaging.

Balanced Diet for School Going Children (ICMR), 2010

S. No.	Food Groups	Quantities (g)		
		7-9 years	10-12 years	
			Boys	Girls
1.	Cereals and Millets	180	300	240
2.	Pulses and Legumes	60	60	60
3.	Milk and Products	500	500	500
4.	Fruits and Vegetables	?	?	?
	Roots and Tubers	100	100	100
	Green Leafy Vegetables	100	100	100
	Other Vegetables	200	200	200
	Fruits	100	100	100
5.	Sugars	20	30	30
	Fats	30	35	35

▲ *Quantities of foods to be consumed by school going children as recommended by ICMR*

6 Diabetes Deficiency of insulin in the body leading to rise in blood glucose and presence of glucose in the urine.

7 Obesity Deposit of excess fat in the body leading to body weight rising above normal levels. This is caused by intake of more calories that can be spent on body metabolism and physical activity.

Sample Diet Plan for Pre-school child

The parents of a 6 years old child can plan and prepare the following meals for a day

- **Breakfast** Milk and cornflakes, rawa upma and an apple or any seasonal fruit.
- **School Tiffin** Grilled sandwich with egg filling, paneer filling (for those allergic to egg) and a seasonal fruit.
- **Lunch** Vegetable pulao, tomato rings and cucumber sticks for salad and butter-milk.
- **Evening Snack** Boiled potato and moong sprout chaat.
- **Dinner** Bengal gram dal or chicken curry, okra and onion vegetable, chapati and raw salad.

Snacks may consist of items made from rice flour with a filling of jackfruit or nuts, both steamed. Snacks may also include murukku for older children.

Traditional Rural Diet

- In **rural areas,** breakfast may include upma (with banana), pootu (with chana curry or banana), idli or dosa (with sambar or coconut chutney), or appams (with potato or chicken curry) in the South. In the North, breakfast options include paranthas with buttermilk or poori with a potato preparation.
- In **tribal areas,** the focus is on foods gathered from the forest, such as nuts, berries and various fruits and flowers.
- Lunch and dinner typically include chapattis and rice, along with a pulse or dal preparation and a vegetable dish.

Factors that Influence Diet Intake of Pre-school-age and School-age Children

Even with careful meal planning, younger children may still miss out on important nutrients. This is often because they are still developing their eating habits, which can be influenced by several factors. Some of the factors are

Family Environment

- Positive parenting practices promote children's overall well-being.
- Families shape food preferences and establish eating patterns, consciously or un-consciously.
- Parents should gain **nutritional knowledge** and use it in planning diets for their children.
- Eating together in a relaxed and happy environment helps children develop good eating habits and get the nutrients they need.

Media Influence

- TV commercials and endorsements by favourite stars significantly impact children's food choices. More exposure, more independence and more understanding of the catchy slogans tempts children of this age.
- Children may prefer foods low in fiber and high in sugar, fat and sodium due to catchy advertising.
- Attractive displays of un-healthy foods during celebrations leads to more snacking, which in turn leads to reduced appetite for proper meals.
- A supportive family environment can help to combat the negative influence of media on food choices.

Peers

- As children start school, they begin to rely more on their friends' food choices rather than their parents' preferences.
- What children eat is often influenced by their peers, not just by what is available at home.
- Children tend to eat better and finish their tiffin when they are with their friends.

- When eating together, children are more willing to try new foods that they might refuse at home.
- To help pre-schoolers develop good eating habits, it's best for them to eat in groups/group settings.

Socio-cultural Influences

- Each region has its own typical foods and flavours.
- Families usually serve children the same meals that adults eat.
- Eating together as a family helps children appreciate both local foods and dishes from other regions. For example, children in Northern India enjoy Southern dishes like idlis and dosas, while Southern children like parathas and rajma-rice from the North.

Erratic Appetite

- It's normal for a child to eat well at one meal and refuse food at another.
- These changes in appetite are usually temporary and not a cause for concern.
- Avoid using bribes, punishments or strict rules, as these can make the situation worse.

Healthy Habits

Good health includes both physical and emotional well-being. Along with getting enough nutrients from food, school children should also develop healthy habits.

- **Establishing Healthy Eating Habits**
  - Children often snack a lot while watching TV and don't get enough exercise.
  - One way to encourage healthy eating is by preparing a big bowl of fruit and vegetable salad.
  - This salad can include lettuce, nuts, sprouts, boiled chickpeas, steamed beans, carrots, tofu or paneer. Adding different dressings and changing the ingredient combinations with fun names makes it more appealing.
- **Encouraging Physical Activity**
  - Healthy eating and physical activity go together. Aim for **45-60 minutes of moderate exercise** each day to promote good health.
  - Limit the time spent watching TV and encourage children to participate in sports and extracurricular activities at school and in the community.
  - Parents should set a good example by leading an active lifestyle and following healthy eating habits.
- **Ensuring Food Safety**
  - Children should be taught to eat in **hygienic conditions**. Food consumed should be clean and safe before eating.
  - They must wash their hands, fruits and vegetables before eating.
  - Involving children in washing, cutting, mixing and cooking helps them develop good hygiene habits while preparing and eating food.
- **Ensure Control Over Quantity Intake**
  - Children aged 9-12 can recognise their hunger levels. It's important not to force them to eat more if they don't want to.
  - Forcing food can prevent them from feeling full. Food should not be used to show love.
  - Skipping a meal is not a problem if the child is healthy, but it shouldn't become a regular habit.

Health and Nutrition Issues of School-age Children

- With proper immunisation and a healthy nutrition pattern, children are generally strong enough to handle colds and coughs.
- Obesity is a growing problem among children, especially those from higher socio-economic backgrounds. This is due to diets high in fatty foods, salt and sugary drinks, combined with a lack of physical activity.
- **Type II diabetes** and hypertension[8] are becoming more common in children due to rising obesity rates.
- Under-nutrition remains a serious issue for children from lower socio-economic groups. Many go to school on empty stomachs, which affects their performance and increases their risk of health problems. They are at a greater risk of morbidity and mortality.
- The **Mid-Day-Meal Scheme (MDMS)** provides free lunches to children in Classes I-VIII. This programme has improved classroom performance and attention spans, increased school enrollment and reduced dropout rates. It has also helped boost female attendance, thus reducing gender gap.
- India faces both **under-nutrition** and **over-nutrition issues**. Promoting healthy nutrition can have long-term benefits for children's health.
- School health programmes that offer free health checks and treatment can further enhance children's overall well-being.
- The overall development of children requires concerned care and quality education.

Quick Test 4

1. Why is breakfast considered a special meal for school children?
2. List any one key factor which influences children's eating habits.
3. What health issue is increasingly common due to rising obesity rates in children?
4. Which scheme provides free lunches to children in India?

8 Hypertension It means high blood pressure.

Mind Map

NUTRITION, HEALTH AND WELL-BEING

1 Nutrition, Health and Well-being During Infancy

Dietary Requirements of Infants
- Nutritional needs are met through breast milk and complementary foods.
- Mother should eat rich diet based on protein, calcium and iron.

Breast Feeding
- Rich in antibodies.
- WHO recommended it for six months.

Benefits
- Provides all necessary nutrients.
- Convenient diet
- Natural immunity
- Protects mother from breast and ovary cancer.

Complementary Foods
- Additional foods along with breast milk.
- They should meet infant's nutritional needs.

Guidelines for Complementary Feeding
- One food should be introduced at a time.
- Fed in small quantities
- Avoid spicy food.
- Provide variety of foods.

Low Cost Complementary Foods
- Indian multipurpose floor.
- Balahar
- Poshak
- Amritham
- Malt food
- Win food
- Amutham

Types of Complementary Foods

Liquid supplementary Foods
- Milk, Juice, soup etc.

Semi-solid Supplementary Foods
- Well cooked and mashed vegetables.
- Cereal's and pulses.

Solid Supplementary Foods
- Given to infants by 10-12 months
- Raw salad, fruits etc.

Immunisation
- It produce antibodies and protects children
- Names of vaccines
  - BCG- Bacillus Calmette Guerin
  - OPV- Oral Polio Vaccine
  - DPT- Diphtheria, Pertussis and Tetanus
  - HE PB- Hepatitis B
  - Hi B

2 Nutrition, Health and Well-being of Pre-school Children

Nutritional Needs
- Require more energy for growth and development.
- Each children's nutritional needs slightly different.

Guidelines for Healthy Eating
- Encourage children to eat with family
- Give them variety of foods
- Regularity in meal time
- Habit of finish the food
- Avoid bribe and punishment to eat certain food.

Balanced Meals
- Three meals and two snacks should be given .
- Provide healthy snacks.
- Low cost snacks **For example** soya bean dal, sweet chikki, upma, dhokla, Poha etc.

Immunisation
- Measles, mumps and Rubella (MMR) vaccine
- Typhoid vaccine
- Booster doses of DPT
- Booster doses of OPV

3 Feeding Children with Special Needs

- Observe the child's likes, how they eat, allergies etc.
- Develop eating skills and encourage them to self-feeding.
- Give soft foods, use feeding tubes if needed.

4 Health Nutrition and Well-Being of School Age Children

- Maintaining energy is important.
- Girls need more protein iron and calcium.
- Boys need more calories.

Planning Diet
- Variety in Diet
- Ensure good nutrition
- Limited intake of saturated fat, salt and sugar
- Ensure eating breakfast
- Involve children in meal planning

5 Factors Influence Diet Intake of Pre-School Age and School Age Children

- Family environment influence children's eating habits.
- Advertisement make them to prefer unhealthy foods.
- Peers influence their food choices.
- Local food shape their taster.
- Their appetite changes so, don't force them to eat.

6 Healthy Habits

- Establish healthy eating habits.
- Encourage physical activity.
- Ensure food safety.
- Ensure control over quantity intake.

7 Health and Nutritional Issue of School Age Children

- Obesity
- Diabetes
- High blood pressures.

NCERT Folder

Intext Questions

1. What do DPT, OPV and BCG vaccines stand for?

Ans. **DPT** stands for Diphtheria, Pertusis and Tetanus vaccine.

OPV stands for Oral Polio Vaccine.

BCG stands for Bacillus Calmette Guerin Vaccine (anti TB).

2. How does diarrhoea result in dehydration?

Ans. Diarrhoea results in dehydration due to the continuous depletion of electrolytes and water from the infant's body.

3. Why is the mother's health and nutrition important to avoid deficiency diseases in infants?

Ans. The mother's health and nutrition is important to avoid deficiency diseases in infants because infants are totally dependent on their mother's milk for nutrition.

An unhealthy mother may not be able to give adequate nutrition to her infant, thus leading to deficiency diseases in the infant.

4. Classify complementary foods.

Ans. Complementary foods can be classified into three forms; liquid, semi-solid and solid. Examples of each type are

(i) **Liquid** Milk diluted with boiled water in the ratio 3:1, citrus juices, vegetable soups, dals, clear soups etc.

(ii) **Semi-solid** Well cooked and mashed vegetables, pulses and cereals well cooked separately or in combinations, egg yolk, minced and cooked meat and fish etc.

(iii) **Solid** Dals, cereals, minced meat cooked in various combinations, raw salad and fruit etc.

5. How many Kcal of energy is required by a 4 years old child?

Ans. 1690 Kcal of energy is required by a 4 years old child.

6. What is the importance of iodine, iron, calcium and protein in the diet of pre-school children?

Ans. In the diet of pre-school children, these nutrients have the following importance

- **Iodine** It prevents Iodine Deficiency Disorders like; cretinism, enlargement of thyroid gland etc.
- **Iron** It prevents anaemia.
- **Calcium** It develops strong bones and teeth and prevents diseases like rickets.
- **Protein** It prevents PEM (Protein Energy Malnutrition) diseases like poor weight gain.

7. Which are the three aspects to be taken into account while planning diets for pre-schoolers?

Ans. The three aspects to be taken into account while planning diets for pre-schoolers are

(i) **Variety** Variation in textures, tastes, smells and colours broaden a child's nutritional intake and eating experience.

(ii) **Balance** Intake of complex carbohydrates, lean proteins and essential fats should be in balance.

(iii) **Moderation** Fast foods rich in fats and refined flours, sweets and ice creams should be taken in moderation.

8. Why are snacks important in a pre-schooler's diet?

Ans. Snacks are important in a pre-schooler's diet because it is hard for the pre-schoolers to eat enough in three meals. Healthy snacks in between meals provide the calories and nutrients they need. Besides, snack time is a good time to introduce new foods.

9. What is MMR vaccine for?

Ans. The MMR vaccine is for Measles, Mumps and Rubella diseases.

Exercise

1. Why should we limit the intake of saturated fats, excess sugars and salt in a school child's diet?

Ans. We should limit the intake of saturated fats, excess sugars and salt in a school child's diet for the following reasons

(i) Diets rich in fats and sugars increase the risk of obesity and other related problems.

(ii) Foods with added sugars cause dental problem and eventually, diabetes.

(iii) A high sodium intake (due to excess salt) may increase blood pressure, leading to major risks of stroke, kidney and coronary diseases.

2. How does involving children in meal planning help in healthy eating?

Ans. Involving children in meal planning helps in healthy eating as it interests them. Encouraging children in age-appropriate tasks like cooking and serving their meals can get them excited and also enable them to develop healthy and positive concepts about food.

3. 'Childhood obesity is on the increase'. Give reasons.

Ans. Childhood obesity is on the increase because

(i) Children are easily attracted by the messages conveyed by commercials. They insist on foods which are low in fibre and high in sugar, fat and sodium. Besides, they consume cold drinks having excess sugar.

(ii) Children have developed sedentary activities like sitting and watching TV programmes excessively, playing video games, etc., and have lost interest in outdoor games and other forms of exercise. Thus, their metabolism has slowed down and the excess fat gets stored in the body, causing obesity.

4. How has the Mid-Day-Meal Scheme boosted children's health as well as school performance?

Ans. The Mid-Day-Meal Scheme has boosted children's health as well as school performance because

(i) The scheme provides free lunch to students of Classes I to VIII in the school. Most of these children are from poor families and may not have eaten any breakfast before going to school. Thus, it has improved their nutritional status, boosting their health.

(ii) It has helped in improving children's performance as they are properly fed to focus. Proper nutrition has helped increase their attention span too.

Activity

1. Ask your parents/grandparents/aunt about the traditional complementary foods of your region. Do you think these foods are nutritious? Give reasons for your answers. (Pg 157)

Ans. I asked my grandmother about traditional complementary foods in our region. She shared some delicious and nutritious options

(i) **Dal-Rice Porridge (Dal-Chawal Ka Pani)** A mixture of lentils, rice and water, cooked to perfection.

(ii) **Khichdi** A blend of split lentils, rice and vegetables.

(iii) **Parantha-Sabzi** Whole wheat flatbread with vegetable fillings.

(iv) **Laddu** Made from wheat flour, gram flour and ghee (clarified butter).

(v) **Halwa** A sweet dish made from wheat flour, ghee and milk.

I believe these traditional complementary foods are nutritious for several reasons

- they use locally sourced, whole ingredients
- they are rich in essential macro-nutrients and micro-nutrients
- they support healthy digestion and gut development
- they are easy to prepare and digest
- they are culturally relevant and socially acceptable

2. You are asked to take care of a 4 years old child for a day from 10 am to 6 pm. Keeping a balanced diet in mind suggest what you will serve to her/him for meals and snacks. (Pg-162)

Ans. The following is a sample meal plan for a 4 years old child keeping in mind the balanced diet requirement

(i) 10:00 am – 10:30 am: Breakfast
- Whole wheat toast with scrambled eggs
- Glass of milk

(ii) 11:30 am – 12:00 pm: Tiffin (Mid-Morning Snack)
- Whole wheat sandwich (cheese/vegetable filling)
- Fresh fruit juice (orange/apple)

(iii) 12:00 pm – 1:00 pm: Lunch
- Whole wheat roti
- Mixed vegetable sabzi
- Dal fry
- Fresh fruit salad

(iv) 3:00 pm – 3:30 pm: Snack
- Veggie sticks
- Whole grain biscuits

(v) 6:00 pm – 7:00 pm: Dinner
- Whole wheat roti
- Chicken or vegetable biryani
- Raita (curd with cucumber, cumin)
- Mixed fruit salad

3. Suppose you have a 9 years old sister and an 11 years old brother, and both are vegetarian. Suggest what you will serve them for breakfast and dinner. (Pg-167)

Ans. I will serve the following items keeping in view their nutritional requirements

Day	Breakfast	Dinner
Monday	Whole wheat toast with cheese and fruit	Vegetable roti rolls
Tuesday	Poha (flattened rice) with nuts and banana	Dal fry with whole wheat roti
Wednesday	Whole grain cereal with milk	Vegetable rice bowl
Thursday	Vegetable dosa (fermented rice and lentil crepe)	Grilled vegetable sandwiches
Friday	Whole wheat pancakes with honey	Whole wheat pasta with vegetable sauce
Saturday	Yogurt with granola and fruit	Mixed vegetable sabzi with whole wheat roti
Sunday	Idlis (steamed rice cakes) with coconut chutney	Vegetable khichdi (mashed lentil and rice dish)

Exam Pattern Questions

Objective Type Questions

Multiple Choice Questions (MCQs)

1. What is the component of food which helps our body to fight against infections called?

(a) Proteins (b) Fats
(c) Carbohydrates (d) Starch

2. What is the primary source of nutrition for infants during the first 6 months?

(a) Breast milk (b) Complementary foods
(c) Formula milk (d) Solid foods

3. What does breast-milk protect an infant from?

(a) Gastro-intestinal infection
(b) Urinary infection
(c) Chest infection
(d) All of the above

4. What is the process of gradually introducing other foods along with breast milk?

(a) Complementary feeding (b) Colostrum
(c) Vegetables (d) All of these

5. Which of the following are benefits of breastfeeding?

I. Provides natural immunity
II. Helps prevent breast and ovarian cancers
III. Increases risk of allergies
IV. Lowers IQ **Competency Based Que**

Codes

(a) I and II (b) I, II and III
(c) I and IV (d) III and IV

6. Which among the following protects children from various diseases?

(a) Immunisation (b) Feeding
(c) Caring (d) None of these

7. What does BCG stands for?

(a) Born Cytoskin Group
(b) Blind Cell Group
(c) Bonded Cell Group
(d) Bacillus Calmette-Guerin

8. Your friend's 4-months old son has just been diagnosed with ricket.
Which deficiency, according to you, is the cause of this? **Competency Based Que**

(a) Vitamin D (b) Vitamin A
(c) Protein (d) Iodine

9. Which among the following diseases do children suffer from if protein, vitamin A and iron respectively are lacking in their meals?

(a) Protein-Energy Malnutrition (PEM)
(b) Xerophthalmia
(c) Anaemia
(d) All of the above

10. Which of the following is not a deficiency disease that may occur in childhood due to malnutrition?

(a) Protein Energy Malnutrition
(b) Anaemia
(c) Cholestrol
(d) None of the above

11. Choose the correct pair. **Competency Based Que**

(a) Protein Energy Malnutrition (PEM) – Vitamin A deficiency
(b) Protein Energy Malnutrition (PEM) – Growth delays and infections
(c) Anemia – Excess iron intake
(d) Rickets – Protein deficiency

12. What is the recommended dietary allowance of energy for preschool children (1-3 years)?

(a) 1000 Kcal (b) 1240 Kcal
(c) 1500 Kcal (d) 2000 Kcal

13. Which of the following is an aspect that a pre-schooler's diet should include?

(a) Variety of texture, tastes, smells, etc.
(b) Balance of intake of carbohydrates, lean proteins and essential fats.
(c) Moderation of intake of fast foods and refined flours.
(d) All of the above

14. Which of the following vaccines is recommended at 15-18 months?

(a) MMR (b) DPT (c) OPV (d) Typhoid

15. Your best friend is a nutritionist. A woman named Namita visited yesterday. She has a 7 years old girl and she asked your friend to suggest some food items for her child. **Competency Based Que**
What would your friend's suggestion be?

(a) Well cooked and mashed vegetables
(b) Raw salad and fruits
(c) Half a teaspoon of egg yolk
(d) Both (a) and (c)

16. In present, which disease is becoming very common among youngsters? **Competency Based Que**

I. Type II diabetes II. Hepatitis B
III. Hypertension IV. Osteopenia

Codes
(a) I and II (b) II and III
(c) III and IV (d) I and III

17. Find the incorrect statement **Competency Based Que**

(a) Anemia is caused due to the deficiency of iron.
(b) Vitamin A deficiency can cause nutritional blindness.
(c) Goitre is caused due to the deficiency of vitamin D.
(d) Protein energy Malnutrition can lead to diarrhea and dehydration.

18. Match the following. **Competency Based Que**

List I		List II	
A.	Protein	1.	For healthy bones
B.	Calcium	2.	For muscular growth
C.	Iron	3.	For growth and expansion of blood volume
D.	Vitamin C	4.	For healthy skin

Codes

	A	B	C	D
(a)	1	2	3	4
(b)	2	1	3	4
(c)	3	2	1	4
(d)	3	1	2	4

Assertion-Reason Questions

Direction (Q. Nos.19-23) In the questions given below, there are two statements marked as Assertion (A) and Reason (R). Read the statements and choose the correct option.

Codes
(a) Both A and R are true and R is the correct explanation of A.
(b) Both A and R are true, but R is not the correct explanation of A.
(c) A is true, but R is false.
(d) A is false, but R is true.

19. **Assertion** (A) Infants require exclusive breastfeeding for the first 6 months.
Reason (R) Breast-milk provides all necessary nutrients and protects against infections.

20. **Assertion** (A) Malnourished children don't perform very well in school.
Reason (R) It is a serious health hazard among lower socio-economic groups.

21. **Assertion** (A) Children with special needs do not require any dietary modifications.
Reason (R) Some children have altered senses of taste or smell, affecting food acceptance.

22. **Assertion** (A) Pre-school children need vaccinations to protect against communicable diseases.
Reason (R) Vaccinations provide lifelong immunity against diseases like measles, mumps and rubella.

23. **Assertion** (A) Moderate physical activity of 45-60 minutes everyday is very good for a school-going child.
Reason (R) Too much screen time and indoor-activities can be harmful for children as they hinder physical growth and development.

Case Based Questions

24. Read the passage given below and answer the following questions.

Nidhi's baby was born with a weight of 1.8 kg. The health problem faced by such babies are that they have poor sucking and swallowing reflexes. Their absorption capacity is also very low.

Answer the following questions based on above information.

(i) Nidhi's baby suffered from ....
(a) malnutrition
(b) low birth weight infant
(c) weak infant
(d) None of the above

(ii) The absorption capacity is very low because of ....
(a) low weight
(b) small size of stomach and intestine
(c) Both (a) and (b)
(d) None of the above

(iii) The dietary supplements than can be given to the infant include which of the following?

I. Fats II. Calcium
III. Iron IV. Carbohydrates

Codes
(a) I and II
(b) II and III
(c) III and IV
(d) I and IV

(iv) Given below are two statements labelled as Assertion (A) and Reason (R).
Assertion (A) The absorption capacity of baby born with a weight of 1.8 kg is very low.
Reason (R) Breast milk is nutritionally tailor -made for meeting an infant's nutritional needs.

Codes
(a) Both A and R are true and R is the correct explanation of A.
(b) Both A and R are true, but R is not the correct explanation of A.
(c) A is true, but R is false.
(d) A is false, but R is true.

25. Read the passage given below and answer the following questions.

With the concerted efforts of parents in following immunisation schedules and healthy nutrition pattern the child by this time is strong enough to fight occasional colds and cough.

You may know that obesity is a growing health risk among children now. This is largely due to a diet rich in fatty foods high in salt, low in fiber and beverages with added sugar. Non-active lifestyle further complements the situation. The problem is more among children from higher socio-economic sections of our society.

Type II diabetes and hypertension, earlier rare among children, are becoming more common among youngsters nowadays. This is attributed to the rise in childhood obesity.

Under-nutrition still remains a serious health hazard among lower socio-economic groups. Children from poor families go to school on an empty stomach. The result is that these malnourished children are not likely to perform well in school. Instead they are at a greater risk of morbidity and mortality.

In our country we face the dual problem of unde-rnutrition as well as over-nutrition. So if we continue to spread the benefits of healthy nutrition it will have an impact in the long run. Besides 'School Health' programmes providing free health checks and treatment will increase overall well-being of children.

On the basis of the information given above answer the following questions.

(i) A diet rich in fatty foods high in salt, low in fiber and beverages with added sugar is a major cause of ....
(a) rickets (b) malnutrition
(c) diabetes (d) obesity

(ii) Childhood obesity causes which among the following?
(a) Anemia (b) Hypertension
(c) Tetanus (d) Goitre

(iii) Malnourished children are at a greater risk of ....
(a) morbidity (b) mortality
(c) Both (a) and (b) (d) None of these

(iv) **Assertion** (A) Skipping breakfast negatively affects a child's physical and mental performance.

Reason (R) The loss of nutrients and calories cannot be made up later in the day.

Codes
(a) Both A and R are true and R is the correct explanation of A.
(b) Both A and R are true, but R is not the correct explanation of A.
(c) A is true, but R is false.
(d) A is false, but R is true.

Answers

1. (a) Protiens
2. (a) Breast milk
3. (d) All of the above
4. (a) Complementary feeding
5. (a) I and II
6. (a) Immunisation
7. (d) Bacillus Calmette-Guerin
8. (a) Vitamin D
9. (d) All of the above
10. (c) Cholestrol
11. (b) Protein Energy Malnutrition (PEM) – Growth delays and infections
12. (b) 1240 Kcal
13. (d) All of the above
14. (a) MMR
15. (b) Raw salad and fruits
16. (d) I and III
17. (c) Goitre is caused due to the deficiency of vitamin-D.
18. (b) 2 1 3 4
19. (a) Both A and R are true and R is the correct explanation of A.
20. (b) Both A and R are true, but R is not the correct explanation of A.
21. (d) A is false, but R is true.
22. (a) Both A and R are true and R is the correct explanation of A.
23. (b) Both A and R are true, but R is not the correct explanation of A.
24. (i) (b) low birth weight infant
(ii) (b) small size of stomach and intestine
(iii) (b) II and III
(iv) (b) Both A and R are true, but R is not the correct explanation of A.
25. (i) (d) obesity (ii) (b) Hypertension
(iii) (c) Both (a) and (b)
(iv) (a) Both A and R are true and R is the correct explanation of A.

Subjective Questions

Very Short Answer Type Questions

1. What is nutrition?

Ans. Nutrition is 'food at work', a process by which we obtain nutrients and metabolise them for growth, repair and well-being.

2. What are two important aspects to be considered in a mother's diet during the breastfeeding time?

Ans. The two important aspects of a mother's diet at this time are

(i) A mother must eat a diet rich in protein, calcium and iron.

(ii) A mother must consume adequate quantities of fluids like milk, soups, fruit juices and water.

3. What is colostrum?

Ans. Colostrum refers to the yellow colour fluid produced in the mother's breasts during the first 2-3 days after giving birth.

4. What factors result in malnutrition?

Ans. Malnutrition is the result of factors including female illiteracy, poverty, ignorance about the nutritional needs of an infant and poor access to health care.

5. Which disease is caused due to an iron deficiency?

Ans. Anaemia is caused due to an iron deficiency.

6. What problems increase the infant's susceptibility to infectious diseases in rural areas?

Ans. Poor access to health centres, climatic conditions, local customs and use of untested traditional methods of treatment increase the infant's susceptibility to infectious diseases in rural areas.

7. Priya, a 12 years old girl, is experiencing growth spurts. What nutrients should her diet focus on during this period? **Competency Based Que**

Ans. Priya should focus on protein, calcium and iron to support bone growth and overall health. Foods like dairy, leafy greens and legumes will be beneficial.

8. Ananya, age 8, often skips breakfast. What are the effects on her energy levels and concentration in school? **Competency Based Que**

Ans. Skipping breakfast can lead to low energy, poor concentration, and decreased academic performance. Ananya should prioritise a nutritious breakfast for better cognitive function throughout the day.

9. How is the growth pattern of children during the age of 7 to 12 years?

Ans. During the age of 7 to 12 years, the growth pattern is rather slow compared to that of earlier years. Instead, body changes occur gradually, especially from 9 to 10 years onwards, when boys and girls show different growth patterns.

10. Why should healthy eating habits be developed in pre-school children?

Ans. Healthy eating habits should be developed in pre-school children since they are still developing their eating habits and working on their chewing and swallowing skills. Healthy eating habits formed during these years are likely to be reflected in their food behaviour throughout their lives.

Short Answer Type Questions

1. What are four benefits of adequate nutrition for children?

Ans. The benefits of adequate nutrition for children are

(i) Proper functioning of the organs and systems of the body.

(ii) Good cognitive performance.

(iii) Good ability of the body to fight diseases and restore healing.

(iv) Development of a pleasant and positive attitude.

2. Rani recently gave birth to an infant baby girl.

(i) Rani's infant was born weighing 2.3 kg. What special nutritional considerations should she keep in mind for her low birth weight baby?

(ii) She's unsure how much breast milk her baby needs in the first month. What should she know about breastfeeding in this period? **Competency Based Que**

Ans. (i) Rani should ensure her baby receives frequent breastfeeding to meet high calorie needs. Complementary foods rich in nutrients like vitamins and minerals may be introduced later, emphasising a high-calorie diet.

(ii) She should know that infants can self-regulate their milk intake. Exclusive breastfeeding is recommended for the first six months, providing all necessary nutrients and hydration without needing additional water.

3. Which communicable diseases may cause death of infants? How can infants be made immune to such diseases?

Ans. The communicable diseases that may cause death of infants are polio, diphtheria, tuberculosis, pertussis (whooping cough), measles and tetanus.

Infants can be made immune to such diseases by giving them suitable immunisation vaccines at different stages of the first year of life.

4. During a family gathering, Anjali's 1 year old is refusing to eat the new vegetable dish. How should Anjali respond to encourage her child to try it?

Competency Based Que

Ans. Anjali should respond in the following ways

- Anjali should remain patient and avoid forcing her child to eat the vegetable dish.
- She can offer the new food along-side familiar favourites to make it more appealing.
- She should initially include small portions.
- If the child resists, Anjali can try again later without showing any personal dislikes toward the food.

5. In what way, should special diets be arranged so that pre-school children with special needs develop their eating skills properly?

Ans. For children with special needs, the special diet should be arranged by thickening thin liquids, by chopping dry or lumpy foods and/or by softening food to make it easy to swallow.

A feeding tube may be used, if required. Children with autism have an altered sense of taste or smell, which affects their acceptance of food.

Accordingly, extra fat, limited liquids, special formula or other dietary changes should be provided.

6. Amrita is keen to ensure her 8 years old son and 10 years old daughter develop healthy eating habits. Her son tends to favour sugary snacks, while her daughter is resistant to trying new vegetables. How can Amrita effectively guide her children toward making healthier choices while keeping mealtime enjoyable?

Competency Based Que

Ans. Ways through which Amrita can effectively guide her children towards making healthier choices are as follows

- **Aim for Variety** Amrita should introduce a range of foods, including fruits, vegetables and whole grains, to increase the likelihood of her children accepting new foods.
- **Ensure Good Nutrition** She can emphasise the importance of protein, calcium, iron and iodine, encouraging her kids to include nutritious options in their meals to support their growth and health.
- **Limit Sugars and Fats** Amrita should help her son reduce sugary snacks by offering healthier alternatives while maintaining a balanced diet low in saturated fats and salt.
- **Involve in Meal Planning** Engaging her children in meal planning and cooking will make healthy eating fun and educational, fostering positive attitudes toward nutritious foods.

7. What is the result of implementation of the mid-day meal scheme in schools?

Ans The implementation of the mid-day meal scheme in schools has shown good results. Classroom performance and attention spans of children have improved significantly due to the implementation of this scheme.

Additionally, school enrollment has increased and drop-out rate has declined. It has reduced the gender gap in education by boosting female attendance in schools.

8. How do the nutritional requirements vary for different age groups and genders of school-going children?

Ans. The nutritional requirements are the same for both boys and girls upto the age of 9 years. After this, the energy requirements for girls remain almost the same throughout but they need increased amounts of protein, iron and calcium to help bone growth and preparation for menarche.

Boys of 10-12 years age need enough calories to maintain adequate reserves for the spurt in their growth during adolescence.

Long Answer Type Questions

1. Enumerate five benefits of breastfeeding to the infant.

Ans. For answer refer to the text under the heading 'breast feeding' on page no. 169 and 170.

2. You are a nutritionist. A mother brings her newborn baby weighing less than 2.5 kg to you.

(i) What are the problems of low birth weight infant?

(ii) What are complementary foods? At what age can these be introduced?

(iii) Discuss in brief, what is immunisation?

Competency Based Que

Ans. (i) The low birth weight infant have poor sucking and swallowing reflexes. Their absorption capacity is also very low because of the small size of their stomachs and intestines, but they have a relatively high calorie requirement.

Breast-milk produced by their mothers has all their essential requirements and thus, can optimally fulfill all their dietary needs.

(ii) Complementary foods involves slowly introduce other foods along with the breast milk. These can be introduced by 6 months of age.

(iii) Immunisation protects children from various diseases. When a vaccine containing an inactive form of a bacterium/virus/toxin made by the germ is injected in a child, it induces white blood cells to produce antibodies. These antibodies then kill the germs if/when they attack a child's system.

3. Describe five nutritional deficiency diseases which malnourished children may fall prey to.

Ans. Nutritional deficiency diseases which malnourished children may fall prey to are

(i) **Diarrhea** It results in depletion of water and electrolytes from the infant's body, which is a major cause of infant mortality.

(ii) **Primary Herpes Simplex** It is an infectious disease caused by a virus which attacks the mouth.

(iii) **Protein Energy Malnutrition** (PEM) It leads to growth retardation and infections leading to diarrhoea and dehydration.

(iv) **Nutritional Blindness** It is a result of vitamin A deficiency.

(v) **Rickets and Osteopenia** They are bone-related diseases which occur due to shortage of vitamin D and calcium.

4. What are the aspects that a pre-school children's diet should emphasise? What are the diseases they will suffer due to diet deficiencies?

Ans. The aspects that a pre-schooler's diet should emphasise are

(i) **Variety** Variation in textures, tastes, smells and colours will broaden a child's nutritional intake and eating experience.

(ii) **Balance** Intake of complex carbohydrates, lean proteins and essential fats should be in balance.

(iii) **Moderation** Fast foods rich in fats and refined flours, as well as sweets and ice creams should be taken in moderation.

Children might suffer from Protein-Energy Malnutrition (PEM), Xerophthalmia (vitamin A deficiency), Anaemia and Iodine Deficiency Disorders if protein, vitamin A, iron and iodine, respectively, are lacking in their meals.

5. During a parents-teacher meeting, the school nutritionist emphasises the importance of establishing healthy eating habits for children. Many parents express concerns about their children's food choices, particularly with the rise of fast food and sugary snacks. The nutritionist suggests that parents work with their children to develop better eating habits. What are four healthy eating habits that school-going children should cultivate to promote their overall well-being and academic performance? **Competency Based Que**

Ans. Four healthy eating habits which school-going children should develop are

(i) **Sensible Eating** They should eat snacks with less fat, sugar and salt while relaxing or watching TV.

(ii) **Increased Physical Activity** Moderate activity of 45-60 minutes everyday promotes good health. Screen time should be limited and children should be encouraged to take part in sports and in extra-curricular activities in the school and the community.

(iii) **Ensure Food Safety** Children should be trained to eat under hygienic conditions. Food consumed should be clean and safe before eating. They must wash their hands before eating.

(iv) **Control Quantity Intake** Children of 9-12 years can gauge how hungry they are. We must never force them for eating more. Skipping a meal is no problem as long as the child is healthy and it does not become a habit.

SELF ASSESSMENT TEST

Objective Type Questions

1. The communicable diseases that may cause death of an infant are ....
   (a) Polio (b) Tuberculosis (c) Measles (d) All of these
2. At what age is exclusive breastfeeding recommended by WHO?
   (a) 3 months (b) 12 months (c) 6 months (d) 9 months

Very Short Answer Type Questions

3. What is the recommendation of WHO regarding breastfeeding of infants?
4. In what way can good nutrition be observed?
5. What are the results of nutritional deficiency during infancy.
6. What precautions should be taken while serving infants complementary foods?
7. How can interest in food be stimulated in pre-school children?
8. How do peers affect the choice of food in school-going children?

Short Answer Type Questions

9. What changes in weight and body dimensions take place in the infant during the first year of life?
10. Explain are the four guidelines for complementary feeding?
11. How should the eating skills of children with special needs be developed?
12. How has obesity affected school-going children? Explain.

Long Answer Type Questions

13. Which vaccines should be given to the infant soon after birth? How many times should they be repeated and after what intervals? Name the diseases that are prevented by each of these vaccines.
14. Explain the immunisation schedule in pre-school children for the four vaccines continued from infancy. Name the diseases prevented by each such vaccine.
15. Discuss the recommendations of ICMR for the daily intake of foods from the five food groups for pre-school children of the age groups 1 to 3 years and 4 to 6 years.

10

CHAPTER

Clothing plays a vital role in our daily lives, serving purposes like comfort, protection and expression.

Our Apparel

YOUR STUDY GOALS

10.1 Clothing Functions and the Selection of Clothes
10.2 Factors Affecting Selection of Clothing in India
10.3 Understanding Children's Basic Clothing Needs
10.4 Clothing Requirements at Different Childhood Stages
10.5 Clothes for Children with Special Needs

YOUR PRACTICE GOAL

- Objective Type Questions (23 Qs ; MCQs, A-R, Matching, Case Based)
- Subjective Questions (10 VSAs, 7 SAs, 6 LAs)

Our posture, walk, smile, frown and other body language all contribute to the impression we make. Among these, clothing creates the first impression. Looking good is important. To appreciate the true significance of clothing, we should reflect on how we feel when we wear different outfits.

10.1 Clothing Functions and the Selection of Clothes

The weather may determine clothing choices. School activities, family events or gatherings with friends might affect the selection of clothes. Everyone wears different types of clothing. It is important to understand why certain clothes are chosen. The reasons for this are

Modesty

- The main reason for wearing clothes is modesty. In our society, people do not go without clothes. Young children often don't feel embarrassed being without clothing. They learn the need to cover their bodies as they grow.
- Ideas about modesty may vary by society. What is considered modest[1] in one society may not be in another.

1 Modest It means having or showing a moderate opinion of one's own value, abilities achievements.

- For example, in some communities, women who do not cover their heads are seen as immodest. While, in other communities, women who do not cover their legs are viewed as immodest.

Protection

- Clothing protects us from the environment, including harsh weather, dirt and pollution.
- People change their clothes according to the seasons. In hot summer months, lightweight cotton clothes are worn. Sometimes we even cover our heads to protect from the Sun. In winter, layers of woolen clothing are used for warmth and protection.
- Clothing can also protect against physical harm. For example, fire-fighters wear special gear to guard against fire, smoke and water.
- Many sports require specific clothing to protect players from injury. Players often wear arm guards, leg guards and wristbands along with their regular uniforms for extra protection.

Status and Prestige

- Clothes can signify a person's **social status**. In the past, clothing often showed economic and social status. Historical films show how kings and courtesans dressed differently from common people.
- Everyone's sense of identity includes a feeling of social status. Clothing is one way to express this. In India, during festivals and important family events, people wear clothes that may reflect their social status.
- Today, stylish clothing is available at reasonable prices, allowing more young people to afford them. Similar clothing (like T-shirts, jeans and salwar-kurtas) have become available to all. This helps to reduce social class differences, thus, promoting **social equity** in a democratic society.

Adornment

- People wear clothes to look attractive. Good clothing enhances appearance. The desire to decorate the body is a common practice in all societies, it is universal. **Body decoration methods** include ear piercing, nail polishing, tattooing and hair braiding or knotting, which is considered attractive varies by society.
- There are many types of fabrics available, each are suitable for different clothing and uses. The choice of clothing not only considers fabric characteristics, but also takes into consideration style and accessory details.

10.2 Factors Affecting Selection of Clothing in India

The final decision in the selection is depend on the **geographical features, climate and seasonal features** of the area where they have to be used. It is also affected by easy availability, cultural influences and even more strongly the family traditions.

Factors that affect selection of clothing are as follows

Age

- Age is a key factor in selecting clothes at all the stages of life, especially for children. Parents or family members make these decisions for kids.
- Children's **physical growth, motor development** and activities must be considered for their comfort and safety.
- As children grow, they interact more with people outside their family and become aware of others' clothing and opinions.
- Conformity to peers becomes important during **middle childhood** and increases with age. Clothing helps children to feel a sense of belonging and acceptance.

- As children approach **adolescence**, rapid physical growth leads to more differences in clothing for boys and girls. Adolescents also recognise cultural norms and trends, believing that their popularity depends on wearing the **'right clothes'**.

Climate and Season

- Protection from the environment and weather is a key reason for wearing clothes, so children's clothing must suit the climate.
- Clothing needs for cold weather are very different from those for warm or temperate climates and also differ for areas with heavy rain or high humidity.
- Some clothes and fabrics may only be suitable for a few months each year, so their cost and quantity should be considered carefully.
- This is especially important for growing children, as they may outgrow clothes by the next season.

Occasion

- The selection of clothes depends on the occasion and time of day. There are unwritten rules and traditions for clothing for each occasion.
- Most schools have uniforms and rules regarding not wearing accessories and ornaments. Wearing very formal or sporty clothes can lead to disciplinary issues or teasing from peers or may be deterred from joining group activities.
- During social gatherings and parties, children like to wear nice apparel[2] to express their individuality. Family events, like weddings, often require following traditional dress norms.
- In many communities, rites and ceremonies related to important life events still follow certain customs, though some may be changed or modified with time.
- Clothing choices reflect not just style, but also fabric type, texture, colour and accessories.
- Concepts of modesty and protection change are based on the occasion, activity and time. It is important to wear the right outfit at the right time.

Fashion

- Fashion is a style that is popular and appealing to many people or masses today.
- Children are becoming more aware of fashion due to TV and media, which makes them **conscious of trends**.
- Fashion can be influenced by famous people, social or political leaders, movie stars and significant events in the country.
- This can include types of fabric, colours, designs, shapes of clothing and accessories like scarves, bags and belts.
- Some trends, known as fads[3], often appeal to children and adolescents. They exaggerate or highlight some features of clothing.

Income

- The amount of money available also affects the selection of clothing.
- The money a family has influences their clothing choices, including the initial cost, how long the clothes last (durability) and how much care they need.
- The number of children, their ages and their gender can also affect what clothes are chosen. Families with higher incomes usually have a greater variety of clothing, especially for special occasions.

---

2 Apparel Clothing or garments worn by individuals for various occasions.

3 Fads It means a style or activity that suddenly becomes popular but which usually does not stay popular for very long.

- In families with modest or low income, the clothes of older siblings are recycled and worn by younger ones to reduce the expenditure on clothes.
- Schools require uniforms to **reduce visible differences** in wealth among students.

Quick Test 1

1. How are ideas about modesty shaped?
2. What would be an appropriate choice of clothes for a social gathering?
3. Which style has contemporary appeal for the masses?
4. Name the fashions that are very short lived.

10.3 Understanding Children's Basic Clothing Needs

- As children grow, they want to dress like their friends or adults they admire. This is an important and emotional experience for them.
- Children's clothes should be appropriate for their various activities and allow them the freedom to play, which is essential for their physical growth.
- The clothing needs change as children grow, from infancy to adolescence.

Comfort

- The most important requirement for children's clothing is comfort. They need to move freely, rolling, crawling, climbing, running and jumping, without their clothes getting in the way.
- Children should be able to play without worrying about getting their clothes dirty. Elastic bindings should not be so tight as to cause pain. Tight clothes can restrict movement and affect blood circulation, so they should be avoided.
- Choose lightweight clothes made of materials like, acrylic and nylon for winter to keep them warm without being bulky or heavy, which can be tiring to wear.
- Clothes should allow for bending and stooping, with enough space in the crotch for comfortable movement. Clothing that hangs from the shoulders is usually more comfortable than those which hangs from the waist.
- Necklines should be wide enough to avoid straining the throat. Sleeves with tight bands can restrict movement and be irritating, so they should be avoided.
- Organdy collars for girls' frocks and heavily starched shirts for little boys are uncomfortable to wear. Raglan sleeves offer more freedom and room for growth compared to fitted sleeves.
- Fabrics should be soft and absorbent for a child's sensitive skin. Avoid overly large or small clothes. Choose garments that fit well and also allow the growth.

Safety

- Comfort and safety are both important for children's clothing. Clothes that are too large can be uncomfortable and unsafe.
- Loose garments are more likely to catch fire, especially near cooking areas, as compared to fitted clothes.
- Hanging sashes and trims can get caught in moving parts of toys like tricycles, which can be dangerous.
- Bright colours are safer for kids because they are more visible to drivers than dark or gray colours. Also, loose buttons and trims can be a choking hazard for infants and toddlers who tend to put things in their mouths.

Self-help

- Allowing children to dress and undress themselves helps them to build their confidence and self-reliance.
- Sometimes clothes are too difficult to put on or take off by the children themselves. It becomes frustrating for a child who wants to dress on her/his own.
- The most important feature for self-help is **having a large opening** in the dress so the child can easily get in and out. Front openings are the easiest for them to manage.
- Buttons should be large enough for a child to grasp/hold. Designs should be distinct on the front and back, helps the child to learn and to recognise how to wear the garment.
- Small snaps, hooks and eyes and bows tied at the waist or the neck and small buttons with thread loops can make it hard for children to dress themselves.

Appearance

- Children have their own ideas about clothing and they should be allowed to express their preferences. Exercising some choice at the younger ages helps them learn to select appropriate clothes.
- Bright colours for outerwear make it easier to spot a child on the playground or street, enhancing their safety.
- Lines in clothing should highlight desirable features and hide those features that are less desirable.
- Fabric designs should match smaller figures. Small checks, stripes, plaids and dainty prints work best, as large designs can overwhelm a small child.

Allowance for Growth

- Children's clothing should allow for growth, especially in length. Buying clothes that are too large is neither safe nor comfortable.
- It's better to select clothes that fit well but have extra room for lengthening as the child grows.
- Fabrics that don't shrink are ideal. Trousers can have cuffs that can be let down to add length and skirts should have adjustable straps.
- Raglan sleeves provide more room for growth compared to set-in sleeves. Tucks and pleats at the shoulders can also allow for extra width as the child grows.

Easy Care

- Children are happier when they don't have to worry about getting their clothes dirty.
- Mothers appreciate clothes that are easy to wash and require little or no ironing.
- **Flat seams**[4] are important because they are last longer than regular seams. Places that get a lot of wear or strain, like knees, pocket corners and elbows, can be made stronger.

Fabrics

- Soft, tightly woven or knitted fabrics that are easy to care for and comfortable against the skin are best for children's clothing.
- Avoid clothes that need to be dry cleaned.
- Printed fabrics, corduroy and textured fabrics show less wrinkles and dirt/soil. Cotton is the most common choice because it's washable and comfortable.
- Wool is warm but needs special care and can irritate delicate skin, so it shouldn't be worn directly on the skin.
- Polyester, nylon and acrylic are durable and easy to care for. Cotton-polyester blend is often more comfortable than pure polyester because it absorbs moisture better.

---

4 **Flat seams** It is a strong seam with two lines of stitching showing on the right side that is produced by folding one raw edge under the other and stitching it flat or slip-stitching it on the wrong side.

10.4 Clothing Requirements at Different Childhood Stages

Each stage of childhood has specific characteristics that need to be kept in mind while selecting their clothes.

Infancy (Birth to Six months)

- During the early months, warmth, comfort and hygiene are the most important factors for infants, who mainly feed, sleep and eliminate.
- Clothes should be easy to put on and take off. Options that open in the front or have large openings are better than those that slip over the head. Avoid draw strings around the neck to prevent entanglement. Fasteners should be easy to reach and safe for the baby. It is advisable to have plenty of garments that need to be changed often like shirts and diapers.
- Babies have delicate skin, so their clothes should be soft, light and simple to put on and take-off. Fabrics with sizing can scratch the skin, and all-wool flannel can be irritating.
- Thus, a baby flannel i.e. a mix of wool and cotton or silk is preferred for winter. Since infants grow quickly, don't buy too many clothes in smaller sizes.
- Diapers are the first and most essential requirement for infants. These have to be soft, absorbent and easy-to-wash.

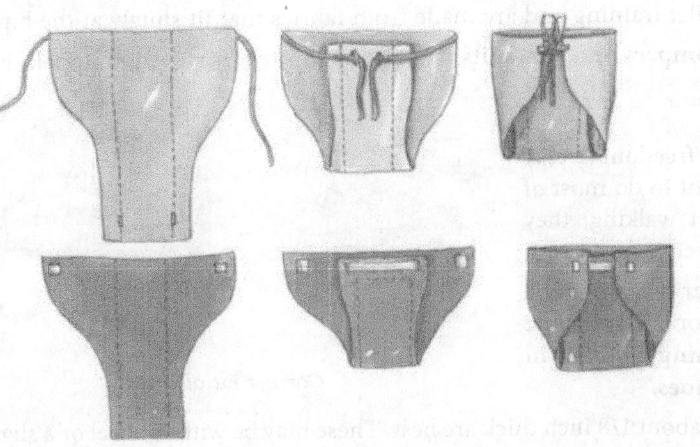

▲ *Pre-shaped Diapers*

- Many families make cotton diapers at home. If old cotton sheets are used for the purpose, they need to be well **sterilised**[5] and disinfected. Many families have replaced homemade diapers with **gauze**[6] and bird's eye diapers that are available in the market.
- Pre-shaped diapers are also available but one should be certain about the fit for the baby.
- Most infants wear undershirts. Depending on the weather and geographical location, the material for the undershirt should be selected suitably. Cotton is suitable for warm weather and a soft wool-cotton blend is suitable for cold weather.
- Shirts and diapers are the main clothes for infants. Cotton shirts that are easy to slip-on are preferred. In rural areas, infants often wear simple, homemade clothes made from used materials.

Creeping Age (6 months to 1 year)

- From 6 months to 1 year, babies start showing signs of independence. They pull themselves up, reach for objects and try to sit or stand on their own.
- Clothes for this age must allow **free movement**. They should be loose and non interfering or comfortable. Knitted and cut garments are ideal because they stretch and accommodate growth.
- It's important to choose clothes that support good posture. Avoid bulky clothing, as it can hinder movement. Lightweight garments are better than tightly knitted or woven ones. They are easier for children to play in and keep them warmer by trapping air, especially in winter. Don't make children wear too many clothes.

---

5 **Sterilised** Made free from bacteria or other living micro-organisms.
6 **Gauze** Thin, lightweight fabric used for dressings or clothing.

- Clothes should be made from soft, smooth fabrics that don't get dirty easily. They should be easy to care for i.e. wash and iron. Fabrics like knits and seersucker (crimped striped material) are great because they don't need ironing. Some cottons and rayons are wrinkle resistant as they are treated with special finishes.

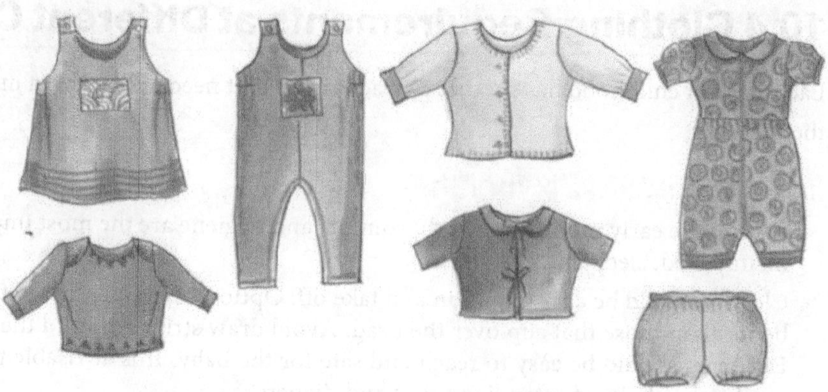

▲ *Apparel Designs Suitable for Crawling Age*

- Since children play a lot, their clothes will get dirty and need to be changed often. They look for garments with convenient openings to make changing easy.
- Choose clothes that are the right size and loose enough so they don't restrict movement. During the crawling stage, soft-soled shoes can be worn for warmth.
- Training pants are helpful during toilet training and are made from fabrics that fit snugly at the hips.
- The best garments for this age are **rompers and sun-suits** made from knitted or woven material.

Toddlerhood (1-2 years)

- Toddlers are very active and need the freedom to play both indoors and outdoors. They want to do most of the things themselves. As they start walking, they want to reach out for anything they see.
- Shoes become essential as toddlers start walking. The right fit of shoes and socks is crucial for their comfort and foot health. **The principle clothing concern in the toddler age is the selection of shoes.**

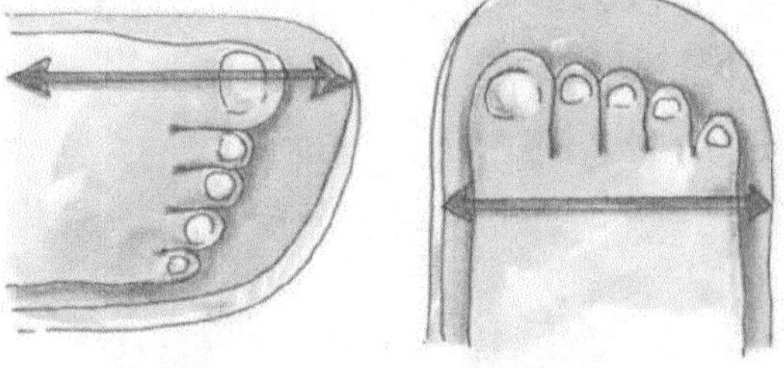

▲ *Correct Fit of Shoe*

- Flexible-soled shoes with rough soles about 1/8 inch thick are best. These may be without heel or a slight heel and should be full and puffy in the toe area.
- Shoes must be carefully selected and fitted because a child's soft bones can be injured by poorly fitting or badly shaped shoes. Consider the length, width, height of toe space and fit of the heel.
- To ensure a proper fit, shoes should be tried on the child. Well-fitting shoes support good body skills, helping with balance, climbing and running. Since children grow quickly, it's important to replace their shoes often to prevent foot problems.
- Overalls are ideal for toddlers, as they need to be loose enough for diapers. By the age of two, children want to dress themselves, so it's important to choose clothes with features that help them to do this easily.

Pre-school age (2-6 years)

- The health and comfort of pre-schoolers are important when choosing their clothes. Clothing should be suitable for active play and able to withstand wear and tear. Clothes should be made from lightweight materials that are pre-shrunk and easy to care for. **Cotton is the best choice** because it is hygienic, absorbent and easy to wash.
- Pre-school clothing should be designed for easy maintenance. Avoid dresses with complicated trimmings that are hard to wash and iron. Clothes should be able to handle many washes.

- Since pre-schoolers grow quickly, it's wise to buy only a few garments that can be used for different occasions. While buying expensive clothes, look for clothes that allow for growth. This will enable a garment to be worn over a longer period of time.
- **Pre-schoolers start to show preferences for colours and styles.** Personality plays an important role in children's choice of clothing. Girls may prefer feminine styles with frills, while boys may want to dress comfortably like other boys.
- It is observed that, at this stage, girls are permitted to wear pants/jeans/shorts like boys, although the opposite is not true for boys.
- Respect each child's individuality when choosing their cloths. Identical twins should not be dressed alike unless they want to be.
- It's important for pre-schoolers to express their clothing choices. Involve them in the shopping process to make them feel included.
- Clothing should have features that help children become more independent and self-reliant. This includes one-piece garments with front openings, large buttons and roomy necklines and armholes.
- Therefore, clothes for pre-schoolers should be comfortable, easy to care for, durable, allow for growth, look attractive and encourage self-reliance.

▲ *Apparel for Pre-schoolers*

Quick Test 2

1. Children clothing should have allowance for what aspect, especially in length?
2. What are the most important factors to be considered, during the infancy (birth-6 months) phase?
3. What is the time period of creeping age?
4. At what age, do children start showing interest in their clothing?

Elementary School Years (6-11 years)

- During middle childhood, children are very active and interested in sports. Clothing is important for their **social and emotional development** at this stage.
- Comfortable clothes are essential. Boys often prefer rugged outfits that can handle rough play, while girls might choose either 'boyish' clothes or more feminine dresses.
- Many children want to choose their own clothes and may not like suggestions from their parents.
- Children start developing preferences for certain styles to gain acceptance from their peers. Parents should recognise that a sensitive child may feel embarrassed or lose confidence if their clothes are very different from what their friends wear.

- While selecting cloths for school children fitting is an important aspect to be considered. A poorly fit dress is often discarded by the children. However, some children may select a dress on the basis of style even if it is not comfortable.
- To meet their physical needs, children require **absorbent fabrics** that can soak up sweat/perspiration. The best options are cotton and voile.
- When choosing clothes for school-going children, factors like safety, easy care, growth allowance and how well the clothes fit their bodies are also important, just like for younger children.

▲ *Sporty and comfortable Dresses for 5-8 years, Comfortable Clothing for Elementary School-age Group*

Adolescents (11-18 years)

- During adolescence, growth happens quickly because different body parts grow at different rates. A minimal wardrobe is advisable since clothes will be outgrown rapidly.
- Teenagers prioritise fit and style in their clothing. They often focus more on trends than on the quality of fabric or construction.
- Adolescents are eager to follow fashion and create their own styles. They may spend a lot of money on clothes and often dress like their peers or role models to establish their identity.
- When dressing for sports or workouts, it's important to choose comfortable clothes and shoes that prevent problems such as strains, blisters, sprains and sore legs and ankles.
- Fabrics should be easy to wash, as simple hygiene can save the skin from irritation and rashes.
- Garment design and fabric should allow for free movement and absorption of perspiration or sweat.

▲ *Apparel Designs for Adolescents*

10.5 Clothes for Children with Special Needs

- Clothing not only protects children but also helps them to develop independence and a sense of self. It allows them to express themselves to others.
- For children with disabilities, dressing is an important task. Some can dress themselves, which gives them pride and satisfaction. However, those with severe disabilities may need help from a caregiver, making it a longer and more challenging process.
- Clothes for children with special needs[7] should be chosen based on their specific disabilities. **Comfort** is the most important factor. Cotton is preferred for summer and fabrics like velvet and corduroy for winter. The clothes should be durable enough to withstand wear from orthotic devices or wheelchairs.
- Garments should have **reinforcements** at specified areas for calipers and braces. Openings should be easy. Hence, velcros and zippers with key chains are good choices. They should be also easy to wash.
- Design features like wider necklines, elastic waistbands and front openings and pockets make them easier to put on and take off.
- The clothes should have an **aesthetic appeal** and look attractive, well-stitched and suitable for any child. They should come in appealing colours and prints to make the wearer feel good. The best clothing is made to meet the individual needs of both the child and caregiver.
- Thus, overall, what children wear plays a significant role in their personality development. Clothes should be visually appealing, comfortable and appropriate for their cultural and ecological context.

Quick Test 3

1. Why do some children want to dress independently?
2. Why minimal wardrobe is advisable during adolescence?
3. Give two factors to be considered while choosing fabric for clothes of an adolescent.
4. Mention the reason due to which the clothes for children with special needs require to be durable.

7 **Children with special needs** Children requiring additional support due to disabilities or challenges.

Mind Map

OUR APPAREL

1 Clothing Functions and the Selection of Clothes

Modesty
- Ideas about modesty may vary by society.
  For example In some communities women's who don't cover their heads are seen as immodest.

Protection
- It protects us from the harsh weather.
- Clothing changes according to the season.
- It also protects us from physical harm.

Status and Prestige
- Clothes reflect a person's social status.
- Today stylish clothing is available at reasonable prices, which reduce class differences.

Adornment
- Good clothing enhances appearance.
- Many types of fabrics available for different clothing.

2 Factors Affecting Selection of Clothing in India

Age
- Key factors in choosing clothes.
- Child's physical growth and motor development must be considered.
- During middle childhood conformity to peers become important.
- In adolescence, rapid physical growth leads to differences in clothing.

Fashion
- Fashion is a style.
- It is appealing to people.
- It includes types of fabric, colour, design etc.
- Fads is a type of fashion which is short lived.

Climate and Season
- Protect from the environment.
- It is important for growing children.

Occasion
- Selection of clothes depends on the occasion.
- There are unwritten rules and tradition of clothing for each occasion.

Income
- Money affects the selection of clothes.
- Schools require uniforms to reduce visible differences in children.

3 Understanding Children's Basic Clothing Needs

Comfort
- Clothes should be comfortable.
- Choose right weight clothes.

Safety
- Clothes should not be too large.
- Loose garments are more likely to catch the fire.

Self-help
- Allow children to dress and undress themselves.
- Front opening are easiest for them to manage.

Appearance
- Children should be allowed to express their preferences.
- Choices help them to learn to select appropriate clothes.

Allowance for Growth
- Children's clothing should allow for growth, in length.
- Clothes should be fit well but have extra room for lengthening.

4 Clothing Requirements at Different Childhood Stages

Infancy
- Clothes should prioritise warmth, comfort and hygiene with light weight.

Crawling Age
- Loose, light weight and non-restrictive clothes that allow free movement.

Pre-school Age
- Easy to care cotton garment's with self-help features.

Elementary School Age
- Casual clothes suitable for, physical activity and peer acceptance.

Adolescents
- Stylish clothes that reflects fashion trends, allow free movement.
- Suit physical growth.

5 Clothes for Children with Special Needs

- They may need clothing that supports their specific needs and ensures comfort.
- Cotton is best for summer.
- Clothes should be strong enough to withstand wear from orthotic devices.
- Design features like wide neckline, front openings make dressing easier.
- Clothes should look attractive to boost confidence in children.

Apparel Designs for Adolescents

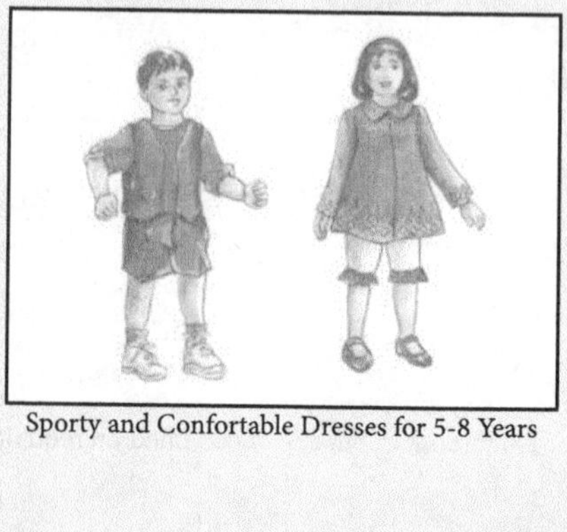

Sporty and Confortable Dresses for 5-8 Years

NCERT Folder

1. Give any three reasons for why you wear clothes.

Ans. Three reasons for wearing clothes are

(i) **Due to Modesty** In our society, people do not go around without them; we wear clothes to cover ourselves.

(ii) **For Protection** We wear clothing to protect ourselves from the harsh environment and to prevent physical harm to us.

(iii) **To Enhance Our Status** People tend to identify others' economic status by observing the clothes that they wear.

2. What are the factors that affect the selection of clothing for children?

Ans. The factors that affect the selection of clothing for children are

(i) Comfort while carrying out all activities.

(ii) Safety under all conditions.

(iii) Ease of dressing and undressing by the child itself.

(iv) Having an attractive appearance.

(v) Having allowances for growth in height and bulk.

(vi) Ease in washing and ironing.

(vii) Made of a suitable fabric.

3. Discuss any four clothing needs of children.

Ans. The four clothing needs of children are

(i) **Comfort** The most important requirement for children is comfort. They need to roll, crawl, squat, climb, run and jump without being hindered by clothes. They need to play without fear of getting their clothes dirty.

(ii) **Safety** Comfort and safety go hand-in-hand for children's clothing. Clothes which are too large may be uncomfortable and may also be unsafe.

Loose garments can catch on fire more easily (than fitting clothes) around the cooking area. Hanging sashes and trims can get caught in the moving parts of the tricycle or objects.

(iii) **Appearance** Children have their own ideas about their clothing and they should be allowed to express their preferences. Exercising some choice at the younger ages will help them to develop their ability to select appropriate clothes. Bright colours for outer wear make it easier to spot a child on the playground or street.

(iv) **Easy Care** Children are happier if they do not have to be worried about getting their clothes dirty. Even mothers appreciate easy care clothes, ones which can be easily washed and need little or no ironing.

4. Why do children's clothing requirements change with age? Discuss the clothing features of children at infancy, pre-school age and elementary school years.

Ans. Children's clothing requirements change with age owing to their physical growth, motor development, association with people and other things around them. The change is also due to the activities they indulge in.

All of this has to be taken into consideration from the point of view of comfort and safety. Thus, the clothing requirements also change.

The clothing features of children at infancy, pre-school age and elementary school years are

(i) **Infancy**

- The clothes should open down the front or have large openings to avoid slipping the dress over the heads of infants.
- The fasteners should be easily reachable and should be of a kind that cannot injure a baby in any way.
- As the baby's skin is very delicate and sensitive, it demands the clothes to be very soft, light-in-weight and simple to put-on and take-off.
- Diapers have to be soft, absorbent, easily washable and quick in drying.
- Cotton diapers can be made at home.

(ii) **Pre-school Age**

- The clothes should be comfortable to wear, easy to maintain, durable to use and provide allowance for growing needs.
- They should also look attractive in design and colour and encourage self-reliance.

(iii) **Elementary School Years**

- The clothes should be rugged so that they can withstand their rough and tumble play activities.
- Proper fitting is an important feature because a poorly fitted dress is often discarded.

5. What should be the features of clothes for children with special needs?

Ans. The features of clothes for children with special needs should be

- They should be comfortable. Cotton is the most preferred fabric for summer. Velvet, corduroy and cotswool can be used in winter.

- In case, the children use orthotic devices or wheelchairs, the garments should be strong enough to withstand abrasion.
- Garments should have reinforcements at specified areas for calipers and braces.
- Openings should be easily accessible and easy to fasten. Hence, velcros and zippers with keychains are good choices.
- Wearing and taking off should be simple. So wider necklines, waist belts with elastics, front open plackets and front pockets are preferred.
- The garment should be appealing in colour and print so that the wearer feels good.

Activity

1. Can you identify the clothing that is needed in the rainy season? What type of fabrics, garments and accessories are needed in that weather? Make a list and discuss with your friends. (Pg 172)

Ans. The kind of fabrics suitable for the rainy season are

- Water-repellent fabrics (e.g., nylon, polyester)
- Breathable fabrics (e.g., cotton, linen)
- Quick-drying fabrics (e.g., polyester blends)

Garments for rainy season are

- Waterproof jackets or windcheaters
- Lightweight, breathable tops (t-shirts, tunics)
- Water-resistant trousers (track pants, leggings)
- Raincoats or ponchos
- Waterproof shoes or sandals with good grip
- Lightweight, quick-drying socks
- Umbrella-proof hodies or caps

Accessories for rainy season are

- Compact umbrellas
- Water-resistant bags (backpacks, sling bags)
- Waterproof phone cases

2. Observe children of various age groups and note what clothing they wear at ages 2 years, 5 years, 11 years and 16 years. (Pg. 178)

Ans. The kind of clothing worn by children in different age groups are as follows

Age 2 years

- **Tops** Cute T-shirts, onesies or lightweight kurta-pyjamas
- **Bottoms** Comfortable pants, leggings or rompers
- **Footwear** Soft shoes or sandals with straps
- **Accessories** Baby caps, mittens and bibs
- **Fabrics** Soft cotton, breathable fabrics
- **Example** A 2 years old boy might wear a bright yellow T-shirt with cartoon prints, paired with lightweight blue pants and soft sneakers.

Age 5 years

- **Tops** Colorful T-shirts, tunics or short-sleeved shirts
- **Bottoms** Shorts, skirts or comfortable trousers
- **Footwear** Sneakers, sandals or school shoes
- **Accessories** Hair clips, simple jewellary or watches
- **Fabrics** Cotton, polyester blends
- **Example** A 5 years old girl might wear a pink frock with white flowers, paired with black shoes and hair clips.

Age 11 years

- **Tops** Graphic T-shirts, school uniforms or casual shirts
- **Bottoms** School trousers, jeans or track pants
- **Footwear** School shoes, sneakers or sports shoes
- **Accessories** Simple jewelry, watches or backpacks
- **Fabrics** Cotton, polyester blends or denim
- **Example** An 11 years old boy might wear a school uniform consisting of a white shirt, navy blue trousers and black shoes.

Age 16 years

- **Tops** Trendy T-shirts, hoodies or formal shirts
- **Bottoms** Jeans, trousers or skirts
- **Footwear** Sneakers, boots or formal shoes
- **Accessories** Fashion jewelry, watches or stylish bags
- **Fabrics** Denim, cotton or blends
- **Example** A 16 years old girl might wear a trendy black top with distressed jeans, sneakers and a silver necklace.

3. Make a size chart of toddlers according to weight and height by measuring four children in this age group, two girls and two boys. (Pg. 181)

Ans. Toddlers' Size Chart (Age 2-3 years)

Weight (Kg)	Height (Cm)
10-12	80-86
12-14	86-90
14-16	90-94
16-18	94-98

General Guidelines

- **Small** 10-12 kg, 80-86 cm
- **Medium** 12-14 kg, 86-90 cm
- **Large** 14-16 kg, 90-94 cm
- **Extra Large** 16-18 kg, 94-98 cm

Sample Measurements

- **Girl 1** 12 kg, 86 cm
- **Girl 2** 10 kg, 80 cm
- **Boy 1** 14 kg, 90 cm
- **Boy 2** 12 kg, 84 cm

Exam Pattern Questions

Objective Type Questions

Multiple Choice Questions (MCQs)

1. Select the incorrect statement. **Competency Based Que**

(a) Clothing can also protect us from physical harm.
(b) Ideas about modesty are shaped by the society in which we live.
(c) What is considered modest in one society might not be considered as modest in another.
(d) None of the above

2. Clothes can also serve as a status symbol. It is true that dress might reveal a person's ....

(a) political status
(b) social and economic status
(c) geographical status
(d) All of these

3. What is a kind of body decoration?

(a) Ear piercing
(b) Nail polishing
(c) Tattooing
(d) All of these

4. .... is an important factor to be considered at all stages of life. It becomes more important while selecting clothes and apparel for children, since it is parents or elders of the family who are taking the decision regarding their clothes. **Competency Based Que**

(a) Climate and Season
(b) Occasion
(c) Age
(d) Fashion

5. Children and adolescents are often likely to be taken up by an exaggerated short-lived fashion known as what?

(a) Fads
(b) Fashion
(c) Style
(d) None of these

6. Why children's clothes must be suitable for the different activities? **Competency Based Que**

I. It gives them freedom to play
II. It is essential for their physical growth
III. It helps them in looking good
IV. They can easily workout

Choose the correct option.

(a) I and II
(b) II and III
(c) III and IV
(d) I and IV

7. The most important requirement for children is .... They need to roll, crawl, squat, climb, run and jump without being hindered by clothes. They need to play without fear of getting their clothes dirty. **Competency Based Que**

(a) safety
(b) self help
(c) comfort
(d) appearance

8. Dresses with what kind of sleeves provide more freedom as well as room for growth?

(a) Long
(b) Raglan
(c) Short
(d) Cotton

9. Which fabric is most widely used because it is easily washable and comfortable to wear?

(a) Polyester
(b) Nylon
(c) Wool
(d) Cotton

10. What are the factors to be considered while selecting a five months old infant's clothes? **Competency Based Que**

I. They should trap heat.
II. They should be comfortable.
III. They should be a sign of status
IV. They should be faishonable

Choose the correct option.

(a) I and II
(b) II and III
(c) III and IV
(d) I and IV

11. Rohit's family is planning a trip to the beach. What type of fabric is suitable for his clothing? **Competency Based Que**

(a) Heavy and dark
(b) Lightweight and breathable
(c) Thick and water-resistant
(d) Itchy and rough

12. Which of the following clothing can be made at home?

(a) Cotton undershirt
(b) Cotton diapers
(c) Raglan undershirt
(d) Raglan diapers

13. What should be the thickness of the sole of a toddler's shoes?

(a) 1.8 inch (b) 1/8 inch (c) 18 inch (d) 0.18 inch

14. Clothes for pre-schoolers should be .... to wear, easy to maintain, durable to use that provides allowance for growing needs, look attractive in design and colour, and encourage self-reliance. **Competency Based Que**

(a) fashionable
(b) comfortable
(c) visionary
(d) None of these

15. Aisha, a pre-schooler, wants to wear clothes that allow her to move freely. Which type of clothing is ideal for her? **Competency Based Que**

(a) Tight-fitting dresses with long sleeves
(b) Loose-fitting pants with elastic waistbands
(c) Bulky jackets with stiff fabrics
(d) Short-sleeved shirts with tight collars

16. Select the incorrect statement. **Competency Based Que**

(a) Individuality of each child should be respected through clothes, even if they are twins.

(b) Identical twins should not be dressed a like unless they wish to.

(c) It is important that pre-schoolers be given a chance to express their choice while making a purchase for their clothing.

(d) Self-help features do not help the child to become more independent and self-reliant.

17. Match the following. **Competency Based Que**

Stages of Childhood		Age	
A.	Creeping Age	1.	11-19 years
B.	Toddlerhood	2.	2-6 years
C.	Pre-school Age	3.	1-2 years
D.	Adolescents	4.	6 months-1 year

Codes

	A	B	C	D		A	B	C	D
(a)	1	2	3	4	(b)	2	3	4	1
(c)	4	3	2	1	(d)	3	4	1	2

Assertion-Reason Questions

Direction (Q. Nos.18-21) In the questions given below, there are two statements marked as Assertion (A) and Reason (R). Read the statements and choose the correct option.

Codes

(a) Both A and R are true and R is the correct explanation of A.

(b) Both A and R are true, but R is not the correct explanation of A.

(c) A is true, but R is false.

(d) A is false, but R is true.

18. **Assertion** (A) Stylish clothing available at reasonable prices can help to reduce social class differences.

Reason (R) Layering clothes is helpful in summer months to combat heat.

19. **Assertion** (A) Flat seams in clothes last longer than regular seams.

Reason (R) Wool can irritate delicate skin hence it should not be worn directly on the skin.

20. **Assertion** (A) The clothes of a boy of four years of age should be able to withstand the wear and tear that he might give.

Reason (R) Children during pre-school age become very naughty and mess around with everything, including their clothes.

21. **Assertion** (A) In teenage years, children start recognising cultural norms as well as contemporary trends.

Reason (R) A person's social and economic status can be identified by the clothes they wear.

Case Based Questions

22. **Read the passage given below and answer the following questions.**

Children's clothing should have allowance for growth, especially in length. It is not advisable to buy a much larger size as they are neither comfortable nor safe. It is better to choose clothes to fit with the provision to increase length. Select fabrics which do not shrink. Trousers can have cuffs at the hemline which can be later let down to increase the leg length.

(i) What is the most important aspect of clothing?

(a) It should be comfortable.

(b) It should have a pleasing and attractive appearance.

(c) It should allow for a child's growth.

(d) All of the above

(ii) Which of the following is mandatory for a girl's skirt?

(a) Adjustable stress (b) Raglan waist

(c) Pleats (d) Cuffs at the hemline

(iii) Given below are two statements labelled as Assertion (A) and Reason (R).

Assertion (A) Young children need clothes that do not shrink in time.

Reason (R) Rapid physical growth can be seen in children at a young age. **Competency Based Que**

Codes

(a) Both A and R are true and R is the correct explanation of A.

(b) Both A and R are true, but R is not the correct explanation of A.

(c) A is true, but R is false.

(d) A is false, but R is true.

(iv) Tight-fitted clothes should not be bought for infants. Which of the following is not an appropriate reason for the above statement? **Competency Based Que**

(a) It would be difficult to clean.

(b) It would be restrictive to its movements.

(c) It would be an obstacle in its growth.

(d) It would be very uncomfortable.

23. Read the passage given below and answer the following questions.

The term 'fashion' is identified with a style which has contemporary appeal for the masses. With children's constant exposure to TV, even they become quite fashion conscious. Fashion may be inspired by important personalities, social or political leaders, film stars or even important national events. These can be reflected in apparel in terms of fabric type, colour and design of the material, shape or cut of the garment or simply the accessories (like scarves, bags, badges, belts, etc.) that go with it. Certain fashions that highly exaggerate some features of dress or may affect only part of the society or a specific area are very short lived. These are known as 'fads'. Children and adolescents are quite likely to be taken up by fads.

On the basis of the information given above answer the following questions.

(i) Constant exposure to .... makes children fashion conscious.

(a) TV (b) radio
(c) songs (d) None of these

(ii) Fashion may be inspired by ....

(a) important personalities
(b) political leaders
(c) film stars
(d) All of the above

(iii) **Assertion** (A) Wearing the right thing at the right time is most important.

Reason (R) Concepts of clothing in terms of modesty and protection vary with occasion, activity and time of the day. **Competency Based Que**

Codes

(a) Both A and R are true and R is the correct explanation of A.
(b) Both A and R are true, but R is not the correct explanation of A.
(c) A is true, but R is false.
(d) A is false, but R is true.

(iv) **Statement I** Clothing is also affected by the number of children in a family, their age gaps and gender.

Statement II Fads are fashions that are sustainable and long lived. **Competency Based Que**

(a) Statement I is true, but II is false.
(b) Statement II is true, but I is false.
(c) Both the Statements are true.
(d) Both the Statements are false.

Answers

1. (d) None of the above
2. (b) social and economic status
3. (d) All of these 4. (c) Age
5. (a) Fads
6. (a) I and II
7. (c) comfort
8. (b) Raglan
9. (d) Cotton
10. (a) I and II
11. (d) Lightweight and breathable
12. (b) Cotton diapers
13. (b) 1/8 inch
14. (b) comfortable
15. (b) Loose-fitting pants with elastic waistbands
16. (d) Self-help features do not help the child to become more independent and self-reliant.
17. (c) 4 3 2 1
18. (c) A is true, but R is false
19. (b) Both A and R are true, but R is not the correct explanation of A.
20. (c) A is true, but R is false.
21. (a) Both A and R are true and R is the correct explanation of A.
22. (i) (a) It should be comfortable.
(ii) (a) Adjustable stress
(iii) (a) Both A and R are true and R is the correct explanation of A.
(iv) (a) It would be difficult to clean.
23. (i) (a) TV
(ii) (d) All of the above
(iii) (a) Both A and R are true and R is the correct explanation of A.
(iv) (a) Statement I is true, but II is false.

Subjective Questions

Very Short Answer Type Questions

1. Give an example of clothing preventing us from physical harm.

Ans. Clothing can project us from physical harm. For example, fire fighters wear special clothing for protection from fire, smoke and water.

2. Ananya's family has limited income. How does their financial situation impact their clothing selection for her and her siblings? What role do school uniforms play in addressing socio-economic differences? **Competency Based Que**

Ans. Ananya's family's limited income influences their clothing choices, leading to the recycling of older sibling's clothes.

School uniforms half minimise visible socio economic differences, thus, promoting equality among students.

3. Name some factors considered while selecting clothing and fabric for children?

Ans. The factors considered while selecting clothing and fabric for children are age, climate and season, occasion, fashion, income.

4. As the new school year begins, what factors should Mrs. Patel consider while selecting uniforms and everyday clothes for her 7 years old son? **Competency Based Que**

Ans. Mrs. Patel should consider factors like age, climate, season, occasion, family traditions, cultural influences and social status while selecting uniforms and everyday clothes for her 7 years old son.

5. What determines selection of clothing based on assessment of clothing needs in India?

Ans. Selection of clothing is based on assessment of clothing needs in India and is determined by geographical features, climate and seasonal features of the area where they have to be used, easy availability and family traditions.

6. For which purpose should children's clothes be suitable?

Ans. Children's clothes should be suitable for the various activities they do and must give them freedom to play, which is very essential for their physical growth.

7. At what age, do shoes and footwear become essential?

Ans. At the age of 1-2 years, i.e. toddlerhood, shoes and footwear become essential.

8. 'Mrs. Sharma wants to buy summer clothes for her pre-school daughter'. Why should she prioritise cotton fabrics? **Competency Based Que**

Ans. She should prioritise cotton fabrics as cotton is hygienic, absorbent, easy to wash and suitable for active play, making it an ideal choice for pre-schoolers.

9. Why do elementary school boys wear rugged clothes?

Ans. Elementary school boys are very active. Rugged clothes can withstand for their rough play.

10. What is a primary criterion of clothes for children with special needs?

Ans. 'Comfort' is a primary criterion for clothes for children with special needs.

Short Answer Type Questions

1. Describe four factors related to comfort hygiene and warmth which need to be considered for clothing of children below six months of age. **Competency Based Que**

Ans. Four factors related to comfort, hygiene and warmth which need to be considered for clothing of infants are

(i) The dresses should open down the front or have large openings to avoid having to slip the dress over the head of the infant.

(ii) As the baby's skin is very delicate and sensitive, it demands very soft, lightweight and simple to put-on and take-off clothes.

(iii) Diapers should be soft, absorbent, easily washed and quick drying.

(iv) Undershirts should be worn in most climates. A cotton undershirt is worn in a warm climate and soft wool-cotton blend undershirts are worn in a cold climate.

2. Aarav is ready to take his first steps, and his parents are looking for the right footwear. What are the essential requirements of footwear for toddlers that they should consider? **Competency Based Que**

Ans. The requirements of footwear for toddlers are

(i) Shoes or footwear become essential at this age. The correct fit in shoes and socks for a small child is essential for foot comfort and health.

Flexible soled shoes with rough soles of 1/8 inch thickness should be worn while walking. These may be without heel or a slight heel and should be full and puffy in the toe area.

(ii) Shoes that fit well helps to build good body skills in balancing, climbing and running. As children outgrow their shoes quickly, these should be frequently replaced to avoid foot related health dangers.

3. Emily, a toddler, is learning to dress herself.

(i) What features should Emily's clothes have to support her self-dressing efforts?

(ii) Why is it essential to consider Emily's comfort while selecting her clothes?

(iii) How can Emily's parents balance their desire for stylish clothing with her need for comfort and practicality? **Competency Based Que**

Ans. (i) Emily's clothes should have features that make dressing easier and more manageable for her, such as

- Large openings and roomy necklines for easy head and arm passage.
- Front fasteners, simple buttons and zippers for effortless closure.
- Elastic waistbands for comfortable fit and easy adjustments
- Simple, uncomplicated designs to minimise frustration.

(ii) Considering Emily's comfort while selecting her clothes is crucial for several reasons

- Comfortable clothes allow Emily to move freely, engage in physical activities without restrictions.
- Discomfort can lead to irritability and distraction from learning and development.
- Comfortable clothing promotes self-confidence, independence and a positive self-image.
- Properly fitting clothes also support physical development, preventing issues like skin irritation or joint strain.

(iii) Emily's parents can balance style with comfort and practicality by

- Choosing clothes with simple designs, soft fabrics and easy-to-maintain materials.
- Prioritising functional features like adjustable waistbands and snap buttons.
- Selecting clothing with breathable fabrics.
- Involving Emily in the shopping process, ensuring her input on comfort and preferences.
- Considering versatile, mix-and-match clothing.

4. 'During middle childhood, clothing plays a significant role in a child's social and emotional development.'

(i) Why is clothing important for children's social development during this stage?

(ii) What factors should parents consider when selecting clothing for school-going children during middle childhood? **Competency Based Que**

Ans. (i) Clothing helps, children to gain acceptance from peers, express personal style and develop self-confidence. Inconsistent or uncomfortable clothing may lead to humiliation and decreased confidence.

(ii) Parents should consider factors such as comfort, safety, easy care, growth allowance, suitability to physique and absorbent fabrics (like cotton, voile).

Additionally, they should respect their child's preferences and involve them in the selection process to promote autonomy and self-expression.

5. Aisha, 13 years old, is choosing new clothes for herself. What four key factors would she consider while selecting her outfits? **Competency Based Que**

Ans. Four points which Aisha would consider while selecting clothes for herself are

(i) To wear the latest styles as well as to create new styles of her own. Thus she would follow fashions as well as 'fads'.

(ii) Spend large sums of money for her clothing. As long as a dress looks good expense won't necessarily matter.

(iii) To dress the way her peers are dressed or imitate their role models in dress.

(iv) Prefer dresses which fit, while disregarding the fabric quality or its construction.

6. While selecting clothes to be used in physical activity like sports and workouts, what are the four important factors which should be considered?

Ans. Four important factors which should be considered while selecting clothes to be used in physical activity are

(i) Clothes and shoes chosen should be comfortable.

(ii) Clothes and shoes chosen should prevent strains, blisters, sprains and sore legs or ankles.

(iii) Fabrics should be easy to wash, as simple hygiene can save the skin from irritation and rashes.

(iv) Garment design and the fabric used should allow for free movement and absorption of perspiration.

7. How is dressing and undressing an important consideration for children with special needs?

Ans. For answer refer to the text under the heading 'Clothes for Children with Special Needs' on page no. 201.

Long Answer Type Questions

1. Kavya is curious about the resons behind her clothing choices and those of her friends. Why do different people wear different types of clothing? Give four reason **Competency Based Que**

Ans. Different people wear different types of clothing for

Modesty In our society, people do not go around without them; thus, we wear clothing to cover ourselves. However, what is considered modest in one society might not be considered as modest in another.

Protection We wear clothing to protect ourselves from the harsh weather conditions, dirt and pollution. We change our clothing according to the different seasons. A few particular clothings can also protect us from physical harm.

Status and Prestige Clothes can also be a sign of status, as we tend to identify people's social and economic status by their clothing. The manner of dress is one way by which this can be accomplished.

Adornment We also wear good clothes to enhance our appearance and look attractive. The need to decorate and adorn the body can be found to some degree in all societies.

2. Explain five important factors affecting selection of clothing in India.

Ans. Five important factors affecting selection of clothing in India are

(i) **Age** Clothing is different for persons in different stages of life. For instance, clothes for babies less than two years old must take into account their comfort and safety in relation to their physical growth, motor development, association with people and things around them and the activities they indulge in.

(ii) **Climate and Season** To ensure that clothes are suited to the climate, for the winter season or for those living in a cold climate, the dresses would be very different from those for a warm or temperate climate.

(iii) **Occasion** It is important to wear the right clothes at the right time. Thus, selection of clothes depends a lot on the occasion, time of the day or may be governed by some rules.
For example, school uniforms, dresses for religious ceremonies and those used for parties and other social functions.

(iv) **Fashion** It may be inspired by important personalities, social or political leaders, film stars or even important national events. It decides the fabric type, colour and design of the material, shape or cut of the garment or simply the accessories.

(v) **Income** The amount of money that a person has affects the selection of clothing. Besides the purchase cost, it also includes its use for varied purposes, durability care and maintenance requirements.

3. Your niece has her first birthday next month and you are planning to gift her some cute clothes.

(a) What is this stage of the child between 6 months to 1 year called? Describe.

(b) What kind of apparel for children in this group has to be?

(c) What are the things to remember for selecting the correct clothes? **Competency Based Que**

Ans. (a) The stage of 6 months to 1 year when child begins to show the signs of independence by pulling themselves upto the furniture to stand, or to reach out to objects or sit on their own is called creeping age.

(b) Apparel for children in this age group has to be such that it allows for free movement. Thus, the clothes need to be loose and non-interfering. For clothes to fit loosely, both knitted and bias cut garments are most suited as they stretch, allowing for some growth.

(c) While selecting the correct clothes one must remember that

- Too much bulk in clothes can hamper motor movement. The garments should not come in the way of the child's movements.
- Tightly knitted clothes should be avoided. Lightweight garments are easy to wear during playing games and are good in winter as they are comparatively warmer.
- Do not make children wear too many clothes.
- The clothes should be made of a soft and smooth fabric which does not collect dirt readily.

4. Explain four requirements of garments related to durability, ease of maintenance, having allowance for growing needs and encouraging self-reliance for children of pre-school age.

Ans. Four requirements of such garments for children of pre-school age are

(i) **Durability** As such children play a lot, the garments should be able to withstand the wear and tear that the average child will give them. The clothes should be able to withstand many launderings and hard wear.

(ii) **Ease of maintenance** The clothes should be made from lightweight materials that are pre-shrunk and are easy to launder and iron, like cotton.

(iii) **Having allowance for growing needs** The clothes should have growth features, like trousers having cuffs at the hemline which can be later opened out to increase their length, adjustable straps on skirts, raglan sleeves, tucks and pleats. This will enable a garment to be worn for a longer period of time.

(iv) **Encouraging self-reliance** Self-help features in the dress like a one piece garment with front long openings that can be easily reached, large buttons, large and comfortable necklines without a collar and large armholes, all help a child to become more independent and self-reliant.

5. Rohan, a 10 years old with cerebral palsy, requires specialised clothing to accommodate his physical needs while promoting independence and self-esteem.

(i) Discuss the importance of independent dressing for children with special needs like Rohan, highlighting its impact on their emotional well-being and autonomy.

(ii) Describe the key considerations for selecting garments for children with special needs, ensuring comfort, accessibility and aesthetic appeal. **Competency Based Que**

Ans. (i) Independent dressing is crucial for children with special needs as it fosters emotional satisfaction, pride, autonomy and competence. This enhances their self-esteem and confidence, promoting a positive self-image.

For children like Rohan, dressing independently, even with adaptations, encourages self-reliance and motivation.

(ii) When selecting garments for children with special needs, primary considerations include

- **Comfort** Choosing breathable fabrics (cotton, velvet, corduroy)
- **Accessibility** Easy-to-use fasteners (velcros, zippers), wide necklines and front-open plackets
- **Durability** Reinforced areas for calipers and braces, abrasion-resistant materials
- **Aesthetic appeal** Appealing colours, prints and well-stitched designs
- Ecological and socio-cultural appropriateness
- **Individualised needs** Garments constructed to cater to the wearer's and carer's specific requirements.

6. Describe four preferences of clothes by children in the middle childhood stage of life.

Ans. Four preferences of clothes by children in the middle childhood stage of life are

For answer refer to the text under the heading 'Elementary School' years (6-11 years) on page no. 199 and 200.

SELF ASSESSMENT TEST

Objective Type Questions

1. Which among the following is not a function of clothing?
   (a) Protection (b) Status and Prestige
   (c) Adornment (d) None of these
2. Loose garments can catch .... more easily around the working area.
   (a) dirt (b) stains
   (c) fire (d) insects
3. Which of the following gives children a feeling of confidence and self-reliance?
   (a) Dressing (b) Undressing
   (c) Folding (d) Both (a) and (b)
4. Which type of clothes do mothers appreciate?
   (a) Easy to wash (b) Little/No ironing
   (c) Dry cleaned (d) Both (a) and (b)

Very Short Answer Type Questions

5. What are the characteristics of diapers suitable for infants?
6. Brifely explain the characteristics of infants' clothes in rural areas.
7. Name the most essential self-help feature in a dress for a pre-schooler.

Short Answer Type Questions

8. Why should children at the creeping stage wear clothes with convenient openings ? Give two reasons.
9. At which stage in life, do children develop posture? What qualities in clothes will enable children to develop a good posture?
10. Explain the four features of clothes regarding shoulder fitting, necklines and sleeves that create comfort for a child who is wearing the clothes.

Long Answer Type Questions

11. Describe features of three types of fabrics which are commonly used for children's clothes. Which properties of fabrics make them easy-to-wear? Which fabrics should be avoided? **Competency Based Que**
12. What three activities do children mostly indulge in during infancy? What are the features in their clothes which facilitate each of these activities?
13. Compare four features which are different in clothes for middle childhood children and for adolescents. Give reasons for the difference in each case. **Competency Based Que**
14. Suggest five features of clothes which should take care of the needs of a physically disabled 11 years old child with one leg amputated above the knee. The child walks with the help of crutches. **Competency Based Que**

11
CHAPTER

Health and Wellness

Health and wellness are fundamental aspects of a good life, serving as the foundation for overall happiness and fulfillment. They include physical fitness, mental and emotional well-being.

YOUR STUDY GOALS

11.1 Introduction
11.2 Healthy and Unhealthy Diet
11.3 Fitness
11.4 Wellness
11.5 Stress

YOUR PRACTICE GOAL

- Objective Type Questions (21 Qs ; MCQs, A-R, Statements, Matching, Case Baded)
- Subjective Questions (15 VSAs, 6 SAs, 5 LAs)

11.1 Introduction

Health can be described as, the state of being free from illness or injury and **wellness** is the maximum capacity of individual to lend a well balanced life related to good health.

Maintaining a balanced diet ensures the body receives essential nutrients, while regular physical activity promotes fitness and vitality. Additionally, effective stress management techniques, such as mindfulness or relaxation exercises, can enhance mental clarity and emotional resilience.

Together, these components contribute to a more vibrant, balanced lifestyle.

Importance of Health and Fitness

Health and fitness are essential components of a fulfilling life. They play a vital role in enhancing physical well-being, mental clarity and emotional stability. Importance of health and fitness are as follows

Improves Energy

- Staying fit significantly boosts your energy levels, making daily activities feel easier and more manageable. Regular exercise enhances your endurance, allowing you to perform tasks without feeling fatigued.
- This increased energy, which can positively impact both your personal and professional life, leading to greater productivity.

Enhances Mood

- Engaging in regular physical activity has a powerful effect on your mood. Exercise stimulates the release of endorphins, which are hormones that promote feelings of happiness and reduce stress.
- By incorporating regular workouts into your routine, you can experience lower levels of anxiety and a more positive outlook on life.

Prevents Illness

- Adopting a healthy lifestyle through regular exercise is crucial for preventing chronic diseases[1]. Conditions such as diabetes, heart disease and obesity can be mitigated by maintaining an active lifestyle.
- By prioritising fitness, you strengthen your immune system and enhance your overall health, reducing the risk of serious health issues.

Promotes Healthy Weight

- Fitness plays a vital role in maintaining a healthy weight. Regular physical activity helps to **burn calories and build muscle,** which can prevent weight gain and promote fat loss.
- A balanced approach to exercise and nutrition ensures that you remain within a healthy weight range, contributing to overall well-being.

Strengthens Bones and Muscles

- Exercise is essential for building strong bones and muscles. Weight-bearing activities, such as running or strength training help increase bone density.
- Additionally, strengthening your muscles supports for better balance and co-ordination, keeping you active and reducing the likelihood of injury.

Improves Sleep

- Regular physical activity has been shown to enhance sleep quality. Engaging in exercise can help you fall asleep faster and enjoy deeper sleep, which is crucial for overall health and recovery.
- Better sleep leads to **improved mood and increased focus** during the day, making you feel more energised.

Increases Longevity

- Maintaining a healthy lifestyle through fitness can contribute to a longer life.
- By staying active, you not only enhance your physical health but also improve your **quality of life** as you age.

11.2 Healthy and Unhealthy Diet

Healthy Diet

- A healthy diet throughout life is essential for preventing malnutrition and reducing the risk of **non-communicable diseases (NCDs)** such as diabetes, heart disease and cancer.
- It emphasises a variety of nutrient-rich foods, including fruits, vegetables, whole grains and lean proteins, suited to individual needs based on age, gender and lifestyle.
- Establishing healthy eating habits early, such as breastfeeding and balanced nutrition, contributes to better growth, cognitive[2] development and long-term health outcomes.
- Healthy individuals tend to be more physically active, cheerful and resilient[3], with strong immune systems and lower fatigue levels.

1 Chronic disease According to National Cancer Institute, it is a disease or condition that usually lasts for 3 months or longer and may get worse over time.

2 Cognitive Related to thinking, understanding, learning and remembering.

3 Resilience Ability to recover quickly from difficulties or stress.

Unhealthy Diet

- Increased production of processed foods, rapid urbanisation and changing lifestyles have led to a shift in dietary patterns.
- People are now consuming more foods high in energy, fats, sugar and salt, and avoid eating fruits, vegetables and other dietary fibres such as whole grains. This diet pattern is unhealthy.
- Such type of diet when consumed in a higher amount than normal, coupled with low or no physical activity, results in various non-communicable diseases. Hence, people should be made aware about better and preventive lifestyles.

Body Mass Index (BMI)

- Body Mass Index (BMI) is a measure of body fat based on height and weight of the person.
- BMI is calculated by dividing a person's weight in kilograms by the square of their height in meters. For instance, if someone is 1.75 meters tall and weighs 70 kg, their BMI would be 70 divided by (1.75 × 1.75), which equals 22.9, indicating a normal weight.

$$\text{BMI} = \frac{\text{Body Weight (in kg)}}{\text{Body height(in m}^2)}$$

- Being overweight or obese increases the risk of serious health issues like diabetes, heart disease and high blood pressure in both youth and adults.
- As Body Mass Index (BMI) increases, the associated health risks also rise. Higher BMI is linked to harmful changes in the body, such as increased fat (adipose tissue), reduced glucose tolerance and alterations in blood cholesterol levels.
- To assess weight-related health risks, BMI is divided into these categories: **underweight, normal weight** and **overweight** and obese, with specific cutoff points[4] for each category.
- BMI is a **universal measure** that applies to adults regardless of age or gender, although different ethnic groups may have varying risks at the same BMI level. For example, South-East Asians may face higher health risks than other populations at the same BMI.
- Understanding BMI can help individuals to make informed decisions about their health and seek guidance if they fall into the overweight or obese categories. Regular monitoring can help in maintaining a healthy lifestyle.

International Classification of Adult Underweight, Normal weight, Overweight and Obese according to BMI

Classification	**BMI (kg/m²)**	
	Principal cut-off points	**Additional cut-off points**
Underweight	**< 18.50**	**< 18.50**
Severe thinness	< 16.00	< 16.00
Moderate thinness	16.00-16.99	16.00-16.99
Mild thinness	17.00-18.49	17.00-18.49
Normal range	**18.50-24.99**	**18.50-22.99**
		23.00-24.99
Overweight	**≥ 25.00**	**≥ 25.00**
Pre-obese	25.00-29.99	25.00-27.49
		27.50-29.99

4 Cut-off Point It is the value which indicate the range of normal levels for weight or blood cholesterol or blood glucose and so on. Anything below the minimum value or above the maximum value becomes abnormal. In other words, such values 'cut off' the abnormal from the normal values.

Obese	**≥ 30.00**	**≥ 30.00**
Obese class I	30.00-34.99	30.00-32.49
		32.50-34.99
Obese class II	35.00-39.99	35.00-37.49
		37.50-39.99
Obese class III	≥ 40.00	≥ 40.00

Do's and Don'ts for Health Promoting Diets

Do's

- **Increase Fruits and Vegetables** Aim to eat more fruits and vegetables as part of your daily diet.
- **Incorporate Legumes and Whole Grains** Add more legumes, whole grains and nuts to your meals for better nutrition.
- **Balance Energy Intake and Expenditure** Ensure that the calories you consume match the calories you burn through physical activity.
- **Use Iodised Salt** Opt for iodised salt in cooking to help meet nutritional needs.
- **Stay Hydrated** Drink plenty of water throughout the day.

Don'ts

- **Limit Fat and Oil Consumption** Avoid excessive use of fats and oils, such as butter on bread or ghee on parathas and reduce fried foods like pakodas, puris and samosas.
- **Reduce Saturated and Trans Fats** Minimise the intake of saturated fats (which are solid at room temperature) and trans fats (like vanaspati).
- **Cut Down on Salt Intake** Avoid consuming too much salt, especially from processed foods like chips, sauces and pickles.
- **Limit Sugary Foods and Beverages** Refrain from indulging in sweets, chocolates and soft drinks, as they can contribute to unhealthy weight gain and other health issues.

Quick Test 1

1. Which three aspects are included under health and wellness?
2. Give two benefits of maintaining health and fitness.
3. Name the diseases which can be prevented through a healthy diet
4. What does BMI stands for?

11.3 Fitness

- While many people often equate health and fitness, it's important to recognise that they are distinct yet interconnected concepts. One can be fit without being healthy and vice versa. Health is promoted not only through a well-balanced diet but also through regular exercise and physical activity.
- Maintaining physical health and well-being in adulthood is crucial, particularly as the body undergoes various changes with age.
- Regular physical activity, combined with a balanced diet, plays a significant role in promoting health, enhancing quality of life and preventing a range of illnesses.

Importance of Exercise and Physical Activities in Adulthood

Physical Health

- Regular exercise helps burn excess calories, reducing the likelihood of weight gain and fat accumulation.
- It enhances the functioning of the heart and lungs, improving circulation and respiratory efficiency.
- Engaging in regular physical activity can help prevent chronic conditions such as obesity, hypertension and diabetes.
- Helps to maintain bone mineral density and thus reduces the risk of fractures.
- It reduces the risk of acute and chronic illness, thereby.

Mental Health

- Exercise has been shown to alleviate symptoms of depression and anxiety, promoting a positive frame of mind.
- Physical activity can improve cognitive function, helping to prevent issues such as cognitive impairment and enhancing overall mental clarity.
- Regular workouts can lower levels of tension and stress, contributing to overall psychological well-being.

Quality of Life

- Many individuals report better sleep patterns as a result of regular physical activity.
- Exercise boosts **stamina**[5] and overall fitness, making daily activities easier and more enjoyable.
- Regular physical activity may help delay the onset of disabilities and chronic illnesses, potentially extending healthy life expectancy.

Categories of Exercise

Exercises can be grouped into three main categories

Endurance/Aerobic Exercises	**Examples** Brisk walking, cycling, swimming and team sports. **Benefits** Improves stamina, helps in weight loss, enhances cardio-respiratory function, improves sleep, regulates blood sugar levels and promotes a positive mood.
Strength/Resistance Exercises	**Examples** Weightlifting, push-ups and resistance training. **Benefits** Increases muscle strength, enhances bone mass and improves overall body firmness and posture.
Balance/Flexibility Exercises	**Examples** Yoga, stretching and activities like climbing stairs. **Benefits** Improves flexibility, reduces stiffness and enhances balance and mobility.

Yoga and Fitness

Yoga is an ancient practice that originated in India, focusing on physical, mental and spiritual well-being. Through various **yogic asanas** (postures), individuals can enhance flexibility, strength and balance. Additionally, yoga incorporates meditation, which promotes mental clarity and reduces stress. Practicing yoga offers an effective way to stay fit, improve concentration and cultivate a sense of peace in their daily lives.

The **WHO** has declared 6 April every year to be observed as **'World Physical Activity day'** and 21 June as **'World Yoga Day'**.

5 **Stamina** Physical or mental ability to keep going for long.

11.4 Wellness

- The **World Health Organisation** (WHO) defines wellness as 'The optimal state of health of individuals and groups'. It is concerned with achievement of physical, mental, social, emotional, intellectual, spiritual and environmental well-being.
- Wellness is directed towards a positive and an affirming life. It is an approach to prevent ill-health and dependence on doctors and medicines.

Wellness Approach Help

- Wellness reduces the risk of disease, disability, discomfort and distress throughout the life cycle, thus, improving **'quality of life'.**
- The first and foremost requirement in wellness approach is that the individual should take the responsibility of quality of one's own life. This begins with a conscious decision to live a healthy lifestyle that leads to high levels of well-being and life satisfaction.

Wellness can also be understood in following ways

- **Wellness is a choice** It is a decision made to achieve optimal health.
- **Wellness is a way of life** It is a lifestyle that helps a person to reach one's goals and realise one's potential.
- **Wellness is a process** It is a sequence of decisions and behaviours that lead to health, well-being and happiness.
- **Wellness is holistic** It is an approach to integrate the body, mind and spirit with the appreciation that all our beliefs, thoughts, feelings and actions greatly influence us in every way.

Wellness is wholehearted **acceptance of self, one's situations and circumstances** with all of one's weaknesses, strengths and challenges.

Qualities of a Person Rated High on Wellness

Persons rated 'high' on the wellness and well-being profile have in common the following qualities

- High self-esteem, a positive outlook and a sense of purpose
- A strong sense of personal responsibility and commitment
- A good sense of humour
- A respect for the environment
- Absence of addictive behaviours
- An ability to continue to learn
- An ability for effective communication
- A concern for others
- A physically fit and an integrated healthy lifestyle
- A capacity to cope with life's challenges
- A capacity to love and an ability to nurture

Dimensions of Wellness

According to the WHO, wellness has two concerns

The achievement of individuals' fullest potentials physically, psychologically, socially, spiritually and economically;

- Carrying out individuals' expectation in the family, community, place of worship, workplace and other settings.

  The dimensions of wellness are

  (i) **Social Aspect** It emphasises on **connecting and engaging** with others and our communities in meaningful ways and having happy, satisfying and stable relationships with others. It promotes the idea of community welfare over individual welfare. One should better live in harmony with others and our environment.

(ii) **Physical Aspect** It means nourishing a healthy body through adequate physical exercise, nutrition, sleep, etc. and involves deliberately following a wellness routine and lifestyle. Making such wellness choices is beneficial for the health and quality of life.

(iii) **Intellectual Aspect** It involves engaging in learning, problem-solving, creativity, stimulating mental activities, etc. Intellectual wellness can be achieved by being open to new ideas, thinking critically, being creative and curious and being motivated to master new skills.

Using the resources available to expand knowledge to improve skills along with sharing with others is the quality of an 'intellectually well' person. Benefits include improved job performance, better problem solving, more knowledge and a better chance at being successful in life.

(iv) **Occupational Aspect** This dimension of wellness encourages personal satisfaction and enrichment in one's life through work, which gives an adult a feeling of comfort and satisfaction in life.

Employers, these days, are emphasising upon the occupational well-being to ensure better employee health, well-being and productivity.

(v) **Emotional Aspect** It implies being aware of, accepting and expressing our feelings and understanding the feelings of others. It means having the ability to manage one's emotions (both positive and negative) in a constructive way, to cope up with stress, to feel positive and enthusiastic about one's life, and to include a realistic assessment of one's limitations.

Emotional well-being helps an individual to recognise, understand, experience and express a full range of emotions. In adulthood particularly, living with chronic illness such as heart disease or cancer, has mental health implications.

(vi) **Spiritual Aspect** It involves searching for meaning and higher purpose of life and living. Spiritual wellness involves possessing a set of guiding beliefs, principles or values that help give direction to one's life. Spirituality relates to better mental health, greater well-being and higher quality of life.

Spirituality can help persons to cope up with problems related to physical health. A spiritually well person seeks harmony between what lies within as well as the forces outside.

(vii) **Environmental Aspect** This deals with the **interaction and interdependence** between humans and the environment. Awareness of the critical role the environment plays in our individual well-being and that all human activity affects the environment is required.

Environmental degradation and destruction by human beings has reduced the availability of natural resources leading to several major problems that will compromise the quality of human life.

(viii) **Financial Aspect** Financial wellness involves the process of decision making and learning how to successfully manage financial expenses. Money plays a critical role in our lives and not having enough of it impacts health as well as overall well-being.

Every individual has to work hard and be productive to have sufficient finances, both at the **micro-level,** i.e., individual and family, and at the **macro-level**, i.e., community, region, state and national levels. The holistic approach to well-being is described in the diagram that portrays the dimensions or focal areas for a healthy lifestyle

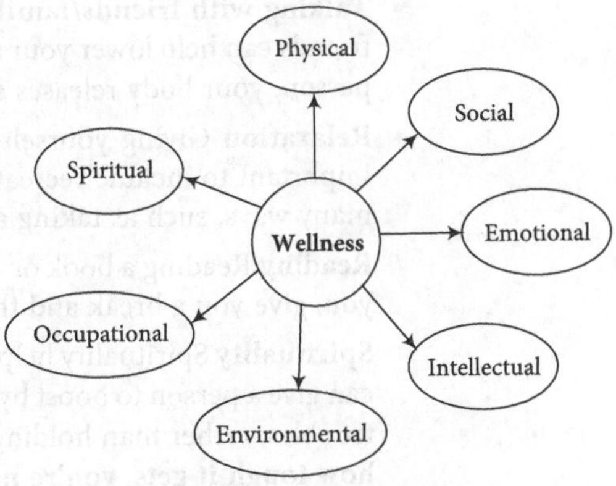

▲ *Dimensions of a Healthy Lifestyle*

Quick Test 2

1. Write any one benefit of aerobic exercise.
2. What ancient practice focuses on holistic well-being?
3. When is the world yoga day celebrated?
4. Define the spiritual aspect of wellness.

11.5 Stress

- Stress is the body's response to personal mental and emotional pressure. While some stress can motivate us, too much stress can harm our health and efficiency.
- Stress is a normal part of daily life. It can have both **positive and negative effects.**
- There are many ways in which stress can affect an individual negatively. It may contribute to irritability, indigestion, loss of sleep, headache, increased blood pressure and reduced appetite.

Types of Stress

Stress can be classified into two main categories

(i) **Eustress** Positive stress that helps you perform better.

For example, when exams are near, you study hard and in a focused way because of the stress. This in turn leads to high marks, which motivates you to continue working hard.

(ii) **Distress** Negative stress that can lead to health problems.

For example, when feeling distressed, you might argue with friends, lose your appetite or have trouble focusing on your studies.

Simple Techniques to Cope up with Stress

There are various stress management techniques which can benefit every human being. The decision to use one or more techniques is a matter of individual choice. They are

- **Talking with friends/family** If things are bothering you, talking about them to family members and friends can help lower your stress. It is a natural way to calm yourself. When you connect with people in person, your body releases a hormone that **stops your fight-or-flight response** and relaxes you.
- **Relaxation** Giving yourself some time to relax from your busy schedule can help relieve stress. It is important to include recreation and relaxation time in your daily time plan. Relaxation can be done in many ways, such as taking a shower, sleeping, meditation, spending time in nature, etc.
- **Reading** Reading a book or a novel of your interest can divert your mind from stress. This can entertain you, give you a break and thus, lower your stress.
- **Spirituality** Spirituality helps in dealing with stress and improving mental health. Having a spiritual side can give a person to boost by allowing **reliance on God or a higher power** and surrendering worries and troubles, rather than holding on so tightly to stress. With a spiritual practice you'll find that no **matter how tough it gets, you're not alone.**
- **Music** Listening to music can relax us in following ways
  - Lower our heart rate and cortisol levels.
  - Release endorphins and improve our sense of well-being.
  - Distract us, reducing physical and emotional stress levels.
  - Reduce stress-related symptoms, whether used in a clinical environment or in daily life.

- **Hobby** Setting aside time every day for things you enjoy makes you feel good, and it will help relieve stress. It doesn't have to be a lot of time – even 15 to 20 minutes will do. Relaxing hobbies include things like knitting, drawing, painting, cooking, etc.
- **Yoga** Performing yoga regularly is one of the best ways to relax body and mind. The asanas that focus on slow movement, stretching and deep breathing are best for lowering anxiety and stress and improving mood.

  Thus, research has shown that people who take care of themselves and adopt healthier lifestyles are more productive, have fewer absences from work and make fewer demands for medical services. It is not medical care alone, rather consistent self-care which promotes better health and an improved quality of life.

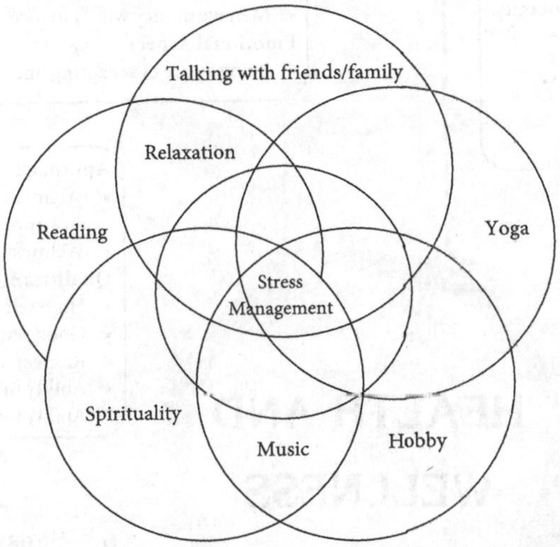

▲ *Simple techniques to cope up with stress*

Quick Test 3

1. Give one example of positive effect of stress.
2. What is distress?
3. Mention any three techniques of coping with stress.
4. What are the two benefits of listening to music?

Mind Map

1 Importance of Health and Fitness

- It improves energy.
- It prevents from illness.
- It strengthens bones and muscles.
- It increases longevity.
- It enhances mood.
- It promotes healthy weight.
- It improves sleep.

2 Healthy and Unhealthy Diet

Body Mass Index (BMI)

- It is an indicator use to classify underweight overweight and obesity.
- It is defined as weight in kgs divided by height in meter square.
- It calculates rate of metabolism of food in the body.
- It has no relation to age.
- It is same for both males and females.
- It may vary with the variations in genetics and races.

Do and Don'ts for Health Promoting Diets.

Do's

- Increase fruits and vegetables.
- Incorporate legumes and whole grains.
- Balance energy intake and expenditure.
- Use iodised salt.
- Stay hydrated.

Don'ts

- Limit fat and oil consumption.
- Reduce saturated and trans fat.
- Cut down on salt intake.
- Limit sugary foods and beverages.

HEALTH AND WELLNESS

3 Fitness

Physical Health

- Regular exercise prevents weight gain and improves heart and lung function.
- Reduce the risk of chronic illness.

Mental Health

- Exercise relieves stress and depression.
- Physical activity improves cognitive functions.

Quality of Life

- Physical activity enhances sleep and boosts stamina.
- Increases healthy life expectancy.

Yoga and Fitness

- It is an ancient practice
- It focuses an physical, mental and spiritual well being.

Categories of Exercise

Endurance/Aerobic Exercise

- **For examples** brisk walking, cycling etc.

Strength /Resistence Exercise

- **For examples** weight lifting, push-ups etc.

Balance/Flexibility Exercise

- **For examples** yoga, stretching etc.

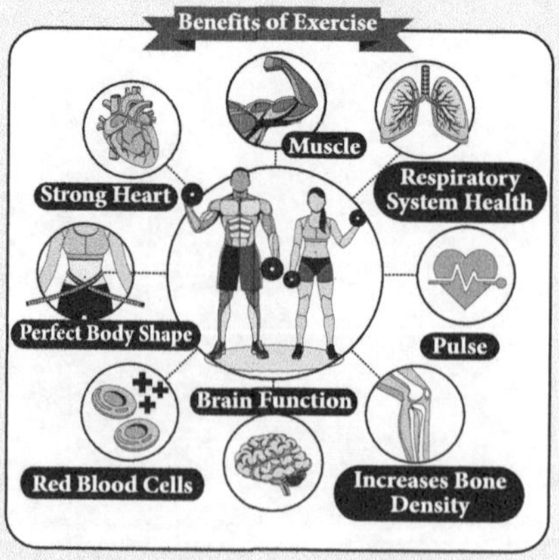

Importance of Exercise

4 Dimensions of Wellness

Physical Aspect

- Maintain a healthy lifestyle through regular exercise and balanced diet.

Social Aspect

- Building meaningful and happy relationships.

Intellectual Aspect

- Develop critical thinking

Spiritual Aspect

- Understand the purpose of life and living with meaning.

Financial Aspect

- Manage money wisely to meet the needs.

Emotional Aspect

- Being aware of accepting one's emotions.

Approach

- Wellness reduces the risk of disease, disability and improves 'quality of life'.
- Wellness is a holistic approach and away of life.

Qualities of a Person Rated High on Wellness

- High self-esteem.
- Positive outlook
- Good sense of humour
- Respect for the environment
- Ability to nurture
- Ability for effective communication

5 Stress

- It is a normal part of daily life.
- Both positive and negative effects.

Types of Stress

Eustress

- Positive stress that helps you perform better.

Distress

- Negative stress that can lead to health problems.

Simple Techniques to Cope with Stress

- Positive thinking
- Yoga
- Happiness
- Learn to say No
- Honestly self-analyse
- Exercise
- Creating work
- Music
- Lessons from Mistakes

Dimension of Wellness

NCERT Folder

1. **Mark the following statements as True or False.**

(i) **You need to be physically active only when you need to lose weight.**

(ii) **Physical fitness requires membership in a gym, special equipment and clothes.**

(iii) **Without 60 minutes of exercise every day, physical fitness cannot be achieved.**

(iv) **Endorphins are chemical substances that make a person depressed.**

Ans. (i) False (ii) False (iii) False (iv) False

* This chapter is deleted from latest rationalised NCERT so the given NCERT Folder is related to previous edition only.

Exam Pattern Questions

Objective Type Questions

Multiple Choice Questions (MCQs)

1. **What are the indicators of being healthy?**

(a) Physically fit and active
(b) Cheerful in overall outlook
(c) Adequate immunity against infections
(d) All of the above

2. **Consider the following statement about promoting health diets.**
Select the incorrect statement. **Competency Based Que**

(a) Increase consumption of fruits and vegetables.
(b) Increase intake of legumes, whole grains and nuts.
(c) Match energy intake to energy expenditure.
(d) Consume too much fat/oil (butter on bread, ghee on parathas) or fried foods.

3. **The risk of developing diseases such as diabetes, heart disease and hypertension in youth and adults is higher. These disease can occur to individual who are suffering from ……… .** **Competency Based Que**

(a) obesity (b) malaria (c) dengue (d) fatigue

4. **Arshad is a college going student. He skips his breakfast every morning and consumes street foods available in or near his college. For lunch as well, he prefers dishes like chhola bhatura and in the evening he drinks coke with his dinner. Which of the following diseases is he susceptible to in the long run?** **Competency Based Que**

(a) Obesity
(b) Heart diseases
(c) Diabetes and high blood pressure
(d) All of the above

5. **Read the following statements**

I. **Health professionals commonly use anthropometric indicators to assess nutritional status and risk.**

II. **BMI is defined as the weight in kilograms divided by the square of the height in centimetres (kg/cm^2).** **Competency Based Que**

Choose which of the above statement(s) is/ are true.

(a) Only II (b) Only I
(c) Both I and II (d) Neither I nor II

6. **WHO has recommended use of 'cut-off points' for determining whether individuals are underweight, overweight, obese or normal. The classifications are**

I. **if a person's BMI is below 18.5, he/she is classified as underweight.**

II. **If a person's BMI is above 25.00, he/she is classified as overweight.** **Competency Based Que**

Choose the correct option.

(a) Only I
(b) Only II
(c) Both I and II
(d) Neither I nor II

7. **'Rahul wants to improve his diet'. Which of the following should he DO to promote better health?** **Competency Based Que**

(a) Limit fruit and vegetable intake
(b) Increase consumption of legumes and whole grains
(c) Reduce water intake
(d) Use non-iodised salt

8. **What is a fundamental means of improving physical and mental health?** **Competency Based Que**

(a) Physical activity
(b) Diet
(c) Stress
(d) Meditation

9. **Rohan wants to improve his mental health and quality of life. What benefit can he expect from regular physical activity?** **Competency Based Que**

(a) Increased stress levels
(b) Release of endorphins, promoting feelings of pleasure and happiness
(c) Decreased energy levels
(d) Poor sleep quality

10. **Find the incorrect pair** **Competency Based Que**

(a) Strength exercises : Push-ups
(b) Endurance exercises : Weightlifting
(c) Balance exercises: Yoga
(d) Aerobic exercises : brisk walking

11. **Which of the following statements is incorrect?** **Competency Based Que**

(a) Exercise reduces the risk of acute and chronic illness through improving body composition, affecting metabolism and cardio-respiratory fitness.
(b) Exercises decreases disability by improving endurance, muscle mass, muscle strength, agility and flexibility. It helps to prevent and treat common.
(c) Exercise can help prevent and treat depression, sleeplessness, anorexia, constipation and cognitive impairment, all of which are frequent and often difficult to treat in older persons.
(d) None of the above

12. **Which among the following are aerobic exercises?**

I. Weightlifting
II. Resistance training
III. Swimming
IV. Brisk walking

Choose the correct option **Competency Based Que**

(a) II and III (b) I and II
(c) I and III (d) III and IV

13. **Ayush is a 28 years old office going male. He is physically fit and does not suffer from any diseases or illness. But, his productivity at office is less and he often feels fatigued while doing his office work. What could be the possible reason for this?** **CBQ**

(a) Mentally unwell
(b) Emotionally unwell
(c) Suffering from underlying diseases
(d) Both (a) and (b)

14. **Match the following.** **Competency Based Que**

Dimensions of Wellness	Terms associated with
A. Social	1. Interdependence
B. Physical	2. Balanced diet
C. Intellectual	3. Mental activity
D. Emotional	4. Awareness and Acceptance

Codes

	A	B	C	D		A	B	C	D
(a)	1	2	3	4	(b)	2	3	4	1
(c)	4	3	2	1	(d)	3	2	1	4

Assertion-Reason Questions

Direction (Q. Nos.15-19) In the questions given below, there are two statements marked as Assertion (A) and Reason (R). Read the statements and choose the correct option.

Codes

(a) Both A and R are true and R is the correct explanation of A.
(b) Both A and R are true, but R is not the correct explanation of A.
(c) A is true, but R is false.
(d) A is false, but R is true.

15. **Assertion** (A) BMI categories apply uniformly across all ethnic groups.

Reason (R) Because BMI is a universal measure that ignores age, gender and ethnicity.

16. **Assertion** (A) People tend to see exercise as a punishment.

Reason (R) Exercise has no role in improving mental well-being.

17. **Assertion** (A) Regular yoga practice can reduce anxiety and stress.

Reason (R) Because yoga combines slow movement, stretching and deep breathing.

18. **Assertion** (A) Conscious decision of adopting a healthy lifestyle is required to have overall well-being.

Reason (R) Adopting a lifestyle forcefully persuaded by others provides no benefits.

19. **Assertion** (A) Financial wellness guarantees lifelong happiness.

Reason (R) Because financial stability reduces stress, improves mental health, and enhances quality of life.

Case Based Questions

20. **Read the passage given below and answer the following questions.**

Experts caution that viewing exercise as a punishment can hamper its benefits. On the other hand, exercise should be enjoyed. The physical pain and soreness that one feels in the first few days gradually disappear. In India, yoga and meditation have been traditionally used to achieve mental health and well-being. Yogic asanas help the body become more flexible. Researchers have shown that yoga also has benefits for conditions such as diabetes and high blood pressure.

(i) **Endorphins, released by brain during and after exercise, are body's natural painkillers and ....**

(a) increase the anxiety and stress level
(b) increase the feeling of happiness
(c) help in losing weight
(d) help in feeling tenses

(ii) **How does exercise promote mental well-being?**

(a) By helping persons who are overweight/obese to lose weight
(b) By controlling blood sugar levels and blood pressure
(c) By postponing disability by as much as 15 years
(d) By boosting confidence as well as reducing anxiety and stress

(iii) **Why does one feel physical pain and soreness in the first few days of new exercise regime?**

(a) Due to stretching of stiff muscles
(b) Due to new exercise regime
(c) Due to taking exercise as a punishment
(d) All of the above

(iv) **Given below are two statements labelled as Assertion (A) and Reason (R).**

Assertion (A) Yoga has benefits for conditions such as diabetes and high blood pressure.

Reason (R) Yogic asanas improve overall physical and mental well-being, thereby help in preventing and combating various non-communicable diseases.

Codes **Competency Based Que**

(a) Both A and R are true and R is the correct explanation of A.
(b) Both A and R are true, but R is not the correct explanation of A.
(c) A is true, but R is false.
(d) A is false, but R is true.

21. **Read the passage given below and answer the following questions**

Health is promoted not only by appropriate, well balanced diets but also by physical activity and fitness. As the human body advances in age, certain changes take place resulting in various changes including decline in capacities and body functions. Exercise and some physical activity are of utmost importance for maintenance of physical fitness and to sustain a healthy life as well as to establish a certain quality of life. Regular exercise makes a person fit. Persons who exercise regularly experience a sense of well-being and sleep better. Exercise also makes the heart and lungs work more efficiently, improving circulation and respiration. Exercise carried out for about 20 minutes at least three times a week is beneficial. Older people should undertake exercise regularly so as to prevent and control several of the diseases like obesity, hypertension, diabetes, etc. In fact youth and young adults should begin to take precautionary health regimen to save themselves of diseases at a later stage.

(i) **Given below are two statements labelled as Assertion (A) and Reason (R).** **Competency Based Que**

Assertion (A) Health is promoted by a well-balanced diet.

Reason (R) If you eat less you don't need to exercise to stay fit.

Codes

(a) Both A and R are true and R is the correct explanation of A
(b) Both A and R are true, but R is not the correct explanation of A
(c) A is true, but R is false
(d) A is false, but R is true

(ii) **Which of the following is not a benefit of exercising regularly?**

(a) Eating junk food without guilt
(b) Have a good physique
(c) Immune against non-communicable diseases
(d) Good mental health and better sleep

(iii) **...... is a precautionary measure so as to not catch heart or respiratory diseases at a later stage of life.**

(a) Training
(b) Education
(c) Blood testing
(d) Exercise

(iv) **Wellness improves .... by reducing risk of disease, disability, discomfort and distress throughout the life cycle.**

(a) quantity of life
(b) legality of life
(c) quality of life
(d) purpose of life

Answers

1. (d) All of the above
2. (d) Consume too much fat/oil (butter on bread, ghee on parathas) or fried foods.
3. (a) obesity
4. (d) All of the above
5. (b) Only I
6. (c) Both I and II
7. (b) Increase consumption of legumes and whole grains
8. (a) Physical activity
9. (b) Release of endorphins, promoting feelings of pleasure and happiness
10. (b) Endurance exercises : Weightlifting
11. (d) None of the above
12. (d) III and IV
13. (d) Both (a) and (b)
14. (a) 1 2 3 4
15. (d) A is false, but R is true.
16. (d) A is false, but R is true.
17. (a) Both A and R are true and R is the correct explanation of A.
18. (b) Both A and R are true, but R is not the correct explanation of A.
19. (d) A is false, but R is true.
20. (i) (b) increase the feeling of happiness
    (ii) (d) By boosting confidence as well as reducing anxiety and stress
    (iii) (a) Due to stretching of stiff muscles
    (iv) (a) Both A and R are true and R is the correct explanation of A.
21. (i) (c) A is true, but R is false.
    (ii) (a) Eating junk food without guilt
    (iii) (d) Exercise
    (iv) (c) quality of life

Subjective Questions

Very Short Answer Type Questions

1. What do health professional use to assess the nutritional health states and risk?

Ans. Anthropometric indicators are used by professionals to assess the nutritional health states and risk.

2. Sahil is a factory worker with a weight of 80 kg and a height of 160 cm. Calculate Sahil's BMI and classify him accordingly. Is Sahil at higher risk of non-communicable diseases than 'normal' persons? If so, why? **CBQ**

Ans. Sahil's BMI = 80 (kg) /1.602 (m^2) = 31.25.

As Sahil's BMI is greater than 30 but less than 35, he will be classified as 'Obese class I'. So, Sahil is at higher risk of non-communicable diseases than 'normal' persons because his weight is much more than 'normal' persons of the same height as him.

3. Which ethnicity of persons are at a higher risk than others for the same BMI?

Ans. For the same BMI, ethnic Asians are at a higher risk compared to other ethnic populations.

4. How does wellness improve the 'Quality of Life'?

Ans. Wellness improves the 'Quality of Life' by reducing risk of disease, disability, discomfort and distress throughout the life cycle.

5. How physical activity significant in promoting health?

Ans. Regular physical activity, combined with a balanced diet, plays a significant rule in promoting health, enhancing quality of life & preventing form illnesses.

6. Sonia is concerned about osteoporosis as she ages. How can physical activity help? **Competency Based Que**

Ans. Physical activities and regular exercise maintains bone mineral density, reducing the risk of fractures and osteoporosis.

7. What builds stamina, improves fitness and help in weight loss or control?

Ans. Aerobic exercises builds stamina, improves fitness and help in weight loss or control.

8. 'Mona wants to improve her flexibility and balance'. What ancient Indian practice can help her achieve this? **Competency Based Que**

Ans. Mona should practice the ancient Indian technique known as Yoga. It includes various yogic aasanas (postures), enhances flexibility, strength and balance.

9. What is wellness and how is it achieved?

Ans. The World Health Organisation (WHO) defines wellness as 'The optimal state of health of individuals and groups'. Wellness is directed towards a positive and afferming life. It is concerned with achievement of physical, mental, social, emotional, intellectual, spiritual and environmental well-being, which in turn, helps an individual to achieve an optimum level of functioning.

10. Aprajita wants to understand the dimensions of wellness. What two concerns does the WHO highlight regarding wellness? **Competency Based Que**

Ans. WHO highlights the following two concerns regarding wellness

(i) Achieving individuals' fullest potentials (physically, psychologically, socially, spiritually, economically)

(ii) Meeting expectations in various settings (family, community, workplace).

11. What is a 'wellness lifestyle' associated with?

Ans. A 'wellness lifestyle' is associated with good physical health, emotional stability, healthy relationships with family, friends and peers as well as productivity and satisfaction in one's work and workplace.

12. 'Mohit wants to assess his wellness level'. What are some key qualities of individuals with high wellness ratings? **Competency Based Que**

Ans. Some key qualities of individuals with high wellness ratings are high self-esteem, positive outlook, sense of purpose, personal responsibility, good sense of humour, concern for others and respect for environment.

13. What are the two opposite forms of stress?

Ans. The two opposite forms of stress are 'eustress', which has a positive effect, and 'distress', which adversely affects performance physical health and mental health.

'Stress is a normal part of daily life that can have both positive and negative effects on an individual's physical and mental well-being'.

14. 'Stress is a normal part of daily life that can have both positive and negative effects on an individual's physical and mental well-being'.

Explain the difference between eustress and distress, providing examples of each. **Competency Based Que**

Ans. Eustress is positive stress that enhances performance, while distress is negative stress leading to health problems.

Eustress Example Studying hard for exams due to stress, leading to high marks.

Distress Example Feeling overwhelmed by workload, causing anxiety and fatigue.

15. After a long day of studying for her exams, Aditi decided to join a dance class for stress relief. While dancing, she felt a wave of joy and energy. Which hormones are responsible for this and how are they beneficial. **Competency Based Que**

Ans. Endorphins are released from the brain during and after exercise. These are the body's natural painkillers and also increase feelings of happiness and well-being.

Thus, they are beneficial for health.

Short Answer Type Questions

1. Anjali, a 27 years old software developer in Bangalore, wants to improve her health. She hears about Body Mass Index (BMI) as a tool for assessing nutritional status and risk. **Competency Based Que**

(i) Define BMI for Anjali

(ii) Explain how it can be used to evaluate her health and identify any potential risks?

Ans. (i) Body Mass Index (BMI) is a simple calculation used to determine if someone is underweight, normal weight, overweight or obese based on their weight and height. It is calculated by dividing weight in kilograms by the square of height in meters.

(ii) For Anjali, understanding her BMI can help identify her weight category and associated health risks, such as diabetes and heart disease. By monitoring her BMI, she can make informed lifestyle choices to improve her overall health and well-being.

2. Neha, a 25 years old, weighs 85 kg and stands 1.70 meters tall. She wants to assess her weight-related health risks.

(i) Calculate Neha's BMI and categorise her weight status.

(ii) Explain the health risks associated with Neha's BMI category. **Competency Based Que**

Ans. (i) $\text{BMI} = \text{Weight (kg)} / \text{Height (m)}^2$

$= 85 \text{ kg} / (1.70 \text{ m})^2$

$= 85 / 2.89$

$= 29.4$

Neha's BMI falls into the 'Overweight' category.

(ii) As Neha's BMI is 29.4, she falls into the 'Overweight' category. This increases hir risk of serious health issues like diabetes, heart disease and high blood pressure.

Higher BMI is linked to harmful changes in the body, including increased fat, reduced glucose tolerance and altered blood cholesterol levels. Regular monitoring and lifestyle adjustments can help mitigate these risks.

3. What are the three main categories of exercise? How can each category contribute to overall fitness?

Ans. The three main categories of exercise are endurance/aerobic, strength/resistance and balance/flexibility exercises.

- Endurance exercises, like brisk walking and cycling, improve stamina and cardiovascular health while aiding weight loss.

- Strength exercises, such as weightlifting and push-ups, increase muscle strength and enhance bone mass.
- Lastly, balance and flexibility exercises, including yoga and stretching, improve flexibility, reduce stiffness and enhance overall mobility.

4. Describe the contribution of yoga and meditation in improving mental and physical well-being.

Ans. Yoga and meditation have been used traditionally for a long time in achieving mental health and well-being. Further, practising yogic asanas regularly helps the body become more flexible and benefits people with diabetes and high blood pressure.

Performing yoga regularly is one of the best ways to relax body and mind. The ones that focus on slow movement, stretching and deep breathing are best for lowering anxiety and stress and improving mood.

5. What do you understand by emotional wellness and well-being? What are four features of emotional wellness?

Ans. Emotional wellness is the degree of awareness and acceptance that one has of one's own feelings. Emotional well-being allows an individual to recognise, understand, experience and express a full range of emotions.

Four features of emotional wellness are

(i) The extent to which one feels positive and enthusiastic about one's self and life.

(ii) The capacity to appropriately handle and express one's emotions (both positive and negative).

(iii) How one copes with stress.

(iv) Being able to realistically assess one's limitations.

6. Aarav, a 35 years old marketing executive in Mumbai, feels fatigued and often experiences stress at work. After reading about the importance of health and fitness, he wonders how improving his fitness could benefit him.

What advantages can Aarav expect from adopting a healthier lifestyle? **Competency Based Que**

Ans. By adopting a healthier lifestyle, Aarav can expect several benefits.

- Regular exercise will boost his energy levels, making daily tasks feel more manageable and enhancing his productivity at work.
- Additionally, physical activity releases endorphins, improving his mood and reducing stress.
- Staying fit will also help prevent chronic illnesses, promote a healthy weight, strengthen his bones and muscles, improve sleep quality and increase longevity.
- Overall, these changes can lead to a more fulfilling and balanced life.

Long Answer Type Questions

1. After reaching 50s, Ravi noticed a decline in his energy levels and overall fitness. Concerned about his health, he considered including regular exercise into his routine. In what ways can exercise benefit Ravi in adulthood? **Competency Based Que**

Ans. The exercises can benefit Ravi in following ways

- Disability can be postponed by as much as 15 years. Even inactive persons, derive considerable health benefits once they begin to do small amounts of exercise.
- Helps him to maintain his weight.
- Helps in controlling blood sugar levels and blood pressure.
- Helps him to maintain bone mineral density and thus, reduces the risk of fractures and disability.
- Helps him in enhancing muscle strength in both upper and lower limbs (training for a couple of months can help to increase strength of our lower limbs).

2. After experiencing low energy and frequent colds, Arjun consulted a nutritionist for advice on improving his diet. He wanted to know the essential do's and don'ts of a health promoting diet. What specific guidelines should he follow to enhance his well-being and boost his immune system and what common mistake should he avoided. **Competency Based Que**

Ans. For answer refer to the text under the heading 'Do's and Don'ts of Health Promoting Diets' on page no. 216.

3. A local community center aims to launch a wellness program for its residents, focusing on holistic well-being and disease prevention.

(i) Explain the concept of wellness and its significance in the community.

(ii) Discuss the dimensions of wellness relevant to the community program, highlighting two benefits of each. **Competency Based Que**

Ans. (i) Wellness is a holistic approach to health, encompassing physical, mental, social, emotional, intellectual, spiritual and environmental aspects. It enables individuals to achieve optimal health, prevent ill-health and enhance quality of life.

For the community, adopting a wellness approach can foster a supportive environment, promote healthy habits and reduce chronic disease risks. It emphasises on connecting and engaging with others in our communities in meaningful ways promotes harmony and positive environment.

(ii) For answer refer to the text under heading 'Dimensions of wellness' on page no. 218 and 219.

4. What are ten personality traits of people rated high on the wellness and well-being profile?

Ans. Ten personality traits of people rated high on the wellness and well-being profile are

(i) High self-esteem, a positive outlook and a sense of purpose.

(ii) A strong sense of personal responsibility and commitment.

(iii) A good sense of humour.

(iv) A concern for others.

(v) A respect for the environment.

(vi) A physically fit and an integrated healthy lifestyle.

(vii) A capacity to cope with life's challenges.

(viii) An ability to continue to learn.

(ix) A capacity to love and an ability to nurture.

(x) An ability for effective communication.

5. Briefly explain the stress coping techniques.

Ans. The various stress coping techniques are

(i) **Talking with friends/family** If things are bothering you, talking about them to family members and friends can help lower your stress. It is a natural way to calm yourself. When you connect with people in person, your body releases a hormone that stops your fight-or-flight response and relaxes you.

(ii) **Relaxation** Giving yourself some time to relax from your busy schedule can help relieve stress. It is important to include recreation and relaxation time in your daily time plan.

Relaxation can be done in many ways, such as taking a shower, sleeping, meditation, spending time in nature, etc.

(iii) **Reading** Reading a book or a novel of your interest can divert your mind from stress. This can entertain you, give you a break and thus, lower your stress.

(iv) **Spirituality** Spirituality helps in dealing with stress and improving mental health. Having a spiritual side can give a person a boost by allowing reliance on God or a higher power and surrendering worries and troubles, rather than holding on so tightly to stress. With a spiritual practice you'll find that no matter how tough it gets, you're not alone.

(v) **Music** Listening to music can relax in following ways

- Lower our heart rate and cortisol levels.
- Release endorphins and improve our sense of well-being.
- Distract us, reducing physical and emotional stress levels.
- Reduce stress-related symptoms, whether used in a clinical environment or in daily life.

SELF ASSESSMENT TEST

Objective Type Questions

1. In which of the following exercise/activities can cycling be put?
   (a) Endurance building exercise
   (b) Strength building exercise
   (c) Balancing exercise
   (d) None of these
2. .... is a state of optimal well-being.
   (a) Happiness
   (b) Wellness
   (c) Hopefulness
   (d) All of these
3. Which of the following is not a dimension of healthy lifestyle?
   (a) Physical
   (b) Spiritual
   (c) Environmental
   (d) Educational

Very Short Answer Type Questions

4. What are healthy and unhealthy diets?
5. In how many categories is BMI divided. What should a person having a BMI of 18.2 be classified as?
6. What are two examples each of endurance building exercises, flexibility exercise and strength building exercise?
7. How does exercise contribute to psychological health and well-being?

Short Answer Type Questions

8. Explain Do's and Don'ts for Health Promoting Diets.
9. Explain the benefits of exercise in maintaining physical fitness.
10. How do persons who take care of themselves improve their quality of life? Give four ways.
11. 'Ajit has a very stressful job as an Air Traffic Controller (ATC) at an international airport. However, he manages his job successfully by employing some stress management techniques'. Mention six such techniques which Ajit may be using to manage his stress. **Competency Based Que**

Long Answer Type Questions

12. Define the following
    (i) Healthy people
    (ii) Wellness
    (iii) Financial aspect of wellness
13. Explain any five dimensions of wellness in not more than two sentences each.
14. Briefly explain four stress coping techniques.

12 CHAPTER

Financial Management and Planning

The quality of life that a family can achieve depends not just on the total income but also on steady and reliable income. Therefore, it is important to learn the skill of managing finances and planning.

YOUR STUDY GOALS

YOUR PRACTICE GOAL

- Objective Type Questions (22 Qs ; MCQs, A-R, Matching, Case Based)
- Subjective Questions (12 VSAs, 6 SAs, 5 LAs)

12.1 Introduction

Financial Management

- Financial management for a family means management of finances. This includes all kinds of income a family can have, such as salaries, wages, rent, interest, dividends, bonuses, retirement benefits and any other money received.
- The process of planning, controlling and evaluating about how to use this income is called **financial management**. Its main purpose is to help the family get the most satisfaction from the resources they have.

Financial Planning

- **Financial planning**[1] is a key part of financial management. A budget is often used during the planning stage. When families create budgets, they ensure their income meets their current needs while also considering their long-term goals.
- Families are able to achieve their objectives by optimising the use of their resources. Financial planning also helps reduce spending on non-essential items, allowing families to save some of their income for the future.

1 **Financial Planning** It is the task of determining how a family will afford to achieve its strategic goals and objectives.

- For this to work, families need to regularly check or monitor and evaluate their financial plans. It's also very important for all family members to be committed to the financial plan for it to be effective.

Management

- Management is about using what you have (resources) to achieve what you want (goals and objectives).
- Family resources are what individuals or families have at a specific time to help them to reach their goals.
- These resources include
  - **Human Resources** Knowledge, skills, health, time and energy.
  - **Material Resources** Housing, money and investments.
  - **Community Resources** Libraries, parks, community centers, hospitals and more. To make the best use of these resources, it's important to manage them well.
- A family acts as both a **consumption unit** and a **social unit**. Its purpose is to manage finances for the well-being of its members. Money is an important family resource; without enough money, a family cannot live comfortably.
- Learning to manage money effectively to meet current needs and future goals is an important skill.

12.2 Family Income

- Family income is the **total income** from all sources and types for all family members over a specific time period.
- This can be calculated on an annual, monthly, weekly or daily basis.
- For official purposes, family income is usually considered as the annual income, which is typically measured from April 1st to March 31st of the next year.
- These different types of income contribute to the overall financial resources of the family.

There are three types of family income.

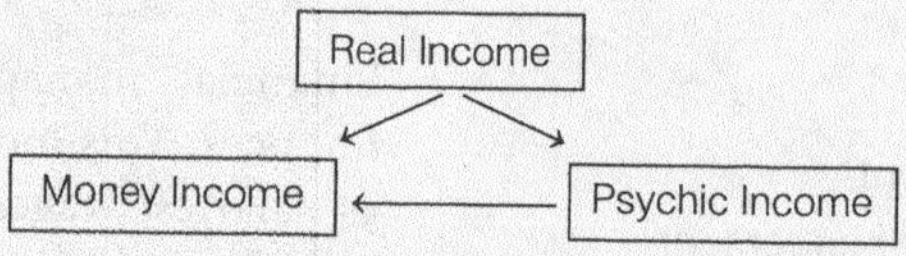

Money Income

- Money income is the **purchasing power** in rupees and paisa that goes into a family's finances over a certain period. It comes from various sources, including wages, salaries, bonuses, commissions, rent, dividends, interest, retirement income, royalties and other allowances given to family members.
- Families use this money to buy goods and services needed for daily living, and they often save part of it for future use or invest it. The frequency and pattern of flow of money income varies from family to family. For example, a person having a job will have regular income every month however income of a farmer is not regular.

Functions of Money

Money is defined by what it does. The two most important functions of money are

(i) **Medium of Exchange** Money is used to buy and sell goods and services.

(ii) **Measurement of Value** Money helps determine the value of different items.

Thus, money is anything which is generally acceptable in exchange of commodities and in terms of which the value of other commodities is determined.

Importance of Money

Money is important in following ways.

- **Standard of Value** Money provides a common denominator in terms of which the value of all other commodities is expressed.
- **Standard of Deferred Payments** Money helps with savings and investments, which are important for building capital and improving living standards.
- **Storage of Value** Money can be saved over long periods, it is thus durable. This allows families to accumulate wealth for future investments and improve standard of living for the family.

Real Income

It is defined by economists as a **flow of commodities and services available** for satisfaction of human wants and needs over a given period of time. This means the amount of goods and services available to meet people's wants and needs over a certain time. It has three key points

(i) **Flow of Goods and Services** Real income represents a continuous supply of goods and services. It is not stagnant means it doesn't stay the same.

(ii) **Availability** It includes both goods and services that may or may not require money to obtain. For example, food grown on your own land or services performed by family members are part of real income.

(iii) **Time Period** Real income is measured over a specific period, like a month or a year.

Real income can be divided into two types

(i) **Direct Income** This includes goods and services available to family members without spending money.

For examples, services provided by family, such as cooking or cleaning, as well as having a fully paid-off house or access to community facilities like parks and libraries.

(ii) **Indirect Income** This is the material, goods and services which are available to the family only after some means of exchange (ordinarily money) has been obtained.

For example, includes the use of money to buy good quality vegetables because it involves one's skill and ability to select.

Psychic Income

It is the satisfaction from owning and using goods and services. It can be defined as the satisfaction derived from real income. It's hard to measure psychic income in rupees. Psychic income is a **hidden, intangible and subjective form** (based on personal feelings) of income. It is important for quality of living.

12.3 Income Management

- Income management may be defined as **planning, controlling** and **evaluating** the use of all types of income.
- The goal is to get the greatest satisfaction from available resources.
- No two families will have the same needs and desires, even if they have the same income. Thus, each family should create their own expenditure or spending plan based on their goals, needs and wants.
- For effective income management, families must recognise and analyse all their available resources.

Budget

- A budget is a common tool for planning about how to use money. It is a plan for future expenditure and is the **first step in managing money**.
- A family budget gives in detail the income and the expenditure of a family for a month or a year.
- It mentions all the sources of income during the period and also all the items of expenditure under different headings, such as food, clothing, housing, entertainment, travel, education, health & medicine and savings.
- Its success depends upon the following
  - Being realistic and flexible.
  - Being suitable for the specific group it is made for.
  - The quality of the control and evaluation steps that follow.

Steps in Making a Budget

There are mainly five steps in making a budget. They are as follows

(i) **List Needs** Write down all the goods and services based on the needs of the family. Group similar items into categories like food, housing, education, transportation, clothing, medical and savings.

(ii) **Estimate Costs** Calculate the costs for each category and the overall budget. General market trends must be considered while making these estimates. For example, if prices are showing an upward trend, sufficient margin should be allowed to cover such increases.

(iii) **Estimate Income** Determine the total expected income, dividing it into **assured income** (guaranteed) and **possible income** (uncertain). Ensure that necessary expenses are covered by assured income and the 'nice but not necessary' items can be obtained from possible income

(iv) **Balance Income and Expenses** Make sure your total expenses don't exceed your income. There are two ways to bring them into balance. One can either increase the income (for example by taking up an extra job/work) or cut expenditures (less frequent outings or less expenditure on festivals).

(v) **Check Plans** Review your budget to ensure
- it meets your family's needs
- allows for emergencies
- assures solvency (ability to pay bills)
- recognises long-term goals.
- the national and world-wide conditions have been considered (e.g., global economic recession).

Advantages of Planning Family Budgets

- Planning Family Budgets[2] enables a family to take an overview of the use of their income.
- Families can examine how much money is allocated to different categories compared to their total income.
- A budget allows families to focus on achieving their most important goals. On the other hand, spending without a plan can lead to wasting money.
- With a budget, family members are less likely to be influenced by impulse (sudden or quick) decisions, enabling them to make choices that fulfill their long-term goals.

Quick Test 1

1. Name some community resources.
2. What are the resources that are available to the individual or the family at a particular time?
3. Mention the types of family income.
4. How economists defined real income?

2 Family Budget A family budget gives in detail the income and the expenditure of a family for a month or a year.

12.4 Control in Money Management

After planning, the next step of managing money is controlling it. Control involves two main actions: checking how well the plan is progressing and making adjustments when necessary.

Checking Progress

This is important to see how the plans are going and where changes might be needed. There are two types of checks

- **Mental Checks** It involves **breaking down your budget** into specific items related to actual spending. For example, ₹ 1,000 might seem like a lot to a student, but when they need to buy shoes, a dress for a festival and some books all at once, it becomes clear that careful selection and pricing are necessary based on the total money available. This way, mental checking helps visualise what each amount must cover.
- **Mechanical Check** It involves **setting aside a specific amount of cash** for a particular expense or item. For instance, many homemakers use a food purse to hold the monthly food budget. All food expenses come from this envelope and if the money runs out quickly, it indicates how fast the spending is happening.

Records and Accounts

- These show how money is spent. They can be informal, like keeping daily notes or receipts or formal, like detailed accounts. The main purpose of records for a family is to track how money is spent and compare it with the budgeted amounts for different items.

The advantages of record keeping for a family are

- Monthly spending can be compared to the budget which helps to identify where adjustments are needed to avoid overspending.
- It helps pinpoint categories where spending is too high or too low, allowing for better future budgets.
- Some methods require keeping bills and receipts, providing proof of payment if there's a complaint about a product or service.

The single sheet method is a simple and flexible way to keep records, where all expenses are noted on one sheet.

Adjusting and Evaluation

- **Adjusting** the budget is crucial to keep it on track. Changes may be necessary if the original plan was poor or weak due to factors beyond the family's control, such as emergencies, unexpected shopping sprees or poor tracking that doesn't reveal much of a gap between the budget (allocated money) and actual spending.
- **Evaluation** is the final step in managing money. It focuses on how satisfied the family is with their spending, which is key to measuring the success of the budget. Evaluation considers specific goals like
  - Getting fair value for money spent.
  - Being able to pay bills on time.
  - Planning for the future.
  - Improving the family's economic status

Records of expenditures may be kept on a **single, double or multiple sheets**. This method is simple and flexible. Also the sheet can be tacked on the back of a door or cabinet with a pencil hanging nearby, which makes it convenient. Although the double and multiple sheet methods can be more adequate than single sheet, yet if the single sheet is well worked out it may include essential data. Consider the following example

Single Sheet Method for the Month of December 2024

Category	Amount Allocated	Amount Spent	Total
Amount Spent .			
1. **Food** Grocery, Milk, Fruit/veg., Meat-poultry, Eating out			
2. **Housing** Rent, Repair, Loan			
3. **Clothing** Children's clothing, Adults' clothing, School Uniform			
4. **Education** Fees, Notebooks, Books			
5. **Medical**			
6. **Any other**			

12.5 Savings

- Savings means keeping aside some of your money or resources for future use or for investment. Savings help families prepare for future needs. They are also important for any economy to survive and grow as savings lead to capital formation and accumulation. This happens when savings are put to productive purposes, like starting a business or depositing in banks.
- A family's savings are determined by two factors
  - (i) A family's ability to save depends on their income. Main factor which influences saving is the **per capita[3] income**. Higher-income families can save more than lower-income families, who often have little left after meeting basic needs.
  - (ii) Willingness to save is influenced by the family's long-term goals and their readiness to give up some luxuries now for future benefits.

Thus, saving money requires discipline, planning, co-operation and hard work from all family members. Saving is important for family security and happiness, but it should have a clear purpose. Savings are meaningful only when there's a well-planned goal understood by all family members, and the money is wisely invested for future use.

12.6 Investment

- Investment means using money to create more wealth or production. Simply keeping savings hidden, like in a saree or pitcher, does not lead to investment. It should be invested for productive use.
- Investments are two types financial assets and physical assets
  - **Financial Assets** These include savings in bank accounts, post offices, shares, securities, and insurance policies. They help provide **financial security** to families and are considered productive for the economy.
  - **Physical Assets** These include purchases like land, property, houses, gold and durable goods. While these investments may not be economically productive or contribute to capital formation, they often yield **positive long-term returns.**

3 Per Capita Income It is a measure of the amount of money earned by per person in a nation or geographical region.

Principles Underlying Sound Investments

Families work hard to save money over their lifetime. It is important to invest those savings wisely for good returns while ensuring safety and availability when needed.

The key principles for sound investments

- **Safety of the Principal Amount** The original amount of money (principal) should be safe to earn interest. To ensure safety
  - **Invest in government and private sector securities** like National Savings Certificates (NSCs) and Public Provident Fund (PPF).
  - Diversify investments across different geographical areas and companies.
  - **Invest in a variety of assets,** such as real estate, stocks and bonds.
  - Research the reputation of the investment options.
  - Understand the current business cycle.
- **Reasonable Rate of Return** Higher the rate of return on an investment, the greater the risk, i.e., safety of principal and rate of return are inversely related.
  - For those depedent on investments for income,having a steady income is often more important than aiming for higher returns that might vary. **Compare interest rates and risks** before investing. This is determined by the selection of securities. Therefore, before investing money one should compare the rate of interest and the associated risk under various schemes and options.
- **Liquidity** It is the **ability to convert the securities into cash** without sacrificing value. The more liquid an investment is, the higher is its price, or in other words, the lower the return to the investor. Hence income and liquidity must be balanced.
- **Recognition of Effect of World Conditions** Changes in business trends affect how much protection is needed for investments and the methods to provide it. A family's savings choices can influence the economy and their willingness to invest during different economic phases can help stabilise economic fluctuations.
- **Investment Knowledge** When choosing investment options, families must consider the knowledge required for success. Lack of understanding can lead to losses if they don't anticipate the challenges of managing investments like securities or properties.
- **Investing in Needed Commodities** Families should consider when their investments will mature. While investing money, families should purchase securities of lengths and durations so that they mature close to the time of their needs , such as funding a child's higher education.
- **Tax Efficiency** Families should invest in instruments that offer tax savings. Various provisions in the **Income Tax Act** allow for tax savings, including investments in insurance policies, Employees Provident Fund, and PPF, which provide built-in tax rebates with specific limits.
- **After Investment Service** When choosing an investment, good customer care should be a key factor. This includes easy encashability of securities and effective communication.
  - Good customer service involves timely dispatch of interest or dividend payments, prompt/quick disbursal of funds after the investment period and keeping customers informed about policy changes and interest rates.
  - A customer-friendly company offers the necessary support and protection to investors when needed.
- **Time Period** The lock-in period is an important factor to consider before making an investment.
  - Generally, longer investment periods offer higher returns.

    For example, fixed schemes usually provide higher interest rates for long-term deposits compared to short-term ones.
  - Investors need to decide between a higher return with a longer wait or a lower return with a shorter lock-in period, depending on their family's needs.

- **Capacity** One should not invest more than they can afford to avoid financial strain. It's important to balance current needs with future needs and security.

Savings and Investment Avenues

The list of saving and investment options which are available to an Indian consumer is as follows

- Post Office
- National Savings Scheme
- Bonds
- Public Provident Fund
- Pension Schemes
- Banks
- National Savings Certificates
- Mutual Funds
- Chit Fund
- Gold, House, Land
- Unit Trust of India
- Shares and Debentures
- Provident Fund
- Life Insurance and Medical Insurance

Quick Test 2

1 Write the process of doing mental checks in controlling money.
2 What helps in identifying the categories in which expenditure is too high or too low, enabling to make better budgets in future?
3 What does the money for further production imply?
4 Give two principles underlying sound investments.

12.7 Credit

- Although families save and invest money, they have to sometimes use credit to meet their needs or obligations. Families make use of credit to avail of goods and services whose initial cost is too high to bear/pay at once.
- The word **credit** comes from the Latin word **CREDO**, meaning **I believe**. It refers to receiving money, goods or services now and paying for them later.
- Credit is essentially a **process of postponed payment**, which can sometimes come with high costs.
- Using credit increases purchasing power, allowing families to buy more than they could with just the cash they have.
- It is, therefore, important for families to understand how credit works, as they will need to repay the borrowed amount along with interest eventually.

Need for Credit

- Families use credit to meet their needs or obligations, which can be real or imagined. If the cost of an item seems too high to save for, families might borrow money to buy it immediately, such as land.
- Borrowing allows families to spread the cost of a purchase over a longer period. This enables them to use the item while making payments.
- Families also borrow money for emergencies, like a family member's illness or for obligations such as weddings or funerals.
- A self-supporting and self-sufficient family can use credit in emergencies and do so confidently.
- Lenders, such as banks or financial institutions, will only give loans if they believe the borrower can repay the money.
- The decision to grant credit to individuals and families is based on the four C's.

Four C's of Credit

- **Character** It refers to the willingness and determination to repay a loan as agreed, even if it costs more or is more inconvenient than expected.
- **Capacity** This means the ability to meet loan obligations when due, which usually depends on income. A family's ability to repay is determined by the difference between their income and necessary expenses. The capacity of a family to repay a loan is determined by the difference between what the family receives and what it spends.
- **Capital** It refers to the net worth. A family's capital is determined by the difference between what it owns and what it owes. Having capital provides safety for the lender, as it can be used to repay the loan if income is insufficient.
- **Collateral** This refers to specific assets that are pledged as security for a loan. Typically, these assets are given to the lender, who can sell them to recover their money if the borrower fails to repay the loan as agreed.

Sources of Credit

- Main sources of credit include commercial banks, co-operative banks, agricultural banks and credit unions.
- One can also take credit from **self-help groups** after becoming its members.
  - The members of this self-help group contribute some money every month and make a **corpus amount.**
  - From this credit, loans are given to the needy member based on her/his requirement and repaying capacity.
  - These groups have members known to each other and hence **no collateral is needed** and the interest rate is nominal.

Considerations Before Using Credit

- Families should think about not just the immediate satisfaction of having a goods or services. They should also consider the future impact on their budget due to loan repayments.
- This includes knowing when to use credit and recognising when it becomes excessive.
- Credit can be a helpful resource if understood properly. If used carelessly, credit can lead to serious problems for a family. The goal should be to minimise credit use and borrow at the lowest possible cost.

Quick Test 3

1. What is the meaning of Latin word 'CREDO'?
2. Mention the four C's of credit.
3. What does collateral refers to ?
4. Mention one source of credit in rural areas.

Mind Map

FINANCIAL MANAGEMENT AND PLANNING

1 Financial Management
- Means management of finances.
- It includes all types of incomes, salary, wages, rent etc.

2 Financial Planning
- Key part of financial management.
- Budget is used during the planning stage.
- It takes care of long -term goals.

3 Family Income
Types of Family Income

Money Income
- Purchasing power in rupees and paisa that goes into family income.

Real Income
- It is a flow of commodities and services available for satisfaction of human needs.
- It is divided into two parts.
  (i) Direct income
  (ii) Indirect income

Psychic Income
- It is the satisfaction from owning and using goods and services.

Money and It's Functions

Importance of Money
- It is a medium of exchange.
- It is used as standard of value.
- It helps in savings and investments.
- It can be saved over long periods and it is durable.

4 Income Management
- It includes planning, controlling and evaluating the use of all types of income.

Budget
- It is the first step in managerial process.
- It is realistic and flexible.
- It is the plan for future expenditure.

Steps in Making a Budget
- List Needs
- Estimate Costs
- Estimate Income
- Balance Income and Expenses

5 Control in Money Management
- It is the second step of money management.
- It includes checking to see how well the plan is progressing.
- It includes Adjustment according to the need.

Advantages of Record Keeping for a Family
- It helps to identify where adjustments are needed.
- It helps to plan for better future.

6 Savings and Investment Avenues
- Post office
- Banks
- Unit trust of India
- Public Provident fund
- Life insurance and medical insurance.
- Pension schemes
- Shares and debentures
- National savings scheme
- Gold, House, Land.

7 Principles of Underlying Sound Investments
- Recognition of effect of world conditions
- Easy accessibility and convenience
- Investing in needed commodities
- Safety of principal amount
- Reasonable rate of return
- Capacity
- Tax efficiency
- Time period
- Liquidity

8 Credit
Need for Credit
- It allows families to spread the cost of a purchase over a longer period.
- It helps family during emergencies like sickness of a family member.
- It helps to meet obligations like marriage of children.
- It helps to perform rituals.

4 Cs of Credit
- Character
- Capacity
- Capital
- Collateral

Sources of Credit
- It includes commercial banks, co-operative banks, agricultural banks and credit unions.

Considerations Before Using Credit
- Think about home loan repayment will affect your budget.
- Use credit only when needed.
- Avoid too much borrowing.
- Use credit wisely.
- Borrow as little as possible and at the lowest cost.

Profit

Savings

NCERT Folder

1. Indicate if the following statements are 'True' or 'False'.

(i) Budget is the first step in money management.

(ii) Money serves as a medium of exchange of commodities.

(iii) Profits from business and gifts are a form of income.

(iv) One should first estimate the cost and then list the commodities and services needed while making the budget.

(v) Savings in physical assets are productive in economic terms.

(vi) The trend in business cycle is an important consideration under the principal of safety.

(vii) The time period may be ignored while considering and deciding on an investment.

(viii) The four C's of credit are character, capacity, capital and collateral.

(ix) Nature of enterprise is not an important safety consideration.

Ans. (i) True (ii) True (iii) True
(iv) False (v) False (vi) True
(vii) False (viii) True (ix) False

2. What do you understand by 'management of finances'?

Ans. 'Management of finances' means planning, controlling and evaluating the use of all types of incomes such as salary, wages, rent, interest, dividends, bonus, retirement benefits and all other forms of monetary receipts.

3. Discuss the different types of income.

Ans. The different types of income are as follows

(i) **Money Income** It is the purchasing power in rupees that goes into the family treasury in a given period of time. It is in the form of wages, salary, bonus, commission, rent, dividends, interest, royalties and any other allowances to any member of the family. The frequency and pattern of flow of money income varies among different families.

(ii) **Real Income** It is defined by economists as the flow of commodities and services available for satisfaction of human wants and needs over a given period of time.

Thus, it is not stagnant and includes goods and services for which money may not be needed. Thus, real income is of two types

(a) **Direct Income** It consists of those goods and services available to the family members without the use of money. Examples are self-cultivated vegetables, cooking the family's meals, etc.

(b) **Indirect Income** It consists of those material goods and services which are available to the family only aftersome money has been spent on them.

(iii) **Psychic Income** It is the satisfaction that results from the ownership and utilisation of goods and services i.e. the satisfaction derived from real income. It is a form of hidden income which is subjective and improves our quality of life.

4. Discuss the steps in making a budget.

Ans. The steps in making a budget are

(i) **List the Commodities and Services Needed** The commodities and services with the quantities required by the family during the specified time period should be listed.

(ii) **Estimate the Cost** It is the total of the costs expected for the desired items under the classifications made and also the budget as a whole.

(iii) **Estimate total Expected Income**

We may list the income under assured income (like salaries) and possible income (like commissions, donations, etc). The budget should be made so as to ensure that necessities are taken care of from the assured income and the 'nice but not necessary' items can be obtained from the possible income.

(iv) **Balance Income and Expenditure** If initially the expenditure seems more than the income, the two ways to balance them are as follows

(a) Increase the income (e.g. do overtime work).

(b) Reduce the expenditure (e.g. less outings).

(v) **Evaluate/Check the Plans** To ensure that the budget or plans have a reasonable chance of success or not.

5. What are the controls that can be exercised in money management?

Ans. Controls that can be exercised in money management are

- Checking, mental and mechanical as well as records and accounts, to see how well the plan is progressing.
- Adjusting the plan or the expenditure wherever necessary.
- Evaluating the success of the budget in terms of specific goals met.

6. Discuss the principles underlying sound investments.

Ans. Following are the principles underlying sound investments

(i) **Safety of the Principal Amount** The principal itself has to be safe if it is to earn interest or dividends. Safety of the principal amount can be ensured by
- Owning securities like National Savings Certificates (NSCs), Public Provident Fund (PPF), Kisan Vikas Patras (KVPs), fixed deposits in banks, mutual funds, etc.
- Varying the kind of securities purchased agricultural land, real estate, stocks, bonds, fixed deposits etc.
- Investing in more than one company and in different geographical zones.
- Owning shares and bonds in different companies.
- Studying the market reputation of the issues of the securities.
- Understanding the prevailing phase of the business cycle.

(ii) **Reasonable Rate of Return** In general, the higher the rate of return on an investment, the greater the risk i.e. safety of principal and rate of return are inversely related. To some people, particularly those depending upon investments as their major source of income, regularity of income is more important than a higher but fluctuating return. This is determined by the selection of securities. Therefore, before investing money one should compare the rate of interest and the associated risk under various schemes and options.

(iii) **Liquidity** It is the ability to convert the securities into cash without sacrificing value. Usually more liquid investments give less returns. Hence, income and liquidity must be balanced.

(iv) **Recognition of Effect of World Conditions** Changes in business trends over the world will affect
- The amount of protection needed.
- The ease of providing it.
- The methods chosen to provide it.

Keeping this in mind, a family must recognise the effect of their savings on the economy. Their willingness or unwillingness to invest in business enterprises at various stages in the cycle may well have an effect in reducing the extremeness of the cycle.

(v) **Easy Accessibility and Convenience** While choosing an investment option for family funds, one must consider the knowledge required for its success. A family may choose an investment which might result in loss simply because they did not foresee the problems involved in the management of security or property acquired.

Exam Pattern Questions

Objective Type Questions

Multiple Choice Questions (MCQs)

1. Finances are all types of income available to a family which include salary, wages, rent, interest, dividends, bonus, retirement benefits and all other forms of monetary receipts. Planning, controlling and evaluating the use of all these types of incomes is called as .... **Competency Based Que**

(a) Financial planning (b) Financial management
(c) Income management (d) Economic planning

2. What are the elements of human resources? **Competency Based Que**

I. Knowledge II. Money
III. Health IV. Parks

Choose the correct option.

(a) I and II (b) II and III (c) I and III (d) II and IV

3. 'It serves as a medium of exchange and also as a measurement of value'. What is the statement referring to? **Competency Based Que**

(a) Budget (b) Income
(c) Money (d) Coins

4. It is the purchasing power in rupees that goes into the family treasury in a given period of time. Which type of income is being referred in the statement? **Competency Based Que**

(a) Real income (b) Money income
(c) Psychic income (d) Actual income

5. Direct income and indirect income are part of which income?

(a) Psychic income (b) Money income
(c) National income (d) Real income

6. **Riya sold all the old newspapers and magazines at a recycle station. What is the money that she earned by selling these called?** **Competency Based Que**

(a) Direct income (b) Psychic income
(c) Indirect income (d) None of these

7. **Rohan buys a new smartphone and feels satisfied with its features and performance. What type of income is he experiencing?**

(a) Monetary Income (b) Psychic income
(c) Real income (d) Social income

8. **Consider the following advantages of planning family budgets. Which of the following statements are correct?** **Competency Based Que**

(a) Amounts allocated to various categories can be studied in relation to total income.
(b) Planning enables a family to take an overview of the use of their income.
(c) Family members are less likely to be swayed, as they can make rational decisions which are reflective of long term goals of the family.
(d) All of the above

9. **What is the first step in making a budget?**

(a) Estimate the cost
(b) Evaluate the plan
(c) Balance income and expenditure
(d) List the commodities required

10. **Controlling comes next to planning in the money management process. What are the two kinds of checks involved in the process?** **Competency Based Que**

(a) Mental and Mechanical (b) Economic and Social
(c) Accounts and Finance (d) Scientific and Economical

11. **If the original planning was poor due to factors beyond the family's control, such as emergencies, family members going on an unplanned shopping spree or insufficient checking mechanisms that do not alert the family to a significant gap between the plan and its execution, alterations may be required.**

What is the phenomenon that is being talked about in the passage? **Competency Based Que**

(a) Evaluation (b) Management
(c) Adjustments (d) Planning

12. **Which of the following are saving and investment options available to an Indian consumer ?** **Competency Based Que**

I. Post office II. Gifts
III. Provident fund IV. Chit fund

Choose the correct option

(a) I and III (b) II, III and IV
(c) I, III and IV (d) I, II, III and IV

13. **What are the main sources of taking credit?** **Competency Based Que**

I. Commercial banks
II. Co-operative banks
III. Charity
IV. Insurance policies

Choose the correct option

(a) I and II (b) II and III
(c) III and IV (d) I and IV

14. **Which of the following statements are incorrect?** **Competency Based Que**

(a) Management is using what you have to achieve what you want
(b) The term budget is often used for the planning stage in financial management
(c) Families are able to achieve their objectives by optimising the use of their resources
(d) None of the above

15. **Match the following.** **Competency Based Que**

	List I		List II
A.	Capital	1.	Self-cultivated vegetables
B.	Direct Income	2.	Material goods and services
C.	Indirect Income	3.	Fixed deposits in banks
D.	Investment	4.	Net worth

Codes

	A	B	C	D		A	B	C	D
(a)	3	4	2	1	(b)	2	1	4	3
(c)	4	1	2	3	(d)	3	2	1	4

Assertion-Reason Questions

Direction (Q. Nos. 16-19) In the questions given below, there are two statements marked as Assertion (A) and Reason (R). Read the statements and choose the correct option.

Codes

(a) Both A and R are true and R is the correct explanation of A.
(b) Both A and R are true, but R is not the correct explanation of A.
(c) A is true, but R is false.
(d) A is false, but R is true.

16. **Assertion** (A) A budget is a plan for future expenditure and is meant for money management.

Reason (R) Budgeting is successful only if it is realistic and flexible.

17. **Assertion** (A) Higher income families have a higher potential to save as compared to lower income families.

Reason (R) A family's savings are determined by ability to save which is determined by the per capita income.

18. **Assertion** (A) The longer the period of investment the higher is the rate of return.

Reason (R) One should try to invest beyond one's capacity in order to secure future.

19. **Assertion** (A) Income and liquidity must be balanced.

Reason (R) Usually, more liquid investments give less return.

20. **Assertion** (A) Character and capacity are two most important things for a borrower.

Reason (R) A lender will only offer a loan if he/she is confident that the borrower will repay the money borrowed.

Case Based Questions

21. Read the passage given below and answer the following questions.

Meera, a housewife saves some money every month from her husband's salary and keeps it behind the almirah in a box so that she doesn't spend on unnecessary stuff. On the other hand, Seema, a teacher saves some part of her salary and deposit it in a fixed deposit account that she has.

With reference to the passage, answer the following questions.

(i) **Is the money saved by Meera considered an investment?**

(a) Yes (b) No (c) Maybe (d) Can't say

(ii) **........... have to be put to productive use to result in investment.**

(a) Money (b) Income
(c) Property (d) Savings

(iii) **What is the ability to convert the securities into cash without sacrificing value called?**

(a) Investment (b) Principal
(c) Return (d) Liquidity

(iv) **Assertion** (A) The higher the rate of return on an investment, the greater the risk.

Reason (R) Safety of Principal and rate of return are directly related.

Codes

(a) Both A and R are true and R is the correct explanation of A.
(b) Both A and R are true, but R is not the correct explanation of A.
(c) A is true, but R is false.
(d) A is false, but R is true.

22. Read the passage given below and answer the following questions.

A family budget gives in detail the expected income and the expenditure of a family for a time period like a month or a year. It mentions all the sources of income during the period and all the items of expenditure under different headings; such as food, clothing, housing, entertainment, travel, education, health and medicine and savings.

In the light of the above passage, answer the following questions.

(i) **Which of the following is not a step in making a budget?**

(a) Listing the commodities needed
(b) Estimation of cost
(c) Estimate total income
(d) None of the above

(ii) **Budgeting is successful if ....**

(a) it is realistic and flexible
(b) it is suitable for the group for which it is prepared
(c) it includes good quality control and evaluation steps
(d) All of the above

(iii) **If the expenditure is more than the income, it can be balanced by increasing the income and reducing the expenses.**

(a) The above statement is false.
(b) The above statement is true.
(c) Nothing can be said as the information is insufficient.
(d) None of the above.

(iv) **Assertion** (A) A family budget gives in detail the expected income and the expenditure of a family for a time period like a month or a year.

Reason (R) Family members are less likely to spend wastefully, as they can make rational decisions which will affect the long term goals of the family.

Codes

(a) Both A and R are true and R is the correct explanation of A.
(b) Both A and R are true, but R is not the correct explanation of A.
(c) A is true, but R is false.
(d) A is false, but R is true.

Answers

1. (b) Financial management
2. (c) I and III
3. (c) Money
4. (b) Money income
5. (d) Real income
6. (c) Indirect income
7. (b) Psychic income
8. (d) All of the above
9. (d) List the commodities required
10. (a) Mental and Mechanical
11. (c) Adjustments
12. (c) I, III and IV
13. (a) I and II
14. (d) None of the above
15. (c) 4 1 2 3
16. (b) Both A and R are true, but R is not the correct explanation of A.
17. (a) Both A and R are true and R is the correct explanation of A.
18. (c) A is true, but R is false.
19. (a) Both A and R are true and R is the correct explanation of A.
20. (a) Both A and R are true and R is the correct explanation of A.
21. (i) (b) No (ii) (d) Savings
    (iii) (d) Liquidity (iv) (c) A is true, but R is false.
22. (i) (d) None of the above
    (ii) (d) All of the above
    (iii) (b) The above statement is true.
    (iv) (a) Both A and R are true and R is the correct explanation of A.

Subjective Questions

Very Short Answer Type Questions

1. What does finances include?

Ans. Finances include salary, wages, rent, interest, dividends, bonus, retirement benefits, etc.

2. What do families ensure when they make a family budget for a fixed time period?

Ans. When families make a family budget for a fixed time period, they ensure that the family income is used in a manner that fulfils all the present needs of the family members and also takes care of the long term goals of the family.

3. Rahul's family consists of four members, with a monthly income of ₹ 50,000. Explain how effective management of family resources can help Rahul's family achieve their goals. **Competency Based Que**

Ans. Effective management of family resources involves utilising human resources (knowledge, skills, health), material resources (money, housing) and community resources (libraries, hospitals). Rahul's family can allocate 50% of income for necessities, 30% for savings and 20% for discretionary spending.

Prioritising needs, budgeting and wise financial decisions will help achieve family goals and ensure well-being.

4. What is family income? Give three examples of family income received usually on monthly basis.

Ans. Family income is the sum total of the income of all types from all sources of all the family members during a given time period like a day, week, month or year.

Three examples of family income received usually on monthly basis are salaries/ wages, rent from properties and pensions.

5. What is the meaning of 'income management'?

Ans. Income management can be understood as planning, controlling and evaluating the use of all types of income with the objective of getting the greatest satisfaction from the resources at hand.

6. Arjun wants to enhance his financial management skills and is learning about the various stages involved. What is the term used for planning stage in financial management? **Competency Based Que**

Ans. Budget is the term used for planning stage in financial management.

7. Ramesh, a software engineer, receives a monthly salary of ₹ 80,000, while his wife, Rohini, a farmer, earns ₹ 200,000 twice a year from selling her crops. Explain the difference in the frequency and pattern of their money income. **Competency Based Que**

Ans. Ramesh's money income is regular, received monthly ₹ 80,000. Rohini's income is irregular, received twice a year ₹ 200,000 after harvesting rabi and kharif crops. This variation affects budgeting, spending and savings.

Ramesh's steady income ensures consistent expenses, while Rohini's intermittent income requires careful financial planning and management.

8. What basic principle should an investor follow to earn the maximum return on his investment?

Competency Based Que

Ans. The basic principle of an investor should follow to earn the maximum return on his investment is to make a through appraisal of all the options available before making the investment.

9. Define savings. What is meant by savings?

Ans. Savings are defined as that part of the present income that is put aside for use in future or for further production.

10. Priya is looking to grow her wealth and secure her financial future. What are some savings and investment options available to Indian consumers like her?

Competency Based Que

Ans. Post office, Provident Fund, Banks, Bonds, Mutual Funds, etc are some options available for saving and investment that are available to an Indian consumer.

11. What is the use of credit?

Ans. The use of credit is to increase purchasing power and thus makes possible the provision of more goods or services than the cash available would allow.

12. Name the four C's of credit.

Ans. Character, Capacity, Capital, Collateral are the four C's of credit.

Short Answer Type Questions

1. Ramesh, a newly married individual, has just started managing his household finances. He wants to ensure effective financial management to secure his family's future.

(i) What is financial management and how is it relevant to Ramesh's situation?

(ii) To effectively manage his budget, what three steps should Ramesh take to exercise control over his finances?

Competency Based Que

Ans. (i) Financial management refers to the process of planning, organising, directing and controlling financial resources to achieve financial goals and objectives. It is crucial for Ramesh to manage his household finances efficiently.

(ii) The three steps to be taken to exercise control in financial management of a budget are

(a) Checking to see how well the plan is progressing.

(b) Adjusting the plan or the expenditure wherever necessary.

(c) Evaluating the success of the budget in terms of specific goals met.

2. Differentiate between Money Income and Real Income by giving two differences.

Ans. The differences between Money income and Real income are as follows

Money Income	Real Income
It is the cash available to a family from all sources over a period of time.	It is the flow of goods and services available to the family over the same period of time.
It is tangible and used for purchasing goods and services for the family.	It is derived from possessions owned by the family, skills, efforts and abilities of the family members and through community facilities.

3. Give four examples of sources of money income which can help a family to improve its standard of living.

Ans. Four examples of sources of money income which can help a family to improve its standard of living are

(i) Giving out a portion of a house or the full house on rent.

(ii) Giving tuitions to students.

(iii) Doing a part-time or full-time job.

(iv) Making articles at home and selling them.

4. Raghav has created a family budget and wants to ensure it has a reasonable chance of success. What four key points should he check in the budget to make sure it is effective and realistic? **Competency Based Que**

Ans. To ensure that the budget has a reasonable chance of success, he should check the following points

(i) The needs of the family have been met.

(ii) The budget allows for emergencies.

(iii) The bills or debts can be paid on the due dates.

(iv) The national and world-wide economic conditions have been considered.

5. Anjali has been diligently saving money for emergencies. List any 4 situations in which her savings prove beneficial?

Competency Based Que

Ans. Four examples of emergency situations for which her savings can come in handy are

(i) Accident to a member of the family.

(ii) An illness in the family.

(iii) Loss of job of a family member.
(iv) Requirement of surgery for a family member.

6. What are two major requirements of families for which they require to avail credit facilities from banks or other financial institutions?

Ans. Two major requirements of families for which they require to avail credit facilities from banks or other financial institution are

(i) To meet their needs for goods or services whose initial cost is too high to bear at once.
(ii) To meet obligations like marriage of children or performing rituals regarding death of a family member.

Long Answer Type Questions

1. Describe four important functions of money.

Ans. Four important functions of money are

(i) **Medium of Exchange** Many is used to buy and sell goods.
(ii) **Standard of Value** Money serves as a standard of value i.e. a common denominator in terms of which the value of all other commodities is expressed.
(iii) **Allows Capital Formation** Money works as a standard for deferred payments, facilitating savings and investments. These are the basis for capital formation and hence for a better standard of living.
(iv) **Facilitates Accumulation** Storage in terms of money is durable for long time periods, facilitating accumulation for investment in production and an improved standard of living for the family.

2. Rohan wants to create a family budget to manage his finances better. What is the first step he should take and what are the eight categories under which he can list his expenses? **Competency Based Que**

Ans. The first step in making a family budget is to list what is required. The commodities and services with the quantities required by the family during the specified time period should be listed under various heads of expenditure.

Eight examples of heads under which expenses on various services availed by a family can be listed are

(i) Housing (ii) Education
(iii) Transportation (iv) Recreation
(v) Laundry and dry cleaning services
(vi) Courier services
(vii) Cellphone network services
(viii) Electricity and water charges

3. Explain the important information which should be given in a family budget. Under what conditions will you consider budgeting successful?

Ans. The important information which should be given in a family budget includes

- Details of the expected income and the expenditure of a family for a time period like a month or a year.
- All the sources of income during the period and all the items of expenditure under different headings, such as food, clothing, housing, entertainment, travel, education, health and medicine and savings.

The conditions under which I will consider budgeting successful are as follows

- The budge is realistic and flexible.
- It is suitable for the group or family for which it is prepared.
- It includes good quality control and evaluation steps which will be used while implementing it.

4. Ram recently got married and started a family. He spends a lot on travelling, shopping, etc and by the end of the month is left with nothing even for basic home needs. **Competency Based Que**

(i) What is Income Management?
(ii) What are the advantages of planning family budgets?

Ans. (i) Income management is defined as planning, controlling and evaluating the use of all types of income with the objective of getting the greatest satisfaction from the resources at hand.

(ii) Budget planning has the following advantages

- It enables a family to understand the use of their income.
- Amounts allocated to various categories can be studied in relation to total income.
- It helps families use their income to first attain those goals which they consider most important.
- Family members are less likely to spend wastefully, as they can make rational decisions which reflect the long term goals of the family.

5. Briefly explain the four C's of credit.

Ans. For answer refer to under to the heading 'Four C's of Credit' on page on. 239.

SELF ASSESSMENT TEST

Objective Type Questions

1. It is the cash available to a family from all sources. Identify the type of income.
   (a) Real income (b) Money income
   (c) Psychic income (d) None of these
2. .... are defined as that part of income that is put aside for use in future or for further production.
   (a) Savings (b) Investment
   (c) Rent (d) Money
3. .... increases purchasing power.
   (a) Interest (b) Tax
   (c) Liquidity (d) Credit

Very Short Answer Type Questions

4. What are finances?
5. How do we ensure maximum utilisation of resources?
6. Mention two differences between direct and indirect income.
7. How should we estimate the expected income while making a budget? Briefly explain the term money.

Short Answer Type Questions

8. What are mental and mechanical checks in money management? Highlight their differences.
9. Explain how financial assets and physical assets can be considered as investments?
10. Describe the adjusting and evaluating steps in managing a family budget.

Long Answer Type Questions

11. Explain four advantages of planning family budgets.
12. Devise a weekly format of an 'Income and Expenditure Account' of a family. Insert one item of income and ten items of typical expenditure under four heads in it so that the budget is balanced.
13. Customer care is an important factor while deciding about a sound investment to be made by an investor. Why is it so? Write a few benefits which an investor will get if the investment agency has good customer care facilities. **Competency Based Que**
14. How do self-help groups provide credit to their members? Explain the factors to be considered by a family before availing credit.

13

CHAPTER

Fabric play a key role in daily life, providing comfort and protection proper care and maintenance help to preserve their appearance, quality and functionality over time.

Care and Maintenance of Fabrics

▼ **YOUR STUDY GOALS**

13.1 Introduction
13.2 Removal of Dirt in the Cleaning Process
13.3 Methods of Washing
13.4 Finishing
13.5 Factors Affecting Fabric Care
13.6 Care Label

▼ **YOUR PRACTICE GOAL**

- Objective Type Questions (22 Qs ; MCQs, A-R, Statements, Matching, Case Based)
- Subjective Questions (12 VSAs, 5 SAs, 5 LAs)

13.1 Introduction

Fabrics hold great importance in our lives. They protect us and enhance our surroundings. Taking care of fabric products, like clothing and furnishings, is essential.

- When selecting and buying any product, people often focus on its appearance–like colour and texture–along with its quality and functionality. It's important to maintain these characteristics throughout the life of the material.
- **Care and maintenance include**
  - Keeping the material free from physical damage.
  - Removing stains and dirt without harming its colour.
  - Preserving or restoring its brightness and texture, such as softness or stiffness.
  - Keeping it wrinkle-free or maintaining creases or removing wrinkles and adding creases when needed.

Mending

- Mending is the general term used for keeping materials free from damage that occurs during normal use or by accident. It includes
  - Repairing cuts, tears and holes.
  - Replacing buttons/fasteners, ribbons, laces or decorative items.
  - Restitching seams and hems if they come undone.
- It's best to take care of these issues as soon as they occur.

- It's important to address them before washing, as the strain from laundering[1] can cause more damage to the fabric.

Laundry

- Every day care of the fabrics generally consists of washing to keep it clean and ironing to get a smooth wrinkle free appearance.
- Many materials need special treatments to remove stains, fix grayness or yellowness from repeated washings and add stiffness or crispness.
- **Laundering includes**
  - Stain removal
  - Preparing fabrics for washing
  - Washing to remove dirt from clothes
  - Finishing to improve appearance, such as blueing and starching
  - Finally, pressing or ironing to create a neat look, so they can be stored and ready for use.

Stain Removal

- A stain is an unwanted mark or discoloration on a fabric caused by contact and absorption of imporities (foreign substances). It cannot be removed by regular washing and it requires special treatment.
- To effectively remove a stain, it's important to identify it first. Stains can be identified based on their **colour, smell and texture**. They can be classified as
  - **Vegetable Stains** These include tea, coffee, fruits and vegetables. They are acidic and can be removed using an **alkaline solution**.
  - **Animal Stains** These consist of blood, milk, meat and eggs. They are protein-based and should be removed with **detergents** in cold water.
  - **Oil Stains** These come from oils, ghee, butter, etc. They can be removed using **grease solvents** and absorbents.
  - **Mineral Stains** These include ink, rust, coal tar and medicine. They should be washed first in an **acidic solution** and then in an **alkaline solution**.
  - **Dye Bleeding** This occurs when colour from other fabrics bleeds onto the material. These stains can be removed using either **dilute alkalis or acids**, depending on the type of fabric.

Removal of Stains-General Considerations

- Stain is best removed when fresh.
- Identify the stains and use the right procedure for its removal.
- For unknown stains, start with a simple process and move to a complex one.
- Repeated use of milder reagent[2] is better than one time use of a strong agent.
- Dry fabrics in the sun as sunlight acts as natural bleach.
- For delicate fabrics try out the chemicals on a small portion; if the fabric gets damaged, do not use them.

Techniques of Stain Removal

- **Scraping** Built up surface stains can be scraped lightly by using a blunt knife.
- **Dipping** The stained material is dipped into the reagent and scrubbed.
- **Sponging** The stained area is placed on a flat surface. The reagent is applied with a sponge on the stained area and absorbed by the blotting paper laid underneath.
- **Drop Method** The stained cloth is stretched over a bowl. The reagent is put on it with a dropper.

1 Laundry It is process of washing and caring for fabrics.
2 Milder reagent It is a chemical that is less harsh or less reactive compared to other reagents.

Stain Removers/Reagents for Stain Removal

The different substances or agents used for removing stains should be applied in liquid form and at the recommended concentrations/amounts for best results. These reagents can be grouped as follows

- **Grease solvents** Turpentine, kerosene, white petrol, methylated spirit, acetone, carbon tetrachloride
- **Grease absorbents** Bran, Fuller's earth, talcum powder, starch, French chalk
- **Emulsifiers**[3] Soaps, detergents
- **Acidic Reagents** Acetic acid (vinegar), oxalic acid, lemon, tomato, sour milk, curds
- **Alkaline Reagents** Ammonia, borax, baking soda
- **Bleaching Agents**[4]
  - **Oxidising bleaches** Sunlight, sodium hypochlorite (javelle water), sodium perborate, hydrogen peroxide
  - **Reducing bleaches** Sodium hydrosulphite, sodium bisulphate, sodium thiosulphate

Methods of Stain Removal

Stain	Method of Removal
Adhesive tape	Harden with ice, scrape off, apply any solvent.
Blood	▪ Fresh stain–wash with cold water ▪ Old stain–soak in salt solution, rub and wash
Ballpoint pen	Keep a blotting paper under it and sponge with methylated spirit.
Candle wax	Soak in cold water immediately, scrape off, dip in white vinegar, rinse with cold water.
Chewing gum	Apply ice, scrape off, soak in cold water, sponge with a solvent.
Chocolate	Soak in cold water, in hypochlorite bleach (javelle water)
Curry (Turmeric and oil)	Wash with soap and water and then bleach in Sun. ▪ Keep blotting paper under fresh stain and iron it. Then wash with soap and water. ▪ Old stains can be removed by soaking in javelle water.
Egg	Wash with cold water, wash with soap and lukewarm water.
Fruits and Vegetables	▪ Apply starch paste on fresh stain. Then rub and wash. ▪ Use borax, salt and hot water to remove it.
Grease	▪ Dip in or sponge with grease solvents–petrol, spirit or kerosene oil. Wash with hot water and soap. ▪ Apply starch paste and dry in shade. After doing it 2-3 times it will be removed. ▪ Soak in javelle water and wash with soap and water.
Ink	▪ Fresh stain can be removed by soap and water. ▪ Apply lemon juice, curd or sour milk and salt and dry. ▪ Javelle water can remove stain. ▪ Rub in potassium permanganate solution and then dip in oxalic acid.
Ice-cream	Sponge with a grease solvent, wash in hot soapy water.
Lipstick	▪ Soak in methylated spirit, wash with soap and water. ▪ Rub glycerine, wash with soap.
Medicines	▪ Dip in methyl alcohol or in a dilute solution of oxalic acid. ▪ Wash with hot water
Mildew	▪ Sponge with hypochlorite bleach

3 **Emulsifiers** It means substances that help mix oil and water for cleaning.
4 **Bleaching Agents** It means substances used to whiten or lighten fabrics.

Stain	Method of Removal
Milk or cream	▪ Sponge with a solvent, Wash in cold water
Paint or polish	▪ Rub with kerosene and/or turpentine oil ▪ Bleach with sodium thiosulphate
Rust	▪ Soak in oxalic acid and rub ▪ Treat like ink stain
Scorch	▪ Sponge with hydrogen peroxide. Stain will not be removed if fibre has been damaged.

Stain removal is the preparatory step in laundry. It must be followed by washing or dry-cleaning.

Quick Test 1

1. Which process is used to keep the material free from damage which may occur in normal use or due to accident?
2. Name some techniques of stain removal.
3. How can be the milk spilt on the shirt removed?
4. When is the best time to remove the stain?

13.2 Removal of Dirt in the Cleaning Process

- Dirt refers to grease, grime and dust trapped within the fabric structure. There are two types: **loose dirt,** which can be easily removed and **tightly held dirt,** which is attached by sweat and grease.
- Loose dirt can be brushed or shaken off or removed by soaking in water. Tightly held grease requires special reagents to loosen it.
- There are three main methods: **using solvents, absorbents** or **emulsifiers**. When using solvents or absorbents, it is called dry cleaning. Regular cleaning involves washing with water, soap and detergents, which emulsify the grease into smaller particles that can be rinsed away.
- **Water** It is the most important agent used in laundry.
  - It has a natural ability (adhesion) to stick to fabrics.
  - When fabrics are soaked, water penetrates them and causes wetting.
  - Pedesis or the movement of water particles helps to remove non-greasy dirt.
  - Washing with just water, along with agitation from hand or machine, can remove some loose dirt and particles.
  - Increase in temperature of the water, increases its pedesis and its penetrating power. It is especially helpful for greasy dirt.
  - However, water alone cannot remove the dirt because is not soluble in water. It also cannot keep dirt suspended, which can lead to the dirt getting redeposited onto the fabric. This redeposition is a major reason why fabrics become gray after multiple washes.
- **Soaps and detergents** These are the most important cleaning agents used in laundry.
  - Soap is made from a reaction between natural oils or fats and alkali. If alkali is used in excess it is released when soap is used on the fabric.
  - Synthetic detergents are made from chemicals.
  - Both soaps and detergents come in powder, flake, bar and liquid forms. The choice of soap or detergent depends on the type of fabric, its colour and the kind of dirt on it.

- Both soaps and detergents share a critical chemical property. They are surface-active agents or surfactants, meaning they reduce the surface tension of water. This allows water to soak into clothes more easily and removes stains and dirt more effectively.
- Surfactants and other ingredients in laundry detergents also help keep dirt suspended in the wash water, preventing it from redepositing on clean fabrics. This helps stop fabrics from becoming gray.
- There are some differences between soaps and detergents.
- Soaps are natural products and are less harmful to the skin and the environment. They are biodegradable and do not pollute rivers and streams. However, soaps are not effective in hard water, which can lead to waste. They are also generally less powerful than synthetic detergents and can lose their cleaning strength over time.
- Detergents, on the other hand, can be specifically designed for different cleaning tasks and can be used in various types of washing machines.

13.3 Methods of Washing

- After soap or detergent has mixed with the grease and dirt, it needs to be kept suspended in the water until it can be rinsed out. Some dirt may stick closely to the fabric.
- The washing methods help in two ways: **removing the dirt** from the fabric and **keeping it suspended** in the water. The method chosen depends on the fibre content, the yarn used and the size and weight of the item being washed.

The washing methods include

- **Friction Washing** It is the most common method and works well for strong fabrics like cotton. This method involves rubbing one part of the garment against another using hands. Brush can be used to clean dirty areas, either by holding the fabric in hand or on a scrubbing board if it's a larger item. However, friction washing should not be used on delicate fabrics like silk and wool or on textured surfaces like pile, loops or embroidery.
- **Kneading and Squeezing** It involves gently rubbing the fabric in a soap solution with hands. Since very little pressure is applied, this method won't damage the texture, colour or weave of the fabric. It's great for cleaning delicate fabrics like wool, silk, rayon and coloured items. However, this method is not effective for heavily soiled fabrics.
- **Suction Washing** This method is used for articles like towels where brush cannot be used and when it is too big or heavy to be handled by kneading and squeezing technique.

  In this method, the item is placed in a soap solution in a tub. A suction washer is then pressed down and lifted repeatedly. The vacuum created by this action helps loosen the dirt particles from the fabric.
- **Machine Washing** Washing machines are helpful devices that save labour, especially in large places like hotels and hospitals. There are many types of washing machines available of different companies, but they all work on the same principle. They create movement in the clothes to loosen dirt.

  The washing machine provides pressure through the movement of either the drum or a central rod. The time it takes to wash varies based on the type of fabric and how dirty it is (soiled). Washing machines can be manual, semi-automatic or fully automatic.

13.4 Finishing

After washing, it's crucial to rinse the item in clean water until all soap or detergent is completely removed. Sometimes, additional substances are added in the final rinse to restore the fabric's freshness or brightness. Other reagents can enhance the fabric's body, stiffness or crispness.

Blues and Optical Brighteners

- With repeated washing, white cotton fabrics can lose their brightness and turn yellow, while synthetic fabrics often become gray.
- To combat yellowness and restore whiteness, blues are recommended. However, they do not fix grayness. Blues are sold as ultramarine blue in powdered form or as a liquid dye.
- Optical Brightening[5] Agents or Fluorescent brightening agents are compounds with low grade or weak dyes that possess the property of fluorescence. These compounds can absorb light at a shorter wavelength and re-emit them at a longer wavelength. They can make fabrics appear intensely white, helping to counteract yellowness and grayness. They can also be used on coloured printed fabrics.
- Optical brighteners are sometimes called whiteners but do not bleach or destroy colour.

Starches and Stiffening Agents

- Regular washing can cause fabrics to lose their body, gloss and shine. Starching[6] or using stiffening agents helps make the fabric firm, smooth and shiny, improving its appearance and texture.
- Starching protects the fabric from dirt and makes future washing easier, as dirt tends to cling to the starch instead of the fabric.

The most common stiffening agents are

- **Starch** It is obtained from wheat (maida), rice arrow-root, tapioca etc. They are available in powder form in the market and must be cooked before use. Commercially prepared starches are easy to use and do not necessarily require hot water for preparation. Starch is used only for stiffening cotton and linen clothes.
- **Gum Acacia or Gum Arabic** It is the natural gum obtained from the Acacia plant (babool tree). The stiffening solution is prepared by soaking it overnight to dissolve it and then sieving it to get a lump free solution. It gives only light stiffening, which is more in the nature of crispness. It is used for silks, very fine cottons, rayons and silk and cotton blends.
- **Gelatin** It is easy to make and use, but is more expensive than homemade starches.
- **Borax** Adding a small quantity of borax in the starch solution helps to improve its stiffening action.

  When the fabric is ironed after starching, borax melts and forms a thin film on the surface of the fabric which repels water, thus maintaining crispness in humid conditions.

  Precautions to be taken while starching and stiffening. These are

  – Application of stiffening agents depends on the fibre content and the specific use of the article.

  – Care has to be taken when applying the starch solution that the correct consistency of the starch is taken and the fabric is in a thoroughly wet (but not dripping) condition.

  – The fabric is kneaded well in the solution, excess solution is squeezed out. The fabric is dried before it can be ironed and stored.
- **Drying** Sun dries the clothes faster and also acts as an antiseptic; for white fabrics, it also acts as a bleaching agent. However, silks and woollens cannot be hung for too long in the Sun, as strong sunlight damages these fabrics.

5 Optical Brighteners It means chemicals that enhance the whiteness of fabrics.
6 Starching It means applying starch to fabrics to make them stiff and shiny.

Synthetic fibres lose their strength when exposed to sunlight for a prolonged period. These fabrics also tend to turn yellow when exposed to sunlight, which is irreversible. So it is best to dry these fabrics indoors.

Ironing

- After washing, articles often have wrinkles and unwanted creases. Ironing removes these wrinkles and creates desired creases.
- Effective ironing needs three key elements high temperature, moisture and pressure.
  - **High temperature** An iron provides a high temperature. It can be a charcoal iron or an electric iron. While charcoal irons are cheaper, they can stain clothes and do not allow for temperature control.
  - **Moisture** It can be provided by ironing clothes while they are still damp from washing. If the items are dry, water can be sprinkled on them and they can be rolled in a towel for even moisture distribution.
  - **Pressure** It is applied manually by moving the iron over the fabric. Iron is generally moved on the clothes along the length. Pressing can also be used for setting of any folds like creases, hems, pockets, plackets and pleats.
- The ironing table should be well-padded yet firm, with an even surface at a comfortable height.
- After ironing, articles should be folded or hung based on available storage space. It's important to have them ready in a finished state for use when needed.

Dry-cleaning

- Dry-cleaning is the process of cleaning fabrics using a liquid that is not water (non-aqueous).
- Unlike wet cleaning, where water can be absorbed by fibers causing shrinkage, wrinkles and colour bleeding, dry solvents do not swell the fibers. This makes dry-cleaning safer for delicate textiles.
- The most common solvents used in dry-cleaning are **perchloro-ethylene**, a petroleum solvent and fluorocarbon solvents.
- Dry-cleaning is usually done in industrial settings, not at home. Items are taken to the cleaner, where they are tagged with special instructions.
- Items are inspected before cleaning and stains, especially those that are water-soluble, are treated on a spot board. Customers can help by identifying stains, which makes the cleaning process easier and increases satisfaction.
- Many dry cleaners also offer extra services like replacing buttons, minor repairs and applying finishes such as sizing, water **repellency**[7], permanent creases, moth proofing and cleaning fur and leather.
- Some dry cleaners also clean and sanitise feather pillows, blankets, quilts, carpets and draperies.

Storage of Textile Products

- The weather in our country varies throughout the year, so we have different clothes for different temperatures.
- When not in use, clothes need to be cleaned and dried before storage.
- Woolen items should be brushed well and dry-cleaned before storing. Remove all stains and mend any tears.
- Turn pockets inside out, and fold trousers and sleeves. Check for dust, grit or soot and clean the items as needed. Clothes should be shaken, brushed, washed, ironed and folded properly.
- Pack clothes loosely in cupboards or trunks to avoid permanent creases from tight packing.
- Shelves, boxes or closets used for storage should be clean, dry and free from insects, as well as away from dust and dirt

7 **Repellency** It means the ability of a fabric to resist water.

- It's important to store clothes in an environment with very low humidity, as different fabrics require specific care to prevent damage from microorganisms.

Quick Test 2

1. Define optical brightenning.
2. Whiteners are also known as?
3. Where are stiffening agents derived from?
4. Which method is opted for cleaning delicate textiles?

13.5 Factors Affecting Fabric Care

- The selection, use and care of fabrics depend on many factors.
- Fibre content, yarn structure, fabric construction, colour application and finishing are the important factors considered for the product.
- Each type of fabric has its own individual characteristics and hence needs specific care.

Yarn Structure

- The structure of yarn, including its twist, can influence maintenance. **Yarns with a high twist** tend to shrink, while novelty and complex yarns may catch, snag or become abraded.
- When dealing with **blended yarns,** it is essential to care for both types of fibers. For instance, when washing cotton blended with polyester, very hot water should be avoided as it can cause shrinkage. However, this blend typically resists wrinkling, making it easier to iron.

Fabric Construction

- Fabrics that are closely woven are generally easy to maintain.
- Fabrics with fancy weaves, such as satin or those featuring long floats, are prone to snagging during washing.
- Knitted materials may stretch out of shape and often require re-blocking.
- Sheer fabrics, lace, nets, felt and non-woven materials must be handled with care to prevent damage.

Colour and Finishes

- Colour is crucial in fabric care. Dyed and printed fabrics can lose their colour during cleaning and may also stain other items.
- It is advisable to test the colour of the fabric before use. Proper care should be taken to maintain its appearance.
- Many finishing treatments can change how fabrics behave. While some finishes may enhance the fabric, others can lead to problems. Certain finishes might need to be renewed after each wash.
- The important factors for all fabric products include fibre content, yarn structure, fabric construction, colour application and finishing treatments.
- These factors work together to influence the fabric's appearance, comfort, durability and maintenance needs.
- The significance of appearance, comfort, durability and maintenance varies. It is essential to evaluate a fabric's qualities based on its intended end-use to make informed decisions about its care and usage.

Fibre Properties that Affect Care and Maintenance of Fabrics

Fibre	Properties	Care Requirements
Cotton and Linen	Strong fibres, stronger when wet, can withstand hard friction.	
	Resistant to alkalis, can be easily washed with strong detergents.	
	Can withstand high temperatures, if necessary can be boiled.	
	Resistant to organic solvents and bleaches, acidic substances weaken the fibre.	Acidic reagents used should be rinsed and neutralised.
	Gets crushed easily, have to be ironed properly to remove the wrinkles.	Needs to be damp for ironing or may scorch.
	Fungus and mildew may attack them.	Should be completely dry and stored in low humidity atmosphere.
	If heavily starched, it can be attacked by silverfish.	Need to be de-starched if stored over long periods.
Wool	Weak fibre and when it is wet, weakens further.	Should be handled gently during laundering.
	Easily damaged by alkaline substances.	Strong detergents or soaps should be avoided.
	Dry-cleaning solvents and stain removing agents have no harmful effect.	Bleaches have to be used with care.
	When wool is subjected to mechanical action like agitation during washing, they have a tendency to felt and shrink.	Washing in cold water with minimum handling is advised.
	Knitted articles in wool can stretch out of shape while washing.	An outline of the garment is made before washing and after washing the article is stretched back to outline.
	Has good resilience and does not wrinkle, may not require ironing.	No direct ironing of the fabric, if needed it may be steam pressed.
	Wool protein is particularly susceptible to damage by insects like cloth moths and carpet beetles.	Repeated spraying with chemicals can prevent the damage during storage; naphthalene balls are effective for prevention of insect infestation.
Silk	Strong fibre but it is weaker when it is wet; careful handling is required in washing of silk.	Only gentle friction should be used while washing.
	Damaged by strong alkalis, organic acids are used in the finishing.	Mild detergents should be used for washing.
	Dry-cleaning solvents and spot removing agents do not damage silk.	Bleaches have to be used with care.
	Does not stretch or shrink on washing, has medium resilience due to which it wrinkles during use.	Needs to be ironed.
	Scorches easily if ironed at high temperature using dry heat.	It should be thoroughly damp and ironed at low temperature.
	Perspiration also damages the fabric.	Need to be dry-cleaned and aired properly before storage.
	Silk gets weakened if exposed for long time to sunlight.	Should not be dried in the Sun.
	Resists attack by mildew and bacteria but are eaten by carpet beetles.	Should not be stored if soiled.
Rayon	Strength of most of the rayons is relatively low and further decreased when the fibres are wet.	Require careful handling in laundering.
	Chemically identical to cotton, but may be damaged by strong alkalis.	It is safer to use mild soaps and detergents.

Fibre	Properties	Care Requirements
	It is resistant to dry-cleaning solvents and stain removing agents.	
	Rayon shrinks on washing.	Care has to be taken while laundering.
	Fabrics made of rayon tend to wrinkle and stretch easily as their elastic recovery and resilience are low.	It is easy to iron.
	Mildew and silverfish are harmful to rayon, they are subject to harm by the rot producing bacteria.	Should be stored in absolutely clean and dry condition.
Nylon	Very good strength, retains much of its strength when wet.	It requires no special care.
	Is not affected by alkalis but acids may destroy the fiber.	Should be rinsed well if acidic reagents are used.
	Dry cleaning solvents, stain removing agents, detergents and bleaches can be used safely.	
	Can absorb dirt from other soiled articles.	Should be washed separately.
	Does not absorb water and therefore dries up quickly.	
	Sunlight is destructive to nylon and causes a marked loss of strength after extend exposure.	Not recommended for window curtains or draperies.
	Nylon is highly resistant to attack by most insects and microorganisms.	
Polyester	No loss of strength when polyester is wet; can be easily washed.	
	Good elastic recovery and resilience.	Does not require hot ironing.
	Develops small balls in its surface, which cannot be removed.	
	Polyester does not absorb water easily.	Causes discomfort during hot and humid weather.
	Oil stains are difficult to remove from polyester.	Oil stains need to be handled carefully.
	It is resistant to microorganisms and insects.	
Acrylic	Strength is similar to cotton.	Can be washed easily without any special care.
	Has high elongation with good elastic recovery, so it does not get wrinkled easily.	
	Moisture regain of acrylic is low and the fabrics dry quickly.	
	It has good resistance to most alkalis and acids and most of the dry-cleaning solvents do not damage the fibre.	
	The fibres have excellent resistance to sunlight, all types of soaps, synthetic detergents and bleaches.	
	It is not affected by moths.	
	It catches fire readily and unlike other synthetic fibres continues to melt and burn.	Care needs to be taken; can prove hazardous for children.

13.6 Care Label

- A care label is a **permanent tag** that provides important information and instructions for caring for a garment.
- It is attached in a way that ensures it will not come off and will remain easy to read or legible for the entire life of the garment.

Washing Instructions on Care-labels

Washing Instructions	Meaning
89° For 29°C 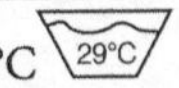	Use cold water or set temperature of machine at cold
90°-110° For 32°-43°C 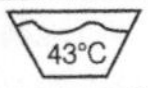	Use warm water or set temperature of machine at warm
150° For 60° C 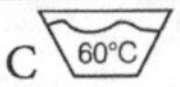	Use hot water or set temperature of machine at hot
WASH CYCLE	
Delicate cycle	Time of agitation is reduced and speed of agitation is slow
Wash separately	Wash like colours together
Wash inside out	Reverse the garment before washing
Warm Rinse	Use warm water for rinsing
Cold rinse	Use cold water for rinsing
Do not spin	Do not put in a spinner
Do not wring	Do not twist the garment
Hand wash	Wash by hand, kneading and squeezing method
Machine wash 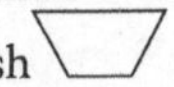	Can put in machine for washing
DRYING	
Tumble dry 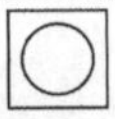	Can dry in a front loading machine (the clothes spin clockwise)
Drip dry	Dry for short while without wringing the water (used for synthetics)
Line dry	Hang on a drying line
Dry flat	Dry on a flat surface (used for woollens)
Dry in shade 	Do not dry in Sun (for coloured clothes)
PRESSING AND IRONING	
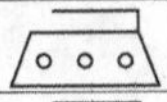	Set temperature of iron at 210°C (hot)
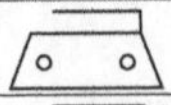	Set temperature of iron at 160°C (moderate)
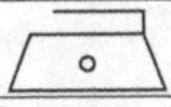	Set temperature of iron at 120°C (low)
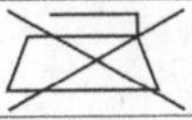	Do not iron
BLEACH 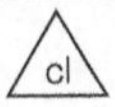	Clorine bleach
	Do not bleach

DRY CLEANING	
Ⓐ	Use all solvents
Ⓟ	To be dry-cleaned with only white spirit or choroethylene
Ⓟ	Special care has to be taken while dry-cleaning as they are sensitive to dry-clean
Ⓢ	Use white spirit only
⊗	Do not dry-clean

Quick Test 3

1. Which type of weave in fabric make them prone to snagging during washing?
2. Give two properties of cotton fibre.
3. Which is a strong fibre but is weaker when wet?
4. What is the permanent tag that provides information and instructions for caring for a garment called?

Mind Map

CARE AND MAINTENANCE OF FABRICS

1 Care and Maintenance

Mending
- It includes removing accidental damage.
- Repairing cuts, tears, holes.
- Replace buttons, ribbons etc.

Laundry
- It includes daily care of textiles like washing and ironing of goods.

2 Stain

Techniques for Stain Removal
- **Scraping** Surface stain can be scraped lightly using a blunt knife.
- **Dipping** The stained material is dipped into the reagent and scrubbed.
- **Sponging** The reagent is applied on the stained area by sponge.
- **Drop Method** The stained cloth is stretched over a bowl. The reagent is put on it with a dropper.

Methods of Stain Removal
- **Blood** Fresh stain should be wash with cold water. Old stain should be soak in salt solution, rub and wash.
- **Chocolates** Soak in cold water then bleach.
- **Lipstick** Soak in methylated spirit and then wash.

Stain Removal Instrument
- **Grease Solvents** White petrol, turpentine, acetone etc.
- **Emulsifier** Soaps, detergents
- **Alkaline Reagents** Ammonia, borax etc.

Stain spots

Vegetable Stains
- **For examples** fruits, vegetables, tea etc.

Animal Stains
- **For examples** blood, milk, meat etc.

Oil Stains
- **For examples** oils, ghee, butter, etc.

Mineral Stains
- **For examples** ink, rust, coaltar, etc.

3 Removal of Dirt

Dirt Type
- **Loose Dirt** It can easily removed by brushing.
- **Tightly Dirt** It needs special reagents like solvents etc.

Cleaning Method
- **Dry Cleaning** uses solvents .
- **Regular Cleaning** uses water, soap etc.

Water in Laundry
- Warmer water cleans greasy dirt better.
- Water alone can't dissolve all dirts.

Soaps and Detergents
- **Soaps,** Natural and environment friendly which removes dirts.
- **Detergents,** They are synthetic and strong to remove dirt.

4 Methods of Washing

Friction Washing
- It includes rub clothes with a brush which is suitable for strong cotton fabrics.

Kneading and Squeezing
- It includes gently rub clothes in soapy water.

Suction Pump Washing
- It clean thick fabrics like towels.

Machine Washing
- It clean clothes by movement or rotation.

5 Finishing

Rinsing and Brightening
- Rinse well after washing.
- Use blues for cotton to restore whiteness.

Starching and Stiffening
- Use starch to add firmness and shine.

Precautions for Stiffening
- Choose the right agent, mix properly, knead well and dry before ironing.

Drying
- Dry clothes in sunlight, but keeps delicate fabrics indoors to avoid damage.

Storage of Textile Products
- Cleaning before storage to remove stains.
- Preparing the clothes and fold neatly.
- Use clean and dry storage place.
- Keep clothes in low-humidity areas.

6 Factors Affecting Fabric Care

- Textile type
- Fabric construction
- Yarn structure
- Colour and finishes

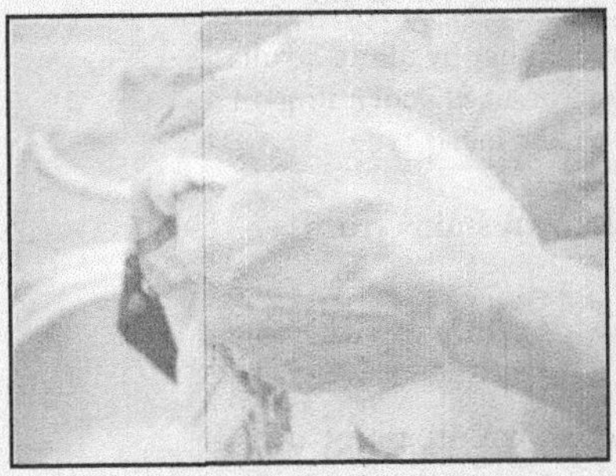

General care and maintenance of fabric

Fabric Finishing

NCERT Folder

1. What are the different aspects of care and maintenance of fabrics?

Ans. The different aspects of care and maintenance of fabrics are

- Keeping the material free of physical damage.
- Retaining its appearance by
  - removing stains and dirt without damaging its colour.
  - retaining or refurbishing its brightness and textural characteristics such as softness, stiffness or crispness.
  - keeping it free from wrinkles, retaining creases, or removing wrinkles and adding creases, where required.

2. Define the term 'stain'. What are the different types of stains and what techniques can be used for removing them?

Ans. The term 'stain' can be defined as an unwanted mark or colouration on a fabric caused by contact and absorption of foreign matter, which cannot be removed by normal washing process and requires special treatment.

Different types of 'stains' and the techniques used for removing them are given in the table below

Type	Caused by/nature	Can be removed by
Vegetable	Tea, coffee, fruits and vegetables/ acidic by nature	Alkaline medium
Animal	Blood, milk, meat, eggs etc./protein in nature	Detergents in cold water only
Oil	Oil, ghee, butter, etc.	Grease solvents and absorbents
Mineral	Ink, rust, coal tar, medicine, etc.	Washed first in acidic medium and then in alkaline medium
Dye bleeding	Colour from other fabrics	Either by dilute alkalis or acids depending on the fabric type

3. Write the steps in removing unknown stains from fabrics.

Ans. We can use the steps given below for removing unknown stains from fabrics.

(i) Place the stained portion face down on a blotting paper and initially, apply a dilute stain removing chemical in a circular motion.

(ii) If the stain does not go away, soak the stained portion in plain cold water for some time and then wash it.

(iii) Soak the stained portion in warm soapy water for sometime and wash it normally.

(iv) If the stain still does not go away, bleach the stain by exposing it to sunlight for some time.

(v) Treat the stain with a dilute alkaline solution and then with a dilute acidic solution.

(vi) Next apply oxidising bleach and lastly, a reducing bleach, which removes oxygen from the stain to make it colourless.

4. What is dirt? How do water, soaps and detergents combine to remove dirt from fabrics?

Ans. Dirt is the term applied to grease, grime and dust jammed between the fabric structure. Dirt is of two types water, soaps and detergents combine to remove both type of dirt from fabrics as given below

(a) **Held Loosely to the Fabric** It can be simply brushed or shaken off or will be removed by steeping in water. During steeping, water penetrates into the fabric and causes wetting. The movement of water particles helps to remove the non-greasy dirt from the fabric.

(b) **Held Tightly by Sweat and Grease** It can be loosened by steeping in water, but requires reagents that will act upon the grease to loosen the dirt. Soaps and detergents emulsify the grease, i.e., break it into very small particles. Then the fabric is rinsed with water.

5. How does finishing after washing improve the brightness and textural characteristics of fabrics?

Ans. Finishing after washing is done in the last rinse. With help of following

(i) Optical brightening agents are applied to the fabric in a thoroughly wet (but not dripping) condition, which is free of the folds of wringing. They are compounds with low grade or weak dyes that possess the property of fluorescence.

(ii) Treating a fabric with an optical fluorescent brightener can give it an intense bright whiteness, which can counteract both yellowness and greyness.

(iii) Similarly, to improve the textural characteristics of fabrics, starches and stiffening agents are used. Application of stiffening agent depends on the fibre content and the specific use of the article.

6. What is dry-cleaning? What are the types of fabrics where dry-cleaning is recommended?

Ans. Dry-cleaning is the cleaning of fabrics in a non-aqueous liquid medium.

The types of fabrics for which dry-cleaning is recommended are delicate fabrics which may shrink, form wrinkles or bleed colour while washing with water.

Exam Pattern Questions

Objective Type Questions

Multiple Choice Questions (MCQs)

1. "It must be attended to before laundering because the stain of washing may lead to greater loss to the fabric". What must be done before laundering, with respect to the statement? Competency Based Que

(a) Stain Removal (b) Mending
(c) Finishing (d) Washing

2. 'An unwanted mark or colouration on a fabric caused by contact and absorption of foreign matter'. What is it? Competency Based Que

(a) Dirt (b) Starch
(c) Stain (d) None of these

3. Choose the incorrect pair Competency Based Que

(a) Oil stains : grease solvents
(b) Animal stains : detergents
(c) Vegetable stains : acidic solution
(d) Mineral stains : acidic and alkaline solution

4. Which among the following can be removed by alkaline medium? Competency Based Que

I. Ghee **II. Coffee**
III. Tea **IV. Butter**

Choose the correct option.

(a) I and II (b) II and III (c) III and IV (d) I and IV

5. The stained area is placed on a flat surface. The reagent is applied wth a sponge on the stained area and absorbed by a blotting paper laid underneath. What is this process called? Competency Based Que

(a) Sponging (b) Scraping
(c) Dipping (d) Dropping

6. Which of the following statements is incorrect regarding stain removal techniques?

(a) Scraping involves using a blunt knife to remove built-up surface stains.
(b) Dipping requires scrubbing the stained material in the reagent.
(c) Sponging involves applying heat to the stained area.
(d) Drop Method involves applying the reagent with a dropper.

7. Which among the following can be used to remove old blood stains on coloured cotton fabric?

(a) Soak in salt water (b) Soak in glycerin
(c) Soak in hot water (d) Wash with soap and hot water

8. Old tea stain on white cotton fabric can be removed by............

(a) use salt water
(b) soak in glycerin
(c) soak in lime juice
(d) pouring boiling water over borax

9. Tanu went to attend a wedding and while eating dinner, her dress get a stain from chicken curry. What is the method of removal for curry stains? Competency Based Que

(a) Wash with cold water
(b) Apply starch paste on fresh stain
(c) wash with soap and water, bleach in Sun
(d) Sponge with a grease solvent

10. Lipstick stain can be removed by............

(a) use of salt water
(b) soak in ammonia
(c) sponge with methylated spirit
(d) wash with hot water and soap

11. Rust stain can be removed by............

(a) use of salt water
(b) soak in oxalic acid and rub
(c) soak in methylated spirit
(d) wash with soap and cold water

12. Rohan prioritises environmental sustainability when choosing laundry cleaning agents. What should he opt for? Competency Based Que

(a) Synthetic detergent (b) Natural soap
(c) Powdered detergent (d) Liquid soap

13. What is used to counteract yellowness and to restore whiteness?
(a) Gelatin (b) Borax
(c) Blues (d) Starch

14. Which of the following is a common solvent used for dry-cleaning?
(a) Perchloro-ethylene (b) Dichloro-ethylene
(c) Chloro-fluorocarbon (d) None of these

15. Match the following. **Competency Based Que**

List I (Stain)	List II (Method of Removal)
A. Milk	1. Sponge with grease solvent
B. Paint	2. Sponge with hydrogen
C. Ice cream	3. Sponge with a solvent
D. Scorch	4. Rub with kerosene

Codes

	A	B	C	D		A	B	C	D
(a)	2	1	3	4	(b)	3	4	1	2
(c)	4	3	1	2	(d)	2	1	4	3

Assertion-Reason Questions

Direction (Q. Nos.16-20) In the questions given below, there are two statements marked as Assertion (A) and Reason (R). Read the statements and choose the correct option.

Codes
(a) Both A and R are true and R is the correct explanation of A.
(b) Both A and R are true, but R is not the correct explanation of A.
(c) A is true, but R is false.
(d) A is false, but R is true.

16. Assertion (A) Emulsifiers are effective in removing tightly held grease from fabrics.
Reason (B) Emulsifiers break down grease into smaller particles that can be easily rinsed.

17. Assertion (A) Water alone can effectively remove all types of dirt from fabrics.
Reason (R) Water's penetrating power and pedesis help loosen and remove dirt.

18. Assertion (A) Wool have a tendency to shrink when subjected to mechanical action like agitation.
Reason (A) Wool should be steam pressed instead of direct ironing.

19. Assertion (A) Colourfastness is crucial in fabric care.
Reason (R) Dyed fabrics can lose colour or stain other items during cleaning.

20. Assertion (A) Yarn structure may affect maintenance.
Reason (R) Yarns with high twist would shrink, complex yarns may snag.

Case Based Questions

21. Read the passage given below and answer the following questions.

Priya had an interview day before yesterday. She was so nervous that even after getting ready for the interview, she was writing and revising the topics. While doing so, she stained her white cotton sari with ink. She had to hurry to buy a similar sari but instead of cotton, she had to manage with a silk sari which was available in a clothing store nearby.

With reference to the passage, answer the following questions.

(i) If Priya had time, how would she remove the ink stain?
(a) Harden with ice, apply any solvent
(b) Fresh stain can be removed by soap and water
(c) Dip in methyl alcohol
(d) Apply starch

(ii) Match the type of fabric given in List I with their properties in List II. **Competency Based Que**

List I (Type of fabric)	List II (Property)
A. Cotton	1. Can stretch out of shape during washing
B. Silk	2. Resistant to microorganisms and insects
C. Wool	3. Can withstand high temperatures and if necessary it can be boiled
D. Polyester	4. Resists attack by mildew and bacteria but are eaten by carpet beetles.

Codes

	A	B	C	D		A	B	C	D
(a)	2	4	1	3	(b)	3	4	1	2
(c)	2	1	4	3	(d)	3	2	1	4

(iii) Stain removal must be followed by .... so that all traces of chemicals are removed.
(a) washing or dry cleaning
(b) dry cleaning or finishing
(c) removal of dirt
(d) drop method

(iv) Assertion (A) Silk is damaged by strong alkalis.
Reason (R) It does not stretch or shrink on washing and has medium resilience. **Competency Based Que**

Codes

(a) Both A and R are true and R is the correct explanation of A.

(b) Both A and R are true, but R is not the correct explanation of A.

(c) A is true, but R is false.

(d) A is false, but R is true.

22. Read the passage given below and answer the following questions.

Dry-cleaning can be defined as the cleaning of fabrics in a non-aqueous liquid medium. The important difference between dry and wet solvents is that white water is absorbed by the fibres, which causes shrinkage, wrinkle formation and colour bleeding: the dry solvents do not cause fibre swelling. Hence, dry-cleaning is a safe method for cleaning delicate textiles. For dry-cleaning, the most common solvents used are perchloro-ethylene, a petroleum solvent or a fluorocarbon solvent.

Dry-cleaning is generally done in industrial establishments and not at the domestic level. The items are brougth to the cleaner's and identified with a tag that includes special instructions. Items are first inspected and treated at a spot board. Because a solvent is used, stains that are water-soluble and other hard-to-remove spots must be treated on the sopt board. Customers who identify the stains for the dry cleaner make the cleaning task easter and ultimately improve their satisfaction with the cleaned product.

Additional treatment that many dry cleaners are equipped to do include replacing buttons. doing minor repairs to items, replacing sizing. Water repellency and other finishes like permanent creases. Moth proofing and cleaning fur and leather. Some dry cleaners also clean and sanitise feather pillows, blankets, quilts and carpets and clean and press draperies.

On the basis of the information given above answer the following questions.

(i) Dry cleaning involves the use of a which kind of liquid medium to clean the fabric.

(a) oil based (b) quasi solid
(c) non-aqueous (d) None of these

(ii) The most common solvent for dry cleaning is **Competency Based Que**

I. perchloro-ethylene II. fluorocarbon
III. Ethyl peroxide IV. Methylated spirit

Choose the correct option.

(a) I and II (b) II and III
(c) III and IV (d) I and IV

(iii) Water solvents can cause which of the following effects.

(a) shrinkage (b) colour bleeding
(c) wrinkle formulation (d) All of these

(iv) Assertion (A) A stain is a decorative mark or colouration on a fabric.

Reason (R) Identification of stains can be done on the basis of colour, smell and feel. **Competency Based Que**

(a) Both A and R are true and R is the correct explanation of A.

(b) Both A and R are true, but R is not the correct explanation of A.

(c) A is true, but R is false.

(d) A is false, but R is true.

Answers

1. (b) Mending 2. (c) Stain
3. (c) Vegetable stains : acidic solution
4. (b) II and III 5. (a) Sponging
6. (c) Sponging involves applying heat to the stained area.
7. (a) Soak in salt water
8. (d) pouring boiling water over borax
9. (c) wash with soap and water, bleach in Sun
10. (c) Sponge with methylated spirit
11. (b) soak in oxalic acid and rub
12. (b) Natural soap 13. (c) Blues
14. (a) Perchloro-ethylene 15. (b) 3 4 1 2
17. (d) A is false, but R is true.
16. (a) Both A and R are true and R is the correct explanation of A.
19. (a) Both A and R are true and R is the correct explanation of A.
18. (b) Both A and R are true, but R is not the correct explanation of A.
20. (a) Both A and R are true and R is the correct explanation of A.
21. (i) (b) Fresh stain can be removed by soap and water
(ii) (b) 3 4 1 2
(iii) (c) removal of dirt
(iv) (d) Both A and R are true but R is not the correct explanation of A.
22. (i) (c) Non-aqueous
(ii) (a) I and II
(iii) (d) All of these
(iv) (d) A is false, but R is true.

Subjective Questions

Very Short Answer Type Questions

1. What operations are included in mending?

Ans. The operations included in mending are
- Repairing cuts, tears, soles, etc.
- Replacing buttons/fasteners, ribbons, laces or fancy attachments.
- Restitching seams and hems if they open up.

2. What is repairing cuts, replacing buttons, etc. before laundering called?

Ans. The process of repairing cuts, replacing buttons etc. before laundering is called mending.

3. Ramesh accidentally spilled coffee on his favorite shirt. What laundry process should he use immediately to remove the stain? Competency Based Que

Ans. Ramesh should use stain removal process immediately to remove the coffee stain. This involves applying a stain remover or laundry detergent directly to the stain and washing the shirt as soon as possible.

4. How should we remove a grease stain from a white cotton bedsheet?

Ans. We should first wash the fresh stain with hot soapy water. Then we should apply some wheat flour or starch solution on the stain and dry it in the shade.

Finally, we should thoroughly rinse the bedsheet to remove the stain.

5. Which stain can be removed by soaking the fabric in methylated spirit?

Ans. Lipstick stain can be removed by soaking the fabric in methylated spirit.

6. Asha wants to remove loose dirt from her cotton scarf. What method would you recommend?

Ans. I would recommend brushing or shaking off the dirt or soaking the scarf in water.

7. When you gently rub the fabric in the detergent solution with the hands, what is it called?

Ans. It is called kneading and squeezing.

9. Why should we dry the clothes in the Sun?

Ans. We should dry the clothes in the Sun because it acts as an antiseptic.

8. Why should the kneading and squeezing method be used for washing a woollen sweater?

Ans. The woollen sweater should be kneaded and squeezed by hand so that its delicate woollen fibre is not damaged. It will also prevent shrinkage in the sweater.

10. Ritika wants to dry her silk and woollen garments but is concerned about sunlight damage. What risks do these falerics face when exposed to strong sunlight? What is the best drying method for them? Competency Based Que

Ans. Silk and woollen fabrics can be damaged by strong sunlight, leading to loss of strength and yellowing. To preserve their quality, it is best for her to dry these delicate garments indoor.

11. What are two common types of solvents used for dry-cleaning clothes?

Ans. Two common types of solvents used for dry-cleaning clothes are perchloro-ethylene, a petroleum solvent and fluorocarbon solvents.

12. Rahul purchased a new woolen sweater and wants to know how to wash and maintain it. Where should he look for guidance? Competency Based Que

Ans. Rahul should check the care label attached to the sweater for washing and maintenance instructions.

Short Answer Type Questions

1. A stain is an unwanted mark or discoloration on a fabric caused by contact and absorption of foreign substances.

(i) How are different types of stains found on fabrics classified?

(ii) What are the different techniques for stain removal?

Ans. (i) Stains on fabrics can be classified into five main types

(a) Vegetable stains (e.g., tea, coffee) are acidic and can be removed with an alkaline medium.

(b) Animal stains (e.g., blood, milk) are protein-based and require cold water and detergents for removal.

(c) Oil stains (e.g., butter, ghee) need grease solvents and absorbents.

(d) Mineral stains (e.g., ink, rust) should be washed first in an acidic medium, followed by an alkaline wash.

(e) Dye bleeding occurs when colour transfers from one fabric to another. They can be treated with dilute alkalies or acids, depending on the fabric.

(ii) Different techniques used in removal of stain are as follows

(a) **Scraping** built up surface stains can be scraped lightly using a blunt knife.

(b) **Dipping** The stained material is dipped into the reagent and scrubbed.

(c) **Sponging** The stained area is placed on a flat surface and then the reagent is applied with a sponge on the stained area.

(d) **Drop Method** The stained cloth is stretched over a bowl. The reagent is put on it with a dropper.

2. Ira accidentally spilled coffee on her new cotton blouse while rushing to work. Concerned about ruining the fabric, she needs to know the best way to remove the stain without causing damage. List down the general considerations for her to follow to effectively treat the stain. **Competency Based Que**

Ans. Some general considerations that Ira needs to follow to effectively remove the stain are as follows

(i) She should act quickly, as fresh stains are easier to treat.

(ii) She should test any cleaning solution on a small portion first.

(iii) It's better to use milder reagents repeatedly rather than a strong agent at once.

(iv) After treatment, she should wash the blouse with a soapy solution to remove any residue and then dry it in the sun, as sunlight acts as a natural bleach.

3. Name 2 grease-absorbents which are used to remove stains from garments. How should they be applied?

Ans. The grease absorbents which are used to remove stains from garments are talcum powder, chalk, fuller's earth and starch. Any of these absorbents are first applied by rubbing on the stains. Then, with the help of a blotting paper and an iron, these stains are transferred to the blotting paper which is kept below the stain.

4. Aditi has a delicate silk dress that she wants to clean before an upcoming wedding. She's worried about water damage, as it may shrink or lose colour. After researching, she considers using a dry-cleaning service. What steps should Aditi take to ensure her dress is dry cleaned properly? **Competency Based Que**

Ans. Aditi should clearly communicate her concerns about the silk dress to the cleaner and mention any visible stains. It's important for her to inspect the dress before handing it over and to confirm any special care instructions on the tag. After cleaning, she should ask about proper storage to maintain the dress' quality.

Finally, Aditi can consider asking about additional services like minor repairs or fabric treatments to enhance the dress' longevity.

5. Ravi is preparing to store his winter clothes as the summer season approaches. He remembers that his woollen sweaters need special care before packing. What steps should Ravi follow to ensure his clothes are properly stored? **Competency Based Que**

Ans. Ravi should start by thoroughly cleaning and drying all his winter clothes. For woollens, he should brush them and consider dry cleaning to remove any stains.

Next, he should turn pockets inside out and inspect the items for dust and grit.

After shaking, brushing, washing and ironing, he should fold the clothes loosely and pack them in clean, dry storage, ensuring that the environment is free from insects and low in humidity to prevent damage.

Long Answer Type Questions

1. State two reasons for the need for washing woollens using the kneading and squeezing method. What are the requirements for the water and soap/detergent used for washing wool? **Competency Based Que**

Ans. Two reasons for the need for washing woollens using the kneading and squeezing method are

(i) Wool requires gentle handling because it is a weak fibre and its strength reduces even more when wet.

(ii) Agitation of wool while washing may cause felting and shrinkage, so agitation should be avoided.

The requirement for water is that it should not be hot. It should only be warm and its temperature should remain constant during the washing process.

The requirement for soap/detergent to be used for washing wool is any mild, neutral detergent, as strong alkaline soaps will damage wool.

2. How should blues and Optical Brightening Agents (OBAs) be applied to enhance the whiteness of fabrics, and what are their specific functions?

Ans. Blues and Optical Brightening Agents (OBAs) are effective in enhancing fabric whiteness. Blues, like ultramarine blue, are primarily used to counteract yellowness. They are available in powdered or liquid forms and should be added during the last rinse.

The powdered form must be mixed with water immediately to prevent settling, ensuring an even distribution. The fabric should be thoroughly wet but not dripping before being immersed in the blue solution for a brief period.

OBAs are fluorescent compounds that absorb short wavelengths of light and re-emit them as longer wavelengths, creating a brightening effect that combats both yellowness and grayness.

They are suitable for use on coloured fabrics and should not be confused with bleaching, as they do not change the fabric's inherent colour. Proper application is important for achieving the desired brightness with both agents.

3. Shreya got a dress on her birthday and she loves that dress so much that she has already worn the dress multiple times. Now, she wants to wear it again on family trip but the dress has lost its shine and gloss.

(a) What should Shreya do to get the shine back?

(b) What is finishing?

(c) State in brief the most common stiffening agents? **Competency Based Que**

Ans. (a) To get the shine back starching of fabric can be done. Starch is obtained from, rice arrow-root, tapioca etc. They are available in powder form in the market and must be cooked before use. Commercially prepared starches are easy to use and do not necessarily require hot water for preparation. Starch is used only for stiffening cotton and linen clothes.

(b) After washing, rinse the article in clean water till it is absolutely free of soap or detergent. In the last rinse, some other reagents are added which can help to restore the freshness and brightness of the fabric. Other reagents may add to the body of the fabric to improve its stiffness or crispness is called finishing.

(c) For common stiffening agents refer to text under the heading 'Starches and Stiffening Agents'.

4. Anjali has just washed her family's clothes and noticed they're wrinkled and creased. She wants to iron them effectively but isn't sure how to proceed. What steps should Anjali take to achieve the best results while ironing? **Competency Based Que**

Ans. Anjali should start by ensuring her clothes are slightly damp, as moisture helps in ironing. If they're completely dry, she can sprinkle water or roll them in a towel to distribute moisture evenly.

Using an electric iron is ideal for temperature control, allowing her to adjust the heat based on fabric type. As she irons, she should apply pressure by moving the iron along the fabric, pressing delicate items instead of ironing to avoid stretching.

Finally, Anjali should use a padded ironing board for comfort and proper folding or hanging of the clothes afterward to keep them ready for use.

5. What factors influence the care and maintenance of dyed and printed fabrics and how do they impact their overall performance?

Ans. The care and maintenance of dyed and printed fabrics are influenced by several key factors, including fiber content, yarn structure, fabric construction, colour application and finishing treatments.

Dyed fabrics may lose colour during cleaning, potentially staining other materials, so it's crucial to test for colourfastness before use.

Finishing treatments can enhance the fabric's performance, but some may require renewal after washing impacting long-term maintenance. Ultimately, the interplay of these factors determines the fabric's appearance, comfort, durability and maintenance needs.

Understanding these characteristics is essential for evaluating the fabric's suitability for its intended use.

Careful consideration of these aspects helps in making informed decisions regarding the proper handling and cleaning methods necessary to preserve the fabric's integrity and appearance over time. By doing so, users can ensure optimal performance and longevity of the fabric in its specific application.

SELF ASSESSMENT TEST

Objective Type Questions

1. Which type of stains can be removed by first washing in acidic medium and then in alkaline medium?
   (a) Vegetable stains
   (b) Mineral stains
   (c) Oil stains
   (d) Dye bleeding
2. .... washing is suitable for strong fabrics like cotton.
   (a) Friction
   (b) Squeezing
   (c) Suction
   (d) Machine
3. When the stained cloth is stretched over a bowl and the reagent is put on it with a dropper, what is the method called?
   (a) Scraping
   (b) Dipping
   (c) Dripping
   (d) Drop method

Very Short Answer Type Questions

4. Blotting paper is used in which method of stain removal?
5. Give three examples of solvents used for removing stains.
6. What common stiffening agent is used for cotton and linen garments?

Short Answer Type Questions

7. Differentiate between stains and dirt by giving two differences.
8. Give two advantages each of washing clothes with soap and detergent.
9. What are four precautions to be adopted while storing woollen coats for a long time?

Long Answer Type Questions

10. What four precautions should we adopt while laundering coloured cotton clothes?
11. There are some tea and ball pen ink stains on a cotton dress. Suggest one suitable chemical each along with six important precautions we should adopt for removing these stains. Name two more types of stains for which these two chemicals can be used. **Competency Based Que**

PRACTICAL WORK

PRACTICAL -1

Understanding Oneself

(Part A and B-Physical Development and Sexual Maturity)

Aim Study of one's physical self.

Tasks

1. Recording the physical parameters like height, weight, hip size, chest/bust circumference, etc.
2. Recording the age of menarche (girls).
3. Recording the age of growth of facial hair and change in voice of boys.
4. Recording the colour of hair and eyes.
5. Compare your development with reference to the standard average parameters.

Purpose of Practical

Keeping in mind the physical growth and development during adolescence, this practical will help you to

- understand your body changes during this stage.
- know the average rate of growth and development of adolescents in your class as you compare your data with those of others.
- The measurements stated in Task 1 above are also important for you to know the size of garment.

Conducting the Practical

Take your own measurements as stated in Task 1 above. Alternatively your can take each other's measurements in the class.

Procedure

1. Take a measuring tape and take the body measurement of each other in your group
   - (i) **Measurement of Height** Use a measuring tape and measure the height from the floor to the top of the head.
   - (ii) **Measurement of Weight** Use a weight scale (machine) and follow some steps like-wear minimal clothes, don't wear shoes and then record your weight.
   - (iii) **Measurement of Hip Size** Use a measuring tape around the widest portion of the hips with two fingers between the tape and the body.

(iv) **Measurement of Bust/Chest Circumference** Hold the tape and measure across the fullest part of the bust/chest. Hold tape firmly but not tight.

(v) **Measurement of Waist** Hold the tape around waist and let it settle into the smallest portion of the body (that is the waistline). Take the measurement with one finger between tape and body. Measure the smallest part of waistline.

(vi) **Measurement around Neck** Lay a still measure tightly around the neck and gently tap it down until the lower edge settles at the base of the neck where the measurement is taken.

(vii) **Measurement across Back** It is measurement taken between the lateral ends of scapulae (shoulder blades). Take one more measurement 10-12 cms below the waist measurement over the fullest part of back.

2. Record information required as per Tasks 1, 2, 3 and 4 in the table below

Name of the Student	:	....	Age of the Student	:	....
Gender	:	....	Colour of Hair	:	....
Colour of Eyes	:	....	Age at Menarche	:	....
Age at growth of Beard, change in voice	:	....	Weight	:	....
Around chest/bust	:	....	Height	:	....
Around neck	:	....	Hip size	:	....
Across back	:	....			

Table for Boys

Age	**Weight** (Kg)	**Height** (cm)
13 years	40.9	153.0
14 years	47.0	160.0
15 years	52.6	166.0
16 years	58.0	171.0
17 years	62.7	175.0
18 years	65.0	177.0

Table for Girls

Age	**Weight** (Kg)	**Height** (cm)
13 years	44.0	150.0
14 years	48.0	155.0
15 years	51.5	161.0
16 years	53.0	162.0
17 years	54.0	163.0
18 years	54.4	164.0

Source Nutritional Requirement and RDA for Indians ICMR 1990.

3. Now create groups of 10 students each and collect and complied the data of all the students of your class. Study the range of measurements like weight, height. Note down separately for boys and girls.

   Make a table of your findings/(observations)

- Note down the range of age of menarche for girls in your class.
- Note down the emergence of facial hair in boys from .... to .... years.
- Note down the age of change of voice in boys from .... to .... years.
- Note down the weight of boys ranges from .... to .... kg.
- Note down the weight of girls ranges from .... to .... kg.
- Height of boys ranges from .... to .... cm.
- Height of girls ranges from .... to......... cm.
- Correlate the size of ready-made garments you purchase with your measurement.

Adolescent Girl's Body Sizing Chart

	Extra Small (XS)	Small (S)	Medium (M)	Large(L)	Xtra Large (XL)	Xtra Xtra Large (XXL)
Bust	30″ – 32″	32″ – 34″	34″ – 36″	36″ – 38″	38″ – 40″	40″ – 42″
Waist	23″ – 25″	25″ – 27″	27″ – 29″	29″ – 31″	31″ – 33″	33″ – 35″
Hip	32″ – 34″	34″ – 36″	36″ – 38″	38″ – 40″	40″ – 42″	42″ – 44″

Adolescent Boy's Body Sizing Chart

	Extra Small (XS)	Small (S)	Medium(M)	Large(L)	Xtra Large (XL)	Xtra Xtra Large (XXL)
Chest	33″ – 36″	36″ – 39″	39″ – 41″	41″ – 43″	43″ – 46″	46″ – 49″
Waist	27″ – 30″	30″ – 33″	33″ – 36″	36″ – 38″	38″ – 42″	42″ – 45″

Size of lower garment is based on the waist size. On the basis of above measurement one can easily find out the size of garment, which they prefer to buy. While buying, they should also select the type of fit that will suit their body type.

Conclusion

1. Compare your physical parameters with the table given by ICMR and draw the inference about your physical development.

   ___

   ___

2. Compare your physical development in reference to the developmental range of your peers in the class and write down your inference.

   ___

   ___

   Students can discuss the reasons for the difference in physical development of adolescents with teacher like heredity, environment, diet, climate, etc.

PRACTICAL -2

Observe the Developmental Norms

Aim Observe and understand the developmental norms (physical, motor, language and social emotions) birth to three years.

Tasks

1. Select a child in your family or neighbourhood and observe the developmental norms regarding physical, motor, language and socio-emotional.
2. Track the child's development with the help of a checklist.
3. Contact with the parents and discuss the development of the child.

Purpose of Practical

To observe and understand the key developmental milestones (Physical, Motor, Language and Social-Emotional) in children from birth to three years, and compare them with normal parameters.

Conducting the Practical

Read and observe the chart on the developmental norms, which is given below and then fill up the personal details of the child.

Name of the child- ________________. Age of the child- ________________.

Gender of the child- ________________. Occupation of mother- ____________.

Occupation of father- ______________. Number of siblings- ______________.

Type of the family (nuclear/joint)- _____. Care of the child- ______________.

Chart on the Developmental Norms

Physical Developmental Norms from Birth to Three Years

0-6 Months	6-12 Months	1-2 Years	2-3 Years
Newborns gain weight rapidly and grow in length.	They try to sit without support.	Children start walking with help, then independently.	Children's run with more confidence and co-ordination.
They start to roll over from tummy to back.	They can roll over both ways (front to back, back to front).	They can squat, stand up, and sit down without help.	They can walk up and down stairs with help.

Practical Work

They try to hold their head steady when sitting with support.	They try to develop better control over head and neck movements.	They start the development of hand-eye co-ordination. For example, drinks from a cup.	They can perform simple self-care tasks like brushing teeth or dressing with some help.
They begin to move their arms and legs more freely.			

Motor Developmental Norms from Birth to Three Years

0-6 Months	6-12 Months	1-2 Years	2-3 Years
Newborns try to move their arms and legs freely.	They try to transfer objects from hand to hand.	Children start to use spoons and forks (with some mess).	They can jump with both feet off the ground.
They begin to develop better hand-control.	They begin to pick up small objects by using their thumb and fingers.	They begin to draw simple lines and shapes.	They can run with more co-ordination and confidence.
		They are able to pick up objects using a more refined pincer grasp.	They can climb stairs using alternate feet with assistance.
		They can push, pull, and carry objects with more strength.	They start to ride tricycles or push toys with wheels.

Language Developmental Norms from Birth to Three Years

0-6 Months	6-12 Months	1-2 Years	2-3 Years
Newborns coos and makes gurgling sounds.	They try to speak words, like 'mama' or 'dada.'	Children start to use simple words, like 'ball' or 'dog.'	Children are able to form short sentences, like 'I want a ball' or 'Where is Mummy?'
They try to respond to familiar voices and sounds.	They try to understand simple words and phrases, like 'no' or 'come here.'	They begin to combine two words, like 'want cookie.'	They start to ask simple questions, like 'What's that?'

0-6 Months	6-12 Months	1-2 Years	2-3 Years
They begin to babble and experiment with different sounds.	They try to respond to their name and familiar sounds.	They understand simple commands, such as 'give me the toy.'	They can use pronouns (I, you, me) correctly.
They smile or make sounds in response to caregivers.		They begin to imitate words and sounds from adults.	They are able to understand basic concepts, like 'big' and 'small.'
They try to recognise and respond to different tones of voice.			

Social-Emotional Developmental Norms from Birth to Three Years

0-6 Months	6-12 Months	1-2 Years	2-3 Years
Newborns start to smile in response to others' faces and voices.	They show attachment to caregivers and may cry when they leave.	Children start to imitate the actions and behaviours of others.	They show more complex emotions, like jealousy, pride, or embarrassment.
They enjoy a comfortable environment provided by their caregivers.	They begin to fear strangers or unfamiliar environments.	They begin to show frustration or anger when things don't go their way. They may show interest in familiar adults or children and imitate their actions.	They show interest in making friends and interacting with peers.
They begin to show preferences for familiar faces, like parents.	They start responding with emotions, like happiness, distress, or excitement.		They start to understand the concept of sharing.
They react to different emotions in others, such as smiling or crying.	They engage in simple social interactions, like laughing or playing.		

Conclusion

1. **Physical Development** Compare the child's physical development with the parameters given in the chart and write your conclusion.

2. **Motor Development** Compare the child's motor development with the parameters given in the chart and write your conclusion.

3. **Language Development** Compare the child's language development with the parameters given in the chart and write your conclusion.

4. **Social-Emotional Development** Compare the child's social-emotional development with the parameters given in the chart and write your conclusion.

PRACTICAL -3

Areas of Agreement and Disagreement

Aim List and discuss areas of agreements and disagreements with mother, father, siblings/friends and teachers.

Tasks

1. Listing the areas of agreements and disagreements
2. Identifying ways of resolving disagreements

Purpose of Practical

- Adolescence is a time when you are forming a sense of your identity. Often, but not always, this process may bring you in conflict with your family members and significant others as your views on particular aspects may be different from theirs. This can cause stress in relationships.
- This practical will help you to identify sources of disagreements and will also encourage you to reflect on how you can minimise and resolve these differences.

Conducting the Practical

Form yourself into groups of 4-6 students. For the first 10 minutes, reflect individually upon your interactions with your family members, friends and teachers in the past few months. Use the following format to record the areas of agreements and disagreements.

Person	Area of Agreement	Area of Disagreement	Comment
Father			
Mother			
Sister			
Brother			
Friends			
Teachers			

Now share your data with the other members of the group and discuss the following

1. (a) Whether there are areas where most of you have disagreements with a particular family member, friends and teachers.
   (b) Why do you think this happens?
   (c) What are you doing presently to resolve the disagreements?
   (d) What can be done to resolve/minimise the differences?

Practical Work

2. (a) Whether there are areas where only you seem to be having differences while the rest of the group members do not have disagreements in that area?
   (b) What could be the reason for this?
   (c) Can you do something to resolve the disagreements?
3. (a) Which are the areas where most of you are in agreement with the family members, friends and teachers.
   (b) Can you use these areas of agreement to build a stronger relationship with the persons around you and thus reduce the areas of disagreements?

Issues of Agreement and Disagreement

Person	Issues of Agreement or Disagreement
Mother	Selection of clothes Different food habits Going late to sleep Waking up late from sleep To be ready on time
Father	Subjects to be chosen for future studies Selection of TV programmes Time spent on gadgets Selection of career and profession Finances
Siblings/Friends	Sharing of personal items Competition in studies and co-curricular activities Selection of an activity to be done together Selection of favorites Selection of food and clothes
Teachers	Maintaining discipline or selecting a monitor Participation in co-curricular activities Following the proper dress code Grades or scores received Overall behaviour in class

Conclusion

After a healthy discussion among the members of the group, write down your conclusion.

___

PRACTICAL -4

Record Own Diet for a Day

Aim Record your own diet for a day and evaluate qualitatively for adequacy.

Task

1. Record the own diet of one day.
2. After recording the diet, evaluate the nutritive value of the diet as per the recommendations given by ICMR.

Purpose of Practical

Health and well-being of an adolescent is important and this practical will help them to understand the following

- The nutritive value of the food they are eating.
- The essential requirement in the modification of diet.
- Evaluate each meal and plan diet in terms of inclusion of the five food groups and the balanced diet.

Conducting the Practical

1. Record your own diet for a day

   Details

   Name- ____________. Age-____________.

   Habit-____________.

   Nutritional Requirements ____________.

   ____________.

   ____________.

2. My one day diet chart

Breakfast	Lunch	Evening Tea	Dinner
1.________	1.________	1.________	1.________
2.________	2.________	2.________	2.________
3.________	3.________	3.________	3.________

Practical Work

Planning a Day's Diet for a 15-year Old Girl

Meal	Menu Measure	Household	Ingredients	Amount (gm.)
Breakfast	Milkshake	1 medium glass	Milk	150
			Chocolate	
			Sugar	
	Stuffed parantha	1 parantha	Onion, Potato	50
			Atta	30
			Ghee	5
			Butter	10
Mid Morning	Fruit	One and Half	Apple	200
	Peanuts chaat	Small plate	Peanuts	50
			Tomatoes	20
			Onion	20
			Coriander	10
			Lemon	5
Lunch	Rajma	1 medium katori	Rajma	50
	Mix veg	1/2 katori	Cauliflower	40
			Potato, Capsicum	25
	Vegetable raita	1 katori	Curd	75
			Cucumber	20
	Rice	1/2 plate	Rice	50
	Chapati	1	Wheat flour	15
			Onion, Tomato	50
Evening Tea	Paneer cutlet	2	Paneer	25
			Besan	15
	Smoothie	1 glass	Potato	25
			Chirva	25
			Onion	20
	Smoothie	1 glass	Banana	50
			Strawberry	25
			Sugar	10
			Milk	50
Dinner	Tomato soup	1 bowl	Tomato	100
	Whole moong dal	2 katori	Moong dal	5
	Mixed vegetable	1/2 katori	Whole among	50
	Chapati	2	Onion	50
	Salad	1/4 Plate	Tomato	50
			Peas	40
	Raita	1/2 katori	Cabbage	40
			Cucumber	50

Evaluate Planned Diet-quantitatively for Adequacy

Evaluate Each Meal of your Above Planned Diet in Terms of Inclusion of The Five Food Groups and Balanced Diet.

Meal/Menu	Name of Food Groups	Comment on whether the meal is balanced or not included
e.g. Breakfast Milkshake	Fruits and Vegetables	Four food groups are included in this meal.
Stuff Parantha	Milk and Milk Products	Meal provides seasonal fruit and vegetable.
	Fat and Sugar	Provides satiety value.
	Cereals	Amount is also sufficient as it provides about 1/4th of nutritional requirement.

After evaluating different meals, take a day's diet as a single unit and then evaluate. From breakfast and evening-tea together, minimum 1/3rd nutritional requirement of the day should be provided and 1/3rd each from lunch and dinner.

Conclusion

The practical to record your own diet and then evaluate for its adequacy will provide a better guide to keep yourself aware and the need for the nutritive rich food.

PRACTICAL-5

Preparation of Different Healthy Snacks for an Adolescent

Aim Prepare some healthy snacks for the adolescents.

Task

Plan and prepare healthy snacks for the adolescents, which are rich in vitamins, calcium, protein and iron.

Purpose of Practical

- The purpose of this practical is to teach students how to prepare simple, nutritious snacks that are healthy for adolescents. These snacks will provide essential nutrients, which help in maintaining energy levels and promote overall well-being.
- By preparing healthy snacks, students will learn how to make better food choices and understand the importance of nutrition during adolescence.

1. Atta Besan Halwa (No. of servings-5)

Ingredients

Atta	:	½ katori (150g)	Besan	:	½ katrori (150g)
Jaggery	:	200g	Groundnuts	:	20g
Ghee	:	2tbsp (30g)	Coconut powder	:	1tsp (5g)

Recipe

1. Roast atta in a kadhai with 1tbsp of ghee on low to medium flame. Stir it continuously till light brown in colour with sweet aroma arising. Put it aside in a plate.
2. Roast besan in a kadhai with 1tbsp of ghee on low to medium flame. Stir it continuously till light brown in colour with sweet aroma arising. Put it aside in a plate.
3. Roast the peanuts and ground them to make powder.
4. Roast coconut powder on a low flame for 2-3 minutes.
5. Prepare thin syrup of jaggery and water in another pan.
6. Combine all the roasted ingredients in a kadhai and add jaggery syrup to the mixture. Stir it continuously and quickly on a medium flame.
7. Stir it till the halwa starts coating the spoon. Turn off the flame.

2. Suji Upma (No. of servings-5)

Ingredients

Suji	:	1 katori (200-250g)	Urad dal	:	1-2 tsp (5-10g)
Groundnuts	:	15g	Sesame seeds	:	1tsp (5g)
Tomato	:	1 finely chopped	Peas (shelled)	:	30g
Carrot (grated)	:	1 medium sized	Curry leaves	:	3-4 leaves
Ghee	:	2tbsp (30g)	Salt	:	to taste
Mustard seeds	:	1 tsp (5g)	Red chilli powder	:	1tsp (5g)
Water	:	2.5 katori			

Recipe

1. Take a kadhai and roast suji in 1tsp ghee. Roast it till a sweet aroma starts coming. Pit it aside in a plate.
2. Roast the groundnuts and urad dal and ground them into granular powder. Put them in plate.
3. Add ghee to the kadhai and splutter mustard seeds and curry leaves in it. Add the vegetables to sauté them.
4. When the vegetables become soft add spices, suji, sesame seeds, ground peanuts and dal while stirring the mixture.
5. Add water slowly while continuously stirring. Stir it till it starts coating the spoon. Turn off the flame.

Note Overheating at this stage can make the upma dry.

3. Hariyali Mathri (No. of serving-5)

Ingredients

Maida/atta	:	1 katori	Bathua leaves	:	50 g
Fenugreek leaves	:	50g	Oil	:	2 tbsp
Salt	:	to taste	Ajwain seeds	:	2 tsp
Oil for deep frying					

Recipe

1. Clean bathua and fenugreek leaves and wash them thoroughly. Grind them to a green coloured paste.
2. Sieve maida/atta thrououghly. Add ajwain seeds and salt to taste.
3. Make a well in between the flour and add oil in it.
4. Mix the oil well so that crumbles of flour can be formed. The mixture should form lumps, when gathered in a fist.

5. Add the green coloured paste in the flour and knead the dough. The dough should be quite firm unlike roti or poori dough.
6. Cover the dough and keep aside for 30 minutes.
7. After 30 minutes, heat oil as required for deep frying in a kadai.
8. Pinch small balls from the dough. Just roll them lightly in your palms to make them even.
9. Flatten each ball with a rolling pin to medium thickness. Prick each mathari with a fork or give cuts with a knife. This makes sure that they do not puff up while frying.
10. Fry about 4 to 6 mathris in medium hot oil till crisp and golden on medium flame.
11. Fry till golden brown.

4. Rainbow Poori (Beetroot, Spinach, Pumpkin)

Ingredients

Whole wheat flour/Atta	: 1 katori (divided into 1/3 katori each)
Bengal gram flour/besan	: 3/4 katori (divide into three equal parts, i.e., ¼ katori each)
Ground Spinach leaves	: 50g
Grated pumpkin	: 50g
Ground Beetroot	: 1 medium sized
Salt	: to taste
Ajwain seeds	: 2 tsp
Oil for deep frying	

Recipe

1. Puree the cleaned spinach leaves and beetroot separately. And grate the pumpkin. Dough making with spinach leaves.
2. Sieve 1/3 katori atta and 1/4 katori besan, and add salt, ajwain seeds and pureed spinach to knead the dough.
3. Add water gradually to make the dough firmer than chapatti dough.
4. Cover the dough and keep it aside for 30 minutes.
5. Repeat the above steps (2-4), replacing spinach with beetroot.
6. Repeat the above steps (2-4), replacing spinach with grated pumpkin.
7. Heat oil in a kadhai as required for deep frying.
8. After 30 minutes, divide the doughs into small balls of medium size.
9. Take one dough ball. Flatten it and spread some oil on both sides of the dough.

10. With a rolling pin, gently roll to a 4 to 5 inches poori. Roll to pooris which are neither thick nor thin.
11. Gently slide one poori in the medium hot oil.
12. Fry till the oil stops sizzling. Then, gently turn over and fry the other side of the poori. Remove when both sides are fried.
13. Prepare other pooris in the same way.
14. The pooris can be served with any vegetable of choice.

Note The pooris will be red, green and light yellow coloured.

5. Paneer Cutlet (No. of servings-5)

Ingredients

Paneer	:	200g	Boiled potato	: 2 medium sized
Chopped onion	:	1/4 katori	Salt	: to taste
Finely chopped spinach leaves	:	1/2 katori	Garam masala	: 1 tsp
Finely chopped coriander leaves	:	1/2 katori	Black pepper powder	: 1 tsp
Chivda	:	150-200g	Sesame seeds	: for coating
Red chilli powder	:	1 tsp	Dhaniya powder	: 1 tsp
Chaat masala	:	1.5 tsp		
Oil for deep frying				

Recipe

1. Wash the chivda in a colander and soak it for 10 minutes till it becomes soft and mushy.
2. Mash the paneer, boiled potatoes in a big bowl.
3. Add chopped onion, spinach and coriander leaves and spices.
4. Add soft and mushy chivda to the mixture and knead the dough without using water.
5. Make small balls or cylinders or any shape you like from the dough.
6. Gently roll the dough over sesame seeds to form a coating.
7. Put the balls in fridge for sometime (10-20 minutes). This will help in proper binding of the balls.
8. Heat oil in a kadhai for frying.
9. Gently put 2-3 balls in the hot oil on medium flame. Do not touch spoon because they will break.
10. Let the cutlets fry for a few minutes before turning them over.
11. Fry till golden brown.
12. The cutlets can be served with ketchup or mint chutney.

6. Healthy Cookie Recipes

Ingredients

Eggs	:	3	Brown sugar	:	¼ cup
Coconut oil	:	1 cup melted	Vanilla essence	:	2 tsp
Sugar free	:	2 tsp	Salt	:	to taste
Baking soda	:	1½ tsp	Quick oats	:	2 cups
Whole wheat flour	:	1 ½ cups			

Recipe

1. Preheat oven to 325 degrees F, and grease the baking sheets.
2. In a medium-sized bowl, whisk eggs for 30 seconds. Then add brown sugar and whisk again. Add vanilla essence, coconut oil and sugar free.
3. In another bowl, mix salt and baking soda together. Add oats and whole wheat flour to the mixture and combine until you get a thick cookie dough.
4. Use an ice cream scoop and place even amounts of cookie dough on the baking sheets.
5. Bake for 10-15 minutes until the edges are golden-brown and a toothpick comes out clean. Remove from the oven and transfer to a cool wire rack.

Conclusion

The snacks planned for adolescents are rich in protein, calcium and iron. These are very important for the growth and development of an adolescents.

PRACTICAL -6

(A) Record of One Day's Activity Relating to Time Use and Work

Aim Record one day's activities relating to time use and work.

Task

- List your daily activities.
- Estimate the time spent on each activity.
- Evalute your time plan.
- Categorise of your daily activities, such as work, rest and leisure time.

Purpose of Practical

The purpose of this practical is to track what you eat and drink in a day to understand your eating habits. And after recording your diet, you will check if it provides all the necessary nutrients, and is balanced for your health.

Conducting the Practical

First students should

(i) List the activities usually done every day.

(ii) Categorise them related to work, rest and leisure activities.

(a) Work includes daily personal, care, eating, sleeping, going to school, doing homework, etc.

(b) Rest includes relaxing, meditating, going for a walk, change in nature of activity for example, when you are tired of studying (mental activity), you can help your mother in kitchen (physical activity) for some time.

(c) Leisure includes outdoor playing, watching TV, reading magazine, spending time with family members, etc.

(iii) Arrange your activities according to priorities, for example, activities related to study and school should be given priority.

(iv) Pick-up one activity and state time for that. You can estimate the time spent in doing specific activity by repeating it 2-3 times.

(v) Specify which of these can be carried out at specific time, like going to school at specific time.

(vi) Allot time for various activities. Some activities are fixed time like going to school, completing assignment, preparing tiffin, etc., and others are flexible.

Record your one day's activities from 6 a.m. onwards. Write down work (activity) one side and time consumed on other side.

(B) Prepare a Time Plan for Yourself

Prepare a Time Plan for Oneself

Time management is important for students. It is the process of organising and planning how to divide your time between different activities.

Conducting the Practical

- Prepare your time plan by writing down estimated time for activity on one side and activity to be done on the other side in the following table.
- Make sure that important tasks are not left out or missed.
- Time to be spent on leisure activities and rest should be separately noted.
- Following are the steps for preparing time plan
  - (i) Prepare a days routine or list your daily activities.
  - (ii) List weekly activities to be done also.
  - (iii) Estimate time required for each activity.
  - (iv) Arrange these activities in order.

Time Plan for a Student

Time Plan for a Child Studying in Grade 11

Time	Activities
6:00 am	Wake up
6:00 am - 7:00 am	Do personal activities (brushing, bathing, getting ready for school)
7:00 am - 7:15 am	Breakfast
7: 15 am - 8:00 am	Reaching School
8:00 am - 2:00 pm	Study in School
2:00 pm - 2:45 pm	Reaching home
2:45 pm - 3:00 pm	Getting freshen up (changing clothes)
3:00 pm - 3:15 pm	Lunch
3: 15 pm - 4:00 pm	Relax (Watch TV or do some other relaxing activity)
4:00 pm - 5:30 pm	Study (take Tuitions)

Time	Activities
5:30 pm - 6:30 pm	Playing outdoor (playing some sport or doing some extracurricular activity)
6:30 pm - 7:00 pm	Evening snack and rest
7:00 pm - 8: 15 pm	Self study
8: 15 pm - 8: 30 pm	Dinner
8: 30 pm- 10: 00 pm	Spending time with family and siblings
10: 00 pm- 10: 15 pm	Preparing for the next day
10:15 pm - 10:30 pm	Getting freshen up (brushing teeth, changing clothes)
10:30 pm	Go to sleep

Evaluate your time plan to see if tasks of priority like finishing of assignment, doing home work or preparation for exam was done or not.

Students have a busy lifestyle as they need to complete their homework, assignment, prepare for exam have some fun, pursue hobbies, etc. Time plan can help to finish all the tasks in a limited time, i.e., 24 hours.

Tips for a Student While Making Time Plan

- Learn to say 'no' to a task if time is short. For example, avoid watching TV during exams.
- Plan to study at that time when you are most productive.
- Relax in between study period.
- Develop and stick to regular study routine.
- Break down task into smaller segments that require less time.
- Avoid doing too many tasks at a time.
- Do not waste time and energy on tasks which are not important.

Conclusion

Recording your activities for one day helps you understand how you spend your time and how much time is dedicated to different tasks. By preparing a time plan for yourself, you can organise your day better, prioritise important tasks, and improve productivity. This practice helps manage time effectively and ensures a balanced routine.

PRACTICAL-7

Budget Planning for a Situation

Aim The aim of this practical is to learn how to plan a budget for a specific situation and manage finances effectively.

Task

Budget Planning for School Farewell

- The first step to budget preparation is to determine a situation and its requirements.
- For a school farewell, one requires graduation caps and coats, awards, decor and food.
- After one has listed the requirements, it is essential to recognise the budget and make plans accordingly.

Purpose of Practical

The purpose is to develop skills in managing money, planning financial resources, and understanding the importance of budgeting for different situations.

Conducting the Practical

List of Requirement

Venue for Farewell : School Auditorium

Number of Participants : 100

Things Required

- Ballons and charts for decoration
- Chairs
- Awards and certificates
- Sashes
- Graduation caps and coats- 40 Pieces
- Food items : soft drinks, water, proper lunch (a combination of Indian and Chinese food items)
- Cutlery
- Maximum Budget: 15,000/-

Budget/Expenditure Plan

The details of the budget plan can be based on the maximum amount that can be spend on a particular item or as per the details acquired by vendor.

S.No.	Item	Cost
1.	Chairs	0.00 (available in school)
2.	Décor (Balloons and Charts)	2000/- Including the charges of the person hired for decoration
3.	Awards, certificates and Sashes	4000/-
4.	Graduation Caps and Coats	3500/-
5.	Food and Cutlery (to be provided by the school canteen)	5000/-
	Total	14,500/-

500/- Rupees can be kept as emergency expenditure.

Remember There might be cases when the expenditure may exceed the maximum budget. In such situations, some things like sashes can be skipped or replaced with other things.

Conclusion

Planning a budget for a given situation helps manage finances effectively by allocating money to different needs and priorities. It ensures that expenses stay within limits, promotes saving and allows for better financial control. This practice is essential for making informed and practical financial decisions.

PRACTICAL -8

Record of Fabrics and Apparel and Their Categorisation

Aim 1. Record the fabrics and apparel used in a day.

2. Categorise them according to functionality.

Task

Record the fabrics and apparel you wear throughout the day and categorise them based on their functionality. For example, casual wear, workwear, sportswear.

Purpose of Practical

The purpose of this practical is to help you understand the types of fabrics and clothing you use for different activities, and how each serves a specific function.

Conducting the Practical

Identify a particular day and note the fabrics that you use throughout the day. Fabric can be used for apparel worn in school or at home or for surroundings like furnishing, bed linen, bath linen, table linen, etc.

You can use the following table for recording the types of fabrics used in a day and their utility for that specific purpose.

Use	Product	Fabric and its Utility
Self	Night suits	Made of cotton, comfortable.
Self	Bath towel	Made of cotton fibre with pile weave. It will absorb water.
Self	School dress-shirt, trousers, socks, etc.	Shirt and trousers are made of terrycot because it is easy to wash and maintain. Socks are of hosiery, cotton or synthetic which has strength and elasticity.
Self	Casual wear at home like leggings, T-shirt, etc.	T-shirt and leggings are made of blended fabric which is stretchable and strong.
Self	Formal wear like skirt and top	Skirt is made of synthetic chiffon which is attractive, flowing and I easy to maintain, top is of satin which is attractive.

Use	Product	Fabric and its Utility
Surrounding	Bed sheet, pillow cover, etc.	Made of cotton because it absorbs sweat and is most comfortable in summers as well as in winters.
Surrounding	Curtains	Made of satin tapestry. It is strong, good drapeability and attractive.
Surrounding	Like umbrella absorbs water.	Made of synthetic fabric, because it has strength and does not.

Students can make groups and discuss the fabrics used for apparel worn by them and fabrics used in other surroundings of their home.

Conclusion

Recording and categorising the fabrics and apparel used in a day helps you see how different clothes are suited for various purposes. This helps in making better clothing choices based on comfort, practicality and functionality.

PRACTICAL -9

Relationship of Fibre Properties to Their Usage

(A) Thermal Property and Flammability

Aim Investigate the relationship between the properties of fibres (specifically their thermal properties and flammability) and their potential applications in various industries.

Task

1. To analyse the thermal properties of different fibres.
2. To evaluate the flammability characteristics of the fibres.

Purpose of Practical

Flammability of fabrics will help to test the behaviour of fabrics in flame and while approaching flame. This will help consumer in taking special care when in use. This is also a way of identifying fibre content of fabrics which are in five composition.

Heat affects different fibres in different ways. Some fibres scorch and flame, others melt and/or flame or shrink. Some fibres are self extinguishing, others are completely non-combustible.

Burning Characteristics of Fibres

Fibre	Approaching flame	In flame	Removed from flame	Odour	Ash or residue
Cotton and Linen	Does not shrink, catches fire	Burns quickly	Continues burning, has an afterglow	Burning paper	Light, soft ash, retains retains shape
Wool and silk	Curls away from flame	Burns slowly	Self-extinguishing	Burning hair	Brittle, curled, small amount, crushable ash
Rayon	Does not shrink, catches fire	Burns quickly	Continues to burn rapidly	Burning paper	Light, fluffy residue, very small amount
Nylon	Shrinks	Melts, catches fire	Continues melting	Acrid	Hard, tan coloured bead
Polyster	Shrinks	Melts, catches fire	Continues melting	Plastic burning	Hard, black coloured bead
Acrylic	Does not shrink, catches fire	Burns rapidly with melting	Continues burning	Acrid	Hard, black coloured, crinkly bead

Practical Work

Conducting the Practical

1. Take a narrow strip of the fabric (½ cm × 5 cm)
2. Hold the strip with a forceps or tongs and do the burning test by bringing it near a burning candle, or low flame of spirit lamp.

   Precaution Perform this experiment on a very low flame of a candle or spirit lamp under the supervision of a teacher.
3. Repeat the process by taking 4-5 samples of different fabrics and record the observations.

Approaching flame	In flame	Removed from flame	Odour	Residue (colour and texture)	Conclusion

Conclusion

The practical demonstrates that the thermal properties and flammability of fibres play a crucial role in determining their suitability for specific applications. These findings highlight the importance of choosing fibres based on their thermal performance to ensure safety and effectiveness in end-use products.

(B) Moisture Absorbency and Comfort

Aim To observe the moisture absorbency property of different fabrics.

Task

1. To measure and compare the moisture absorbency rates of different fibres.
2. To assess the comfort level provided by these fibres based on their moisture absorption capabilities.
3. To evaluate how moisture absorbency influences the performance of fibres.

Purpose of Practical

In hot humid weather, one can feel very uncomfortable, if the clothes do not absorb moisture and sweat. The moisture absorption capacity of textile fabrics has a direct impact on comfort level. Garments which absorb moisture and dry quickly improves' comfort level. An understanding of moisture behaviour of any fabric is therefore important before buying it.

Following tests will help consumers to know

- Absorbency of the fabric
- Comfort level of fabric
- Usage of fabric

Material Required

Square pieces (2″ × 2″) of different kind of fabrics, water.

Conducting the Practical

Drop water on the sample fabric, visually observe its absorbency and touch to feel.

Absorbency Behaviour of Different Fibres

Fabric	Absorbency	Comfort Level
Cotton	Absorbs water quickly and water spreads uniformly in all directions of fabrics, feel wet to touch.	Fabrics are comfortable for summer wear because they absorb sweat and the wearer feels cool.
Rayon	Absorbs water rapidly than cotton	Comfortable in summer.
Silk	Absorbs water, not wet to touch.	Absorptive property of silk contribute to its comfort in warmer weather.
Wool	Initially,water is repelled and can be brushed off. Absorbs water after sometime, not wet to touch.	Comfortable in humid and cold atmosphere.
Nylon	Does not absorb water. Water remains on the surface runs off the smooth surface.	Not comfortable for apparel and used in the production of swim suits, wind cheater, umbrella etc., because they do not absorb water.
Polyester	Water travels along the length of the fabric but not absorbed.	Not comfortable for apparel but blended fabrics can be worn as they absorb water.

Precaution

Same amount of water should be dropped on each sample. Repeat the test using 2,3 samples of each fabric and write down your observations.

Conclusion

The practical showed that moisture absorbency plays a significant role in fiber comfort. Natural fibres like cotton and wool were found to absorb moisture more effectively than synthetic fibres like polyester, which can cause discomfort due to their lower absorbency. fibres with higher moisture absorption capabilities tend to offer better comfort by keeping the skin dry and regulating body temperature. This highlights the importance of selecting fibres with the right moisture absorbency properties for specific end uses, ensuring both comfort and functionality in the final product.

PRACTICAL -10

Care of Garment

(A) Analyse label of garment with respect to; clarity, fibre content, size and care instructions

Aim To analyse the label of a garment in terms of clarity, fiber content, size, and care instructions, and evaluate how effectively it communicates essential garment information to consumers.

Task

Select a garment and then examine and assess its label for key information such as clarity of language, fiber composition, sizing details, and care instructions.

Purpose of Practical

The purpose of this practical is to develop an understanding of garment labeling practices, and how they contribute to informed consumer choices regarding fabric properties, fit and proper care.

Material Required

Readymade shirt, ladies kurta and suit length.

Conducting the Practical

A label of gents shirt is attached with side seam is given below.

- Read this label and assess its effectiveness in terms of ease of understanding and completeness of the information provided.

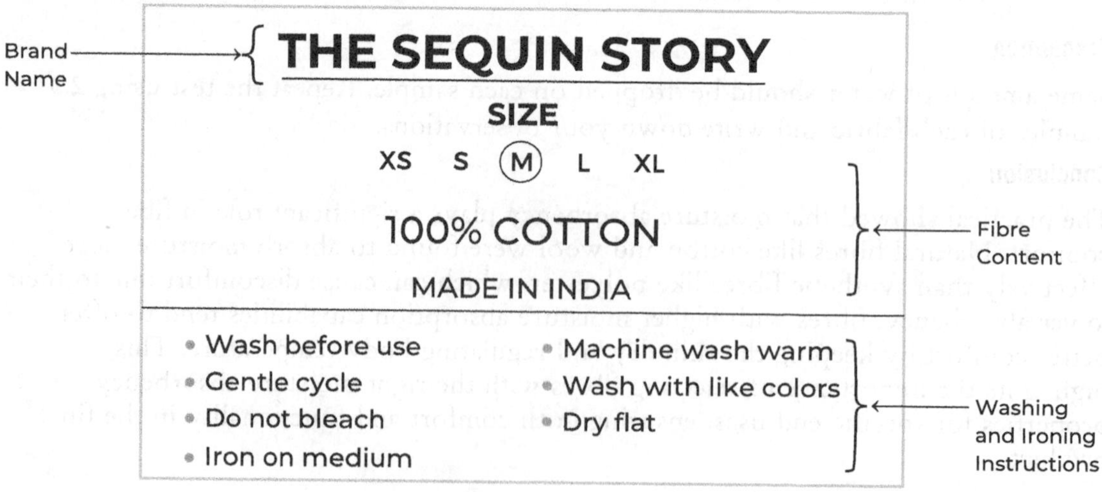

After Studying the label, write your observations in the following table.

Reference	Desired Quality of a Garment Label	Quality of The Label on The Garment
1. Clarity	• Knitted/printed	________
	• Cotton/satin/Damask	________
	• Easy to wash or Not	________
	• Strong or Not	________
	• Shrinkable or Not	________
2. Fibre Content	• Description of Fabric	________
	• Content of Fabric	________
3. Size and Care Instruction	• Size	________
	• Washing Instructions	________
	• Dry-cleaning Instructions	________
	• Bleaching Instructions	________

Conclusion

The practical demonstrates that a well-designed garment label is crucial for conveying important information, such as fibre content, size, and care instructions. Clear labeling ensures that consumers can make informed decisions about their purchases and properly care for their clothing, leading to better garment longevity.

(B) Prepare One Care Label of Any Garment

Aim Prepare a care label for a specific garment, ensuring it provides clear, accurate, and easy-to-follow instructions for washing, drying, ironing and general maintenance.

Task

1. Select a garment and determine the appropriate care instructions based on its fibre content and characteristics.
2. Prepare a detailed care label that includes information about washing, drying, ironing, and any special care requirements.
3. Ensure that the care label is designed with clarity, readability, and universal symbols to facilitate easy understanding by consumers.

Purpose of Practical

The purpose of this practical is to understand the significance of care labels in garment care.

Conducting the Practical

Prepare a care label of any one garment and paste that label in your practical file.

Conclusion

The practical demonstrates that a well-constructed care label is essential for ensuring the proper maintenance and longevity of garments. By preparing a care label, the importance of using accurate and universal care symbols was emphasised, which ensures that the garment's life cycle is prolonged and the consumer experience is enhanced.

(c) Analyse Two Different Fabric Samples for Colour Fastness

Aim Analyse and compare the colour fastness of two different fabric samples and determine how well each fabric retains its colour after exposure to washing and other environmental factors.

Task

Analysis of colour fastness to washing.

Purpose of Practical

The purpose of this practical is to understand the importance of colour fastness in fabrics and how different fibres respond to washing.

Conducting the Practical

- Take four samples each of coloured fabric and white cotton fabric measuring (2" × 4").
- Join coloured samples with white samples to produce (4" × 4") four samples (ABCD)
- Keep (A) as control sample and treat the samples B C D with already prepared 0.5% soap solution in warm water (40° C), rub gently.
- After five minutes rinse and dry.
- Repeat the process for samples C and D. Wash, rinse and dry.
- Repeat the process with sample D and record the observation.

Paste Your Samples in Your File

Sample A- Control Sample	Sample B- After One Wash
Sample C- After Two Wash	**Sample D- After Three Wash**

Conclusion

The practical demonstrates that the colour fastness of fabrics varies significantly between natural and synthetic fibres. This highlights the importance of choosing fabrics with appropriate colour fastness for different garments, especially in garments or textiles that require long-lasting colour.

Observations

Sample	Change in Colours of Test Samples	Staining of White Cloths Attached
A	A Control Sample	
B		
C		

Make a group of 4-5 students and compare the observations of other fabrics also.

Viva Voce Questions

1. ***What is the first step in conducting physical development?***

Ans. The first step is to take measurements of height, weight, hip size, chest/bust circumference, waist, neck and across the back.

2. ***How do you measure height?***

Ans. Height is measured using a measuring tape from the floor to the top of the head.

3. ***What information should be recorded regarding girls?***

Ans. The age at menarche should be recorded for girls.

4. ***What developmental milestone does a child typically reach between 6-12 months in terms of motor skills?***

Ans. Between 6-12 months, children start transferring objects from hand to hand.

5. ***How do children show social-emotional development between 1-2 years?***

Ans. Children begin to show frustration or anger when things don't go their way between 1-2 years.

6. ***What is an example of physical development between 0-6 months?***

Ans. An example of physical development between 0-6 months is when newborns try to hold their head steady when sitting with support.

7. ***What is the aim of the Areas of Agreement and Disagreement ?***

Ans. The aim is to help adolescents identify sources of disagreements with family members, friends, and teachers and reflect on how to minimise and resolve these differences.

8. *How can adolescents resolve disagreements with family members or teachers?*

Ans. Adolescents can resolve disagreements by having open conversations, understanding each other's perspectives, and compromising when necessary.

9. *What is the purpose of recording your own diet for a day?*

Ans. The purpose is to evaluate the nutritive value of the food eaten and understand the essential nutritional requirements for health and well-being.

10. *What are the five food groups that should be included in a balanced diet?*

Ans. The five food groups are cereals, fruits and vegetables, milk and milk products, fats and oils, and proteins.

11. *What is the main nutrient benefit of the Atta Besan Halwa recipe?*

Ans. The Atta Besan Halwa is rich in iron, protein, and healthy fats, which are essential for an adolescent's growth and development.

12. *What nutrients are present in the Rainbow Poori recipe?*

Ans. Rainbow Poori is rich in fibre, vitamins, and minerals, especially from the vegetables like spinach, beetroot, and pumpkin used in the dough.

13. *What is the benefit of preparing healthy snacks for adolescents?*

Ans. Healthy snacks help adolescents meet their nutritional needs, maintain energy levels, and promote overall well-being.

14. *What is the purpose of tracking daily activities?*

Ans. The purpose is to understand how you spend your time and how much time is dedicated to different tasks, which helps in organising your day better and improving productivity.

15. *What factors are considered while categorising fabrics and apparel based on functionality?*

Ans. Fabrics and apparel are categorised based on their use, such as casual wear, work wear, or sportswear.

16. *How can you evaluate the thermal properties of fibres?*

Ans. By conducting a burning test, where fibres are exposed to flame, and observing their behaviour, such as whether they catch fire, burn quickly, or self-extinguish.

17. *What is the significance of moisture absorbency in fabrics?*

Ans. Moisture absorbency is important because it influences comfort; fabrics that absorb moisture keep the wearer dry and comfortable, especially in hot and humid conditions.

18. *What is the importance of garment labels?*

Ans. Garment labels provide essential information like fibre content, size, and care instructions, which helps consumers make informed decisions about the fabric and how to properly care for the garment.

SAMPLE QUESTION PAPERS

SAMPLE QUESTION PAPER 1

A Highly Simulated Sample Question Paper for CBSE Class XI

HOME SCIENCE (SOLVED)

General Instructions

- All questions are compulsory.
- There are total 35 questions.
- Question paper is divided into four sections-A, B, C and D.
- Section A has question no. 1 to 14 (Multiple choice questions) and are of 1 mark each.
- Section B has question no. 15 to 18 (Case based questions) and are of 1 mark each.
- Section C has question no. 19 to 25 of 2 marks each and question no. 26 to 29 of 3 marks each.
- Section D has question no. 30 to 33 of 4 marks each and question no. 34 and 35 are of 5 marks each.
- Internal choices are given in some questions.
- Support your answers with suitable examples wherever required.

Time : 3 hours | Max. Marks : 70

Section-A (Multiple Choice Questions)

1. Food-borne illnesses occur when we consume food that contains disease-causing micro-organisms. Which of the following is essential to prevent food-borne illnesses? (1)

(a) Personal Hygiene
(b) Environmental Hygiene
(c) Good food handling practices
(d) All of the above

2. Which element is natural bleach? (1)

(a) Hydrogen peroxide
(b) Grass
(c) Ammonia
(d) Sunlight

3. The proper utilisation of resources to achieve the goals and objective is called .... (1)

(a) Price (b) Plan
(c) Management (d) Investment

4. A communication process is incomplete without .... (1)

(a) sender
(b) receiver
(c) message
(d) feedback

5. Which among the following is seen as a critical time for identity development? (1)

(a) Childhood (b) Adolescence
(c) Schooling (d) None of these

Or

The construction of self identity is a .... process.

(a) static (b) continuous
(c) evergreen (d) slow

6. Which of the following is NOT a level of communication? (1)

(a) Intra-Personal Communication
(b) Inter-Personal Communication
(c) Informal Communication
(d) Mass Communication

7. "Boys who do not have adequate growth of facial hair, as compared to other boys, often feel peculiar about it". What kind of changes are being referred in this statement? (1)

(a) Cognitive changes (b) Physical changes
(c) Emotional changes (d) Biological changes

8. In which college the study of Home Science was first started at higher level? (1)

(a) Lady Shri Ram College (b) Lady Harding college
(c) Lady Irwin College (d) None of these

9. Three year old Bunty is feeling shy of his uncle. He starts feeling conscious of unfamiliar face around him. Bunty feels extremely comfortable in the presence of his mother. But he feels shy whenever his uncle comes to their place. (1)

What are the ways in which Bunty could react?

(a) He runs and hides himself behind his mother
(b) He gets irritated and it appears on his face
(c) Both (a) and (b)
(d) Neither (a) nor (b)

10. Select correct pair. (1)

(a) Rayon : The first true synthetic fibre, manufactured completely using chemicals.
(b) Acrylic : It is a non-cellulosic man-made fibre which is made from petroleum products.
(c) Linen : It is obtained from the stems of the flex plant.
(d) Nylon : It is a synthetic fibre. It resemble wool.

11. Match List I with List II. (1)

	List-I (Characteristics of Resources)		List-II (Meaning)
A.	Utility	1.	Substitutes of all resources
B.	Accessibility	2.	Resources managed for effective utilization
C.	Interchangeability	3.	Usefulness of resources to achieve the goal.
D.	Manageable	4.	Resources available easily to everyone.

Codes

	A	B	C	D		A	B	C	D
(a)	1	2	3	4	(b)	3	4	1	2
(c)	2	1	4	3	(d)	4	3	2	1

12. Match List I with List II. (1)

	List-I		List-II
A.	Vegetable stains	1.	Milk, meat, egg
B.	Animal stains	2.	Tea, coffee, fruits
C.	Dil stains	3.	Rust, coal tar, medicine
D.	Mineral stains	4.	Ghee, butter

Codes

	A	B	C	D		A	B	C	D
(a)	1	2	3	4	(b)	3	4	1	2
(c)	2	1	4	3	(d)	4	3	2	1

13. What are the dimensions of wellness? (1)

I. Spiritual II. Emotional
III. Distress IV. Eustress

Choose the correct option.

(a) I and II (b) II and III
(c) III and IV (d) I and IV

Or Laundering includes which of the following? (1)

I. Replacing buttons II. Stain removal
III. Pressing or ironing IV. Repairing cuts or holes

Choose the correct option.

(a) I and II (b) II and III
(c) III and IV (d) I and IV

14. Intrinsic factors linked with various diseases are (1)

I. Sex, ethnicity II. Air, water
III. Heredity IV. Plants, animals

Choose the correct option.

(a) I and II (b) II and IV
(c) I and III (d) III and IV

Section-B (Case Based Questions)

Read the following passage and answer the questions no. 15 to 18.

A woven fabric consists of two sets of yarns which are interlaced at right angles to each other, to form a compact construction. It is done on machines called looms. One set of yarns is fitted on the loom, which determines the length and width of the fabric to be woven. These are called warp yarns. The loom helps to maintain these yarns at a fixed tension and even space. The second yarn, which is the filling yarn, is then interlaced to form the fabric. The simplest interlacing is when the filling yarn moves over and under one warp yarn alternately in one row and reverses the process in the second row. By passing the filling yarn over and under different number of warp yarns, in a specified sequence, different designs can be created. Attachments like the dobby or jacquard to the loom can help to create figurative designs as well. These designs become clearer when different coloured yarns are used for warp and filling.

15. In the context of weaving in the process of fabric production, choose the correct pair. (1)

(a) Compact Construction of fabric : Jacquard
(b) Determines length and breadth of the fabric : Warp yarns
(c) Yarn interlaced to form fabric : Dobby
(d) Figurative design : Looms

16. Match the items in list I with their functions in list II. (1)

	List-I (Name of Yarn)		List-II (Function)
A.	Filling yarn	1.	Compact construction of yarn
B.	Warp yarn	2.	Figurative designs
C.	Jacquard	3.	Determines length of the fabric
D.	Loom	4.	Interlaced to form fabric

Codes

	A	B	C	D		A	B	C	D
(a)	2	1	4	3	(b)	3	4	1	2
(c)	4	3	2	1	(d)	1	3	4	2

17. **Assertion** (A) Attachments like the dobby or jacquard to the loom can help to create figurative designs as well.

Reason (R) These designs become clearer when different coloured yarns are used for warp and filling. (1)

Codes

(a) Both A and R are true and R is the correct explanation of A

(b) Both A and R are true, but R is not the correct explnation of A

(c) A is true, but R is false

(d) A is false, but R is true

18. **Assertion** (A) Two sets of yarn are interlaced at right angles to each other, to form a compact construction.

Reason (R) One is used to deterimine the length and width of the fabric and other is filling yarn. (1)

Codes

(a) Both A and R are true and R is the correct explanation of A

(b) Both A and R are true, but R is not the correct explnation of A

(c) A is true, but R is false

(d) A is false, but R is true

Section-C (Short Answer Questions)

19. Riya has normal weight but she is on a slimming diet. She skips meals, take diet pills, binge eats etc. What are the consequences of such dieting? (2)

20. Riya visited a loom as a part of a school educational tour. Here she noticed that the fabric that comes straight from the loom looks different from the clothes we buy in stores. Why does such difference take place? Explain any two functions upon which such appearance changes depend. (2)

Or How does the level of twist in a yarn affect the fabric's strength, elasticity, and drape? State any one example of material based on the yarn twist.

21. How can media serves for the transmission of values? What are the two examples of traditional media used in rural areas? (2)

22. Raghav is an employee in a steel industry. How is money as a resource a good example to him of the fact that availability of resources changes from time to time? (2)

Or List basic steps to Raghav in making a plan to manage resources.

23. "Lack of fresh air in the building may lead to a headache". Which principle of space planning can be used to overcome such a situation? Define the principle.What are the other difficulties that may be faced by the occupants due to lack of fresh air? (2)

24. Explain the concepts which govern the cleanliness and sanitary conveniences principle in space planning. (2)

25. At what time during the day should a student plan study time? (2)

26. Arav has been studying for his maths test for an hour but he fell distracted sometimes when his phone rings. What would be the best thing for Arav to do now? (3)

Or Zeenath is following the time management steps. She just made a list of her tasks and estimated how much time those tasks will take. What she do next?

27. What are the main techniques of fabric construction? Discuss. (3)

28. (i) "The elements of the self and the identity of a girl from a traditional community would be very different from that of a girl living in urban areas". Highlight the role of society and culture in the context of adolescence. (1+2)

(b) Raghav is a teenager who is struggling with his identity and feeling pressured to conform to the peer expectations. Explain how his parents and guardians can foster the feeling of self in Raghav?

29. What are the benefits of regular exercise? Explain in detail. (3)

Or Explain any four benefits of maintaining the optimum BMI range?

Section-D (Long Answer Questions)

30. Namita is an adolescent she is confused about her role or identity.

(i) What kinds of problems can she face?

(ii) What may be two reasons due to which Namita gives more importance to her peers than her family? (1 + 3 = 4)

31. Communication is the process of thinking, observing, understanding, analysing, sharing and transmitting or transferring. It also refer to seeing or watching, listening or hearing and exchanging ides, thoughts, experiences, facts, knowledge, moments, emotions and the like with self or with others.

(i) What do you understand by the word communication? Communication may be classified on what basis? (2 + 2 = 4)

(ii) State the various levels of communication.

32. Why budgeting is important for a family? Explain and write its advantages also. (4)

33. "An educated sender is likely to articulate and express his/her thoughts more effectively". Explain.

Or Why is adolescence accompanied with dilemmas and disagreements? Explain with examples. (4)

34. (i) Why do adolescent girls need high intake of calories, calcium, protein and iron in their diet? Give two reasons for each. (1 + 4 = 5)

(ii) What do you understand by the term RDA? Mention six properties of balanced diet.

Or (i) What are nutrients and how can they be classified?

(ii) What are micro-nutrients? List the micro-nutrients required by the body every day along with any two items of common consumption containing each of these macro-nutrients.

35. Rohan is a 10 years old kid who became the monitor of his class. He came home and told his mother, "I am better than other kids that's why teacher made me the monitor". (2 + 3 = 5)

(i) What are the characteristics of age? Which stage of self is Rohan at?

(ii) Distinguish between early childhood and middle childhood.

Answers

1. (d) All of the above
2. (d) Sunlight
3. (c) Management
4. (d) feedback
5. (b) Adolescence *Or* (b) continuous
6. (c) Informal Communication
7. (c) Emotional changes
8. (c) Lady Irwin College
9. (d) Neither (a) nor (b)
10. (c) Linen : It is obtained from the stems of the flex plant.
11. (b) 3 4 1 2
12. (c) 2 1 4 3
13. (a) I and II

    Or (b) II and III
14. (c) I and III
15. (b) Determines length and breadth of the fabric : Warp yarns
16. (c) 4 3 2 1
17. (b) Both A and R are true, but R is not the correct explanation of A.
18. (b) Both A and R are true, but R is not the correct explanation of A.
19. Consequences of such dieting include its possible association with cycles of weight loss and regain that increase the liklihood of developing eating disorders and obesity, lowered self esteem and other psychological problems. This can lead to increased cardiovascular risk (heart problems) and possible mortality.
20. The fabric that comes out from the loom is different in appearance from the clothes we buy in stores because of the textile finishing.

    A finish is any treatment on the fabric which can change its appearance, its texture or its behavior for specific uses.

    The reasons for change in such appearance is due to the different functions like,

    - **Change textures** Starching or sizing
    - **Change behavior** Wash, water proof, fireproof

    Or

    The level of yarn twist decides the appearance and strength of the fabric. Yarn twist is added to hold the fibers together, and it is indicated by twist per inch. For example, loosely twisted yarns are softer and lustrous whereas tightly twisted yarns are coarser like denim materials.
21. Media can serve for the transmission of values by teaching values through stories shown in cartoon films or through puppetry.

    Two examples of traditional media used in rural areas are traditional folk theatre, also known as drama and puppetry.
22. Money as a resource is a good example for the salaried class of persons who are paid on a monthly basis. Just after receiving their salary every month, money is plentiful for the salaried class. It reduces gradually during the next few days until it becomes the lowest just before the next salary is received.

Or

The basic steps in making a plan to manage resources are
- Identifying the problem.
- Identifying different alternatives for achieving the target.
- Choosing between the alternatives which will make the target achievable.
- Acting to carry out the plan, i.e. putting the plan into action.
- Accepting the consequences.

23. Lack of fresh air in the building may lead to a headache if the building is not well ventilated.Ventilation is the supply of the outside air into the rooms. It can be achieved by placing windows, doors or ventilators. The other difficulties faced by occupants are sleepiness, inability to focus, etc.

24. The concepts which govern this principle in space planning are
(i) The house should be planned to facilitate cleaning and prevention of ingress of dust so that the occupants can maintain it.
(ii) Suitable sanitary conveniences like bathrooms, water closets and lavatories should be provided in a house.

25. A student should plan study time for the time period when the student is able to work best i.e. at the peak time. Some students work best in early morning hours whereas others work most efficiently during the late night.

26. Arav should take a quick break, so he can get a snack and respond to his calls before he goes back to studying.

Or

Zeenath should prioritise her tasks or put them in order of importance.

27. The main techniques of fabric construction involve
- **Weaving** It is the process of interlacing yarns in different ways.
- **Knitting** It is a technique of producing a three-dimensional fabric from a yarn.
- **Braiding** It is a type of fabric made by plaiting three or more yarns in such a way that they cross one another in a diagonal formation.

28. (i) Different sections of the society may respond differently to the physical changes in the body during adolescence. In traditional Indian societies, the onset of puberty creates many restrictions on the girls and their freedom of movement. There are certain sections of entertainment or work which are seen as inappropriate for girls, therefore the elements of self and identity for a girl of traditional community may be different from that of the girl living in urban areas.

(ii) During adolescence identity formation is enhanced by family relationships. Raghav's parents should follow the affectionate parenting by giving him warm, loving and support. They should praise and show excitement to his activities very sensitively. Along with this discipline. This will foster the feeling of independence and self-reliance in Raghav.
Raghav's parents should promote both individuality and connectedness so that he could get greater opportunity to have his own point of view as well as respect and sensitivity towards the opinion of other people.

29. The following are the benefits of regular exercise.
(i) Regular exercise burns up extra calories consumed and therefore, reduce the chance of extra calories being converted into fat and its deposition in the body thereafter.
(ii) The person considers himself/herself healthy and fit.
(iii) Diseases like obesity, diabetes, excess blood pressure can be avoided or controlled.

Or

The four benefits of mainstring optimum range of BMI is as follow
(i) It reduces the chance of diabetes.
(ii) Chances of high blood pressure and heart diseases are reduced.
(iii) A person can be happy, healthy and fit life.
(iv) He/She becomes physically, socially and emotionally fit.

30. (i) If Namita is confused about her role or identity, the kinds of problems can she face are
- Inability to concentrate on the work at hand.
- Difficulty in starting or finishing work on time.
- General difficulty in coping with schedules.

(ii) Two reasons due to which Namita gives more importance to her peers than her family are
(a) **Peer Pressure** During the day, an adolescent spends more time with peers than with family members. Thus, the peers influence directly affects the perspectives and values of the adolescent.
(b) **Pressure to Conform** The adolescent faces the pressure to conform to social norms set by the peer group, irrespective of the family's social outlook. Thus, its behaviour gives more importance to his/her peers.

Or

(i) Child is at Early Childhood Stage. The year range when the child develops these characterisitcs is 2-6 years.

(ii) The child gives concrete self-descriptions, self over estimation other than active-self-description in this stage.

31. (i) The word 'communication' comes from the Latin word, communis meaning common. Thus, it can be defined, as the process of thinking, observing, understanding, analysing, sharing and transmitting or transferring feelings to others through a variety of mediums in diverse settings so that they understand the exact meaning of the content.

Communication may be classified on the following basis

- Type of interaction
- Levels
- Means or modes
- Involvement of number of senses

(ii) The various levels of communications are

- **Intra-Personal Communication** It means communicating with oneself, i.e. thinking.
- **Inter-Personal Communication** It refers to sharing of thoughts and ideas with one or more people in a face-to-face situation.
- **Group Communication** This form of communication is direct and personal as well as between an individual and a group.
- **Mass Communication** It can be defined as the process of multiplying a message with the help of any mechanical or electronic device and disseminating it to a large number of people at the same time.

32. Budget is the first step in managerial process. Its success depends upon

- It's being realistic and flexible
- Suitability to the group for which it is prepared
- Quality of control and evaluation steps which follow.

Family budget gives details of income and expenditure of a family for a month or a year. It mentions all the sources of income during that period and also all the items of expenditure under different headings like food, clothing, housing, entertainment, travel, education, health, medicines and saving.

Advantages

- Planning helps the family to take an overview of use of their income.
- Amounts allocated to various categories can be studied in relation to family income.
- Helps families to use their income to attain those goals which they consider most important.
- Family members are less likely to be swayed as they can make rational decisions.

33. Education broadens one's knowledge scope. It improves a person's ability to understand and apply knowledge, provides access to information and helps people to prepare for careers. All of these advantages increase one's communication capacity and range.

A well-educated sender will be able to articulate and convey her/his thoughts more effectively, and if the listener is also well-educated, good communication will result.

When a teacher teaches a concept to another teacher, for example, the level of cognition is higher than when the subject is explained to students.

Or

Adolescents face dilemmas and disagreements because of conflicting expectations from the people that they interact with. They may be expected to behave in an adult-like manner and begin to take on responsibilities related to family, work or marriage in some traditional cultures. Then the adolescent may rebel against being treated like a child but at the same time may seek comfort as a child would.

The parents too may often tell the adolescent to behave like an adult, but some of their other actions may indicate to the adolescent that they do not think that of him/her as a grown up yet. This may be somewhat different for girls and boys depending on the expectations of the family. Thus, the adolescent experiences conflicting feelings and also receives conflicting messages as well as social expectations.

34. (i) Reasons for requirement of higher intake for adolescent girls are

- Calories due to
  - (a) Involvement in strenuous exercise
  - (b) Greater Metabolic rate.
- Calcium due to
  - (a) Development of skeletal system
  - (b) For even development of body
  - (c) For good appetite
- Protein due to
  - (a) Development of body mass
  - (b) Sexual maturation
  - (c) Increase in height and weight
  - (d) Hormonal changes
- Iron due to
  - (a) Increase in blood volume
  - (b) Replacing monthly blood loss due to menstrual cycle.

(ii) The term RDA means the Recommended Dietary Allowance for a person, which comprises the daily nutritional requirements of a person plus a margin of safety.

Six properties of a balanced diet are

- It includes a variety of food items.
- It meets the RDA for all nutrients.
- It includes nutrients in correct proportions.
- It provides a safety margin for nutrients.

- It promotes and preserves good health.
- It maintains acceptable body weight for the relevant height.

Or

(i) Nutrients are the constituents in food that must be supplied to the body in suitable amounts.

They can be classified as macro-nutrients (required in large amount every day), for example, carbohydrates, fats, proteins and micro-nutrients (required in small amount every day), for example, iodine, minerals, iron on the basis of the required quantity to be consumed by us every day.

(ii) Macro-nutrients are those nutrients which are required in large amount by the body everyday. The nutrients that are needed in large amount are carbohydrates, found in rice and wheat, proteins, available in abundance in pulses and eggs. Fats, in milk and eggs, water, almost all food items contain this in different proportions and fibre, usually found in all cereals and fruits.

35. (i) Some of the characteristics of middle childhood are

(a) **Distinguish Real Self From Ideal Self** They can differentiate between their actual competencies and those that they want to have or those which they think are most important.

(b) **Realistic Self-Descriptions** The self-descriptions become more realistic as compared to those of the pre-school child. This may be because of the ability to see things and situations from the point of view of other(s).

Rohan is at middle childhood stage. At this stage of life, children's self evaluations become more complex.

This stage ranges from 6 to 12 years.

(ii) There are many differences between early childhood and middle childhood. Some of them are

(a) In during early childhood children use physical descriptions of their material possessions to differentiate themselves from other whereas in middle childhood child shift towards describing himself in terms of his/her internal characteristics.

(b) In early childhood they describes themselves in terms of things they can do whereas in middle childhood they define themselves in terms of groups they belong to.

SAMPLE QUESTION PAPER 2

A Highly Simulated Sample Question Paper for CBSE Class XI

HOME SCIENCE (UNSOLVED)

General Instructions

- All questions are compulsory.
- There are total 35 questions.
- Question paper is divided into four sections-A, B, C and D.
- Section A has question no. 1 to 14 (Multiple choice questions) and are of 1 mark each.
- Section B has question no. 15 to 18 (Case based questions) and are of 1 mark each.
- Section C has question no. 19 to 25 of 2 marks each and question no. 26 to 29 of 3 marks each.
- Section D has question no. 30 to 33 of 4 marks each and question no. 34 and 35 are of 5 marks each.
- Internal choices are given in some questions.
- Support your answers with suitable examples wherever required.

Time : 3 hours

Max. Marks : 70

Section-A (Multiple Choice Questions)

1. Old blood stains on coloured cotton fabric can be removed by .... (1)

(a) soak in salt water
(b) soak in glycerin
(c) soak in hot water
(d) wash with soap and hot water

2. About half of our diet should include which of the following? (1)

(a) Fruits and Milk (b) Grains and Vegetables
(c) Milk and Cheese (d) Fats and Sugar

3. What is the core of Home Science education? (1)

(a) Universe development (b) Family eco system
(c) Job assurance (d) None of these

4. A 3 years old carrying a toy and claiming it is his, this shows the attribute of .... (1)

(a) absolute self description
(b) active self description
(c) concrete self description
(d) over estimation

5. .... fibers are synthetic fibers like lycra or spandex. (1)

(a) Acrylic (b) Nylon
(c) Rayon (d) Elastomeric

6. The computer which is used for extension of work, like processing, keeping record of all kinds of information, performing accounting function is known as............ . (1)

(a) Mainframe computers (b) Mini computers
(c) Micro computers (d) Super computers

Or

Which fabric is most widely used because it is easily washable and comfortable to wear? (1)

(a) Polyester (b) Nylon
(c) Wool (d) Cotton

7. Cow dung is considered waste. However it can be used to prepare humus (manure). Which characteristic of resources does this symbolise? (1)

(a) Accessibility (b) Interchangeability
(c) Manageable (d) Utility

8. Match the following. (1)

	List-I (Stain)		List-II (Method of Removal)
A.	Milk	1.	Soak in oxalic acid and rub
B.	Paint	2.	Sponge with hydrogen
C.	Rust	3.	Sponge with a solvent
D.	Scorch	4.	Rub with kerosene

Codes

	A	B	C	D		A	B	C	D
(a)	1	3	2	4	(b)	3	4	1	2
(c)	2	4	3	1	(d)	4	2	1	3

9. Match the following. (1)

List-I (Principles of space planning)	List-II (Meaning)
A. Aspect	1. Placement of the rooms within house
B. Prospect	2. It includes light, cleanliness, ventilation
C. Sanitation	3. It is the look of house from outside
D. Grouping	4. Arrangement of doors/windows.

Codes

	A	B	C	D		A	B	C	D
(a)	1	2	3	4	(b)	2	3	4	1
(c)	4	3	2	1	(d)	3	1	4	2

10. Which of the following falls in the food group of 'Fat and Sugars'? (1)

I. Ghee II. Jaggery

III. Mustard leaves IV. Skimmed milk

Choose the correct option.

(a) I and II (b) II and III

(c) III and IV (d) I, II and IV

Or Communication may be classified on the basis of (1)

I. Type of interaction II. Levels

III. Social life IV. Community

Choose the correct option.

(a) I and III (b) II and IV

(c) I and II (d) III and IV

11. Which of the following are names of vaccine as recommended by ICMR? (1)

I. BCG II. HEPB

III. OPV IV. DPT

Choose the correct option.

(a) I and II (b) II and III

(c) III and IV (d) All of these

12. About half out diet should include which of the following? (1)

(a) Fruits and Milk (b) Grains and Vegetables

(c) Fats and Sugar (d) Milk and Cheese

13. Asbestos is a .... (1)

(a) natural rubber (b) mineral fibre

(c) protein fibre (d) cellulosic fibre

14. Select correct pair (1)

(a) Intra-Personal Communication : It is usually takes place in a highly structured and formal setting.

(b) Inter-Personal Communication : It refers to sharing of thoughts and ideas with one or more people in a face-to-face situation.

(c) Mass Communication : This form of communication is direct and personal as well as between an individual and a group.

(d) Group Communication : It can be defined as the process of multiplying a massage with the help of any mechanical or electronic device.

Section–B (Case Based Questions)

Read the passage carefully and answer the following questions no. 15 to 18.

According to a well-known psychologist Erik H. Erikson, at each stage of our development, from infancy to old age, we have to accomplish certain tasks which enable us to move on to the next stage of development. For example, a task during late infancy and early childhood (between 2-4 years of age) is to achieve bowel and bladder control. Without this, participation in most social and community activities would become impossible for the child. The task during the period of adolescence, according to Erikson is to develop a sense of identity, a satisfactory self-definition. The reason why the stage of adolescence is critical for identity development is because there is an enhanced focus on the development of the self. It is believed that the adolescent faces an identity crisis.

15. In context of the meanings of self, choose the correct pair. (1)

(a) Infancy : Self-descriptions

(b) Early Childhood : Self-awareness

(c) Middle Childhood : Self-understanding

(d) Adolescence : Identity crisis

16. Match the items in list I with their functions in list II. (1)

List-I (Name of Yarn)	List-II (Function)
A. Personal Identity	1. Links with culture
B. Social Identity	2. Bowel and bladder control
C. Early Childhood	3. Makes the person different from others
D. Adolescence	4. Focus on development of self

Codes

	A	B	C	D		A	B	C	D
(a)	2	1	4	3	(b)	3	1	2	4
(c)	4	3	2	1	(d)	1	3	4	2

17. Assertion (A) An adolescent often faces an identity crisis.

Reason (R) This is the time when there is an enhanced focus on the development of the self and the person is pre-occupied with trying to know oneself. (1)

Codes

(a) Both A and R are true and R is the correct explanation of A.
(b) Both A and R are true, but R is not the correct explanation of A.
(c) A is true, but R is false.
(d) A is false, but R is true.

18. Assertion (A) According to a well-known psychologist Erik H. Erikson, at each stage of our development, from infancy to old age, we have to accomplish certain tasks which enable us to move on to the next stage of development. (1)

Reason (R) Without controlling the bowel and bladder, the participation in social and community activities would be impossible for the child.

Codes

(a) Both A and R are true and R is the correct explanation of A.
(b) Both A and R are true, but R is not the correct explanation of A.
(c) A is true, but R is false.
(d) A is false, but R is true.

Section-C (Short Answer Questions)

19. Your sister wants to know more about career options in Home Science. She also thinks that Home Science is a career options for only girls.

(i) What is the significance of Home Science? (2)

20. (i) Rajat is employee in MNC what are the controls that can be exercised by him in money management? (2)

(ii) Shreya is a house wife what are the two advantages of planning family budgets for her.

21. Why have the gadgets used for communication, for instance smart phones, become popular? Explain. (2)

22. What conditions and resources are required to promote the healthy growth of a child from the time he/she is born till he/she completes adolescence? (2)

23. Differentiate between money income and real income by giving two differences. (2)

24. "Childhood obesity is on the increase". Give reasons. (2)

Or How has the Mid-day Meal Scheme boosted children's health as well as school performance?

25. Name four C's of credit. (2)

Or Explain a way to increase psychic income.

26. What are the recommendations of ICMR for daily intake of foods from the five food groups for pre-school children of the age groups 1 to 3 years and 4 to 6 years? (3)

27. What are the implications of the statement, 'All resources are finite'? What is the interchangeability characteristic of a resource? (2 + 1 = 3)

Or Describe four common characteristics of resources and give an example of a resource, explaining why it has each of these characteristics?

28. (i) Explain what is balanced food? (3)

(ii) How dietary pattern changes in adolescence.

(iii) Tendency of consuming fast foods is seen in adolescence. What does this signify?

29. State in brief the meaning of each of the following principles of space planning. (3)

(i) Aspect (ii) Prospect (iii) Grouping

Or How do persons who do not plan their activities misuse their resource?

Section-D (Long Answer Questions)

30. Namita is a pre-school child what a diet plan she must follow for her growth and development? (1 + 3 = 4)

(i) What are the diseases they will suffer due to diet deficiencies?

(ii) What are the aspects that pre-school children's diet should emphasise?

31. What precautions should be taken in washing of woollen clothes and why? (4)

Or List some basic features of silk.

32. Aditya actively takes part in sports activities. He is a fitness freak and goes to gym regularly.

(i) Name some factors responsible for the selection of clothing. (4)

(ii) What are the clothing requirements for adolescents?

(iii) What factors should be considered while selecting clothes to be used in physical activity like sports and workout?

33. What do you understand by language development? At what age a child's language development start? (4)

34. (i) Stress has both positive and negative aspect in poor lives. Explain by giving examples.

(ii) What changes would you like to make in our diet to avoid disease? (5)

Or Tanu went to attend a wedding and while eating dinner, her dress get a stain from chicken curry.

(i) What is the method of removal for curry stains?

(ii) What are the different techniques of stain removal? Discuss.

35. Reema's daughter Ridhi is pre-schooler child.

(i) What guidelines for healthy eating should Reema follow for Ridhi?

(ii) What are the aspects that Reema should emphasise while planning balanced diet for Ridhi. (2 + 3 =5)

Answers

1. (a) soak in salt water
2. (b) Grains and Vegetables
3. (b) Family eco system
4. (c) concrete self description
5. (d) Elastomeric
6. (a) Mainframe computers *Or* (d) Cotton
7. (d) Utility
8. (c) 2 4 3 1
9. (c) 4 3 2 1
10. (d) I, II and IV *Or* (c) I and II
11. (d) All of these
12. (b) Grains and Vegetables
13. (b) mineral fibre
14. (b) Inter-Personal Communication : It refers to sharing of thoughts and ideas with one or more people in a face-to-face situation.
15. (d) Adolescence : Identity crisis
16. (b) 3 1 2 4
17. (a) Both A and R are true and R is the correct explanation of A.
18. (b) Both A and R are true, but R is not the correct explanation of A.

SAMPLE QUESTION PAPER 3

A Highly Simulated Sample Question Paper for CBSE Class XI

HOME SCIENCE (UNSOLVED)

General Instructions

- All questions are compulsory.
- There are total 35 questions.
- Question paper is divided into four sections-A, B, C and D.
- Section A has question no. 1 to 14 (Multiple choice questions) and are of 1 mark each.
- Section B has question no. 15 to 18 (Case based questions) and are of 1 mark each.
- Section C has question no. 19 to 25 of 2 marks each and question no. 26 to 29 of 3 marks each.
- Section D has question no. 30 to 33 of 4 marks each and question no. 34 and 35 are of 5 marks each.
- Internal choices are given in some questions.
- Support your answers with suitable examples wherever required.

Time : 3 hours | Max. Marks : 70

Section-A (Multiple Choice Questions)

1. Apparel for children with special needs should have ....
(a) single stitching
(b) blind stitching
(c) double stitching
(d) raw stitching

2. In noisy environments, Mr. Raman aged 69, find it difficult to determine who is talking and what is exactly being said. Rohan aged 18, may not have any such difficulty. What kind of changes is age-related? (1)
(a) Cognitive changes
(b) Material changes
(c) Functional changes
(d) Structural changes

3. __________ means keeping aside a part of your money or other resource for use in future or for further production. (1)
(a) Investment
(b) Savings
(c) Loan
(d) Debit

4. Tina plans her schedule everyday while Riya wastes her time in doing nothing all day. What is Riya supposed to do? (1)
(a) Implementation
(b) Controlling of resources
(c) Management of resources
(d) Wastage of resources

5. Riya sold all the old newspapers and magazines at a recycle station. What is the money that she earned by selling these called? (1)
(a) Direct income
(b) Indirect income
(c) Psychic income
(d) None of these

6. Which of the following combination is both high and undesirable in fast foods? (1)
(a) Folic acid and Fibre
(b) Calcium and Vitamin A
(c) Riboflavin and Folic Acid
(d) Fat and Sodium

Or Which fabric is most widely used because it is easily washable and comfortable to wear? (1)
(a) Polyester
(b) Nylon
(c) Wool
(d) Cotton

7. What is the main cause of child mortality rate?
(a) Poverty
(b) Ignorance
(c) Lack of medical facilities
(d) Superstition

8. Match the following. (1)

Stages of Childhood		Age	
A.	Creeping Age	1.	11-19 years
B.	Toddlerhood	2.	2-6 years
C.	Pre-school Age	3.	1-2 years
D.	Adolescents	4.	6 months-1 year

Codes

	A	B	C	D		A	B	C	D
(a)	1	2	3	4	(b)	2	3	4	1
(c)	4	3	2	1	(d)	3	4	1	2

9. Match the following. (1)

List-I		List-II	
A.	Capital	1.	Self-cultivated vegetables
B.	Direct Income	2.	Material goods and services
C.	Indirect Income	3.	Fixed deposits in banks
D.	Investment	4.	Net worth

Codes

	A	B	C	D		A	B	C	D
(a)	3	4	2	1	(b)	2	1	4	3
(c)	4	1	2	3	(d)	3	2	1	4

10. Which of the following are included in Human Resources? (1)
I. Knowledge II. Skills
III. Money IV. Housing
Choose the correct option.
(a) I and II (b) II and III
(c) III and IV (d) II and IV

Or Some areas of Home Science are .... (1)
I. Textile Science
II. Food and Nutrition
III. Research
IV. Data Science
Choose the correct option.
(a) I and II (b) II and III
(c) III and IV (d) I and IV

11. Methods of water purification includes (1)
I. Boiling II. Freezing
III. Iodine IV. Chlorine
Choose the correct option.
(a) I and II (b) II and III
(c) III and IV (d) I and IV

12. Which among the following is seen as a critical time for identity development? (1)
(a) Childhood (b) Adolescence
(c) Schooling (d) None of these

13. 'Motivation' is which type of resource? (1)
(a) Non-human resource (b) Human resource
(c) Shared resource (d) Natural resource

14. Select correct pair (1)
(a) Nutrients : It is the lack of proper nutrition caused by either not eating enough of right things or eating too much.
(b) Hygiene : It refers to conditions and practices that helps to maintain health and prevent the spread of diseases.
(c) Sanitation : It is to keep the food safe and free from all contaminants.
(d) Health care : It refers to the provision of facilities and services for safe disposal of garbage and their collection.

Section-B (Case Based Questions)

Read the following passage and answer the following question no. 15 to 18.

A stain is an unwanted mark or colouration on a fabric caused by contact and absorption of foreign matter, which cannot be removed by normal washing process and requires special treatment. In order to use the right procedure for removing the stain, it is important to identify the stain first. Identification may be done on the basis of colour, smell and feel. The stains can be classified as

(i) **Vegetable stains** Tea, coffee, fruits and vegetables. These stains are acidic by nature and can be removed by alkaline medium.
(ii) **Animal stains** Blood, milk, meat, eggs, etc. These are protein in nature and removed by detergents in cold water only.
(iii) **Oil stains** Oils, ghee, butter, etc. These are removed by the use of grease solvents and absorbents.
(iv) **Mineral stains** Ink, rust, coal tar, medicine, etc. These stains should be washed first in acidic medium and then in alkaline medium.

15. In context of stain sources choose the correct pair. (1)
(a) Vegetable stains: Coffee
(b) Oil stains : Ink
(c) Mineral stains : Ghee
(d) Animal stains : Tea

16. Match the type of stains given in list I and their method of removal in list II. (1)

List-I	List-II
A. Mineral stains	1. alkaline medium
B. Vegetable stains	2. detergents in cold water
C. Oil stains	3. first in acidic then alkaline
D. Animal stains	4. grease solvents

Codes

	A	B	C	D		A	B	C	D
(a)	4	2	1	3	(b)	3	1	4	2
(c)	4	3	2	1	(d)	1	3	4	2

17. Given below are two statements labeled as Assertion (A) and Reason (R). (1)

Assertion (A) It is important to identify the stain before attempting to remove it.

Reason (R) Identification of the stain can be done using methods such as washing with hot water.

Codes

(a) Both A and R are true and R is the correct explanation of A.
(b) Both A and R are true, but R is not the correct explanation of A.
(c) A is true, but R is false.
(d) A is false, but R is true.

18. Given below are two statements labeled as Assertion (A) and Reason (R). (1)

Assertion (A) A stain is an unwanted mark or colouration on a fabric caused by contact and absorption of foreign matter.

Reason (R) In order to use the right procedure for removing the stain, it is important to identify the stain first.

Codes

(a) Both A and R are true and R is the correct explanation of A.
(b) Both A and R are true, but R is not the correct explanation of A.
(c) A is true, but R is false.
(d) A is false, but R is true.

Section-C (Short Answer Questions)

19. Manish is a fresh graduate working in a BPO in a big city and living away from his home. He has to manage his own cooking and cleaning. Suggest three methods by which Manish can increase his psychic income. (2)

20. When a child reaches the middle childhood stage in life, it describes itself through its 'internal characteristics'. What does this mean? (2)

Or Shreya is 16 years old adolescent girl, In what two ways is identity influenced by her physical changes?

21. What are the main nutrients supplied by pulses and legumes? Which of these can be classified as micro-nutrients? (2)

22. What are the major nutritional limitations of fast foods? (2)

23. Riya had an interview and she had to wear a thin cotton saree. Before her interview she had to finish that saree fabric with a stiffening agent. Which agent can she use and give the sources from which that agent can be derived? (2)

24. "Nutrition affects productivity, income and quality of life". Write your opinion about the given statement. (2)

Or How is nutrition linked to mental and visual disability and quality of life?

25. What do you mean by management process? Explain briefly planning as a step of management process. (2)

26. Amrita is a football player, while selecting her clothes to be used in physical activity like sports and workouts, what are the four important factors which she should be considered? (3)

27. Describe four factors related to comfort, hygiene and warmth which need to be considered for clothing of children below six months of age. (3)

Or What do you understand by emotional wellness and well-being? What are four features of emotional wellness?

28. (i) What are natural fibres? How many types of natural fibres are there? (2 + 1 = 3)
(ii) How are natural fibres different from manufactured fibres?

29. (i) State the benefits of breastfeeding. (2 + 1 = 3)
(ii) What are the dietary requirements of Infants? Name them.

Or What are four benefits of adequate nutrition for children?

Section-D (Long Answer Questions)

30. The househelp who comes to clean utensils wastes 3-4 buckets of water for a few utensils. (1 + 3 = 4)
(i) Which characteristic of resources is she taking for granted?
(ii) Discuss in brief the main characteristics of resources.

31. State four nutritional deficiency diseases which malnourished children fall prey to. (4)

Or Give the dietary pattern of adolescents.

32. Rekha's teacher teaches the whole chapter in one go but doesn't allow any student to ask doubts. (1 + 1 + 2 =4)
    (i) What kind of communication is taking place here?
    (ii) Communication may be classified on what basis?
    (iii) Differentiate between Intra-personal and Inter-personal Communication.

33. Shivam lives in Himachal Pradesh for his office work. He is looking for a synthetic fibre which is strong and wrinkle resistant because he does not get time to iron his clothes. Which fabric best suits his requirement of climate as well as his formal dress up?

    Mention the other name of this fibre as well as all the properties possessed by such fibre. (1+3=4)

34. (i) What is an example of clothing preventing us from physical harm? (5)
    (ii) How is dressing and undressing an important consideration for children with special needs?

Or (i) How are food-borne illnesses in developing countries caused? What are your intrinsic factors linked with such kind of diseases?
    (ii) How can they be prevented or controlled?

35. Shreya is an active student and takes part in all types of curricular activities. She kept herself busy in sports, debates, etc. whole year and did not take out time to study. The exams are just a week away now. (5)
    (i) What is the important of time management?
    (ii) What mistake did Shreya make?

Answers

1. (d) double stitching
2. (c) Functional changes
3. (b) Savings
4. (d) Wastage of resources
5. (b) Indirect income
6. (d) Fat and Sodium *Or* (d) Cotton
7. (a) Poverty
8. (c) 4 3 2 1
9. (c) 4 1 2 3
10. (a) I and II *Or* (a) I and II
11. (d) I and IV
12. (b) Adolescence
13. (b) Human resources
14. (b) Hygiene : It refers to conditions and practices that helps to maintain health and prevent the spread of diseases
15. (a) Vegetable stains: Coffee
16. (b) 3 1 4 2
17. (c) A is true, but R is false.
18. (b) Both A and R are true, but R is not the correct explanation of A.